Advance Pra

"My experience reading this book was a big 'YES'! By placing her power-ful Sensorimotor Psychotherapy (SP) approach 'in context,' Pat Ogden and her consultants have embraced the challenge and the call for locating mental health practice in an anti-oppression frame. Their commitment to anti-racist practice has inspired a revisiting and revisioning of SP from this ground. I consider this book a must-read for therapists and will be requir-ing it for the graduate students that I train. YES!"

—**Shelly P. Harrell, Ph.D.,** Professor, Pepperdine University
Graduate School of Education and Psychology

"In this eye-opening new book, Pat Ogden, with her consultants, bril-liantly charts the continuing evolution of her work. Based on a solid sci-entific understanding of human development, neuroscience, attachment, and body-mind connections, this book is filled with riveting case exam-ples that illustrate the efficacy of Sensorimotor Psychotherapy. Original, illuminating, and mind-expanding about cultural biases and legacies, it helps us understand how the unexamined use of psychotherapy practices based solely on Western academic models without taking into account the effects of social marginalization and privilege/oppression is prone to lead to profound disappointments and colossal treatment failures. I hope this will become required reading for every therapist and policy maker!"

—**Bessel A. van der Kolk M.D.,** Professor of Psychiatry, Boston
University School of Medicine, President Trauma
Research Foundation, author of #1 NYT
bestseller *The Body Keeps the Score*

"Ogden and her consultants place a quote from James Baldwin at the front of the book: 'Not everything that is faced can be changed, but nothing can be changed until it is faced.' For me, Baldwin saw denial of reality as perhaps the greatest of sins. By focusing on our explicit and implicit theo-ries and states of consciousness, summarized by the phrase Ethnocentric Western approaches to psychotherapy, Ogden forces us to end our denial of what is evident: the inherent bias and limitations of talk therapy, of attachment theory, of trauma theory, of individualism and autonomy, of diagnoses, and more. You may have come to this book solely to see how

Sensorimotor Psychotherapy might affect your way of working—which it will—but you also will find that you have to face up to discord about how you see and know yourself as a therapist and as a person. If you can overcome your denial, avoid a flight into certitude, and begin to make new meaning of yourself in the world, you will change and grow, and become better for grappling with this book."

—**Ed Tronick,** author (with Claudia Gold) of *The Power of Discord: Why the Ups and Downs of Relationships Are the Secret to Building Intimacy, Resilience, and Trust*

"This is a remarkably thoughtful and generous book in which Sensorimotor Psychotherapy, and all analytic psychotherapies, are illuminated and enhanced through their contextualization by race, ethnicity, class, religion, gender expression, and other diversities. Exemplary in its integration of an expansive diversities scholarship into its body-attuned, sophisticated yet accessible account, the book will be of immense value to students as well as experienced practitioners seeking reflective, embodied contextualization of their psychotherapeutic work."

—**Anton Hart, Ph.D.,** FABP, FIPA, Training and Supervising Analyst, The William Alanson White Institute; Co-Chair of the Holmes Commission on Racial Equality in the American Psychoanalytic Association

"A superb text, *The Pocket Guide to Sensorimotor Psychotherapy in Context* highlights the relevance of context in psychotherapy by integrating trauma treatment, culturally responsive methods, somatic approaches, and ecological theories into healing and well-being. This much-needed book is relevant to all clients, especially to those struggling with oppression. A timely and essential contribution to psychotherapy, this text provides an invaluable resource to all therapists. I strongly recommend it."

—**Lillian Comas-Díaz, Ph.D.,** Clinical Professor, George Washington University Department of Psychiatry and Behavioral Sciences, author of *Multicultural Care: A Clinician's Guide to Cultural Competence*

The Pocket Guide to
Sensorimotor Psychotherapy
in Context

THE NORTON SERIES ON INTERPERSONAL NEUROBIOLOGY

Louis Cozolino, PhD, Series Editor
Allan N. Schore, PhD, Series Editor, 2007–2014
Daniel J. Siegel, MD, Founding Editor

The field of mental health is in a tremendously exciting period of growth and conceptual reorganization. Independent findings from a variety of scientific endeavors are converging in an interdisciplinary view of the mind and mental well-being. An interpersonal neurobiology of human development enables us to understand that the structure and function of the mind and brain are shaped by experiences, especially those involving emotional relationships.

The Norton Series on Interpersonal Neurobiology provides cutting-edge, multidisciplinary views that further our understanding of the complex neurobiology of the human mind. By drawing on a wide range of traditionally independent fields of research—such as neurobiology, genetics, memory, attachment, complex systems, anthropology, and evolutionary psychology—these texts offer mental health professionals a review and synthesis of scientific findings often inaccessible to clinicians. The books advance our understanding of human experience by finding the unity of knowledge, or consilience, that emerges with the translation of findings from numerous domains of study into a common language and conceptual framework. The series integrates the best of modern science with the healing art of psychotherapy.

A NORTON PROFESSIONAL BOOK

THE POCKET GUIDE TO
SENSORIMOTOR PSYCHOTHERAPY IN CONTEXT

PAT OGDEN

W. W. NORTON & COMPANY
Independent Publishers Since 1923

Note to Readers: Standards of clinical practice and protocol change over time, and no technique or recommendation is guaranteed to be safe or effective in all circumstances. This volume is intended as a general information resource for professionals practicing in the field of psychotherapy and mental health; it is not a substitute for appropriate training, peer review, and/or clinical supervision. Neither the publisher nor the author(s) can guarantee the complete accuracy, efficacy, or appropriateness of any particular recommendation in every respect. As of press time, the URLs displayed in this book link or refer to existing sites. The publisher and author are not responsible for any content that appears on third-party websites.

For information about permission to reproduce selections from this book, write to Permissions, W. W. Norton & Company, Inc., 500 Fifth Avenue, New York, NY 10110

For information about special discounts for bulk purchases, please contact W. W. Norton Special Sales at specialsales@wwnorton.com or 800-233-4830

Manufacturing by Lake Book Manufacturing, Inc.
Book design by Molly Heron
Production manager: Katelyn MacKenzie

ISBN: 978-0-393-71402-9 (pbk.)

W. W. Norton & Company, Inc., 500 Fifth Avenue, New York, N.Y. 10110
www.wwnorton.com

W. W. Norton & Company Ltd., 15 Carlisle Street, London W1D 3BS

1 2 3 4 5 6 7 8 9 0

For Brennan
With boundless gratitude for all you do,
and even more for all you are.

CONTENTS

ACKNOWLEDGMENTS

I recently learned the phrase "thought partner" from one of my consultants, Sherri Taylor. It's the perfect phrase to describe the many colleagues, friends and family members who challenge how I think, inspire me to innovate, and revise my assumptions. I've been blessed with incredible thought partners throughout my career. And so many people with all sorts of different perspectives and life experiences have stepped up, directly and indirectly, to contribute to *The Pocket Guide to Sensorimotor Psychotherapy in Context.*

At the beginning of my dive into this material, Medria Connolly, Bryan Nichols, Cleonie White and Shelly Harrell were patient and generous in helping me learn as I started to absorb what it means to be white and appreciate the impact of racism and systemic oppression on all of us; Mary Roy and Denise Gallagos gave me difficult and much-needed feedback on my blind spots. These thought partners helped me grow in my awareness of how bias and ignorance manifest personally, theoretically and in my clinical work. So many heartfelt and revealing discussions with friends and colleagues of all ages, including Susan Aposhyan, Ally Joel, Terry Toth, Lily Kurtz, Hana van der Kolk, Christine Caldwell, Bonnie Goldstein, Betty Cannon, Shelly Harrell, Kekuni Minton, Chris Courtois and others, have helped me begin to sort out the many facets of racism, privilege, oppression, sexism, gender nonconformity, religious discrimination and more. I so appreciate how these people continue to challenge and expand my thinking, each in their own unique way.

Warm and humble gratitude goes to my clients, consultees, and students, who have been patient with my learning curve, tolerated my imperfections and lack of knowledge, and often gone out on a limb to give me valuable feedback. Thank you! I have learned so much from you.

Several colleagues read and critiqued the chapters of this book, providing essential feedback. The members of my long-standing study group, Wolfgang Schlage, Betty Cannon, Mark Vick and Rick Slossman, as always, were eager to review what I'd written and give me their invaluable perspectives. Betty's grammatical precision and astute critique and Wolfgang's ruthlessly honest (in a good way) feedback are especially appreciated. Many thanks to my friend and colleague, Bonnie Goldstein, who also read this volume and helped to shape and refine the chapters, and to Lindsay Elin who pointed out ways in which cissexism and transphobia had seeped into sections of writing, and worked with me on their revision. And gratitude goes to Paula Iturra for our discussions on clinical work, for contributing to the composite cases in several of the chapters, and for elucidating a wider world perspective on oppression and racism.

Everyone at the Sensorimotor Psychotherapy Institute (SPI) deserves big thanks—Elizabeth Wood, Lindsay Norden, Holly Milne, Kristi Howard, Deb Gardner, and especially Brennan Arnold, SPI's CEO, all of whom have championed the difficult process of beginning to address the influence of white supremacy on SPI, supporting and encouraging change in institute policies, curriculum, attitudes and more. I am grateful to our trainers as well who have committed to taking the necessary steps to educate themselves and unpack their own inevitable bias in order to better support our diverse student body and to learn to teach a revised curriculum.

A warm thank you to Norton's Mariah Eppes and Sarah McBride Tuohy for all the effort they put into bringing this book to comple-

tion, and to Deborah Malmud, who has always had faith in my
writing, cheered this project on as well as all the others, and provided timely insight. Everyone at Norton went out of their way to
be understanding of my learning curve, my constantly expanding
deadline, and last-minute changes.

I want to extend my deepest appreciation and thanks to my four
brilliant consultants on this project—Sherri Taylor, Laia Jorba, Raymond Rodriguez and Mary Choi—who have spent countless hours
editing, discussing and advising me at every step of the way, rough-
ing in new concepts, co-writing the first chapter and contributing
to the composite case studies. Without their collective wisdom and
sage guidance, this book would not have been possible.

And finally, most of all, my profound gratitude goes to my
extended family who have been there for me through thick and
thin, always supportive of my work: to my mother Martha Ogden,
for her bravery in speaking out against the injustice she saw in our
small town and teaching me by example to be a strong and independent woman; to Paul Joel for his unwavering compassion for
the underdog and innate aversion to oppression of all sorts; to my
goddaughters, Jovanna Stepan and Shira Goldstein (and her parents Bonnie and Jan), for the creativity and optimism they bring
to my life; to my unconventional, amazing, diverse family, Brennan Arnold, Grace Richards, Ally Joel, Daniel Reizenstein, Quin-
sen Joel, Rob Ogden, Redmond Ogden and Matthew Ogden, for
countless discussions over the years on these topics and so many
more, and above all for their everlasting support and inspiration. I
am forever grateful to each of you for all you bring to my life.

PREFACE

The inspiration for this book emerged in 2015, after a UCLA/Lifespan Learning Institute Interpersonal Neurobiology conference on the topic of multiculturalism. In 2014, distressed by the murders of Black people (including Michael Brown Jr., Ezell Ford, Eric Garner, Akai Gurley, Laquan McDonald, Tamir Rice, Yvette Smith) taking place in the U.S., I had proposed that we choose the theme of diversity and culture for the 2015 conference, not realizing that delving into this topic would catalyze a profoundly disturbing, yet rewarding, ongoing learning journey for me and the organization I founded in 1981, the Sensorimotor Psychotherapy Institute (SPI). With an ignorance typical of white people who fancy themselves as not racist, I naively thought I had a handle on diversity issues at that time. In the 1960s, I started my career as the only white teacher in an all-black public school, then taught at the first integrated classroom in Louisville, KY. I passionately participated in the Civil Rights Movement of that era. And, my family is mixed race. But none of these experiences safeguarded me from my own implicit bias, white fragility, and internalized racism, or meant that I had a handle on systemic oppression or white privilege. Through collaboration with Dr. Medria Connelly, Dr. Brian Nichols, and others in preparation for the conference, I had to come to terms with the fact that I had limited awareness of white privilege, what it means to be a member of the dominant culture, privilege/oppression dynamics, or the implicit racial bias that is inherent within myself, in the U.S., in the world, and in my profession. Through presenting at and participating in the conference on culture, I became acutely aware of my own and my white colleagues' lack of knowledge about the impact of white supremacy and its influence in our field. Although racism affects us all in different ways, I realized that it was exactly because of my privilege that I had been protected from suffering the direct effects of the injustice, racism, and systemic oppression. As a white person of privilege, I am not immediately faced with, and therefore often not aware of, the constant disadvantages, pervasive microaggressions, implicit bias, and institutionalized racism that marginalized people face every day—personally, professionally, in the media, and in political discourse. The more I studied and reflected, the more I felt chagrined and ashamed that I had participated as a leader in our field with such a paucity of awareness and knowledge, unwittingly perpetuating Eurocentric perspectives that not only left out but at times sought to dominate most marginalized people and the wisdom of their healing traditions and practices.

Once the veil began to lift, there was no turning back. I wanted to delve more deeply into these issues, both for myself personally and for my school, to examine and change the ways in which I myself and SPI have participated in perpetuating privilege oppression dynamics. I initiated a Think Tank at SPI to explore issues of diversity and oppression that over time came to include the coauthors of the first chapter of this book: Sherri Taylor, Laia Jorba, Raymond Rodriguez, and Mary Choi. Our purpose was to create a process of moving SPI from a reactive position to a proactive position with respect to systemic oppression and racism. It was a process that would involve integrating diversity, inclusion, and cultural humility into SPI culture, into everything we do, with the intention of becoming an organization that upholds an anti-racist and anti-oppression perspective and holds itself accountable to anti-racist and anti-oppressive practices. These four coauthors are a mix of Sensorimotor Psychotherapy Institute graduates, Think Tank members, trainers, consultants, and talented Sensorimotor Psychotherapists who have made social justice and sociocultural awareness the center of their work and who are my teachers in these arenas. Together, we spearheaded an exploration of racist issues and provided consultation and education to the staff and trainers of SPI on anti-racist, anti-oppression lenses, starting with designing and conducting an Inservice on "Racism, Intersectionality and Implicit Bias." We have been meeting regularly now for several years.

When Deborah Malmud, vice president of Norton, suggested I publish a new book, *A Pocket Guide to Sensorimotor Psychotherapy*, consisting primarily of previously published chapters of mine, I immediately knew the focus needed to be on sociocultural sensitivity and skill. I asked my colleagues to coauthor a new chapter, *Sensorimotor Psychotherapy in Context: Sociocultural Considerations*, and to become consultants and collaborators in revising the remainder of the chapters that I had already written to include diversity, cultural humility, and an anti-racism, anti-oppression platform. We worked closely together to incorporate perspectives from the wisdom of each of our various social locations and identities. By the time I wrote the final new chapter on the principles that guide Sensorimotor Psychotherapy practice, a topic dear to my heart, I was able to better incorporate a sociocultural lens myself, integrating what I had learned from them and others.

Our process of writing and collaborating was both intensely rewarding and intensely challenging. With each of us having different voices, different experiences, and different social locations, we experienced the difficulties of conversing about race and oppression. We discussed, debated, agreed, disagreed, sometimes reaching agreement and sometimes not. As often happens, we found that the dynamics of privilege/oppression that we were writing about and hoping to disrupt were influencing our own group. Collectively and individually we confronted our feelings of being imposters, our sense of not knowing enough, of internalized oppression, of privilege, of not being good enough. As a present-moment experience lived every day for BIPOC, internalized oppression is not something that happened in the past and is now resolved, and writing brought these issues to the fore. Additionally, for my collaborators, the topics we addressed in the book at times touched on a lifetime of intergenerational trauma and systemic oppression. We all had our different struggles. Personally, I was faced with the harm white people, the group to which I belong, had perpetrated on others, and felt the pain of inheriting this legacy of oppression and colonization. I constantly doubted my own insights and questioned whether I might be inappropriately exerting my privilege as the only white person in our group, the founder of the work, and the senior, more experienced author. After much feedback from and discussion with my collaborators, I finally began to realize and come to terms with the prejudice and microaggressions against women, and me personally, in my profession and career. Thus, the dynamics of our diverse group were emblematic of the struggles of our society, and we learned and grew through our own grappling with these issues.

As a published author, and as someone who has grown up within a western context, I was fully aware of the pressures, needs, and deadlines related to writing a book. But this individualistic cultural emphasis on productivity sometimes came into conflict with the more collectivist and collaborative perspective of my consultants. As a group, we were repeatedly confronted with each member's experience of linear time and how long each milestone took, and with trying to balance productivity and group process. We had to reconcile our diverse cultural preferences and perspectives in the context of a western publishing structure with its more academic requirements, schedules, and deadlines. Although I was accustomed to a western paradigm, my collaborators had to contend with operating within the time confines of a western white supremacist way of working throughout the project that did not always lend itself to a more open-ended, intuitive process. One of the difficulties in adhering to a timeline was that our work together was not only about knowledge, but also about learning, exploring and refining our personal perspectives and what we wanted to share in the book. We were unpacking complex dynamics and trying to put them into writing in a process that constantly challenged our estimates of the time it would take to complete an assignment.

Who our audience would be was a constant question. More gracefully at some moments than others, we repeatedly asked ourselves, "Who is this book for?" How do we reach the largest audience with the message we want to convey without seeming to disregard the contributions of western perspectives and education, while at the same time honoring the perspectives and healing perspectives and practices of communities that have often been omitted, devalued, and disrespected? We hoped to reach a diverse group of readers but in the end, we collectively felt we were writing primarily for a white audience, because white people, having been protected from the effects of white supremacy by their very whiteness, were more in need of understanding how racism, white privilege, and systemic oppression manifest in the therapeutic context. And we wanted to clarify the history of predominance of Eurocentric western white perspectives in psychology. At the same time, we hoped that what we addressed would be of use to BIPOC, LGBTQ+, and other people who belong to historically marginalized and oppressed groups. We hoped that the book would center the types of conversations these communities had already been having for quite some time.

We questioned how much we could speak clearly and directly to the effects of white supremacy on our clients, profession, and society without alienating our readers and making them feel blamed, which was never our intention. We struggled to find our way through, especially after receiving feedback from an external reader who felt that we were disrespecting the contributions of white people. We had strong and varied reactions to their feedback based on the dif-

ferent identities and social locations we held, but we heard each
other out and stayed with this tough conversation to completion.

For example, at one point, during a discussion with Sherri about
this external feedback, which occurred days after Ahmaud Arbery
had been murdered, I made the statement that I hoped to build
bridges to white people who did not understand systemic oppression. The conversation got heated between us for several moments.
Eventually, Sherri said that for her, a Black womxn, my statement
felt like "wait," and she questioned, "How much more time do
white people need to understand this is urgent?" This was a moment
where Sherri clarified her voice to me, a person whose social location and position as the founder of SP placed me in a role that is
often perceived as more authoritative or senior. Sherri could have
chosen to shut down, and I could have stuck to my position, but
we didn't do that; Sherri spoke up instead of falling silent and I got
quiet and thoughtful instead of digging in my heels. At this moment
I, as a white person, understood and appreciated a deeper connection with the sense that BIPOC have waited hundreds of years for
actions of justice, and thus the sense of urgency that BIPOC have
made complete sense. It was a pivotal moment, and our conversation
could breathe again. We didn't shy away from open and at times
fierce and profoundly vulnerable interpersonal encounters such as
this and appreciated that we could come to deeper connection and
understanding. We both felt it was a full and beautiful conversation
in hindsight, encompassing two worlds coming together. Sherri was
able to speak her truth, and I came to a deeper understanding of
how critical it is for me, as a white person, to hold the intention,
and take the time, to attune to the experience of BIPOC, as white
privilege can cloud my perception despite my best intentions.

The clients we describe throughout the book are composite
clients based on our clinical practices, with the intention of illustrating a Sensorimotor Psychotherapy approach that integrates an
anti-racist/anti-oppression lens and that may be used with all cli-

ents, although there are risks and concerns in doing this. Traditional western therapeutic practice is not often geared specifically toward anti-racism and anti-oppression, and what is written here is meant to elevate the centrality of holding this perspective in clinical work. Complicated decisions had to be made about what we could include and not include, and we needed to accept that this book is just a beginning of attending to these issues. There is so much more to say and explore. We went back and forth about how much and who we represented in our composite cases, such as questioning if we included a composite case of a disabled person, a certain sexual orientation, gender, nationality, and so forth, and once again came to understand that it would not be possible to include representation from every marginalized population and that was not our goal. We struggled with how to honor the complexity of intersectionality instead of reducing our clients to specific categories and to make sure we were combating stereotypes, not contributing to them. We wanted to do justice to the deep and varied complexities and differences within each of the lives, individual histories, cultures, and races of those that had shared their pain and struggles with us. But what was the best way to do that? And how could we make sure we were doing more good than harm? These were the questions we wrestled with.

To this end, choosing terms and language was a repeated topic of debate, and we examined and dissected descriptive words to carefully determine the ones we would use. For example, in the past, I had used the terms "animal" and "primitive" to describe the subcortical defenses elicited in the face of trauma. Then Shelly Harrell pointed out that both these terms had been used to refer derogatorily to BIPOC. We settled on the term "instinctive" instead. We decided to use "Black" instead of African-American to be inclusive of Black people who have their roots in countries other than the United States, to use "LBGTQ+" to include all orientations, instead of "LBGTQIA," which leaves out many other identities such as pansexual, demisexual, and more. We chose to use "they" instead of gendered pronouns unless we were representing a client who identified with gender. We decided on the un-gendered term, "Latinx" instead of "Latino" and "Latina," although there are some who feel "Latinx" disrespects cultures who use gendered nouns, and thus represents a kind of imperialism. If used in the context of oppression, the phrase "window of tolerance" is problematic since no one should "tolerate" oppression, but we decided to keep it to describe arousal tolerance. In our intention to leave behind a medical disease model, we favored the term "client" to "patient." We discussed mindfulness in most chapters and debated when to expound upon the appropriation of the term and concept of "mindfulness" by western culture from Eastern traditions, and settled on discussing the appropriation of the term primarily in the one chapter that is specifically about mindfulness. In each of these cases we also understood that in spite of our intentions and studied choice of wording there is no way to language and represent perfectly all of the nuances and complexities around the human experience.

Throughout, we had to make hard decisions about what we could include and not include, and how much we could expound upon a topic and stay within our page limit. We often felt that we were only grazing the surface and simplifying a topic down to the essential elements. We frequently exclaimed that we could write an entire book about a certain theme, such as bias. We briefly referenced white fragility, for example, but omitted some of the criticism this concept has received from BIPOC communities. We wanted the content to be internationally applicable but ended up using primarily examples from the U.S., hoping that readers will see similarities to the dynamics of systemic oppression in their own country. We deliberated about how much our readers would already know about our topics. With each concept we tried to explain, we realized some readers would already be familiar with it, while others would find their first exposure to it within these pages.

We wanted to be inclusive and generous in our writing, and we accepted that, despite our best efforts to do so, once these conversations are started, controversy is inevitable; it is part of where we are in the U.S. and in the world. Taking a stand will create a critique. And we welcome the critique. We invite the reader to notice their body as they move through the chapters of the book—what speaks to you, what does not, what raises tension, what elicits a deeper breath, what you wish we had said. We acknowledge that this book is imperfect. It is a beginning. We wanted to blow open the discussion in new ways, to keep this conversation going and to critique and expand it.

Upon the culmination of this book, we wanted to come on stronger with our anti-racist, anti-oppression platform. In many ways the world in which we started working on this project is not the same world now, and sadly in some respects, it still very much is. Just as we were completing the book, COVID-19 turned the world on its head, and ongoing police brutality towards Black bodies in the United States once again reached a tipping point. Currently, with the rise of the Black Lives Matter movement, information about racialized trauma and systemic oppression has proliferated, and many white people are earnestly seeking education and resources to help them to understand systemic racism, white privilege, and how to begin to do the work of dismantling a white supremacist society. In the summer of 2019, when we started this project, that was not the case. If we had more time, and were not working under a word limit, we would have wanted to include more topics, such as the need for bringing an anti-oppression, anti-racism lens to group and community work, as individual psychotherapy often restricts access to services for those with limited resources.

The cognitive dissonance that DeGruy (2017) writes about in *Post Traumatic Slave Syndrome* was central to the U.S. justification of slavery and racialized trauma. Enslaved Africans were portrayed in dehumanizing ways, such as not requiring much sleep which justified 16-hour work days, or as having higher pain tolerance which justified exploitation of their bodies by the medical establishment. Such racist beliefs about BIPOC communities remain pervasive into our culture today. The inaccurate portrayal of immigrants as criminals or as stealing jobs from Americans, which then justifies ICE, is yet another example. The extent of the injustice of systemic oppression and colonization, the fact that these harms have been minimized in public discourse and education, the ubiquity of white supremacist culture, and the damage this all causes deserve more attention.

Paradoxically with more knowledge and awareness come more concerns. I have more questions than answers, but I strongly believe that I have the moral, personal, and social responsibility to confront racist ideology in myself and educate myself so that I can begin to hold the space for these difficult conversations and, alongside my colleagues, begin to integrate an anti-racism, anti-oppression lens in all my interactions, teaching, clinical work and other endeavors. Unveiling the many inevitable and far reaching tendrils of racism, systemic oppression and implicit bias is not an endpoint, but an ongoing process that requires challenging oppression and racism in all its forms—personal, interpersonal, systemic, and cultural. I think grappling with these issues in our work and teachings is an essential next step not only for the field of psychology, but in the U.S. and throughout the world. By doing so, we can show up for social justice, motivate others through our example and rather than contributing to the problem, become active participants in creating a more equitable world.

The Pocket Guide to Sensorimotor Psychotherapy in Context

Chapter 1

SENSORIMOTOR PSYCHOTHERAPY IN CONTEXT: SOCIOCULTURAL PERSPECTIVES

with Sherri Taylor, Laia Jorba, Raymond Rodriguez, and Mary Choi

Not everything that is faced can be changed, but
nothing can be changed until it is faced.

JAMES BALDWIN

For the master's tools will never dismantle the master's house.

AUDRE LORDE

Racism, sexism, ableism, homo- and transphobia, ageism,
fatphobia are algorithms created by humans' struggle to
make peace with the body. A radical self-love world is
a world free from the systems of oppression that make it
difficult and sometimes deadly to live in our bodies.

SONYA RENEE TAYLOR

Contemporary psychotherapy as we understand it was first developed in the 19th century by people of European Christian and Jewish ancestry, designed to treat people of that society. Most other psychotherapeutic modalities established over the past century followed a similar trajectory of development, and Sensorimotor Psychotherapy is no exception. This method, a body-based treatment approach that values the "somatic narrative" (the story told by facial expressions, posture, gesture, movement, and eye gaze) as a viable avenue of therapeutic change, was created in the United States in the mid to late 20th century. It implicitly contains the values and bias of white culture and has not been systematically adapted to address the unique perspectives of people of color and marginalized ethnic populations, nor of other historically marginalized groups (e.g., those with disabilities, the elderly, LGBTQ+ communities). "Whiteness" has a complex meaning as it is both a category of racialized identification and a social construction. Best described as "a constellation of processes and practices rather than as a discrete entity (i.e. skin color alone)" (DiAngelo, 2011, p. 56), whiteness allocates power to those considered white, shaping every aspect of our social, cultural, educational, political, and economic institutions. In psychology, the predominance of whiteness and related Eurocentric/Western views throughout the history of psychology research and practice has resulted in an exclusion of diverse perspectives that do not meet the prevailing criteria for health. More recently, the distinct mental health needs of marginalized people have been a frequent topic of exploration in psychology; however, the impact of mainstream psychology values and white supremacist and heteropatriarchal ideologies on marginalized populations remain relatively underexamined both clinically and theoretically.

The purpose of this chapter is to expand the current conceptualization of Sensorimotor Psychotherapy to increase the reader's knowledge of this legacy and to bring awareness to the influence of culture, racism, and biases toward those we perceive to be unlike ourselves. We hope to inspire practitioners to develop a deeper sensitivity to these issues as well as a commitment to ongoing learning within a contextual sociocultural and anti-oppression lens. The chapter is organized around the model pioneered by Sue, Arredondo, and McDavis (1992) that delineates three essential components of a more equitable, inclusive, and culturally sensitive therapeutic orientation: knowledge, awareness, and skill.

INCREASING KNOWLEDGE AND UNDERSTANDING

In this section, we consider a few of the Eurocentric and Western paradigms that inform Sensorimotor Psychotherapy, introducing some of the culture-bound values and their impact on contemporary clinical practice. We believe that examining these values and paradigms will clarify some of the projections and misunderstandings commonly imposed on those for whom these models were not developed.

Contributions and Limitations of Western Developmental Models

Western Eurocentric models in general prioritize the use of empirical data and natural science methodology to understand social phenomena. These European ideologies were exported to other areas of the world through imperialism and colonization, and were presented as intellectually superior to alternative ways of living (Said, 1978). This reflects a belief in the dominance of reason and a devaluation of intuitive and emotional perception as well as the body that has its roots in the Cartesian dualism of mind and body. One way this belief may manifest is that people who use complicated arguments and language might be perceived as more knowledgeable and trustworthy, while those whose reasonings are based on emotions, intuition, or a felt sense in the body, may be dismissed as subjective. Additionally, this kind Westernized thinking also prioritizes individual rights over collective rights and competition over collaboration, and thus seeks to advance an individual's own status and needs rather than those of the group as a whole.

Many researchers, theorists, and clinicians have highlighted the problems of maintaining such a stance. Boykin, Franklin, and

Yates (1979) pointed out the inherent biases that exist in all forms of research, which are especially problematic when the outcomes of the research are presented as objective and universal. Nobles (1986) coined the phrase "conceptual incarceration" to describe the generalization and indiscriminate application of these partial ideas and biases to all individuals and groups of people. The acronym WASP (Western academic scientific psychology) is used to identify theories and scientific approaches that draw upon research based on a rather limited percentage of the people in the world (Berry et al., 1997). However, despite criticism of its bias and limited applicability, the scientific method and quantitative measurement are consistently valued over emotional insight, direct experience, or other forms of sensory-based or qualitative "knowing," which has contributed to a lack of data about alternative ways of knowing.

Elements of this Western scientific methodology and its assumed universality are evident in many developmental models in psychology. With individualism at its very foundation, these models frame human development as a process of maturing into a self-contained individual with agency and autonomy. Western psychology relies upon a sharp distinction between the self and nonself, that is, a dualistic understanding of self as independent from context (Schachter, 2005). In such models, optimal development centers around individualistic and relationally independent orientations (that prioritize the well-being of the individual over the group), while implicitly or explicitly dismissing collectivist and interdependent orientations (that prioritize the well-being of the group over the individual) as inferior or lacking. Successful individuation—described as the achievement of a separate and distinct sense of self—is touted as the direction and telos of human development and a necessary foundation for psychological wellness, vitality, and health across the life span. In contrast, other models founded in ecological theory are increasingly gaining influence and represent an alternative to mainstream individualistic models (Harrell & Gallardo, 2008). These models highlight the multiple contextual and community influences and interactions that impact and shape the child's development, from the most immediate environment of the child to larger sociocultural elements (Harrell & Gallardo, 2008).

Attachment theory is drawn from traditional Western scientific models, but highlights the relational and interdependent aspects of human development. This model, with its focus on the quality of early childhood relationships, has dramatically changed the field of psychology and continues to dominate prevailing perspectives on child development. Innovative in his time, John Bowlby emphasized the importance of early caregiver-child interactions as critical for healthy development, thus challenging Freudian concepts of infant development and the individualistic nature of other models. This emphasis on relationship represented a paradigm shift, as Sroufe and Siegel (2019, para. 1) state:

> By divorcing human attachment from the drive-reduction notions of Freudian theory, Bowlby laid the foundation for a shift from seeing people as individuals somehow standing apart from their social environment to a more fine-tuned grasp of just how deeply relational human nature is.

The contributions of attachment theory have profoundly impacted psychotherapy practice. However, although attachment theory has been extensively examined across cultures, research remains limited, and cultural elements that contribute to attachment outcomes are not apparent (Agishtein & Brumbaugh, 2013).

Bowlby stated that infants were biologically wired to develop a singular relationship with the caregiver. Because attachment is thought to be rooted in biology, it is assumed to be universal across cultures. However, while the survival need for relationship itself is universal, establishing a primary attachment with one particular caregiver is not. Additionally, attachment research often bypasses critical cultural factors relevant to caregiving practices. These include diverse family and community structures, socioeconomic status, family culture and kinship structure, ethnicity, education levels, mental health issues, medical care access, and so forth, all of which strongly influence both the child's development and caregiver availability (Cassidy et al., 2013). Applying generally culture-bound conceptions of family structure of the industrial world (nuclear family, fewer children per family, late first pregnancy, high education, relative financial stability, and so forth), which represent a limited portion of the entire global population, to all cultures fails to account for sociocultural variety. In Keller's (2018, p. 11414) words, "The claim of universality for attachment theory, qualifying one particular view as best for all children in the world is in stark contrast to the actual ecosocial diversity."

Ainsworth's Strange Situation research expanded attachment theory by focusing on the behavior of children when their mothers left them alone with strangers and then returned (Ainsworth & Bell, 1970). Although some of her research was conducted in countries outside of Europe, Western theoretical premises were used as the contrasting baseline norm. Such premises are biased toward ideals of autonomy and individuation of the self, prioritizing a parental style of sensitivity that requires the caregiver to be available and attuned to the signals of the child, and values child behaviors such as social competence and the idea of a secure base connected to one caregiver (Rothbaum et al., 2000). In contrast, infants in non-Western farming societies learn to comply with the directives of multiple caregivers who view an infant not as an independent agent who deserves attuned ministering to their signals (a Western view) but as a "calm, unexpressive, quiet, and harmoniously well-integrated communal agent" (Keller, 2018, p. 4). When judged by the Western standard of sensitivity, caregiver practices adaptive in such cultures are viewed as emotionally distant, harsh, and unresponsive to the child's immediate needs, and parents can be considered inadequate (Morelli et al., 2018). Furthermore, in collectivist cultures, children are not seen as having rights over their caregivers, and "the notion of separating the rights of children from the family or community circle would be deeply and structurally—indeed, ethically—problematic" (Morelli et al., 2018, p. 6).

Bowlby wrote that "the infant and young child should experience a warm, intimate, and continuous relationship with his mother (or permanent mother substitute) in which both find satisfaction and enjoyment" (1951, p. 13). According to attachment theory, failure to form a one-on-one attachment bond with a caregiver, or the disruption of this dyad, is considered detrimental to the development of secure attachment in a nearly deterministic manner, while at the same time stranger anxiety is considered normal. The Strange Situation research showed differences in children's responses to both separation and reunion with the mother, leading to the categorizations of secure, insecure avoidant, and insecure ambivalent; later, a fourth category was added, disorganized/disoriented (Main & Solomon, 1986, 1990). Relevant for technologically advanced cultures, these views do not always take into account the predominant child-rearing practices in non-Western, non-technological communities, and to risk classifying children of these communities with disregard for sociocultural norms and meanings neglects critical factors.

For instance, ethnographic studies in sub-Saharan Africa show that communities in which child-rearing tasks are distributed among many people also produce well-adapted, securely attached children who lack an anxiety response when separated from their biological caregiver and do not experience fear of strangers (Gottlieb, 2004; Otto & Keller, 2014). In another example, among the Efe of Zaire, newborns are cared for by various women, and at six weeks of age are in the company of their birth mother less than with other people, yet grow up to be well-adjusted adults (Tronick et al., 1992). Similarly, Otto's (2008) and Otto and Keller's (2014) research on northwest Cameroonian Nso practices confirms that fostering a child's bonds to older siblings also produces well-adjusted children. In these more collectivist cultures, applying the concepts of attachment theory that reflect an individualist, independent cultural orientation can be misleading. Not surprisingly, most cross-cultural research on attachment patterns systematically finds a higher percentage of securely attached children in Western developed countries (Keller, 2018), although so-called "insecure" patterns are often shown to be adaptive when contextualized. Additionally, Tronick (2007) has noted that infants display different attachment patterns with different caregivers, yet this complexity is not commonly acknowledged. The prevailing view is that a child develops one attachment pattern that remains stable throughout adulthood (Mikulincer & Shaver, 2007). Moreover, it is not only possible to develop different attachment patterns with different people, but also to "earn" secure attachment as an adult (Main, 2000). Both these potentials—to develop different attachment patterns and earn secure attachment—challenge the deterministic nature of attachment patterns in early childhood.

Attachment theory as it is often applied provides an example of how the unexamined use of psychotherapy practices based solely in Western models increases the possibility of misunderstandings, misattunements, and mistreatment of persons, communities, and cultures that do not seek to approximate such standards or those that have been historically defined as "other" by the privileged culture. For example, relational patterns common to extended family systems and collectivistic cultures could be misconstrued as enmeshed and thus evidence of pathology (Kağitçibaşi, 1990). A therapist with an individualistic orientation might view the physical proximity between a mother and child in a more collectivist Asian culture "as symbiotic and overdependent" (Pallaro, 1997, p. 229). A parent from India living in a European country who lifts a hand to the child and firmly demands that the child cease what they are doing—normal parenting practice in Indian culture—may be assessed as abusive by Western social services (Keller, 2018). When clients do not meet Western ideals of relationship or developmental trajectories toward autonomy and independence (e.g., demonstrate less interest in productivity or prefer a relaxed time orientation over a fixed or future time orientation), they may run the risk of being perceived by therapists as underachieving, hostile, lazy, resistant, or generally not committed to therapy. Conversely, a client from an individualistic culture could be perceived by a therapist whose culture is collectivist as selfish or egotistical for strongly asserting their right to personal gratification or achievement. When both therapist and client value an individualistic cultural orientation, qualities such as dependence on others, a desire to blend in, and disinterest in one's unique expression may be faulted or seen as undesirable.

In sum, as Tronick states, "Western models of childrearing and development are extremely limited and narrow" (2007, p. 12). We mental health professionals can challenge claims of universality and expand our lens to include collectivist or even hybrid developmental models. And although attachment theory continues to be valuable, we also need to include the perspective that an adaptive attachment pattern depends on context (Keller, 2013) and congruence with the belief system of the community (Tronick, 2007).

Trauma Theory and Models in Western Societies

The effect and impact of trauma, defined as a threat to safety that elicits instinctive defensive responses and dysregulated arousal (Ogden et al., 2006), is strongly influenced by cultural norms, values, and perspectives. Culture shapes not only whether certain events are experienced as traumatic, but also how an individual makes meaning of those events. For example, the greater the significance of an event to the person and community and/or the level of disruption of cultural practices due to the event (SAMHSA, 2014), the greater the impact. However, in Western psychology, post-traumatic stress disorder (PTSD) is generally identified as a universal phenomenon observed cross-culturally (Figueira et al., 2007; Foa et al., 2009) and thus provides the frame for most of the common understandings of trauma. Although the neural substrates of PTSD are well documented, "there is very little empirical work investigating the impact of culture on these systems" (Liddell & Jobson, 2016, p. 1). Thus, differences in "idioms of distress," a term introduced by Nichter (1982, 2020) in reference to "socially and culturally resonant means of experiencing and expressing distress in local worlds" (Nichter, 2010, p. 405), and alternative explanations for symptoms considered to be related to PTSD by the Western world are areas that requires more exploration and expansion (Jacob, 2019; Kaiser & Jo Weaver, 2019).

Trauma literature often omits the influence of historical trauma, which is defined as "cumulative emotional and psychological wounding, over the lifespan and across generations, emanating from massive group trauma experiences" (Brave Heart, 2003; Brave Heart & DeBruyn, 1998, p. 7). Over the centuries, groups of people have been discriminated against, terrorized, and at times decimated based on one or more of their social identities. The generational aspect of this form of trauma has been described by other authors as transgenerational, intergenerational, cross-generational, and multigenerational. Historical trauma can be found in "numerous colonized indigenous groups throughout the world, as well as . . . many other cultural groups and communities that share a history of oppression, victimization, or massive group trauma exposure" (Mohatt et al., 2014, p. 2). These include the historical trauma of African Americans, described as "post-traumatic slave syndrome" (DeGruy, 2017); the trauma of Native Americans, described as a "soul wound" (Duran et al., 1998); and the experience of descendants of Holocaust survivors around the world (Kellermann, 2001).

Historical trauma (and racialized trauma in particular) is an intrinsic dynamic in any country where there is a political and social cleavage between groups that hold power (e.g., national citizens) versus those who do not (e.g., immigrants). A close examination of the history of the United States reveals a pervasive ideology of white dominance that led to the genocide of Native Americans, the African slave trade, Jim Crow, Japanese internment camps, and the current immigration detention centers, to name a few. The racialized dominance inherent in these actions and policies became further entrenched as this ideology was transformed into normative political, economic, social, and cultural practice and embedded in the very psyche of the United States. Although often covert, such as in the predominance of Western ideas of health and healing and how pathology is defined, racism also presents itself in more overt forms such as in the disproportionate number of Black and Brown people incarcerated or in deliberate discriminatory hiring practices (Alexander, 2020; Quillian et al., 2017). The ideology of white racial dominance is thus institutionalized as normative and natural, and the structural advantages of this privileged group become invisible so that whiteness remains a self-perpetuating cultural structure (Frankenberg, 1993; Lietz, 2015). In psychology, for example, dominance is maintained through policies and practices that privilege white people, which contributes to the lack of diversity among psychiatrists, doctors, and mental health professionals in relation to the population as a whole (Roberts, et al., 2020). Furthermore, racial/ethnic marginalized people and those of lower socioeconomic status have a reduced probability of accessing state-of-the-art psychotherapy from well-trained therapists, receiving the needed number of sessions, reaping the benefit of interventions most applicable to their difficulties, or securing timely treatment (Harrell & Sloan-Pena, 2006).

Racialized trauma and the trauma of systemic oppression are closely related. Systemic or structural oppression refers to the ways in which institutional practices and policies interact to keep specific groups of people at a disadvantage, reducing their options for the future and sometimes even their very survival. It is widespread, with devastating outcomes for those groups, for example when girls

are denied education, immigrants are denied work, Blacks are incarcerated at many times the rate of whites for similar crimes, or when
institutionalized Islamophobia justifies violence and even war. Both
trauma and oppression are perpetrated not only in overt ways but
also in subtle and often intractable ways by people who would not
consider themselves oppressors or racists. The impact of this individual and systemic oppression affects a multitude of groups, including
women, Blacks, Chicanos, Latinx, Arabs, Asians, Native Americans, immigrants, refugees, Jews, lesbian, gay, bisexual, transgender,
and gender nonconforming individuals, older people, working-class
people, those with larger bodies, and the physically and/or mentally
disabled, to name a few. Currently, we are seeing manifestations and
results of systemic oppression in the coronavirus pandemic that disproportionately affects vulnerable, marginalized, and food-insecure
communities who have less access to resources such as shelter, health
care, less financial backup to support them during shelter-at-home
mandates, and less availability of online options (technology, Wi-Fi,
etc.). Concomitantly this global pandemic is fueling fear, breeding
misinformation, and spreading racist scapegoating and accusations
in statements such as, "The Chinese are to blame for this," calling
it the "Chinese virus." Still other racist theories are circulating that
hold Jews responsible for this pandemic as well.

The varied and nuanced responses to the multitudes of traumas
and oppressions, such as those outlined above, may be judged as pathological without understanding their cultural implications or their
relationship to systemic oppression and racialized trauma. As Harrell
and Sloan-Pena state, "The ideology of racism has been embedded
in psychological theory and research since its inception and continues
to influence what is considered normal or abnormal, healthy or maladaptive, functional or dysfunctional" (2006, p. 396). For example,
a tendency to view overactive instinctive survival defenses that are
elicited in the face of threat (cry-for-help, fight, flight, freeze, feigned
death) as needing to be fixed or treated discounts the possibility that

these defenses might be vital and crucial strategies necessary to survival in hostile environments. Emotional numbing and behavioral inhibition, common reactions when confronted with discrimination (Sanders Thompson, 2006), can be adaptive responses when the targeted person perceives that challenging the perpetrators would lead to a negative outcome (Sue et al., 2019). In another example, toughness and its associated qualities (e.g., difficulties with being vulnerable, armoring of the body) might be interpreted as negative or as something to be softened, when an individual may need this protection when confronted with racism or other unsafe situations.

In sum, because institutionalized practices that privilege white cultural groups against people of color and other marginalized groups are usually present in society, it is critical for psychotherapists working with traumatized individuals and communities to understand the dynamics of each sociocultural context and the impact on psychotherapy practice. Awareness of the different idioms of distress, as well as the legacies of racialized trauma, oppression, and historical violence, is essential when addressing individual or community presentations of trauma-related dysregulation.

Western Perspectives on the Body and Nonverbal Communication

Western perspectives on mind-body dualism tend to dominate how we see and experience the body itself. Descartes crystallized the idea of division between the body and the mind by proposing that the body is an instrument without consciousness, a concept that gave birth to modern science and medicine (Mehta, 2011). This view has largely carried through to the present day in the Western viewpoint that the body and the mind are distinct and can be studied and treated separately. The body is usually perceived as lesser than the mind, driven by passion instead of intellect, and considered an enemy to control because it challenges cognitive objective logic by the subjectivity of the senses (Aposhyan, 1999). This perspective has contributed to the development of specialized fields and professions that address problems of the mind and the body as separate from one another.

However, although it is not yet mainstream, an emergent recognition of the mutual interdependence between the body and the mind has started to appear in approaches such as integrative medicine and many models of psychotherapy, including Sensorimotor Psychotherapy. Despite these shifts toward holism, the cultural impacts of mind-body dualism continue to affect perspectives on the body itself. For example, the body is often viewed as something to be controlled, shamed, and objectified. This is apparent in the popular fixation with molding and enhancing bodies through fitness, dieting, and surgery (Hanckock et al., 2000). Norms of what is acceptable and attractive in terms of the body itself as it relates to color, size, ability, age, shape, proportion, posture, stance, and symmetry primarily reflect Western heteropatriarchal values (Hanckock et al., 2000). These idealized Western/European standards of beauty, such as being thin, fair, and blonde, as well as appropriate physical behaviors and how the body is to be adorned, are then imposed upon various cultures and races. Within the confines of these standards, "the body that acts and appears different becomes a marked pariah and disrupter of the social order" (Thompson, 1997, p. 254, in Caldwell, 2013). People whose bodies do not conform to the norms of beauty, color, presentation, and the like will also tend to be seen with more suspicion and biases, even if unconsciously.

The influence of these values is also evident in norms related to which bodies are to be controlled or policed. For instance, one of the myths of "white-body supremacy" (the privileging and elevating of white bodies above all others) is based on the belief that Black bodies are strong and, if not subdued or enslaved, must otherwise be controlled and punished (Menakem, 2017). In contrast, white bodies are seen as more fragile (DiAngelo, 2011), a version of the puritan Victorian ideal of "angels" that need protection by the police.

Culture and context also shape nonverbal patterns of body posture, movement, expression, and nonverbal communication (Bird-whistell, 2010; Hall & Hall, 1959; Knapp, 2006). Physical behaviors of dominance and subordination are learned through countless social interactions over time, and these become procedural habits. Johnson asserts, "asymmetrical interactions are a hallmark of the nonverbal exchanges between individuals from dominant/subordinate social groups" (2015, p. 83). Privilege/oppression dynamics are reinforced through these learned procedures of nonverbal communication (including movement, posture, boundary actions, use of space, gestures, and expression), all of which are used (consciously or non-consciously) to maintain societal norms and power dynamics (Henley, 1977; Henley & Freeman, 1995; Johnson, 2015; Johnson et al., 2018).

Reviews of research in Western cultures confirm that status—determined by different relationships of various factors (such as race, gender, class, economic status, occupational rank, age, and so forth) "is a powerful organizer of proxemic behavior" (Gillespie & Leffler, 1983, p. 141). For example, implicit conventional rules of personal space in Western European culture prescribe that people of the dominant culture are permitted to take up more interpersonal space through expansive postures and movements. Dominance can also be demonstrated by less formality, more variety, flexibility, and ease in gesture and posture, while oppression is indicated by the opposite (Johnson, 2015; Johnson et al., 2018). Eye contact as well serves to modulate and manage social interactions, including power and oppression dynamics. For example, prolonged, direct eye contact is a signal of dominance and often aggression in animals, including humans (Ellyson & Dovidio, 1985). Similarly, the use of touch can reflect power/oppression dynamics. Since physical contact indicates more intimate access to another person, a person deemed to have lower status learns to refrain from touching a person deemed to have higher status, while the person with higher status is permitted to initiate and informally touch the other person (Henley & Freeman, 1995). This is also observed in patriarchal, heteronormative, and gender-binary cultures to reinforce male dominance (Borden & Homleid, 1978), even taking into account cultural differences in touch behaviors (DiBiase & Gunnoe, 2004). However, in "societies where gender roles are less defined," the use of touch for dominance is less clear across the gender category (DiBiase & Gunnoe, 2004, p. 59).

The power of nonverbal language lies in its repetitive nature, which becomes automatic and procedural over time, and thus harder to identify (Johnson, 2015; Johnson et al., 2018; Ogden, Minton & Pain, 2006). The body's language is especially significant when we consider that the impact of nonverbal communication has been shown to be four times stronger than that of verbal language when both are used simultaneously (Argyle et al., 1970). In this sense, seemingly ordinary social gestures replicate and perpetuate histories of cultural domination and subordination.

Awareness of the biases toward the body as well as attention to the nonverbal perpetuation of dominance and submission are often lacking in mental health. As psychotherapists and counselors, we need to account for culture and oppression dynamics and how these are re-enacted through both verbal and nonverbal expressions in the therapy interaction. When they are ignored, the most well-intentioned approaches can, and often do, negatively impact therapeutic formulation, assessment, intervention, and, ultimately, progress.

Assessment and Treatment Considerations

Despite the progress made by including cultural formulations in the current *Diagnostic and Statistical Manual of Mental Disorders* (DSM-5), its main taxonomy of pathology is based on research that privileges the Western and Eurocentric value systems as previously outlined. These cultural formulations are lacking in the *International Classification of Disease* (ICD-11) (Paniagua, 2018), although some argue that "the more flexible language of the *ICD-11* diagnostic guidelines is intended to increase clinical utility by allowing for cultural variations in presentation as well as contextual and health-system factors that may affect diagnostic practice" (Clark et al., 2017, p. 84). Still, because the classifications of diseases were developed with individualistic and Western values in mind, when people are evaluated against these standards, their unique conditions, challenges, and alternative explanations of symptoms can be lost. This has resulted in a history of, at best, inaccurate psychological assessments and diagnoses for individuals and communities that do not align with such standards and, at worst, legitimized the perpetration of physical and/ or psychological violence against those individuals and communities (Barrera & Jordan, 2011; Cosgrove, 2005; Hammack et al., 2013; Kirschner, 2013; Szasz, 1971). Similarly problematic is the fact that even when there is an increasing effort to develop more culturally appropriate methods (i.e., assessments, treatments, theoretical orientations, etc.) in mental health, research continues to show disparities in access, diagnosis, and quality of treatment (Snowden, 2003).

Mental health practitioners' decision making about diagnosis and treatment is influenced by their internal bias and prejudices (Escobar, 2012; Snowden, 2003) as well as cultural misunderstandings of symptoms (Snowden, 2003), which can result in either an "overdiagnostic bias" or an "underdiagnostic bias" (López, 1989). Harrell and Sloan-Pena clarify, "Clinicians may overpathologize racial/ ethnic [marginalized] clients or interpret behavior as deviant when a client is not understood within a cultural context. Alternatively, clinicians may also underpathologize racial/ethnic [marginalized] clients and label a problem behavior as 'cultural' in an attempt to not be perceived as racist" (2006, p. 401). Overpathologizing is well documented in disparities in diagnosing the African American population in the last two decades: for example, African Americans are overdiagnosed with schizophrenia disorders, while research shows less diagnosis of affective disorders (Snowden, 2003). These disparities between privileged and marginalized groups are likely to be present in any country where marginalized groups do not fit the predominant standards of wellness.

Sidhu explains that applying Western models indiscriminately is "a forceful, oppressive endeavor [that] replicates colonization, where Eastern [and other non-Western] ways of healing are disregarded and Western theories are seen as the 'true' ways of healing" (2017, p. 13). Ancient, traditional, and folk healing and alternative forms of diagnosis and treatment of psychological disturbance have been largely neglected and even devalued by dominant conceptualizations of psychotherapy (Sidhu, 2017). This exclusionary focus leaves psychology bereft of a truly nuanced understanding of both the diversity of the human experience and the multiple approaches to healing. Recognizing this ethnocentrism in Western psychology requires us to learn from other ways of thinking about illness and from different practices for assessing and healing beyond hospitals or medical interventions (Christopher et al., 2014). These can include, among others, reiki, curanderismo, rootworkers, Ayurvedic therapies, traditional Chinese medicine therapies, and group practices such as spiritual rituals, and ceremonies like drumming circles, and so forth.

In terms of diagnosis, many cultures formulate explanations of symptoms that are different from those of the *DSM-5*. For example, hearing voices is viewed in certain cultures as the emergence of the person's spiritual giftedness, the need for increased protection of personal energy, or as ancestral communication (Valavanis et al., 2019). Symptoms of dissociative identity disorder, associated in the West with severe trauma, might be accepted in other cultures as an indication of being inhabited by spirits or ancestors (Kirmayer, 1996). Thus, in Afro-Caribbean countries and in many Latin American countries, a person may more readily seek the guidance of a curandero, spiritual diviner, or native healer for a perceived mental health issue than a doctor or psychotherapist.

To increase the utility and effectiveness of Western paradigms of psychotherapy, we need to question when they are applicable, and also to include other sources and approaches to understand wellness, pathology, and healing as conceptualized and practiced by different cultures and subcultures. This is delicate territory, since this dialogue can often lead to appropriation of these practices by those without adequate knowledge of and deference to the ancestral and/or spiritual underpinnings of such practices. For example, "mindfulness" is a commonly utilized term in the field, including Sensorimotor Psychotherapy, but it is often used without recognition of the historical and cultural background of its roots in Eastern practices and spirituality (cf. Chapter 4, this volume). The nuanced variations that occur when these practices are applied in a different cultural context or used to promote particular goals is rarely acknowledged. Such cultural appropriation can reinforce the devaluation of other cultures, maintain privilege/oppression dynamics, and sometimes serve to increase the profit of people in power who commodify cultural artifacts. As mentioned above, one way to address this issue is to cultivate a thoughtful approach to when and how we use contributions originating in other cultures, and to give credit to these sources, while studying and analyzing what changes in meaning occur when we import these practices into our own cultural context. For example, we can acknowledge that mindfulness, in a Western conceptualization, serves a different purpose when applied to psychotherapy than it does in the original contexts. Without such thoughtfulness, we collude with the inherent oppression and colonialism that exists in cultural appropriation.

In sum, mainstream mental health models that inform current evidence-based methods in psychotherapy are founded in Western understandings of illness and health while practices from other cultures are typically undervalued by the dominant culture. Therapists need to consider that much can be learned from unpacking culturally bound assumptions and starting a dialogue with alternative ways of understanding symptoms and pathways to well-being.

DEEPENING AWARENESS AND SENSITIVITY

In this section, we move from theoretical understanding into personal awareness of our bias and how it operates in mind and body. All of us assess the external world according to preconceptions that arise from the norms and customs of the groups to which we belong and from associations we have formed that are reinforced by the dominant culture. These preconceptions obscure understanding of the sociocultural phenomena of privilege and oppression, and also structure and constrict our capacity to form equitable relationships with those we perceive as different. Understanding how introjected values impact our prejudices and behaviors toward our clients begins with awareness of their historical context and the conditionings of explicit and implicit bias. We will explore how to cultivate cultural sensitivity and humility, accept the inevitability of implicit bias, and suggest strategies to increase awareness of our own bias.

Understanding Explicit and Implicit Bias

Bias—defined here as the attitudes, stereotypes, and prejudices we hold toward our own groups of reference and toward groups of people that we perceive as different from ours—can be explicit or implicit. Explicit bias includes conscious opinions and belief systems. Although we may not reveal these to others, they are reflected in our internal thought processes, emotions, and somatic responses. Behaviors based on explicit prejudices vary from more extreme forms of hate and violence to more subtle forms of nonverbal acrimony, animosity, harassment, and discrimination. Explicit biases are often modified to appear more socially acceptable when social norms reinforce values of equality and justice (Perception Institute, 2019). However, expressions of explicit bias increase when there are few social norms in place to restrict prejudice, or when people in power model or endorse such expressions, hence validating previously hidden prejudices of the general population. In contrast, implicit bias encompasses the values, opinions, attitudes, stereotypes, and prejudices we hold toward both our own groups and toward groups of people different from our own that are outside of our awareness, governed by processes that are reflexive and automatic. They can also be described as shortcut assessments that are triggered subcortically, without reflection, to facilitate immediate judgments of people and situations. Hence, implicit bias includes all that "we don't know that we don't know" and "what we don't think that we think."

Bias arises partly because the brain is wired to maximize both efficiency and survival through association and categorization. Before we develop language and narratives about the self, we begin to classify stimuli at a basic level. Even in utero, we learn to categorize prosody and cadence of movement as familiar or unfamiliar, and act accordingly as we physically orient toward safety cues and away from threat cues. Once born, categorization continues: For instance, babies have an innate preference for particular facial traits and learn quickly to recognize the traits of their main caregivers, including the characteristics of their own race or ethnicity (Bobula, 2011; Dunham et al., 2008). However, when infants are exposed to diverse racial groups, they do not show patterns of preference toward their own racial or ethnic group or against others (Dunham et al., 2008).

Categorizing stimuli is elaborated throughout development by imitating others while exploring and adapting to one's specific sociocultural environment. As we mature, we steadily absorb information from a variety of sources: direct interactions with and observations of others, overheard conversations among adults and peers, education both formal and informal, music lyrics, books, news, movies, TV, and, more recently, the internet and social media. Our brains continually compare present-moment sensory stimulation from the environment to this stored information, facilitating lightning-quick unconscious and biased associations upon which we may act without realizing our prejudice. Thus, learned associations and categorizations become procedural and are subsequently applied reflexively and universally regardless of context. This leads to automatic projections between groups that we perceive as "us" versus groups that we perceive as "others" (Tajfel & Forgas, 1981). So, although procedural learning supports survival and belonging, it can also constrain receptivity to new information (Ogden et al., 2006; Tronick, 2007), and in this sense can support and perpetuate bias.

Reshamwala's (2016) short film on bias and race clarifies how we form mental shortcuts that we may not agree with consciously but nevertheless act upon unwittingly. He describes the associations we unconsciously make as pairings typical in a given culture, such as peanut butter being paired with jelly in the United States. All cultural assumptions, but particularly those of the dominant culture, influence our non-conscious perspectives of our own groups and of other groups. In a seminal study, Bertrand and Mullainathan (2004) altered résumés to reflect typically white and typically Black-sounding names and emailed them to potential employers who had explicitly expressed the intention to increase the diversity of their personnel. Despite this conscious intention, potential employers were 50% more likely to respond to those résumés that had a white-sounding male name. Also noteworthy was that employers responded more frequently to résumés with white-sounding names who were rated as average than to résumés with Black-sounding names who were rated as "highly skilled." There are numerous additional studies that also demonstrate that job applicants with ethnic-sounding names working in English-speaking countries like the United States, United Kingdom, and Canada are not hired as much as those with English-sounding names, a phenomenon that has not changed in the last four decades (Quillian et al., 2017). Such bias does not only apply to race and ethnicity. Moss-Racusin, Dovidio, Brescoll, Graham, and Handelsman (2012), who used male and female names for identical student application materials for a laboratory management assignment, found that faculty of both genders rated males as more competent, and offered males both a higher salary and more opportunities for mentoring than female applicants. Although this study only examined binary categories of gender, its results highlight social biases around gender dynamics, in this case in a patriarchal culture.

As these studies reveal, implicit bias operates outside of our awareness and can contradict our explicit attitudes and beliefs, even when negative bias is toward the group to which one belongs. These attitudes and beliefs are reinforced by popular culture, language, the media, social networks, technology, and the like, which often support Western Eurocentric ideas and promulgate them globally, to the exclusion of other perspectives. Disturbingly, the reinforcement of these stereotypes and associations through media and social structures perpetuates systemic oppression, white supremacy, and racism. Some common inaccurate and offensive associations are African American men/violent; Asian/compliant; poor people/lazy; migrants/troublemakers; women/incompetent in business; blonde women/intellectually inferior; Arabs and Muslims/terrorists; gay men/feminine; lesbian/masculine; overweight/unhealthy; disabled/less intelligent; Native American/alcoholic; homeless people/drug addicts; and sadly there are many more. None of us are immune from the cultural conditioning that ingrains such associations in our unconscious, and even with a conscious belief in equality and fair treatment for all people, implicit attitudes and practices of discrimination toward specific groups of people, including one's own, can still occur.

Identifying Microaggression, Denial, and Vulnerability to Bias
Biased associations can lead to microaggressions, defined as "brief and commonplace daily verbal, behavioral, and environmental

indignities, whether intentional or unintentional, that communicate hostile, derogatory, or negative racial, gender, sexual orientation, and religious slights and insults to the target person or group" (Sue, 2010, p. 5). Microaggressions are common occurrences when people who belong to different races, cultures, or religions interact, and are regularly inflicted on groups such as women, LGBTQ+ community members, those with disabilities, the elderly, people with more body fat, and immigrants, but also occur between interethnic groups as well (Sue et al., 2007). Like the studies above show, those who inflict microaggressions are usually unaware that their communications are offensive (Sue et al., 2007). It is important to highlight that microaggressions prevail because the cultural conditioning that drives them upholds and perpetuates "social inequalities and hierarchies that are desirable to the in-group at the expense of the out-group" (Williams, 2019, Defining Microaggressions section). However, because members of the dominant culture are conditioned to avoid recognizing racial and ethnic inequities (Phillips & Lowery, 2018), and because they are not typically the targets of the effects of prejudice and bias, their own and others' microaggressions often remain unnoticed. In addition to all these reasons, microaggressions are more likely to take place when there is a power imbalance, such as in the therapist/client dyad (Sue 2010; Williams, 2019); hence, it is imperative that therapists examine their own biases and how they might play out in the therapy hour.

Denial of bias is common among us all, often occurring where we hold a place of privilege, which renders our bias hidden. Our desire for social acceptability and a need to protect an egalitarian self-image can often lead to this denial. For instance, we may readily identify racism and prejudice in society but fail to recognize racialized implicit biases within ourselves, both because they occur outside of our conscious awareness, and because ignorance of bias maintains congruence with how we want to see ourselves as well as how we want others to see us. When we have tendencies toward explicit bias, our desire to avoid disapproval from others, preserve a positive image of ourselves, and uphold anti-racist, anti-oppression attitudes would have us edit or modify our behavior to be more acceptable. However, when bias is implicit and thus unconscious, we are unable to recognize the need to modify our behavior. Therefore, regardless of our explicit values and good intentions toward others (including our clients), implicit bias can lead to inadvertent microaggressions.

Acting upon implicit bias is particularly prevalent when we have not addressed our internalized privilege or oppression, or become aware of our biases. We can begin to notice implicit bias as a sense of general discomfort or "feelings of anxiety and uneasiness" toward people of different groups (Dovidio & Gaertner, 2004, p. 42). These feelings may also manifest somatically as sweaty palms, longer or shorter eye contact, more blinking, frozen smiles, or unconscious efforts to bypass difference through denial, fixation, or overcompensation. For example, in a dyad between a white therapist and a client of color, denial of color (colorblindness) might lead the therapist to invalidate the client's experience of being a person of color by saying, "I don't see color; I just see you as a person." Or a therapist may demonstrate a fixation on difference when identities are not shared, and continue to misgender a client who is gender expansive. Finally, a therapist's attempt to speak with the vocal intonations, verbal patterns, and/or other phrases stereotypically associated with the oppressed or targeted group may also signal discomfort or attempts to cover up discomfort (e.g., a heterosexual therapist who uses idioms associated with gay and queer culture like "tea," and "hunty," whose origins are from Black and Latinx LGBTQ+ culture). It should be noted that overemphasizing positive qualities can also be microaggressions, as in telling a refugee, "With all you have endured, I'm sure you can deal with this problem too." As with any interpersonal process, these expressions may also be bidirectional and happen from therapist to client and from client to therapist and across variations of difference.

The tendency to employ the mental shortcuts of stereotyped categories is intensified in stressful situations, when access to cortical processes might be more limited and the brain relies on speed over accuracy. Based on our personal and cultural backgrounds and societal messaging, these quick judgments may be predicated on subtle and not so subtle physiological responses to threat, regardless of whether the threat comes from a truly unsafe situation or is assumed to do so. In other words, implicit bias and stereotyping are more active when our arousal is approaching a state of hyper- or hypoarousal. We are also more susceptible to implicit bias when making decisions quickly or without sufficient information, for instance, in rapid action–reaction encounters between law enforcement and Black individuals (Menakem, 2017). However, with intention, we can become aware of our tendencies and develop strategies to mitigate denial and work to reduce their negative impact.

Strategies to Challenge Bias

Understanding bias is facilitated by examining the concepts of social location and intersectionality. Social location refers to each of the groups people belong to, defined by such factors as race, socioeconomic status, gender, age, religion, sexual orientation, ability, education, language, geographic location, immigration status, and the like. Social location answers the questions, "who am I? and who are my people?" (Kirk & Okazawa-Rey, 2013), giving rise to a sense of group membership. While some of these locations may be more visible, such as race, many are not, such as gender, sexual orientation, class, and some disabilities. Some social locations are stable, and some develop and change over a life span. Intersectionality, a term introduced by Crenshaw (1989), describes the process and dynamic by which these social locations interact and come together at any given time and how they are acted upon by the forces of domination and oppression. Considering intersectionality helps us look beyond a single identity of who a person is and instead understand the person as a complex tapestry of identities that have an intersecting impact on the entirety of a person's experience. For instance, a person's male privilege is mitigated by being undocumented, working class, and disabled. Similarly, a working-class person will hold greater privilege when cisgender, heterosexual, and white.

As therapists, our task is to continually work toward understanding our own social locations and the roots of our own identity that is informed by the sociopolitical history of the groups to which we belong and the power and privilege these groups hold. For instance, if we benefit from white privilege, it would be helpful to understand the construction of whiteness and white supremacy, or if we identify as cisgender, to become curious about all the privileges we hold and the ways intersex, transgender, and gender-nonconforming individuals have been oppressed throughout history. We can read and get acquainted with the literature of our own history from a critical standpoint, connect with other people of our own group that can support us in awakening to these privileges, and explore how to use them consciously to decrease inequality. Identifying when our social locations indicate positions of subordination or subjugation and exploring the ways in which oppression, historical and current, impacts us, is also helpful. For example, the social locations of a highly educated, Latino, 35-year-old heterosexual man with documented status, or of a white, wealthy, physically disabled lesbian woman whose first language is English include elements of both privilege and oppression. Examining our privileged locations, we learn to recognize the invisibility of our own implicit bias and how this invisibility has benefited those that share similar social locations, while placing others with dissimilar locations at a disadvantage.

A critical first step is to consider our early learning about differences, including races, ethnicities, cultures, and social groups. In our own self-examination, we have found it valuable to reflect on questions such as these: When did you first become aware that there were different races or cultures? What early messages (verbal and nonverbal) did you receive from those around you about your-self and people different from you? How did those around you respond to those they perceived as other? In your upbringing, was there homogeneity or diversity around various social loca-tions? How were differences acknowledged? Were they valued or ignored, respected or judged, minimized or celebrated? What of these early learnings remain with you and what have you changed? It is also helpful to consider the associations you learned in relation to social locations, particularly considering the locations of your clients and how they differ from yours. There are always differ-ences between a therapist and client who share the same location that may be overlooked, as well as other similarities that can be invisible at the beginning. Terms such as "Asian," "Latinx," "Afri-can," or "European" are commonly used to categorize groups of people but overlook the abundant diversity to be found within each of these cultural groups. Being curious about differences between ethnicities and identifying individual differences in peo-ple of the same culture can help counteract our own stereotypes and associations.

Pondering our tendencies—what we avoid, what challenges us, what we are reactive to, what we minimize—with regard to race, culture, gender, age, and any other differences between us and our clients is essential. Asking ourselves questions like, "Would I prefer a male (or white, physically fit, English-speaking, able-bodied, or heterosexual) doctor, mentor, or client?" can reveal implicit bias. Examining "affinity" bias (Ross, 2017), a subtle form of prejudice that eludes recognition, can elucidate how our perceptions of simi-larity between ourselves and our clients may influence our approach and even the outcome of therapy. We can identify affinity bias by considering which clients we resonate with the most, and why. What aspects of a client do we feel particularly resonant with and empathic toward (or not)? How do those aspects that we are reso-nant with relate to our own social locations? How can we sustain an inquiry into our biases and not bypass them or subsume them under the rubric of countertransference?

As important as knowing our own social location is knowing the history and cultural background of our clients. We all need to educate ourselves about other cultures, being aware that the media is full of biases and prejudices toward marginalized groups. We can learn from original and multiple sources, and also expand our "social context" by "increasing intergroup contact" (Stewart & Payne, 2008, p. 13). A note of caution: Even though it is often helpful to learn directly from people who identify with marginalized social locations, we need to be mindful that doing so may be burdensome to that person.

As therapists, we can aspire to hold an intersectional understanding of the identity of our clients and ourselves and how these intersecting identities interface and show up in the therapy room at different times during treatment. At the same time, from our localized awareness we need to accept the limits of our own knowledge and understanding of others' experiences, bodies, individuals, families, cultures, and communities that are not our own. We strive to cultivate an open mind and attitude of curiosity and self-inquiry that allows new and sometimes dissonant information to affect us and impact our actions.

Mindful Awareness of Biases

Through the use of mindfulness—the ability to notice our present-moment internal experience—we aim to become aware of and challenge both the implicit assumptions of superiority/shame of our privileged identities, and of the internalized shame/oppression of our marginalized identities, at somatic, emotional, and cognitive levels. Ng and Purser (2015, para. 11) state, "If mindfulness teaches us anything, it is the importance of redirecting our attention *continuously* and *repeatedly* to question how forces of conditioning are shaping unacknowledged habitual reactive patterns." The willingness to be tenaciously aware of our own feelings, physical responses, and thoughts that emerge when we meet someone we perceive as different can be a vital teacher in dismantling our own implicit bias. If our heart rate increases, or we notice tension in the belly or in another part of the body, or if we become aware of certain body sensations, micromovements, or impulses, we can reflect on their meaning and how these somatic responses might echo implicit bias and stereotypes. We can examine the emotional response and the reflexive thoughts that emerge in response to difference. Do we feel anxious, critical, or afraid? What are the automatic thoughts and assumptions that emerge in our minds?

As we become mindfully aware of our internal reactions, we can hypothesize what microaggressions we might be prone to enact and actively work toward counteracting them. For example, if we were to lead a workshop on mental health stigma for a group of unsheltered homeless people in an economically impoverished part of town and notice our shoulders tightening, our breath becoming shallow, and tingling in our belly as we approach the location of the event, we can examine the associations. For example, we might be correlating these groups of people with violence and crime. It follows that we may then be inclined to microaggress in particular ways, such as exhibiting surprise, through words or facial expression, upon finding out the workshop participants have families or higher levels of education than we had assumed.

Learning to tolerate discomfort helps us increase our capacity to stay with experiences that are new and unknown. This is especially true for our privileged social locations that give us a sense of safety, and yet we often have little tolerance for discomfort when these locations are named or highlighted by others in the context of discussing oppression. A common example of this occurs when a person is sharing an experience of oppression and this sharing elicits uncontained emotions from a person holding a place of privilege due to their own guilt, which in turn can divert the focus away from the original sharing. In the therapeutic context, an aware therapist versed in an understanding of these dynamics will be able to regulate and contain their reactions to stimuli that elicit strong emotion or arousal.

Dismantling internalized ideas of privilege or oppression might require actively identifying counter-experiences of our own stereotypes or what Stewart and Payne (2008) call "implementation intentions," that is, intentionally and repeatedly finding examples of individuals we know or public figures that counteract our own biases toward that specific community. By doing so, we are deliberately considering "the diversity within social groups and especially the many examples of group members who disconfirm the stereotype" (Blair et al., 2001, p. 838). As the authors highlight, this active strategy has been proven to mitigate the intensity and presence of implicit bias (Blair et al., 2001) more than awareness alone (Bobula, 2011).

Through a concerted effort to be mindful of our reactions to difference, we learn to identify the internal signals of our learned associations and stereotypes, our triggers, and our propensities for microaggressions. After noticing them, the next step is to inhibit these automatic reactions through finding ways to regulate ourselves appropriately and alter our behavior. A good dose of compassion for one's own learning process and growing edges helps us lean gently into the discomfort, and to seek like-minded others for support and challenge. Dismantling internalized privilege and healing from oppression can only occur in the context of a larger container of a supportive and intentional community that helps us grow. We naturally have a tendency to surround ourselves with those that look like us and think like us. Even though we might need kin spaces for resourcing, it is important to actively and authentically increase our exposure to different ways of thinking, feeling, being, and moving to challenge our own assumptions.

Bias and the Body

The body is central in Sensorimotor Psychotherapy; thus it is critical to recognize our bias and preconceived notions toward the body, some of which are described in the first section of this chapter. At this point it should be clear that our own ideas of what constitutes both physical health and desirable physical presentation and movement habits are historically, culturally, and socially constructed. At the same time, the meaning we make from posture and movement is also a result of idiosyncratic and family influences embedded in a community-specific culture (Moore & Yamamoto, 2012). At the most fundamental level, what we feel, see, and recognize in others' nonverbal communication is filtered through what we have personally experienced. We have more familiarity and feel more comfort with the movements and other nonverbal cues of our group of reference. When we recognize familiarity in movement patterns and expression, we experience an increased felt sense of security and resonance; on the contrary, when movements and patterns are not familiar, we may experience a sense of threat.

Naturally, our sense of safety and familiarity affects the way we read other people's movements and somatic expressions, which can lead to misinterpretation when working with people from diverse backgrounds and locations (Caldwell, 2013). For instance, if the therapist assumes a client feels angry or aggressive due to their stiff or armored body posture (when the person is feeling safe) or assumes a client is lying due to a lack of eye contact (when the person is being truthful), the therapeutic relationship could be adversely impacted. Eye contact behaviors are used often when illustrating cultural differences because duration and direction of eye contact is highly influenced by cultural norms, and what is considered respectful or not (Burgoon et al., 2010). Similarly, different cultures have different norms for degree of personal space and amount, placement, and duration related to touch (Burgoon et al., 2010). Movement tendencies, such as more sway in the hips or expressive gestures with the hands, are not common in some cultures, hence, they might be considered "uncontained," "dysregulated," "histrionic," or overly sexualized. Attaching inaccurate meaning to physical characteristics and idiosyncratic movements can be especially salient with clients that are on the autism spectrum, neurodivergent, or otherwise physically atypical.

As therapists, we can seek to become increasingly aware of our perspectives and prejudice toward "different" bodies (race, size, attractiveness, age, ability, etc.) and movements (including nonverbal communication). The more cultural, ethnic, or racial disparity between people, the higher the probability of "body prejudice" (Moore & Yamamoto, 2012): Each of us will be prone to interpret the other person's movement, gesture, posture, and so forth from their own lens, and judge these somatic expressions quickly and unconsciously. We can learn to recognize our own physical reactions to the bodies and movement habits of others and also identify the cognitive descriptors of that prejudice (e.g., "dangerous" or "fragile" bodies). In this way, we become aware of inclinations to label or interpret certain body shapes, colors, movements, gestures, postures, or expressions as pathological, restricted, maladaptive, or conversely optimal, positive, and healthy, with the understanding that as therapists we can only know what is adaptive or not as we explore these patterns with the client in front of us.

Implicit Bias, Transference, and Countertransference

Perceived and actual difference evokes powerful and often unconscious emotions and physical actions that lead to transference, countertransference, and enactments in the therapist-client relationship. Becoming aware of the body-to-body conversation occurring in the therapy space (touch, proximity, initiation/reaction, eye contact, etc.) that perpetuates privilege/oppression dynamics is a first step in uncovering them. We can be mindful of our own body language and what it might be communicating moment by moment. As we notice our client's reactions to our nonverbal expressions and consider what our body language might be communicating, we learn about the undercurrents and habits of our posture and movements, in reciprocal interaction with the posture and movements of our clients. It is important to understand that the person who holds privilege (the therapist) will be likely to demonstrate power nonverbally. Examples include touching first (as in offering a handshake), having more relaxed movements, initiating movement or verbal talk, greater use of space, greater allowance for expression, and initiation of direct gaze (Johnson, 2009, 2015; Burgoon et al., 2010). The therapist–client dynamic is asymmetrical with respect to power and privilege, where the therapist is always, due to their role as therapist, in a position of power in relation to their clients. Exploration of the nuances of this asymmetry in the clinical encounter is often deemed unimportant, discouraged, and even overlooked. However, the therapist's mindful awareness of their power and privilege, and how they express it verbally and nonverbally, can foster trust and strengthen the therapeutic alliance. Conversely, lack of awareness and unconscious misuse of power and privilege can lead to significant or even irreparable damage to the therapeutic relationship.

As Comas-Díaz and Jacobsen (1991) explain, enactments and relational processes between the therapist and the client are influenced by both projections of each person's sociocultural reality onto the other and the discomfort or disorientation that each feels in the presence of difference. The authors identify several common dynamics that occur when the therapist and the client do not share social locations. For instance, either party can be overly compliant or overly friendly to avoid being stereotyped, which can manifest in trying to be a good client or good therapist. If the therapist experiences feelings of anxiety or nervousness, they may find themselves seeking approval, trying to please, or avoiding conflict with the client, or even utilizing the therapeutic relationship in an attempt to prove that they are not racist (Harrell & Sloan-Pena, 2006). We therapists may deny discussion of a client's disability and other locations from the conviction that all clients should be treated equally, from guilt about our own ableism or other privileges we hold, or from fear of exposing our own privilege. Transference can manifest in myriad complex ways. For example, a client of color working with a white therapist may demonstrate "overcompliance and deferring to the therapist, behaviors that are intended to disprove racial stereotypes, [or] hostility toward the therapist" (Harrell & Sloan-Pena, 2006, p. 401). Moreover, marginalized clients who have internalized the racism of society may be apt to disconnect from their own group or seek approval from their white therapist (Harrell & Sloan-Pena, 2006).

Emotions such as guilt and shame, pity, mistrust, suspicion, or even ambivalence toward the therapeutic process can also be part of these dynamics. For example, a documented immigrant therapist experienced guilt over their own status while working with an undocumented client grieving about not being able to travel back to their country for their parent's funeral, which resulted in the therapist unconsciously trying to find similarities to bond with the client and inadvertently overlooking the client's need to work on grief and separation.

When therapist and client share some of the same marginalized sociocultural locations, there may be "a risk of overidentification, a need to rescue, protect, or join with the client in an 'us against them' orientation" (Harrell & Sloan-Pena, 2006, p. 401). Comas-Díaz and Jacobsen (1991) also describe such dynamics, including the therapist's idealization by the client as a perfect parent or savior, an "overidentification" between therapist and client, or feelings of anger or frustration toward the success of the therapist or the client if they share some locations but differ in socioeconomic status. Internalized oppression and racism might also play a role if the therapist has not explored it, which can lead to pressuring the client toward increased effort, such as to focus on individual success for the sake of improving the status of the group that both belong to. In another example, a Black therapist from a working-class or low-income background may experience a form of survivor's guilt about having achieved higher social status when working with a Black client from a similar background. This guilt may cause the therapist to unconsciously focus treatment toward the client's achievement of individual success. Bias is inevitable among mental health professionals. As therapists, it is essential that we identify and reflect on our own bias, cultivate humility and non–defensiveness, and maintain an attitude of beginner's mind since this work is never complete. Learning to accept and welcome the unknown, especially when being confronted or challenged, can help in being compassionate with ourselves. In the next section, we encourage an inner posture of openness and humility to the ways our clinical encounters with clients are nuanced by their (and our) histories of privilege, oppression, and resilience.

THERAPEUTIC ACTION

After reviewing some of the culturally bound assumptions inherent to Western psychology and examining the implications of our personal biases, we have now arrived at the skills that support and strengthen our socioculturally attuned therapeutic practice. In this section, we will explore the significance of cultural humility and radical openness to mitigate the influence of implicit bias and the dynamics of privilege/oppression on our work as therapists. Our emphasis in this chapter is not on perfect practice but on therapeutic action that is grounded in mindful awareness of the effects of many histories of privilege/oppression and resilience present in both the client and the therapist.

Radical Openness and Cultural Humility

The U.S. civil rights movement of the 1950s and 1960s demanded respect for diversity and attention to racial inequality, and was fundamental to the development of the first multicultural competency model in the 1980s (Sue et al., 1982). As stated by Chiarenza, the competency approach often assumes that cultural proficiency and expertise can be "taught, learned, trained, and achieved," (2012, p. 69) leading to greater efficacy in clinical practice. However, Hart (2017, para. 2) writes, "Such [competency] training inherently promotes a defended, prepared manner of addressing difference and otherness, with all their attendant anxieties and defenses, and this represents a major lost opportunity for personal reflections and deeper engagement." He proposes instead an attitude of "radical openness," which entails an ongoing effort "to notice, question, and relinquish presumptions about oneself and the other" (para. 6). Radical openness, like cultural humility (Hook, Davis, et al., 2013; Hook, Owen, et al., 2013; Tervalon & Murray-Garcia, 1998) is conceptualized as a lifelong process emphasizing self-reflection and personal critique. This requires us to realize that we are products of our sociocultural context, accept that we have internalized their biases, recognize the inevitability that we will at times act upon them, and continually examine our own reactions to and actions toward our clients. Hart advises therapists to engage "a stance of openness to the unknown, the unfamiliar, even the frightening, in our patients and in ourselves" (2017, para. 18). Therapeutic action—what we do in clinical practice—emerges from an attitude of radical openness and cultural humility.

Radical openness and cultural humility build the therapist's trustworthiness and credibility. We become trustworthy in our clients' eyes when we recognize the impact of sociocultural and sociopolitical elements on our clients, are willing and able to stay present to issues of oppression and racism, and confront our own bias. As credibility is earned, the client experiences a growing sense of safety in bringing personal and cross-cultural challenges forward. Credibility is fostered by the predictability of the relational dynamics and our demonstration of consistency, goodwill, and care, as well as attention to the specific and concrete needs of the marginalized aspects of our clients (Dilbeck, 2014). We can assume that there will be many moments in cross-cultural and cross-ethnic therapeutic dyads in which therapist and client will not share values and points of view. Embodying radical openness requires us to remain curious about the complexity of these differences and how our own biases play out in our bodies, emotions, and thoughts, as well as about what we might be missing in understanding the interplay of privilege/oppression. All of these may include recognizing, challenging, and at times discussing our own locations and prejudices with our clients. In this way, we become increasingly capable of staying in the relational process during challenge and conflict, instead of focusing on competence, skills, and interventions.

As the therapeutic relationship develops—when credibility with the therapist has been sufficiently established and when the client seems receptive—explicit exploration of the historical and sociocultural context of the client's presenting issues might help to destigmatize pathology as a solely personal deficit. Whether or not the client takes up the therapist's invitation to explore these contexts, when the therapist is able to name these issues, it opens the door for future discussion and signals their relevance to the presenting problem for the client. As therapists, we hold these considerations in our personal consciousness and case formulation regardless of whether we are actively or explicitly working with these issues with the client. We can reflect upon them ourselves, discuss them in supervision, and consider the impact of those factors with other helping providers.

Regardless of intention, without awareness of the dynamics of privilege and oppression therapists may be unskillful or overzealous in exploring sociocultural issues with their clients. It is also possible for a therapist to become fearful of intervening more assertively. Either extreme may be more likely when the therapist holds multiple positionalities of marginalization in contrast to a client's privileged social locations. We strive to recognize our own capacities and stage of development of this awareness along with those of our client in navigating these issues and seek consultation. Culturally informed supervision, especially group supervision, whether it is with peers or led by a mentor, will help us continue to develop skills, learn about our own responses to these issues, and gain insight into the specific intersectionalities between ourselves and our clients. Harrell stresses that supervisors should be selected based on their having "engaged in, and continu[ing] to engage in, the process of examining [their] own race narratives, including racial identity, racism, privilege, interracial encounters and relationships, and beliefs about race and racial groups" (2014, p. 24).

Most importantly, we must track carefully for clients' responses to our interventions, realizing that all clients, but perhaps especially marginalized clients because of the dynamics of privilege/oppression, might conceal their negative responses due to fear of backlash or rejection, or due to conditioned deference to authority (Vasquez, 2007). Negative responses are usually revealed through the body, in facial expressions, tension, or movements, rather than words. As we notice the indicators that may signal an adverse reaction, we share our observations, ask for more information, and adjust our approach in the moment. It is important that we refrain from pushing our own agendas, and particularly that we avoid campaigning for discussions on oppression and injustice when this is not the client's main purpose for therapy. But we can consistently hold an anti-oppression lens in our awareness, use it to broaden our understanding of the client's presenting issues, and discuss it when appropriate. Delineating culturally relevant practical skills and interventions is complex and nuanced. Although power dynamics and identities are always present in the therapy room, when and whether to address these dynamics depend on timing, context, content, and the client's focus and goals, in addition to the client's receptivity and the therapist's credibility. Moreover, specific interventions, both verbal and physical, require great sensitivity and skill. Drawing on Sensorimotor Psychotherapy, the next section explores a few elements of the dynamics of therapeutic action, common pitfalls, and culturally relevant intervention, all within the context of the therapeutic relationship.

Sensorimotor Psychotherapy Skills

It is paramount for the clinician to track the impact of their interventions on the client. Tracking is the skill of noticing changes in the body—in movement, gesture, posture, facial expression, tension, or relaxation. Physical signs of emotions (moist eyes, changes in facial expression or voice tone) and the beliefs that emerge, like the words, "I'm failure" or "I'm not good enough," are accompanied by physical indicators such as looking down at the floor. The Sensorimotor Psychotherapist especially tracks the physical changes that correspond to emotions, thoughts, and narrative. These changes in the body often go unnoticed by the client unless the therapist verbally names them with a contact statement that is intended to demonstrate understanding of the client's experience and convey our curiosity about these physical signs (Kurtz, 1990; Ogden et al., 2006).

For example, when Ejikeme, a male originally from Ghana now living in Western Europe, spoke of the difficulty navigating the culture of his new home to his female therapist, she noticed that his shoulders rounded, his posture slumped, and he looked down. Such physical signs can reflect the legacy of trauma, oppression, and relational stress; other such signals can include hyperarousal, held breath, constriction, collapsed chest and shoulders, or trembling, tension, stillness, or blank expression. Holding these hypotheses in our awareness, the Sensorimotor Psychotherapist does not immediately move to interpreting the client's movement, which would mainly be informed by the therapist's location, but introduces these movements into the client's awareness by contacting what is observed. The contact statements his therapist used— "As you say those words, it seems as if your posture changes. . . . It looks like your head comes down too, huh?"—offered Ejikeme the chance to disconfirm or elaborate the accuracy of the contact statements. This intervention is enhanced by using qualifiers such as "seems like," or "maybe," which convey the tentative nature of the observation and invite the client to modify or correct it. The opportunity to revise the therapist's statements can expose inaccurate interpretations and projections, and is an important invitation for marginalized clients who may not be accustomed to those in authority soliciting their input.

In this instance, Ejikeme nodded in response but said he wanted to continue discussing the problems he was facing. The therapist followed his lead without challenging why he was not interested in exploring the physical indicators. It is important to note that Sensorimotor Psychotherapy, as a relationally focused method, is collaborative and seeks to follow the client's agenda and interest. Instead of labeling a client as resistant or guarded when they reject a suggestion, the therapist recognizes that the client has good reasons for their stance, which in and of itself increases trust in the relationship. Physical signs of trust, openness, or well-being might include a deep, regular breath, a more relaxed or upright posture, or more spontaneous movement and less tension (Ogden et al., 2006). For example, when exploring Ejikeme's resources for the purpose of stabilization, the therapist asked about what was meaningful to him about his culture—the songs he grew up with, his family and the village where he lived as a boy—and he told her the story his elders had taught him: When he was born, he was put outside in nature because his family thought he was dead. Upon hearing the distant roar of a lion, his parents saw that he was breathing, which in their tradition showed how strong he was. As Ejikeme told the story, his shoulders squared, his head lifted, and his spine lengthened upward. His therapist tracked and named the changes in his body, and Ejikeme responded with a big smile and said that he felt proud. This time he resonated with what the therapist had tracked and contacted, and thus the therapist suggested that maybe they could stay with this experience of pride and how his body responded, to which Ejikeme enthusiastically agreed. This intervention of framing is used to collaboratively narrow the focus of exploration at any given moment in the session, in this case to Ejikeme's pride and posture (Ogden, 2014).

Mindfulness, as used in Sensorimotor Psychotherapy, is relationally focused, used to help clients become aware of their internal organization of experience by becoming aware of the five basic building blocks of present experience that make up their internal landscape: thoughts, emotions, internally generated sensory perceptions, movements, and sensations (cf. Chapter 4, this volume). The efficacy of mindfulness interventions is supported by directing the client's attention toward one or more of the building blocks that are thought to be instrumental in meeting therapeutic goals, called "directed mindfulness" (Ogden, 2007, 2009). In the above example, the therapist directed Ejikeme's mindful attention toward the pride and changes in his body when he remembered the story his elders told him with questions like, "Are there images that come up when you remember this story?" (himself as a happy boy, feeling the hot sun of his homeland) and "Are there movements that go with this sense of pride?" (a slight lifting of the arms outward) and "What words might go with this movement?" ("I feel strong!")

The positive feeling, posture, and movement, which were empowering for Ejikeme, were applied in imagination to the difficult situations he faced in navigating the challenges of an unfamiliar culture, specifically an upcoming job interview that evoked anxiety. Ejikeme's therapist asked him, "If you imagine your job interview and at the same time, sense this strength and pride, and let your spine lengthen, and say the words, 'I am strong,' what happens?" Therapeutic experiments in Sensorimotor Psychotherapy are prefaced by phrases such as, "What happens when . . . ?" or "What do you notice when . . . ?" These mindful directives instruct clients to notice the changes in their building blocks in relation to a stimulus, in this case embodying the resource while imagining a challenge. Therapist and client can experiment with words (e.g., saying "no," or "I am strong!") and movements (e.g., reaching out or lifting the spine) that challenge habitual patterns, or engage a pattern to discover more about it (e.g., using Ejikeme's habit of lowering his head as the stimulus led to sensing the part of him that felt anxious and incompetent). When Ejikeme embodied his resource, he reported feeling a little more confidence and a little less anxiety, and both he and the therapist noted the significance of his expressing his strength and pride physically in the presence of a therapist of a different ethnicity. He decided to practice this resource—to lift his chin, lengthen his spine, and recall the sense of pride and strength—as he struggled to navigate the complexities of speaking a new language while trying to secure work. Note that the dance of tracking, contacting, framing, asking mindfulness questions, and conducting experiments always occurs in collaboration with the client, and the client's responses determine the next intervention and direction of the session.

Our task as therapists is complex as we must simultaneously attend to the client, to the content, to the process of the therapy dynamics, and to our own reactions. We track our own bodies for signs of implicit bias, which are highly individual but may include tightening, held breath, pulling back, averting or narrowing the eyes, and so forth. We are mindful as well of our own emotional responses (e.g., aversion, blame, or annoyance) and stereotypical judgmental thoughts (e.g., "You're not trying hard enough" or "Your people all have alcohol problems") that reflect our bias toward the client's group. We are also mindful of how we use our bodies to assert dominance or to act from a position of privilege and how that is impacting the client, or, on the other hand, how our bodies react if the client is enacting a similar dynamic with the therapist. Thus, our ability to track ourselves and use our own mindful awareness reveals critical, often unconscious, indicators of bias, useful information to be explored in the ongoing process of challenging our conditioning.

Opportunities for Exploration

Bryant-Davis states, "Initiating process and being aware of process themes that emerge related to discrimination, migration, language, skin color, gender, sexual orientation, religion, spirituality, age, identity, roles, responsibilities, stigma, and cultural strengths need to be a part of both assessment and intervention" (2019, p. 6). However, therapists often neglect to address these issues, perhaps by failing to pick up on signals, changing the subject, or lacking empathetic contact (Comas-Díaz, 2006). Paying attention to timing and the client's receptivity, we might inquire about family roles, spirituality and religion, migration history, beliefs, values, ancestors, documentation status, intergenerational connections, acculturation, or connection with the client's own culture, as well as ideas of health and healing. In tracking clients' responses to these discussions, simple contact statements, such as, "It must be difficult leaving your homeland, huh?" or "Seems like the values of this culture are quite different from your own," can convey the therapist's interest and understanding of the client's experience, and open the door to exploring these themes. As always, tracking your client's response to any intervention, including contact statements, is critical. If your client's facial expression indicates a lack of receptivity, or if they shift topics, the therapist follows the client's lead and internally notes this shift, while continuing to track for future opportunities for exploration of these issues as trust and credibility deepen. Framing the effects of oppression on beliefs, body, values, life path, and so forth (e.g., "Maybe we can stay with how this struggle to fit in impacts you physically") can open doors to deepen the exploration. Additionally, therapists can surmise that clients from historically marginalized groups have likely experienced multiple forms of discrimination, bias, and misunderstanding. Finding opportunities to bring these encounters forward, including those with other helping professionals, can build trust and credibility and provide a chance to process the effects of oppression while building resources to navigate future encounters from a place of empowerment. The inquiry can include asking about prior relationships with therapists, social services, medical professionals, teachers, or other authorities.

Moreover, people affected by historical trauma may experience reminders of the past in the present time. For example, Williams states that African Americans "have a cultural memory of things that have happened to us going all the way back to slavery—knowing all of that, and then hearing things in the media about unarmed Black men being shot or Black people being killed in a place of worship. These are traumatic for us many times because we have all of this cultural knowledge already" (2014, para. 7). Keeping historical trauma in mind, and taking opportunities to name, discuss, and explore it (while at the same time assessing client receptivity as well as our own credibility and skill) can help place current symptoms and experience in a broader context, and provide opportunities to build resources. For example, when Reyhan (a female Iranian daughter of highly skilled refugees that migrated to Sweden after the Iranian revolution in 1979) mentioned that she had to work harder than anyone else in her workplace to advance professionally, her therapist wondered aloud if this reflected the plight of many immigrants and the effect of anti-Islamic sentiment, to which Reyhan vehemently responded in the affirmative. Through Sensorimotor Psychotherapy, she and her therapist went on to explore how this extra pressure affected her self-esteem, posture, movements, and even her health. This validation allowed the client to soften her own self-judgment and identify the introjected racism that she had experienced at work. By naming this, the client's muscle tension relaxed, and she was able to express her grief about the world's injustices with the support of her therapist.

As previously discussed, the therapist aspires to cultivate an intersectional understanding of social location, and to welcome the tapestry of identities that clients bring to the therapy hour. Everyone holds multiple identities, and trauma "is exacerbated by intersectionality because persons live with multiple oppressed statuses such as African American Muslim women, Jewish transgender men, undocumented Latinas who are differently abled, and homeless Asian American gender-nonconforming adolescents" (Bryant-Davis, 2019, p. 6). Examining intersections such as these and, when appropriate, acknowledging possible privileged identities reveals both strengths and vulnerabilities. We can track and contact the impact of different marginalized identities on the client, including the impact on the body. For instance, we might explore the physical cost (somatic adaptations, physical pains, illness, movement adaptations, and so forth) and invite clients to describe their physical organization in response to different contexts they navigate in their daily life. We might also explore the impact of privileged identities, like higher socioeconomic status, male gender identity, or slim physical appearance, on the body.

Kimberly was an African American female therapist living in the western United States. When her white female therapist asked what she noticed about herself in different contexts, Kimberly spoke about the discrepancies in her body movement and relational capacity when she was at work (at a mental health agency with mostly white people), versus when she was at home with her family. She noticed that she restricted the movement in her body at the workplace, feeling like she needed to "follow authority" and curtail spontaneity, while being "overly friendly" and hyperalert at the same time. These feelings were familiar to her, and she said that they were mostly present when she was in white settings and specifically in front of white male clients in her practice. Therapist and client named Kimberly's feelings related to the oppression she experienced both as a Black person and as a woman. Her therapist asked her to notice, as an experiment, what happened when she imagined being in her clinical practice, and Kimberly reported that her body was more rigid, with truncated movements, and she did not feel confident, had thoughts of wanting to be liked, and felt overly compliant. In contrast, when her therapist asked her to imagine being in her community, she felt more confident, playful, and spontaneous in her movements, and reported an impulse to reach out and connect with others. Part of Kimberly's work in therapy was to recognize and acknowledge the burden on her body when she was in a predominantly white environment, and to identify resources to support her well-being while navigating in a white-dominant cultural context. She placed a picture of her family in her office to remind her of her community and used the somatic resource of a small reaching movement when she felt tense at work. This movement was imperceptible to Kimberly's clients but significant to her, as it connected her to the confidence she felt in reaching out to her community. Exploring different social locations creates an opportunity to examine the privilege/oppression dynamics that exist in society and in the therapeutic relationship, and to acknowledge and develop resources to mitigate the continual invalidation, discrimination, and trauma that marginalized clients experience as connected to the themes of the therapy. One of the goals in Sensorimotor Psychotherapy is to increase this awareness, while at the same time developing the somatic, emotional, and cognitive tools to support resilience.

In treatment, at different times, some of the client's identities and locations will move to the background while others will become more salient, depending on the content the client is bringing forward, which will modify what is played out in the therapeutic relationship. For instance, when exploring relational conflicts with a lesbian client, the heterosexual location of her female therapist created a different dynamic in the therapy room than when discussing the client's documented status with the same therapist (also an immigrant), or when bringing forward the client's Mexican culture in contrast with the Spanish background of the therapist. In the first case of different locations (lesbian and heterosexual), the client's eyes looked to the floor, her body tightened and pulled back, and there was more silence between sentences. Where explorations pertained to similar locations (both had documented immigrant status), the client was smiling, had a softer body posture and a more relaxed stance, often nodding to the therapist, and the verbal exchanges flowed smoothly. When talking about her Mexican background, the client shrank slightly in her body and avoided eye contact with the therapist while stating, "You speak such a nice Spanish," referencing the differences in accent and signaling an introjected prejudice. The dance between these locations can be fluid and ever changing and requires awareness of the landscape that emerges at any given moment and the somatic switches that occur depending on which identities are more salient. Attending and studying these changing dynamics increases awareness around how the client (and therapist) carries their multiple identities both within and outside of the therapy room.

It might also be relevant for a therapist who holds privileged identities (e.g., male, heterosexual, white, able bodied, or higher socioeconomic status, and so forth) to share their own process of learning about oppression and sociocultural complexity with their client, including their own strengths and limitations. This can model humility in addressing these issues, and open the opportunity for conversations on these topics with the client throughout the therapy. It is important that this conversation is not for the benefit of the therapist but for the therapy itself, and in support of the therapeutic relationship. In Sensorimotor Psychotherapy, tracking the client's response and brief contact statements ("I see that you're nodding, and it seems your breath deepened when I talk of this" or "What I'm saying doesn't seem to resonate with you . . .") guide interventions; disclosure can be expanded if it is received with interest by the client, or abandoned if otherwise received.

The Window of Tolerance and Embodiment of Resources

Verbalizing and listening to experiences of oppression can be triggering for clients from both historically marginalized and historically privileged social locations. In Sensorimotor Psychotherapy, a potentially useful way to conceptualize triggers and signs of dysregulation is to consider the "window of tolerance," a term coined by Siegel (1999), described as an optimal zone within which stimuli can be processed (Ogden & Minton, 2000; Ogden et al., 2006). Triggers can cause arousal to enter the hyperarousal or hypoarousal zones, within which integrative capacity is compromised. Through practice and attention to internal signals, we can increase our capacity to regulate and be present to these potentially dysregulating experiences and conversations. As we converse about identities and privilege/oppression dynamics, we can start tracking the signs of regulated and dysregulated arousal in ourselves and in our clients. When the arousal of either the client or therapist threatens to exceed the boundaries of the window of tolerance, progressing toward the hyper- or hypoarousal zones, the primary task becomes to support the return of arousal to the window by using interventions that help to regulate. Since dysregulation is first and foremost a bodily response, somatic resources (breath, centering, grounding, movement, alignment, self-touch, and so forth) and attending to boundaries and space can be useful.

Many trauma-focused approaches are designed to resolve the effects of past trauma and regulate symptoms of dysregulated arousal that emerge in the face of threat but persist long after the trauma is over and the surroundings are now safe. However, people from marginalized groups may suffer continuous oppression in various forms in their current lives, so the threat is never really over. For this reason, although the trauma of oppression will often induce typical PTSD symptoms, historical trauma, the trauma of racism and marginalization, and "intersectional oppression" are not equivalent to PTSD (Bryant-Davis, 2019). In cases such as this, it is important for therapists to acknowledge and process the effects of trauma, as well as to develop resources to increase resilience and navigate the impact of ongoing oppression. For example, Ejikeme experienced anger when he talked about the systemic oppression and discrimination he faced after migrating to western Europe. As he spoke of his anger, his arousal escalated. He reported his energy rising, and he expressed fear of acting upon his aggressive impulses, which he sensed in the tension of his jaw and arms. When his therapist said that his anger made sense in this context of ongoing oppression, Ejikeme felt validated, but repeated that it frightened him. With his therapist's help, he learned to track the internal signs of anger as his arousal threatened to escalate into a hyperarousal zone, and regulate it by putting his hands in his armpits. Lengthening his spine, lifting his chin, and speaking the words, "This is not fair. I don't deserve this treatment," connected him to his resource of pride and helped him maintain arousal within a window of tolerance.

When therapist and client do not share similar social locations, but especially when they are at different levels of cultural and identity awareness development, the ability to tolerate conversations about privilege and oppression may vary considerably. For instance, it is not unusual for white people to have a lower capacity to engage in conversations about racial privilege because, as they occupy a historically privileged location, white people do not need to contend with the stress of racism, prejudice, and discrimination that people of color manage on a daily basis. When these conversations are introduced and white privilege is explicitly named, white people often become defensive. This defensiveness has been referred to as *white fragility*, a term describing the behavioral responses to race stress that "function to reinstate white racial equilibrium" (DiAngelo, 2011, p. 54). Fragility is not limited to whiteness and applies to the defensive behaviors of any person embodying a *privileged* identity, meaning one can demonstrate *male* fragility, *cisgender* fragility, *heterosexual* fragility, *able-bodied* fragility, and so forth. The susceptibility to fragility highlights the importance for members of the privileged groups to explore their own identity and bias, and increase their understanding of the dynamics of privilege and oppression in order to widen their own windows, build their capacity, and skillfully address these topics in therapy nondefensively and with humility. Conversations about power, privilege, oppression, and identity will likely trigger dysregulation, especially when we are in the infancy of our development toward knowing how to engage in these conversations. Referencing the window of tolerance as it relates to conversations about racism and oppression might provide an additional map to facilitate the navigation of these discussions. The challenge is to both resource ourselves as clinicians and support the client in resourcing themselves to stay connected during these conversations. We will need to learn how to hang out at the regulatory boundaries of the window of tolerance and navigate the conflicts, differences, and enactments that may emerge (cf. Chapter 11, this volume). As Menakem (2017) points out, therapeutic practice becomes one of accepting discomfort, being less disturbed in unknown territory, and increasing our capacity to bring curiosity and gentleness to ourselves and to our clients.

The Therapist Role: Beyond Western Perspectives

Bryant-Davis (2019, p. 4) points out that therapists may tend to "define the person through their trauma while overlooking the strengths, resources, culture, and sociopolitical identity of the survivor." Being attentive to indicators of clients' resources, whether they be existing or missing, internal (within the self) or external (within the environment), can provide opportunities to develop and embody resilience (Ogden et al., 2006; Ogden & Fisher, 2015). As Denham (2008) states, the contextualization of historical trauma can also be framed with the "transmission of resilience strategies" within the community. Therapists can inquire about the resources inherent in the client's culture, such as traditions, spiritual or religious elements, food, celebrations, songs, art, and so on. For example, a middle-aged Puerto Rican immigrant client living in New York sat straighter and her face lit up as she spoke of her church and singing in the choir. Her therapist noted her expression, contacted it, and framed it by saying, "This seems really important to you! Let's explore it a bit, shall we?" The client readily accepted the therapist's invitation to explore her experience at church and in choir. The therapist listened with curiosity and warmth as the client shared details about her church, her participation in this community, and the songs she sang in the choir. As the client spoke, the therapist tracked and commented on the client's affect and somatic responses in the moment: "I can sense your happiness as you share about that song" and "As you say that, your hands come together as if to clap." The client followed up by sharing how clapping was a vehicle for audience participation when the choir sang, and it brought her great joy to see her fellow parishioners enjoying the choir and her singing. As she talked about her joy, her chest expanded, and her breathing deepened. Together, the therapist and client identified these physical changes as somatic resources that the client could easily embody and use throughout her day to remind her of her beloved church community and her love for singing.

Current treatment guidelines, which emphasize evidence-based treatment, may fail to pay enough attention to cultural elements; therapists must cultivate "respect for the client and their culture, recognizing that cultures have therapeutic pathways despite the lack of empirical validation for their contribution" (Bryant-Davis, 2019,

p. 5). Some cultural resources and healing practices, such as ritual, songs, dance, and drumming, existed long before the field of psychotherapy itself but have not been acknowledged by contemporary Western standards. These cultural elements can be identified and developed into powerful healing resources. Julieta, originally from Chile but living in western Europe at the time of her therapy, was of both Indigenous and Spanish heritage. In therapy, she learned that the pattern of collapse in her spine and shallow breathing was related to submitting to others. Julieta discovered that she had internalized the historical abuse of the Spanish conquistadors by oppressing and silencing the Indigenous part of her. Impacted by the historical trauma of her ancestry, her challenge was to integrate these two parts of herself. She stated that the Indigenous part of her was grounded in nature, and with help from her therapist she remembered the beloved araucaria tree, a symbol of strength and resilience for the Indigenous people of central and southern Chile for centuries. Remembering this tree, Julieta found that her body became less collapsed, and her chest became fuller with a deep breath. She said as the Indigenous part of her drew upon the strength of the tree, she felt less vulnerable to being dominated. The therapist invited Julieta to imagine a recent moment when she had felt dominated, and her posture immediately began to slump. But when she recalled that moment, and simultaneously visualized the tree and its strength, she could maintain her more erect posture, fuller chest, and deeper breathing. In this way, Julieta moved from a triggering experience (recalling feeling dominated and sensing the tendency to collapse) to a resource (visualizing the tree and embodying a more upright posture, fuller chest, deeper breath). This movement from collapsed posture to the resource of upright posture helped to bring her two sides into a more equal relationship, healing some of the effects of transgenerational trauma.

Additionally, historically marginalized people may have needs beyond those of mental health due to the sociopolitical, structural, and financial consequences of oppression that the therapist may need to address. To support meeting these needs, the therapist can develop a referral network of other services and providers that are socioculturally sensitive, for instance, medical doctors and psychiatrists that are aware of trauma's impact on the body, or agencies that can support clients' access to important resources and connect them with community, such as clothing, food, and housing. At the same time, the therapist might need to utilize their professional position to advocate with and for the client in schools, workplaces, and courts. For example, Sofia, a 54-year-old client originally from Central America living in the United States, spoke broken English and suffered from a work-related injury and PTSD from her husband's suicide. Sofia minimized the pain she was in from her workplace injury and referred to her PTSD symptoms as personal deficits, indicating that she had failed to create a better life for herself and her daughter in the United States. She wanted to appear happy and content in her new country, especially with authorities like doctors, and was not able to obtain disability benefits. Therefore, she needed advocacy to make sure that her doctors understood the severity of her symptoms so she could receive benefits. As her therapist filled out the disability application, she explained what she was writing and why, asking Sofia for input and feedback. When the application was complete, the therapist brought awareness to the relationship as a resource by asking, "What happens when you sense that we did this together?" Sofia brought her hand up to her heart, which her therapist mirrored. Sofia said, "Yes, you are here," patting her heart. Advocacy not only met a real need of Sofia's but also strengthened the therapeutic relationship, and helped Sofia find a somatic resource of connection with her therapist (patting her heart).

Therapists might also need to address and adjust the therapy setting to meet the client's needs; for instance, examining accessibility of therapy offices (including more local venues or online therapy if the client has internet access), addressing transportation needs, child-care coverage, work schedule unpredictability, financial constraints, religious limitations, and so forth. The capacity of the therapist to be flexible and open to adjusting the counseling setting to increase access to mental health care for marginalized populations is an important anti-oppression policy toward increasing equity. Client needs and the expanding role of the therapist can conflict with traditional Western approaches to psychotherapy that tend to establish a clear boundary between professional disciplines, within which advocacy and case management tasks are not traditionally considered in the scope of psychotherapy practice (Comas-Díaz, 2006). These multiple roles that the therapist might need to fulfill also increase the necessity of discussions with the client, supervisors, and consultants as the dance between the different and nuanced dual relationships is negotiated.

Microaggressions in the Therapy Room

Because we cannot escape implicit bias, we are vulnerable to committing microaggressions of all kinds in the therapy hour, both verbal and nonverbal. These may be subtle, through what we contact, emphasize, or fail to acknowledge, and are often based on our own values and biases. For example, we may coach clients to increase their independence and autonomy, not considering that the client's culture is collectivist. We may make biased assumptions ("Did you grow up with a single mom?" for an African American client, or "Since you're Jewish you're probably good with money") or assume similarities ("I understand racism because I have a friend who is a person of color"). We may become silent or avoidant in the face of triggers, as when a white therapist's guilt is triggered as his African American client brings up feelings anxiety and stress from media coverage of excessive violence directed toward Black people.

Our bias, disapproval, and judgment will typically be revealed first on a physical level, and often without our awareness. Our facial expression may be the first indicator: furrowing brows (when a client discloses that they are transgender), a surprised expression (when an immigrant client from South America reports that she is highly educated), a neutral expression (when a client reports the horror of suffering political torture), or a slight frown (when a client reports an experience of discrimination). Our biases and those of our clients will also be revealed in the tension and expression of the body, such as visibly tensing and pulling back (when a gay client is sharing feelings about a sexual encounter or when a gay therapist discloses their sexual orientation to the client), looking down and away (when a client asks for needed advocacy), shrugging one's shoulders and shaking one's head (when a genderqueer client requests use of the pronoun "they" or when the therapist discloses the same thing to a cisgender client) or leaning forward and speaking with a patronizing attitude and prosody (to a disabled adult client). It is important that we therapists understand when and how our bodies commit microaggressions or when they are committed against us as therapists, and what the somatic cues of each are. The more we know about our physical tendencies and how our own body responds, the more we can address how we express our own implicit bias nonverbally.

Jacy was a young Native American man who had been raised on a reservation in the United States. During therapy, his white female therapist became aware of two microaggressions that she had committed. Jacy struggled with alcohol, and she made the comment that she understood the connection between alcoholism and being Native American. Jacy grew silent, and the session stalled. In supervision, the therapist realized that her statement had failed to acknowledge the impact of historical trauma upon his people and instead categorized Jacy's difficulty in terms of stereotypes about his culture. In the next session, she acknowledged this and apologized, thus enhancing her own credibility, and Jacy was visibly relieved (his shoulders relaxed, and he smiled). His therapist's willingness to take responsibility for her own bias initiated a conversation about other microaggressions Jacy experienced on a regular basis. In another incident much later in therapy, Jacy expressed doubts that he could succeed in college, and his therapist said, "Oh, you're so smart, I'm sure you'll do fine." This time she tracked Jacy's subtle disappointed facial expression and squinting eyes, and he again grew silent. Vasquez (2007, p. 880) points out that marginalized people "experience slights and offenses so regularly that there is a tendency for them to 'edit' their responses on a regular basis. That reality, combined with cultural values, may . . . inhibit negative reactions." Therapists must take extra care to track for signals of negative reactions to their interventions and provide opportunities to discover their source. In this case, the therapist made a contact statement ("That didn't quite resonate, did it?"). Jacy shook his head but remained silent. The therapist continued with contact statements and thinking out loud ("It seems that what I said didn't sit well with you"; "Maybe it wasn't quite accurate") and asked Jacy to tell her more about his fear. Jacy's face began to relax, and he said he felt he would have to work twice as hard as anyone else to succeed in college, and he did not know if he could meet that challenge. His therapist then recognized that the statement she had made was a microaggression that reflected meritocracy: the myth that all people have equal opportunity, which ignores the effects of systemic oppression that puts marginalized groups at a disadvantage. Again, she apologized, and again the relationship was strengthened as Jacy felt seen and understood. In both instances, the therapist tracked not only Jacy's body but also her own physical reactions, noticing that her arousal increased, her breath quickened, and her body tensed. She also noticed an impulse to rescue the client and felt guilt about the genocide of Native Americans perpetrated by settler colonialism and the implications of that for her own location as a white woman.

Bias can also be demonstrated by the client. A therapist from a marginalized culture whose client is from the privileged culture may be the target of microaggressions. For example, a white male client of a female immigrant therapist for whom English was a second language showed his bias by challenging her knowledge and competence. Negatively assessing another based on their "foreign" accent is a common form of discrimination (Fuertes et al., 2012). In the face of a microaggression like this, the therapist will need to regulate and ground themselves to be able to name the impact in a way that does not shame the client, and initiate a process of repair, taking into consideration the strength and nature of the therapeutic relationship. In this case, the therapist commented that she understood that the client wanted to receive good care and that he could be scared about that not being that case, which helped the client relax and feel validated. The therapist asked if he was afraid of that because of her accent, and if he wanted to discuss both his assumptions and the qualifications of the therapist openly.

Clients may also express racism, stereotypes, or biases toward other marginalized groups. This can present a dilemma for therapists, who may feel conflicted between refraining from challenging the client's perspective in favor of honoring a core belief of the client's culture; risking damaging the therapeutic relationship by discussing the remark; or going against their own social justice values by not bringing attention to it. For example, Joe, a white, middle-aged, low-income male client, came to therapy to address PTSD from his years of deployment in the Vietnam War, after having served prison time for aggravated assault. In therapy, Joe made hostile racist remarks about the African American men he encountered while incarcerated, calling them violent and stupid. This presented an opportunity to address his dysregulated anger and hyperarousal associated with PTSD, which was also fueled by racism. The therapist has several options at this point, depending on the client and the therapeutic relationship, such as framing ("Let's stay with this perception for a moment") to explore the roots of the client's racism by asking questions like those suggested in the second section of this chapter (e.g., "Do you remember when you first learned about other races?" "What were the attitudes of your family or home-town?" "What personal experiences have you had?"). This line of questioning can help both clients and therapists understand the roots of the biased attitudes, thus reducing judgment and mitigating possible shame the client might feel if directly confronted. The client eventually recognized that he felt closer to the white inmates than to the Black men, due to the similar stories they shared, and that the unfamiliar group had been an outlet for his dysregulated anger. Self-disclosure about the therapist's own bias combined with psychoeducation about oppression and systemic racism can also open the door to a conversation in a nonshaming manner. A third option from a Sensorimotor Psychotherapy perspective would be to work with the memory, in this case, of being with African American men in prison. The client reported that the most triggering incident was a brawl before he went to prison, in which he attacked a group of Black men in a parking lot and received a knife slash on his arm. Client and therapist worked to process the memory, after which the client was able to identify how he had provoked the incident himself, as he sought high intensity and risk before prison, and how he had targeted those against whom he was biased and who happened to be in his immediate proximity.

As always, therapists should also be mindful of their own reactions to the client on somatic, emotional, and cognitive levels, perhaps explore these in supervision, and examine their own motivations and values in relation to the client's prejudicial expressions. Additionally, a therapist always has the option to refer the client if the clash of values and the microaggressions are intense enough that it would compromise the therapeutic work.

Pitfalls and Vulnerabilities

Therapists are vulnerable to a variety of pitfalls in the therapeutic dyad. As mentioned, we may fail to track the signals that our clients are not ready or do not wish to explore sociocultural elements, or we ask too many personal questions, including inquiring about emotional states, expressions of affect, and body language or posture before developing the relationship and building credibility (Comas-Díaz, 2006). And although it is important to learn about a client's cultural background, we are vulnerable to indiscriminately applying this knowledge and making assumptions without being aware of the client's unique or divergent experience. Furthermore, misunderstandings and miscommunications are common when we work with marginalized clients who are not fluent in the privileged culture's language.

We may rely too heavily on our training in Eurocentric approaches and miss opportunities to draw on non-Western healing methods. We may emphasize evidence-based practices, which may or may not work well with diverse groups, considering the paucity of research conducted with these groups (Comas-Díaz, 2006). We may tend to adapt the language of neuroscience indiscriminately in psychoeducation or conceptualization, not understanding that those who developed most of that research often belong to privileged locations within the dominant culture, so it is skewed and biased toward those identities. We may fail to consider alternative explanations of health that might be more relevant to the client. For example, current neuroscience research and literature assume too quickly that reactions to threat or unsafe situations are biologically ingrained, without taking into account that they are also socially primed or conditioned. Language can also be used insensitively in ways that discount or demean a particular group. For example, the words "primitive" or "animal" are racist terms when used in reference to people of color, but are often used as nomenclature for innate subcortical defenses that instinctively emerge when we are threatened. Another example is referencing skin color to refer to changes in the autonomic nervous system. One of the signs of hypoarousal is commonly described as blanching or becoming pale; however, people with darker skin tones rarely demonstrate observable blanching. Recognition of these biases in medical and psychological research is critical when offering the client psychoeducation, as well as when the therapist tracks and contacts the client's body.

As we introduced earlier in the chapter, therapists are also at risk of attributing meaning to the body language of their clients without understanding differences in nonverbal communication of the client's culture. For example, a client's preference for increased proximity (a characteristic of their culture) might be interpreted as indicative of insufficient boundaries. A therapist may explore eye contact as a proximity-seeking, attachment-related action with a client whose cultural norms eschew direct eye contact with authority figures. A client who speaks loudly and expressively may be misread as dysregulated or angry, or a client who speaks softly might be interpreted as weak or lacking confidence. An Asian client whose body was pulled in (described as "hiding") was thought by the therapist to have familial issues with safety, when this was not the case; the client's physical pattern was developed in reaction to the lack of safety in the face of ongoing systemic oppression as a person of color. A client who hailed from Italy, an expressive culture, who gestured widely was thought by his therapist to be dysregulated and lacking self-control. A Latinx client who touched her therapist on the arm upon greeting was thought to have inappropriate boundaries, when frequent physical contact is accepted in their culture. It is important to understand the nonverbal communication norms of the culture of our clients and to initiate open discussions about them in a body-oriented therapy like Sensorimotor Psychotherapy to mitigate the tendency to prematurely make meaning of nonverbal cues.

One can never avoid all these pitfalls, and therapy itself is never a one-size-fits-all endeavor. Therapists must constantly track the effects of their interventions and adjust, and learn what is appropriate for each client. Vasquez points out that "some culturally diverse clients may be unsettled with the egalitarian and nondirective interaction styles of some therapists. Others may be put off by an authoritarian stance" (2007, p. 5). For example, an open-ended and more equal relationship that includes self-disclosure and participation in community endeavors on the part of the therapist may be appropriate for some clients, while others may prefer a therapist who has a more directive stance, assertively takes charge of the sessions, does not self-disclose, and does not expand their boundaries to include community. Some culturally diverse clients may prefer more silence, less questioning, or more small talk, while others may prefer a faster pace, less small talk, and more focused questioning that pertains to specific goals. Thus, it is important for therapists to cultivate variability in style. With careful tracking of the client's response and appropriate adjustments in the Sensorimotor Psychotherapy skills of contacting, framing, directed mindfulness questions, and experiments, clinical practice can be adapted in the moment to meet the client in a culturally sensitive manner.

CONCLUSION

To review, Eurocentric Western approaches to psychotherapy (including developmental models and trauma theory), as well as many perspectives of the body, were primarily developed according to individualistic and privileged Western paradigms. These models of psychological health have generally excluded other cultural understandings and in particular the wisdom of Indigenous and marginalized people. Knowledge of the applicability and relevance of these models for collectivistic cultures and more generally for individuals and communities with different models of consciousness, psychology, and personality is limited. Integration and adaptation of culturally sensitive approaches to understanding presentation of illnesses and therapeutic interventions remains at the margins of psychological theory and practice, which can impact the effectiveness of treatment with persons that do not conform with the norm.

We have seen that our identities, values, and other lenses through which we assess and interact with the world are embedded in the historical, sociopolitical, and cultural context of the group(s) to which we belong. This embeddedness is the result of our brain's adaptability to context and, with all its benefits, makes us vulnerable to cultural conditioning, hence to prejudices and biases. This inevitability can be held with compassion and humility, as well as curiosity toward examining our own cultural background, and how it informs our cognitive, emotional, and physical reactions to ourselves and others. From the first contact, to assessments of our clients, to the therapeutic relationship, to the interventions we put forth, implicit bias affects every aspect of therapy. Trying to suppress our biases or deny their existence only reinforces them, while continuing to impact our interpretations of the world and other people, including our clients, implicitly (Blair et al., 2001). Challenging our bias requires an active interrogation of the associations that inform our way of perceiving others, to compassionately recognize how these may not align with our beliefs, to be curious about how they show up in our lives and in the therapy room, and to actively work to counteract them. Additionally, our responsibility as therapists is to educate ourselves with regard to the impact of privilege/oppression dynamics and to develop the skill to address these dynamics in therapy. Therapists need to engage in a lifelong process of self-reflection and growth (Hook, Davis, et al., 2013; Hook, Owen, et al., 2013). This ongoing aspirational process cannot be sustained without a commitment to the journey of inquiry. What we can gain along this path goes far beyond knowledge; it includes a felt sense of the lived experience of these explorations, in connection with others, deepening our embodied resonance with our fellow human beings.

REFERENCES

Agishtein, P., & Brumbaugh, C. (2013). Cultural variation in adult attachment: The impact of ethnicity, collectivism, and country of origin. *Journal of Social, Evolutionary, and Cultural Psychology, 7*(384). https://doi.org/10.1037/h0099181

Ainsworth, M. D., & Bell, S. M. (1970). Attachment, exploration, and separation: Illustrated by the behavior of one-year-olds in a strange situation. *Child Development, 41*, 49–67.

Ainsworth, M., Blehar, M., Waters, E., & Wall, S. (1978). *Patterns of attachment: A psychological study of the strange situation.* Hillsdale, NJ: Erlbaum.

Alexander, M. (2020). *The new Jim Crow: Mass incarceration in the age of colorblindness.* New York: New Press.

Aposhyan, S. (1999). *Natural intelligence: Body-mind integration and human development.* Baltimore, MD: Williams and Wilkins.

Argyle, M., Salter, V., Nicholson, H., Williams, M., & Burgess, P. (1970). The communication of inferior and superior attitudes by verbal and non-verbal signals. *British Journal of Social and Clinical Psychology, 9*(3), 222–231. https://doi.org/10.1111/j.2044-8260.1970.tb00668.x

Barrera, I., & Jordan, C. (2011). Potentially harmful practices: Using the DSM with people of color. *Social Work in Mental Health, 9*(4), 272–286. https://doi.org/10.1080/15332985.2011.554306

Berry, J. W., Poortinga, Y. H., & Pandey, J. (Eds.). (1997). *Handbook of cross-cultural psychology* (2nd ed.). Needham Heights, MA: Allyn & Bacon.

Bertrand, M., & Mullainathan, S. (2004). Are Emily and Greg more employable than Lakisha and Jamal? A field experiment on labor market discrimination. *American Economic Review, 94*(4), 991–1013.

Birdwhistell, R. L. (2010). *Kinesics and context: Essays on body motion communication.* Philadelphia: University of Pennsylvania Press.

Blair, I. V., Ma, J. E., & Lenton, A. P. (2001). Imagining stereotypes away: The moderation of implicit stereotypes through mental imagery. *Journal of Personality and Social Psychology, 81*(5), 828–841. http://dx.doi.org/10.1037/0022-3514.81.5.828

Bobula, K. A. (2011). *This is your brain on bias . . . or, the neuroscience on bias* [Faculty Lecture Series]. Developing Brains: Ideas for Parenting and Education, Clark College, Vancouver, Washington.

Borden, R. J., & Homleid, G. M. (1978). Handedness and lateral positioning in heterosexual couples: Are men still strong arming women? *Sex Roles, 4*, 67–73.

Bowlby, J. (1951). *Maternal care and mental health.* Geneva: World Health Organization Monograph (Serial No. 2).

Bowlby, J. (1982). *Attachment* (2nd ed., Vol. 1). New York: Basic Books.

Boykin, A. W., Franklin, A. J., & Yates, J. F. (1979). Work notes on empirical research. In A.W. Boykin, A. J. Anderson, & J. F. Yates (Eds.), *Research directions of black psychologists* (pp. 1–17). New York: Russell Sage Foundation.

Brave Heart, M. Y. H., & DeBruyn, L. M. (1998). The American Indian holocaust: Healing historical unresolved grief. *American Indian and Alaska Native Mental Health Research*, no. 2, 60–82.

Brave Heart, M. Y. (2003). The historical trauma response among natives and its relationship with substance abuse: A Lakota illustration. *Journal of Psychoactive Drugs, 35*(1), 7–13.

Bryant-Davis, T. (2019). The cultural context of trauma recovery: Considering the posttraumatic stress disorder practice guideline and intersectionality. *Psychotherapy, 56*(3), 400–408. http://dx.doi.org/10.1037/pst0000241

Burgoon, J.K., Guerrero, L., & Floyd, K. (2016). *Nonverbal communication*. New York: Routledge.

Caldwell, C. (2013). Diversity issues in movement observation and assessment. *American Journal of Dance Therapy, 35*, 183–200.

Cassidy, J., Jones. J. D., & Shaver, P. R. (2013). Contributions of attachment theory and research: A framework for future research, translation, and policy. *Developmental Psychopathology, 25*(4, Pt. 2), 1415–1434. https://doi.org/10.1017/S0954579413000692

Chiarenza, A. (2012). Developments in the concept of "cultural competence." In D. Ingleby, A. Chiarenza, W. Devillé, & I. Kotsioni (Eds.), *Inequalities in health care for migrants and ethnic minorities* (pp. 66-81). Antwerp: Garant.

Christopher, J. C., Wendt, D. C., Marecek, J., & Goodman, D. M. (2014). Critical cultural awareness: Contributions to a globalizing psychology. *American Psychologist, 69*(7), 645–655. https://doi.org/10.1037/a0036851

Clark, L. A., Cuthbert, B., Lewis-Fernández, R., Narrow, W. E., & Reed, G. M. (2017). Three approaches to understanding and classifying mental disorder: ICD-11, DSM-5, and the National Institute of Mental Health's Research Domain Criteria (RDoC). *Psychological Science in the Public Interest, 18*(2), 72–145. https://doi.org/10.1177/1529100617727266

Comas-Díaz, L. (2006). Cultural variation in the therapeutic relationship. In C. D. Goodheart, A. E. Kazdin, & R. J. Sternberg (Eds.), *Evidence-based psychotherapy: Where practice and research meet* (pp. 81–105). Washington, DC: American Psychological Association. https://doi.org/10.1037/11423-004

Comas-Díaz, L., & Jacobsen, F. M. (1991). Ethnocultural transference and countertransference in the therapeutic dyad. *American Journal of Orthopsychiatry, 61*(3), 392–402.

Cosgrove, L. (2005). When labels mask oppression: Implications for teaching psychiatric taxonomy to mental health counselors. *Journal of Men-*

tal Health Counseling, 27(4), 283–296. https://doi.org/10.17744/mehc.27
.4.9eqrq789bllq1dd2

Crenshaw, K. (1989). "Demarginalizing the intersection of race and sex: A black feminist critique of antidiscrimination doctrine, feminist theory and antiracist politics. *University of Chicago Legal Forum, 1989*(1), Article 8. http://chicagounbound.uchicago.edu/uclf/vol1989/iss1/8

DeGruy, J. (2017). *Post traumatic slave syndrome: America's legacy of enduring injury and healing.* Milwaukie, OR: Uptone Press.

Denham, A. R. (2008). Rethinking historical trauma: Narratives of resilience. *Transcultural Psychiatry, 45*(3), 391–414.

DiAngelo, R. (2011). White fragility. *International Journal of Critical Pedagogy, 3*(3), 54–70.

DiBiase, R., & Gunnoe, J. (2004). Gender and culture differences in touching behavior. *Journal of Social Psychology, 144*(1), 49–62. https://doi-org.naropa.idm.oclc.org/10.3200/SOCP.144.1.49-62

Dilbeck, K. E. (2014). Vicarious and source credibility: A cross cultural explanation. *Theses and Dissertations, 589.* https://dc.uwm.edu/etd/589

Dovidio, J. F., & Gaertner, S. L. (2004). Aversive racism. In M. P. Zanna (Ed.), *Advances in experimental social psychology* (Vol. 36, pp. 1–52). New York: Elsevier Academic Press. https://doi.org/10.1016/S0065-2601(04)36001-6

Dunham, Y., Baron, A. S., & Banaji, M. R. (2008). The development of implicit intergroup cognition. *Trends in Cognitive Sciences, 12,* 248–253. https://doi.org/10.1016/j.tics.208.04.006

Duran, E., Duran, B., Heart, B., & Horse-Davis, Y. (1998). Healing the American Indian soul wound. In Y. Danieli (Ed.), *International handbook of multigenerational legacies of trauma* (pp. 341–354). New York: Springer US.

Escobar, J. I. (2012). Diagnostic bias: racial and cultural issues. *Psychiatric Services, 63*(9), 847. doi: 10.1176/appi.ps.20120p847

Ellyson, S. L., & Dovidio, J. F. (1985). Power, dominance, and nonverbal behavior: Basic concepts and issues. In S. L. Ellyson & J. F. Dovidio (Eds.), *Power, dominance, and nonverbal behavior* (pp. 1–27). New York: Springer-Verlag.

Figueira, I., Luz, M., Braga, R. J., Cabizuca, M., Coutinho, E. S. F., & Mendlowicz, M. (2007). The increasing internationalization of mainstream posttraumatic stress disorder research: A bibliometric study. *Journal of Traumatic Stress, 20*(1), 89–95.

Foa, E. B., Keane, T. M., Friedman, M. J., & Cohen, J. A. (2009). *Effective treatments for PTSD: Practice guidelines from the International Society for Traumatic Stress Studies* (2nd ed.). New York: Guilford.

Frankenberg, R. (1993). *White women, race matters: The social construction of whiteness.* Minneapolis: University of Minnesota Press.

Fuertes, J. N., Gottdiener, W. H., Martin, H., Gilbert, T. C., & Giles, H. (2012). A meta-analysis of the effects of speakers' accents on interpersonal evaluations. *European Journal of Social Psychology, 42*, 120–133.

Gillespie, D. L., & Leffler, A. (1983). Theories of nonverbal behavior: A critical review of proxemics research. *Sociological Theory, 1*, 120–154. https://doi.org/10.2307/202049

Gottlieb, A. (2004). *The afterlife is where we come from: The culture of infancy in West Africa.* Chicago: University of Chicago Press.

Hall, E. T., & Hall, T. (1959). *The silent language* (Vol. 948). New York: Anchor.

Hammack, P. L., Mayers, L., & Windell, E. P. (2013). Narrative, psychology and the politics of sexual identity in the United States: From "sickness" to "species" to "subject." *Psychology and Sexuality, 4*(3), 219–243.

Hanckock, P., Hughes, B., Jagger, E., Paterson, K., Russell, R., Tulle-Winton, E., & Tyler, M. (2000). *The body, culture and society: An introduction.* Philadelphia: Open University Press.

Harrell, S., & Gallardo, M. (2008). Sociopolitical and community dynamics in the development of a multicultural worldview. In J. K. Asamen, M. L. Ellis, & G. L. Berry (Eds.), *The SAGE handbook of child development, multiculturalism, and media* (pp. 113–128). Thousand Oaks, CA: Sage. https://doi.org/10.4135/9781412982771.n8

Harrell, S. P. (2014). Compassionate confrontation and empathic exploration: The integration of race-related narratives in clinical supervision. In C. A. Falender, E. P. Shafranske, & C. J. Falicov (Eds.), *Multiculturalism and diversity in clinical supervision: A competency-based approach* (pp. 83–110). Washington, DC: American Psychological Association. https://doi.org/10.1037/14370-004

Harrell, S. P., & Sloan-Pena, G. (2006). Racism and discrimination. In Y. Jackson (Ed.), *Encyclopedia of multicultural psychology* (pp. 396–402). Thousand Oaks, CA: Sage.

Hart, A. (2017). From multicultural competence to radical openness: A psychoanalytic engagement of otherness. *American Psychoanalyst, 51*(1). https://apsa.org/apsaa-publications/vol51no1-TOC/html/vol51no1_09.xhtml

Henley, N., & Freeman, J. (1995). *The sexual politics of interpersonal behavior in women: A feminist perspective.* London: Mayfield.

Henley, N. M. (1977). *Body politics: Power, sex, and nonverbal communication.* Englewood Cliffs, NJ: Prentice-Hall.

Hook, J. N., Davis, D. E., Owen, J., Worthington, E. L., Jr., & Utsey, S. O. (2013). Cultural humility: Measuring openness to culturally diverse clients. *Journal of Counseling Psychology, 60,* 353–366. https://doi.org/10.1037/a0032595

Hook, J. N., Owen, D. E., Worthington, E. L., Jr., & Utsey, S. O. (2013). Cultural humility of therapists is associated with stronger working alliance and better psychotherapy outcomes. *Clinician's Research Digest: Adult Populations, 31*(9), 5.

Jacob, K. S. (2019). Idioms of distress, mental symptoms, syndromes, disorders and transdiagnostic approaches. *Asian Journal of Psychiatry, 46,* 7–8. https://doi.org/10.1016/j.ajp.2019.09.018

Johnson, R. (2009). Oppression embodied: Exploring the intersections of somatic psychology, trauma, and oppression. *USPB Journal, 8*(1), 19–31.

Johnson, R. (2015). Grasping and transforming the embodied experience of oppression. *International Body Psychotherapy Journal, 14*(1), 80–95.

Johnson, R., Leighton, L., & Caldwell, C. (2018). The embodied experience of microaggressions: Implications for clinical practice. *Journal of Multicultural Counseling and Development, 46*(3), 156–170.

Kağitçibaşi, Ç. (1990). Family and socialization in cross-cultural perspective: A model of change. In J. Berman (Ed.), *Nebraska Symposium on Motivation, 1989* (pp. 135–200). Lincoln: University of Nebraska Press.

Kaiser, B. N., & Jo Weaver, L. (2019). Culture-bound syndromes, idioms of distress, and cultural concepts of distress: New directions for an old concept in psychological anthropology. *Transcultural Psychiatry, 56*(4), 589–598. https://doi.org/10.1177/1363461519862708

Keller, H. (2013). Attachment and culture. *Journal of Cross-Cultural Psychology, 44*(2), 175–194. https://doi.org/10.1177/0022022112472253

Keller, H. (2018). Universality claim of attachment theory: Children's socio-emotional development across cultures. *PNAS, 115*(45), 11414–11419.

Kellermann, N. (2001). Transmission of Holocaust trauma: An integrative view. *Psychiatry Interpersonal and Biological Processes, 64*(3), 256–267.

Kirk, G., & Okazawa-Rey, M. (2013). *Women's lives: Multicultural perspectives* (6th ed.). New York, NY: McGraw-Hill.

Kirmayer, L. J. (1996). Confusion of the senses: Implications of ethnocultural variations in somatoform and dissociative disorders for PTSD. In A. J. Marsella, M. J. Friedman, E. T. Gerrity, & R. M. Scurfield (Eds.), *Ethnocultural aspects of posttraumatic stress disorder: Issues, research, and clinical applications* (pp. 131–163). Washington, DC: American Psychological Association.

Kirschner, S. R. (2013). Diagnosis and its discontents: Critical perspectives on psychiatric nosology and the *DSM. Feminism and Psychology, 23*(1), 10–28.

Knapp, M. (2006). An historical overview of nonverbal research. In V. Manusov & M. L. Patterson (Eds.), *The SAGE handbook of nonverbal communication* (pp. 3–20). Thousand Oaks, CA: Sage. https://doi.org/10.4135/9781412976152.n1

Kurtz, R. (1990). *Body-centered psychotherapy: The Hakomi method: The integrated use of mindfulness, nonviolence, and the body.* Mendocino, CA: Life-Rhythm Books.

Liddell, B. J., & Jobson, L. (2016). The impact of cultural differences in self-representation on the neural substrates of posttraumatic stress disorder. *European Journal of Psychotraumatology, 7.* https://doi.org/10.3402/ejpt.v7.30464

Lietz, M. (2015). Whiteness and white identity development. http://cultureandyouth.org/racism/articles-racism/whiteness-white-identity-development

López, S. R. (1989). Patient variable biases in clinical judgment: Conceptual overview and methodological considerations. *Psychology Bulletin, 106*(2), 184–203.

Main, M. (2000). The organized categories of infant, child, and adult attachment: Flexible vs. inflexible attention under attachment-related stress, *Journal of the American Psychoanalytic Association,* 48(4), 1055–1096, 1094.

Main, M., & Solomon, J. (1986). Discovery of an insecure-disorganized disoriented attachment pattern. In T. B. Brazelton & M. W. Yogman (Eds.), *Affective development in infancy* (pp. 95–124). New York: Ablex.

Main, M., & Solomon, J. (1990). Procedures for identifying infants as disorganized/disoriented during the Ainsworth Strange Situation. *Attachment in the Preschool Years: Theory, Research, and Intervention, 1,* 121–160.

Mehta, N. (2011). Mind-body dualism: A critique from a health perspective. *Mens Sana Monographs, 9*(1), 202–209. https://doi.org/10.4103/0973-1229.77436

Menakem, R. (2017). *My grandmother's hands: Racialized trauma and the pathway to mending our hearts and bodies.* Las Vegas, NV: Central Recovery Press.

Mikulincer, M., & Shaver, P. R. (2007). *Attachment in adulthood: Structure, dynamics, and change.* New York: Guilford.

Mohatt, N. V., Thompson, A. B., Thai, N. D., & Kramer Tebes, J. (2014). Historical trauma as public narrative: A conceptual review of how history impacts present-day health. *Social Science Medicine, 106,* 128–136.

Moore, C. L., & Yamamoto, K. (2012). *Beyond words: Movement observation and analysis* (2nd ed.). New York: Routledge.

Morelli, G., Quinn, N., Chaudhary, N., Vicedo, M., Rosabal-Coto, M., Keller, H., Murray, M., Gottlieb, A., Scheidecker, G., & Takada, A. (2018). Ethical challenges of parenting interventions in low- to middle-income countries. *Journal of Cross-Cultural Psychology, 49,* 5–24. https://doi.org/10.1177/0022022117746241

Moss-Racusin, C. A., Dovidio, J. F., Brescoll, V. L., Graham, M. J., & Handelsman, J. (2012). Science faculty's subtle gender biases favor male students. *Proceedings of the National Academy of Sciences, 109*(41), 16474–16479. https://www.pnas.org/content/109/41/16474.abstract

Ng, E., & Purser, R. (2015). White privilege and the mindfulness movement. Buddhist Peace Fellowship: Buddhism and Social Justice. http://www.buddhistpeacefellowship.org/white-privilege-the-mindfulness-movement/

Nichter, M. (1982). *Idioms of distress: Alternatives in the expression of psychosocial distress: A case study from South India.* Culture, Medicine, and Psychiatry, 5, 379–408. 10.1007/BF00054782.

Nichter, M. (2010). Idioms of distress revisited. *Culture, Medicine and Psychiatry, 34,* 401–416. https://doi.org/10.1007/s11013-010-9179-6

Nobles, W. (1986). *African psychology: Toward its reclamation, reascension and revitalization.* Oakland, CA: Black Family Institute.

Ogden, P. (2007). *Beyond words: A clinical map for using mindfulness of the body and the organization of experience in trauma treatment.* Paper presented at Mindfulness and Psychotherapy Conference, Los Angeles: UCLA/Lifespan Learning Institute.

Ogden, P. (2009). *Emotion, mindfulness, and movement: Expanding the regulatory boundaries of the window of affect tolerance.* In D. Fosha, D. Siegel, & M. Solomon (Eds.), The healing power of emotion: Affective neuroscience & clinical practice (pp. 204–231). New York: W. W. Norton & Company.

Ogden, P. (2014). *Beyond conversation in Sensorimotor Psychotherapy: Embedded relational mindfulness.* In V. M. Follette, D. Rozelle, J. W. Hopper, D. I. Rome, and J. Briere (Eds), Contemplative methods in trauma treatment: Integrating mindfulness and other approaches. New York: The Guilford Press.

Ogden, P. (2020). *The different impact of trauma and relational stress on physiology, posture, and movement: Implications for treatment.* European Journal of Trauma & Dissociation, 100172.

Ogden, P. & Fisher, J. (2015). *Sensorimotor psychotherapy: Interventions for trauma and attachment.* New York: W. W. Norton & Company.

Ogden, P., Minton, K., & Pain, C. (2006). *Trauma and the body: A sensorimotor approach to psychotherapy.* New York, NY: Norton.

Otto, H. (2008). *Culture-specific attachment strategies in the Cameroonian Nso: Cultural solutions to a universal developmental task* [Unpublished doctoral dissertation]. Osnabrück, Germany.

Otto, H., & Keller, H. (Eds.). (2014). *Different faces of attachment.* Cambridge, UK: Cambridge University Press.

Pallaro, P. (1997). Culture, self and body-self: Dance/movement therapy with Asian Americans. *Arts in Psychotherapy, 24*(3), 227–241.

Paniagua, F. A. (2018). ICD-10 versus *DSM-5* on cultural Issues. *SAGE Open.* https://doi.org/10.1177/2158244018756165

Perception Institute. (2019). *Transforming perception: Black men and boys* [Executive summary]. https://perception.org/research/explicit-bias/

Phillips, L. T., & Lowery, B. S. (2018). Herd invisibility: The psychology of racial privilege. *Current Directions in Psychological Science, 27*(3), 156–162.

Quillian, L., Pager, D., Hexel, O., & Midtbøen, A. H. (2017). Meta-analysis of field experiments shows no change in racial discrimination in hiring over time. *Proceedings of the National Academy of Sciences, 114*(41), 10870–10875.

Reshamwala, S. (2016). *Peanut butter, jelly, and racism* [Video]. *New York Times.* https://www.nytimes.com/video/us/100000004818663/peanut-butter-jelly-and-racism.html

Roberts, S. O., Bareket-Shavit, C., Dollins, F. A., Goldie, P. D., & Mortenson, E. (2020). *Racial inequality in psychological research: Trends of the past and recommendations for the future.* Perspectives on Psychological Science, 1745691620927709.

Ross, H. (2017). Exploring unconscious bias. https://culturalawareness.com/wp-content/uploads/2017/03

Rothbaum, F., Weisz, J., Pott, M., Miyake, K., & Morelli, G. (2000). Attachment and culture: Security in the United States and Japan. *American Psychologist, 55*(10), 1093.

Said, E. (1978). Orientalism: Western concepts of the orient. New York: Pantheon.

SAMHSA. (2014). *Trauma-informed care in behavioral health services.* Treatment Improvement Protocol (TIP) Series 57. HHS Publication No. (SMA) 13-4801. Rockville, MD: Substance Abuse and Mental Health Services Administration.

Sanders Thompson, V. L. (2006). Coping responses and the experience of discrimination. *Journal of Applied Social Psychology, 36*(5), 1198–1214.

Schachter, E. P. (2005). Context and identity formation: A theoretical analysis and a case study. *Journal of Adolescent Research, 20*(3), 375–395. https://doi.org/10.1177/0743558405275172

Sidhu, G. (2017). The application of Western models of psychotherapy by Indian psychotherapists in India: A grounded theory. *Dissertations and Theses, 377.* http://aura.antioch.edu/etds/377

Siegel, D. (1999). *The developing mind: Toward a neurobiology of interpersonal experience.* New York: Guilford Press.

Snowden, L. R. (2003). Bias in mental health assessment and intervention: Theory and evidence. *American Journal of Public Health, 93*(2), 239–243. https://doi.org/10.2105/ajph.93.2.239

Sroufe, L. A., & Siegel, D. (2011, March/April). The verdict is in. *Psychotherapy Networker*, pp. 34–39, 52–53. https://www.drdansiegel.com/uploads/1271-the-verdict-is-in.pdf

Stewart, B. D., & Payne, B. K. (2008). Bringing automatic stereotyping under control: Implementation intentions as efficient means of thought control. *Personality and Social Psychology Bulletin, 34*, 1332–1345.

Sue, D. W. (2010). *Microaggressions in everyday life: Race, gender, and sexual orientation*. Hoboken, NJ: Wiley.

Sue, D. W., Arredondo, P., & McDavis, R. J. (1992). Multicultural counseling competencies and standards: A call to the profession. *Journal of Multicultural Counseling and Development, 20*(2), 64–88.

Sue, D. W., Bernier, J. E., Durran, A., Feinberg, L., Pedersen, P., Smith, E. J., & Vasquez-Nuttall, E. (1982). Position paper: Cross-cultural counseling competencies. *Counseling Psychologist, 10*, 45–52. https://doi.org/10.1177/0011000082102008

Sue, D. W., Capodilupo, C. M., Torino, G. C., Bucceri, J. M., Holder, A. M. B., Nadal, K. L., & Esquilin, M. (2007). Racial microaggressions in everyday life: Implications for clinical practice. *American Psychologist, 62*(4), 271–286. https://doi.org/10.1037/0003-066X.62.4.271

Sue, D. W., & Sue, D. (1990). *Counseling the culturally different*. New York: Wiley.

Sue, D. W., Sue, D., Neville, H. A., & Smith, L. (2019). *Counselling the culturally diverse: Theory and practice*. New York: Wiley.

Szasz, T. S. (1971). The sane slave: An historical note on the use of medical diagnosis as justificatory rhetoric. *American Journal of Psychotherapy, 25*(2), 228–239.

Tajfel, H., & Forgas, J. P. (2000). Social categorization: Cognitions, values and groups. In C. Stangor (Ed.), *Stereotypes and prejudice: Essential readings* (pp. 49–63). Ann Arbor, MI: Taylor and Francis.

Tervalon, M., & Murray-Garcia, J. (1998). Cultural humility versus cultural competence: A critical distinction in defining physician training outcomes in multicultural education. *Journal of Health Care for the Poor and Underserved, 9*(2), 117–125.

Tronick, E. (2007). *The neurobehavioral and social-emotional development of infants and children*. New York: Norton.

Tronick, E. Z., Morelli, G. A., & Ivey, P. K. (1992). The Efe forager infant and toddler's pattern of social relationships: Multiple and simultaneous. *Developmental Psychology, 28*(4), 568.

Valavanis, S., Thompson, C., & Murray, C. D. (2019). Positive aspects of voice-hearing: A qualitative metasynthesis. *Mental Health, Religion and Culture, 22*(2), 208–225. https://doi-org.naropa.idm.oclc.org/10.1080/13674676.2019.1601171

Vasquez, M. (2007). Cultural difference and the therapeutic alliance: An evidence-based analysis. *American Psychologist, 62*(8), 875–885. https://doi.org/10.1037/0003-066X.62.8.878

Williams, M. (2014). A conversation on racial disparities in MH treatment. New York Association of Psychiatric Rehabilitation Services. https://www.nyaprs.org/e-news-bulletins/2015/a-conversation-on-racial-disparities-in-mh-treatment

Williams, M. (2019). Microaggressions: Clarification, evidence, and impact. *PsychArchives.* https://doi.org/10.23668/psycharchives.2506

Chapter 2

THE IMPACT OF TRAUMA AND RELATIONAL STRESS ON PHYSIOLOGY, POSTURE, AND MOVEMENT

*The history of the body is the history of human beings, for there
is no cultural practice that is not first applied to the body.*

SILVIA FEDERICI

This chapter examines two interrelated categories of adversity: trauma and relational stress. Distinguishing between trauma and relational stress and understanding their interactions helps clinicians prioritize appropriate clinical strategy and technique to maximize therapeutic efficacy (Ogden, 2009a). To ensure survival, children adapt automatically, without conscious intent, to traumatic events, whether perpetrated by individuals, groups, or society as a whole (e.g., systemic oppression). Similarly, they also adapt to the misattunements of caregivers, significant other individuals, or groups of people to maximize the available resources or at least minimize the stress. These adaptations accumulate to leave scars in the form of symptoms and patterns of thinking, feeling, and acting that correlate with each kind of injury. The unique legacy of each category of adversity is revealed physically in patterns of gesture, posture, movement, and physiology; cognitively in a range of limiting, distorted beliefs; and emotionally in both the dysregulated emotions associated with trauma and the unresolved ones associated with relational misattunements that have not been sufficiently repaired. Although these two kinds of injuries are interconnected, clinical intervention appropriate for addressing the effects of each as they emerge in the therapy hour are markedly different. Understanding the differences in their etiology, effects, and symptoms can help guide both general clinical approaches and specific techniques (Ogden, 2009a). These clinical choices become imperative in a relationally focused, trauma-informed, culturally sensitive integrative therapeutic approach.

INTRODUCTION

Our brains are designed to anticipate the immediate future so that we can plan and carry out adaptive actions. From infancy, this capacity is refined through our relationships with our caregivers, others, and the environment. What we learn to expect in the next moment in part determines the action that we execute, be it pushing open a door or pushing away an assailant. Predictions of relational interactions commence in infancy, as Beebe asserts:

> Early interaction patterns are represented pre-symbolically, through the procedural organization of action sequences. Predictability and expectancy is a key organizing principle of the infant's brain. Infants form expectancies of how . . . interactions go whether they are positive or negative, and these expectancies set a trajectory for development (which can nevertheless transform). (2006, p. 160)

For example, if as children we consistently experience disapproval, we will tend to anticipate disapproval in future interactions. Such a prediction not only influences immediate actions, but also affects the physical habits of posture, movement, gait, facial expression, and so forth. A physical habit, such as rounded shoulders, may be formed if curving the shoulders inward is repeated over and over in response to disapproval. Significant physical habits provide a window into the experiences that shaped them, as well into as their meaning and function. Rounded shoulders, for example, may be an attempt to hide in the face of disapproval, or to conceal an aspect of the self. In this way, physical form, in part, follows function. Once learned, these habits become procedural—stable and lasting—and do not "require conscious or unconscious mental representations, images, motivations or ideas to operate" (Grigsby & Stevens, 2000, p. 316). They occur and persevere without our intent, which renders them even more influential because they are unavailable for reflection and revision. Echoing forecasts of a future that is based on past experience, procedural patterns become default actions, engaged without thought or question, preempting actions that might be more adaptive in current situations.

Within a history of normative development, including good enough parenting and the absence of pervasive trauma and societal oppression, expectations, as well as forecasts and actions, "remain to some extent fluid and flexible throughout life; the nature of the consequences that are anticipated for a given action will change as the context of interaction changes and with development of the individual's powers" (Bucci, 2011, p. 6). However, trauma and relational stressors, including strife with early attachment figures as well as the strife of oppression, discrimination, and exploitation that marginalized people experience, have far-reaching neuropsychological effects and may foreshadow future versions of past ordeals. When unresolved, the fallout of each category of adversity generates specific symptoms and patterns that can perpetuate a repeat of the original suffering. Although we are making a clinical distinction between these categories of adversity for the purpose of clarity, they invariably overlap with one another and are not experienced as distinct by the client. Moreover, different dynamics of privilege/oppression will also be impactful depending on the social location of the individual (race, gender, sexual orientation, socioeconomic status, disability, immigration/refugee status, language, education, age, geographic location, and so forth). The interaction of these identities can amplify and perpetuate trauma and relational stress in unique ways for both the marginalized and the privileged.

Therapists and clients are sometimes confused about what constitutes trauma. With the understanding that particular conditions such as abuse are universally traumatic, trauma is defined in this chapter by the effect of an event, rather than by the event itself. If an individual experiences a situation as a threat to safety or existence (whether that threat is actual or presumed), such that subcortical defenses and extremes of autonomic arousal are catalyzed, that event constitutes a trauma for that individual. Therefore, for our purposes, event(s) are deemed traumatic not because of the event per se but because it spurs instinctive defenses and extreme arousal that are not mediated by the cortex; in fact, cortical activity is disabled. Extreme or "vehement" (Janet, 1909) emotions that exceed the regulatory boundaries of the window of tolerance are also stimulated. The symptoms and difficulties of unresolved trauma stem from these extreme physical, physiological, and emotional reactions that remain unintegrated.

It should be noted that events that are traumatic for the victim are traumatic for the perpetrator as well (Menakem, 2017). Harrell (2020) points out "a traumatic incident involves not just the target or 'victim,' but also perpetrators and their descendents, as well as witnesses and 'first responders.'" Often those who have been oppressed become oppressors themselves (Freire, 2007); several studies show that a history of being on the receiving end of interpersonal violence inclines the survivor to be violent toward others (Kar, 2018). Additionally, experiences of being shunned or ostracized have been shown to predict later aggression (Ren et al., 2018; Wesselmann et al., 2017). The function of aggression toward others, whether physical or verbal, may be in part to protect against feelings of vulnerability in the aftermath of one's own past trauma and oppression. For example, trauma symptoms of men who batter their wives were significantly higher than those of the control group (Dutton, 1995). And Dokoupil (2012) proposed that shame and regret associated with perpetrating violence contribute more significantly to PTSD of combat soldiers than fear itself. Thus, treatment of trauma should be all-inclusive, involving perpetrators and victims, as well as the societal structures that hold systemic oppression in place.

Clients come to therapy suffering not only from the effects of trauma, but also from the effects of relational stress that may not be traumatic. Even within a context of normative development and good enough parenting, caregivers will inevitably fail at times to accurately recognize their child's cues and thus will respond in ways that do not meet the child. Misattunements will cause emotional distress for children, which can accumulate when mismatches are repeated and remain unrepaired. As we mature, relational interactions with people other than primary attachment figures, both individuals and groups, can also be hurtful and leave wounds that fester. Although these misattunements are distressing for children and adults alike, they may not be appraised by the recipient as physically dangerous or life threatening, and thus do not technically qualify as trauma according to our definition.

Many clients suffer from the enduring effects of events that took place in the past, but marginalized people suffer from current, ongoing events that are often demeaning, exchanges that perpetuate power/oppression dynamics and are not systemically or interpersonally repaired. These ongoing experiences of misattunement may or may not technically meet the diagnostic criteria required to be described as trauma, but they are (implicity or explicity) informed by deeply traumatic histories of colonization, genocide, slavery, or other violations of human rights that can exacerbate the range of physiological and/or emotional responses to current events. Thus, for marginalized persons, current relational stress is generally complicated by transgenerational trauma, the accumulated histories of collective trauma, and the ongoing structural violence that their communities have suffered (Brave Heart, 2003; DeGruy, 2005; Duran et al., 1998; Kirmayer et al., 2014).

Provided that such distressing events do not evoke instinctive survival defenses and extreme autonomic arousal that endures without reprieve, they do not qualify as immediately traumatic under our definition. In some form and to some degree, all of us will grapple with the lasting difficulties resulting from disturbing interactions and ruptures that are unrepaired. It should be noted that when the stress in relationships, whether between individuals or groups of people, is prolonged or so severe that instinctive defenses and extreme arousal are activated, such stress is considered traumatic for that individual.

Some adverse events are not perpetuated by others, such as natural disasters or accidents like a fall. But most clients come to therapy due to adversity that did involve other people, often caregivers, but also others as well, such as peers, relatives, babysitters, teachers, employers and coworkers, or strangers. Groups of people and even nations can engage in such offenses as bullying, group exclusion, prejudice, hate crimes, racial trauma, and oppression (e.g., colonization, internment camps, slavery, Holocaust, postmigration discrimination and mistreatment, and so forth). Since our identities as individuals and as members of a group are mostly formed by how others view and relate to us, or recognize us, misrecognition, whether by an individual, a group, or society as a whole, can be insidiously harmful and even traumatic. Taylor clarifies:

> a person or group of people can suffer real damage, real distortion, if the people or society around them mirror back to them a confining or demeaning or contemptible picture of them-

selves. Nonrecognition or misrecognition can inflict harm, can be a form of oppression, imprisoning someone in a false, distorted and reduced mode of being. (1992, p. 25)

Often neglected in much of the literature, historical and current massive trauma and profound societal misrecognition, discrimination, and prejudice leave devastating effects across generations. Marginalized people, including ethnic and racial minorities, migrants, refugees, indigenous people, those with disabilities, the LGBTQ+ community, women and girls, the poor, and others who are persecuted by the dominant culture, such as Muslims or Jewish people, to name a few, experience macro- and microaggressions perpetrated by other people and oppressive systems, which profoundly deny their realities (Sue, 2010) and can undermine their well-being, sense of safety, and relational trust.

Experiences of trauma and relational dynamics are the blueprints for children's developing cognition, affect array, regulatory ability, and physical tendencies (the way children learn to move, hold the body, engage particular gestures and facial expressions, and so forth). In clinical practice, different conceptualizations, strategies, and interventions are needed to address the aftermath of both trauma and attachment/relational stress. This chapter will briefly describe the polyvagal theory (cf. Porges) and explore how the legacy of each of the general categories of adversity affect the body's movement, posture, physiology, cognitions, emotional patterns and biases, and dissociation and self-states. A few treatment approaches for the effects of each category of injury as they emerge in the therapy hour will be described through a case study. The effects of the trauma, oppression, and invalidation inflicted on marginalized people will be referenced herein; however, elucidating the profound impact or complex strategies for resolution of these injustices is beyond the scope of this chapter.

THE POLYVAGAL THEORY

Porges's (1995, 2001, 2004, 2005, 2009, 2011) polyvagal theory clarifies how physiological and physical patterns are affected by adversity
of all kinds. This theory describes the autonomic nervous system as
one of hierarchy between sympathetic and parasympathetic systems.
A full-term infant is born with an intact ventral vagal complex, a
branch of the parasympathetic nervous system that supports relationships with others through facial expressions, sounds, gaze, and
the like, rather than through gross motor movement. This social
engagement system is thought to be the basis for the attachment system because it modulates social cueing behaviors that promote relational communication, starting with infants and caregivers (Porges,
2004, 2005).

Porges's (2004, 2011) term *neuroception* explains the automatic,
non-conscious neural process that is neurobiologically programmed
to detect features in the environment and from others that signify
levels of safety, danger, and threat. When safety is neurocepted,
the social engagement system is strengthened. Social interaction
requires that the areas of the brain that organize defenses are inhibited, which is adaptive only in contexts that are safe (Porges, 2011).
If we experience a sufficient degree of safety in childhood, we
develop an effective social engagement system that is able to form
and sustain relationships (Porges, 2004, 2005, 2009, 2011). But children's ability to rest in a feeling of safety is lost when the perpetrator
is a caregiver, or when the child belongs to a marginalized group
that continues to be victimized by society. The social engagement
system's function to elicit care and protection has been overridden
in different ways in each case, and, when the attachment figure is
the perpetrator, children experience overwhelming arousal without
the availability of repair from their caregivers.

In non-traumatic stressful interactions, the social engagement
system does not completely fail, nor is security altogether absent.

However, certain behavioral features of the caregiver or significant person(s), neurocepted by children, can serve to diminish their sense of security. Children have two options in the face of the expectations of caregivers: one, to receive approval by meeting expectations, thus preserving safety, and two, to fail to meet expectations and risk negative reactions such as rejection, disapproval, criticism, disappointment, or even abuse (S. Porges, personal communication, September 13, 2013). Children will usually instinctively strive to preserve safety and connection by modifying their behavioral responses and needs to accommodate the preferences of important or dominant individuals and groups, learning early on what is expected in those relationships and what to do to relieve stress. This "implicit relational knowing" (Lyons-Ruth, 1998) can be applicable in caregiver–child relationships, as well as in privilege/oppression dynamics, where children who belong to a marginalized group learn to adapt to a world that is prejudiced against them. When children attempt to meet expectations, the presence and frequency of behavioral cues from others and the messages they receive from society as a whole that decrease well-being and security typically lessen or disappear, resulting in a neuroception of safety and a degree of social engagement.

TRAUMA AND RELATIONAL STRESS

Bowlby (1969/1982) noted that the attachment system prompts proximity-seeking actions of infants to increase the nearness of caregivers, necessary for the child's survival. Signaling behaviors bring the other person closer to the child, while approach behaviors bring the child closer to the other person. In infancy, proximity relies upon crying, facial expressions, and other forms of signaling, supported by the social engagement system that governs neural regulation of the facial muscles and voice. Facial expressions, eye contact, and conforming to the attachment figure's body all contribute to achieving and maintaining proximity (Ainsworth, 1963; Bowlby, 1988; Lyons-Ruth & Jacobvitz, 1999; Schore, 1994, 2003). As coordinated movement skills mature, children increasingly use their arms and legs to achieve proximity. They crawl toward caregivers, toddle after them, climb on their laps, cling, and sometimes resist separation. Proximity-seeking behaviors adapt "based on that person's forecasts of how accessible and responsive his attachment figures are likely to be should he turn to them for support" (Bowlby, 1973, p. 203). This early learning in the context of interactions with others modifies instinctive proximity-seeking action sequences such as reaching out for help or connection, or seeking eye contact.

Imperfect, yet generally attuned, interactions between children and significant others bolster the social engagement system, and as that system develops, relational bonds are heightened. Children build the capacity to tolerate stress and regulate arousal, with others and alone. With sufficient care, children acquire generally positive expectations of human interactions and become increasingly effective at nonverbal signaling, approach behaviors, engaging, and responding to others (Brazelton, 1989; Schore, 1994; Siegel, 1999; Stern, 1985; Tronick, 2007). Physical habits, such as reaching out, reflect predictions that others will usually respond to them in a desirable manner. Thus, the child's trust in relationships is strengthened.

However, out of necessity this trust may be limited to those of similar social or racial identity, particularly when the child belongs to a marginalized group. Proximity-seeking actions toward people of the dominant culture, or to those who are different from or prejudiced against the group to which the child belongs, will most likely be modified. Code-switching—changing our actions and ways of speaking to adapt to various social contexts—may be conceptualized as both a critical skill in diverse contexts and a response to historical trauma for marginalized people interacting with an often rejecting, patronizing, or hostile world. Code-switching is thought to ensure survival, facilitate adaptation into the dominant culture, and maximize access to resources; however, it can "result in the denial of part or all of one's identity" (Edelman, 2018, p. 187).

All societies and all individuals have shortcomings stemming from difficult and traumatic collective or personal histories and societal norms that are reenacted in some form, often without awareness. Caregivers whose family of origin expected compliance may unwittingly impose the same expectation on their children. Employers who do not consider themselves to be prejudiced may unconsciously ask refugees or people of color to perform menial tasks or bypass them for a raise despite superb job performance. Clients come to therapy hurt or offended by such expectations that do not qualify as traumatic per se because they do not immediately elicit dysregulated arousal and survival defenses. However, such expectations, although indirect and subtle, still leave a powerful impact on the recipient, especially when they are imposed by a person in power, be it a caregiver to a child or a member of the dominant culture to a member of a marginalized group.

Even in a generally attuned, secure relationship, upsetting interactions will occur, without conscious intention or awareness. Significant people may be unwittingly inattentive, too busy, harsh, inconsistent, insensitive, fault-finding, demanding, or expectant of something that the child or other person cannot, or does not want to, provide. Children will display attempts to meet the expectations of the important people in their lives through movement and posture, developing habits that can endure. For example, children whose caregivers stressed compliance and conformity, but disapproved of originality and assertive behavior, will embody these expectations. Perhaps their posture will be pulled in or collapsed; spontaneous proximity-seeking actions, such as reaching out, may be modified; for example, reaching out may be tentative rather than assertive. Movement in general may be subdued, as the body automatically adjusts based on predictions of response. When postures and actions such as these are congruent with meeting expectations, children may be able to avoid negative responses from others and maintain safety and acceptance. Conversely, an erect, upright posture with clear, straightforward eye contact may threaten both safety and acceptance.

Similar postures can also form in response to the misrecognitions and oppression of society at large. Physical interactions between privileged and marginalized people are inherently asymmetrical, nonverbally reflecting power/oppression dynamics. As these are repeated over time, they become modes of interaction that serve to maintain societal norms of privilege/oppression and dominance/subordination (Johnson, 2015). Whether the context is one of relational misrecognition or social oppression, the physical patterns are accompanied varying levels of dysregulation by corresponding beliefs, conscious or not, ranging from, "I shouldn't express myself" or "I need to conform to the wishes of others" to "I must be small [or fight back] to be safe." These physical patterns and their corresponding beliefs modify or curtail impulses and internal needs that are perceived as unacceptable. When repeated over time and across different contexts, they limit the range of affect and movement vocabulary, often diminishing a person's experience later in life when circumstances may have changed.

All our clients come to therapy with difficulties resulting from the inadequacies, misattunements, and injustices, both small and large, of past interactions. Some may minimize needs, feel somewhat uncomfortable or fearful of closeness, and thus shun people or situations that stimulate needs, and avoid eye contact and reaching out in favor of distancing actions, such as pushing away. Instead of seeking proximity under stress, they may find it easier to withdraw. Others may maximize needs and be preoccupied with the availability of other people close to them. However, patterns such as these do not necessarily indicate either trauma or an insecure attachment. Good enough caregivers are inevitably inconsistent in their attunement. At least some of the time, they help the child recover from breaches through interactive repair that restores connection and positive affect following a negative relational experience, offering enough support so the child can manage the frustration and hurt. But even when a child's caregivers have provided sufficient interactive repair, they still favor certain actions and ways of being over others.

If situations or expectations from attachment figures or other people in power are neurocepted as life threatening, instinctive survival defenses and accompanying dysregulated arousal ensue. Thus, trauma affects the body in predictable ways according to the innate defenses aroused. Nontraumatic attachment inadequacies are reflected in cognitive distortions, emotional patterns and body structure, posture, movement, and expression. Events neurocepted as threatening (and thus constituting a trauma) first and foremost affect physiology and movement because trauma calls forth inherent subcortical instincts in the service of survival. Trauma often leaves severe psychological manifestations in its wake, like cognitive distortions of being at fault or bad, and emotions of terror or rage, but it has its roots in the body.

Under threat, the sympathetic nervous system releases adrenaline, increasing heart rate and respiration to provide muscles with the oxygen and energy needed to fuel the active defenses of crying-for-help, fight, or flight. The first instinct of an infant is to cry for help, also called the "separation cry" (Panksepp, 1998; Van der Kolk, 1987) or the "attachment cry" (Steele et al., 2005). Additional instinctive defenses of flight and fight become available as motor capacities mature. However, when these active responses are not effective—when no one comes to help or when fighting or fleeing are impossible and futile—immobilizing defenses are catalyzed. A freeze defense, described as "alert immobility" (Misslin, 2008, p. 58) is characterized by high arousal coupled with a complete cessation of movement except for respiration and movement of the eyes. When all else fails, the dorsal vagal branch of the parasympathetic nervous system is aroused, supporting feigning death or shutdown. The body becomes numb, collapsed, and immobilized. In situations where the attachment figure is also a threat to the child, both the attachment system, with its proximity-seeking actions, and the defense systems, with its protective actions, are evoked. The social engagement system is compromised and its development interrupted. But even when seeking proximity, the child's defensive subsystems of flight, fight, freeze, or feigned death are also catalyzed, while the cry-for-help is truncated since the perpetrator is also the attachment figure.

These responses to threat are initially adaptive, but tend to persist when the trauma is unresolved. Traumatized clients may suffer from hyper- and/or hypoarousal, and may continue to experience immobilizing defenses of freezing, accompanied by hyperalert senses and immobility, or feigned death—feeling distant from their experience, or reporting a sense of deadness. Mobilizing defenses may persist in the form of altered, exaggerated, or chaotic impulses to fight, flee, or cry-for-help.

It is important to understand the influence of societal group membership on the occurrence and the symptoms of trauma. As Bryant-Davis states, "Marginalized community members are more likely to experience interpersonal trauma, to develop severe PTSD, and to face barriers to safety, justice, and mental health services" (2019, p. 401). Ongoing misrecognition, discrimination, and invalidation can lead to dysregulation. While the field of psychology has a long tradition of viewing particular behaviors as evidence of pathology, for marginalized people, however, such behaviors can also be seen as strategies that have grown over time in response to oppression (Watts et al., 1999). Thus, although symptoms of trauma may be influenced by the norms and customs of each culture, they may present in even more nuanced and unique ways for marginalized people. Additionally, although overactive survival defenses are often viewed as pathological, marginalized people often need these defenses to navigate the ongoing trauma that persists over a lifetime. Even if a person has not been directly harmed, knowing that victimization is always a potential due to marginalized group membership can elicit survival defenses.

EMOTION

Emotions are complicated. Therapists may be confused whether to help clients regulate, contain, soothe, or fully express their emotions. Understanding the difference between trauma-related emotions and the emotions that have been pushed away because they have not been adequately regulated or accepted by important others can help clear up some of this confusion. Janet's (1909) vehement emotions associated with trauma "have a disintegrating effect on the entire organism [and] constitute an integrative failure" (Van der Hart & Rydberg, 2019, p. 9), and cannot be resolved through emotional expression. Other kinds of emotions add motivational coloring to experience and, although intense, do not have a disintegrating effect and can be integrated through their expression.

Conceptualizing vehement emotions as designed to fuel instinctive defenses is one way to understand their intensity. Once danger is neurocepted, terror, rage, or panic, which are all vehement emotions, arise to reinforce the function of these defenses (Frijda, 1986; Hobson, 1994; Ogden, 2009a; Rivers, 1920). For example, fear can fuel a flight defense and rage a fight defense; panic often accompanies cry-for-help; terror can provoke a freeze defense; and despair or detachment from emotion can reflect a feigned death, shutdown defense. All these emotions are adaptive in the moment of immediate peril because they support the action and goal of a specific instinctive defensive response. However, they can linger after the danger is over and can be repeatedly triggered by traumatic reminders. Clients may report that the rage associated with a fight defense is catalyzed with minimal provocation, or that they continue to feel terrified (even when they know cognitively that they are no longer in danger) or desperate for someone to rescue them, a cry-for-help defense. Repeated feelings of helplessness and terror correlated with a freeze defense may continue, while frequent subjective detachment from or absence of emotion that go along with a feigned death defense may persist. People may vacillate between outbursts of rage or panic or overpowering shame or despair, or feel flat or detached from their emotions, or powerless to manage them. Some may feel nothing even when they are in a dangerous situation, despite their mind telling them that they should be afraid. As stated, these vehement emotions should subside when the danger is passed, because the defensive responses they fuel are no longer needed.

However, for marginalized people, defensive responses are warranted in a continually unsafe, persecutory society. For example, an African American client expressed that they immediately felt threatened when they saw a police officer, knowing that racial profiling was a real possibility; a Jewish person felt afraid in their own synagogue after recent threats; an undocumented immigrant experienced panic each time there was a knock at their door, fearing authorities who would deport them. In situations such as these, instinctive defenses and the emotions that fuel them are needed because the possibility of danger and threat is ever present in society at large.

Trauma-related vehement emotions interface with those associated with close interpersonal relationships. Bowlby stated that "many of the most intense emotions arise during the formation, the maintenance, the disruption, and the renewal of attachment relationships" (1980, p. 40). However, when needs are not met or it is not safe to freely express emotion, procedurally learned inhibitory emotional responses develop. Children initially experience unrestrained emotion, but when this "core affect" (Fosha, 2000) elicits negative responses from a caregiver (criticism, withdrawal, hatred, dismissal, anger, disappointment, disapproval, and so forth), children then experience their own negative affect: shame, humiliation, rejection, confusion, bewilderment, fear, anger, and the like. If this sequence is consistent over time, the child may lose hope in the efficacy of spontaneous core emotions to achieve desired results, and form habitual emotional defenses against them in order to avoid the negative responses from others.

These patterned emotional defenses are sometimes described as dysfunctional reactions that typically defend against or impede the expression of core emotion and interfere with resolution (Safran & Greenberg, 1991). Thus, they can be conceptualized as relational defenses (distinguished from instinctive defenses to trauma) against the core emotions that elicit negative responses from others. Such patterned emotions serve to

> mask or suppress a deeper [core] emotion, recapitulate early affect–laden interactions with caregivers, and limit affective experience, array and expression. These emotions have a repetitive quality, and often disguise and defend against a deeper level of feeling, having been formed as successful strategies for meeting needs where direct authentic emotional communications proved unsuccessful. (Ogden, 2009a, p. 228)

Fosha describes affective competence as "being able to feel and process emotions for optimal functioning while maintaining the integrity of self and the safety-providing relationship" (2000, p. 42). However, even in secure attachments, certain emotional responses are favored over others. For example, some families or social groups may welcome vulnerable emotions of sadness, hurt, and disappointment, while others frown upon these but may welcome anger, pride, or assertion. In either case, children may curtail their core affect and develop patterned emotions in order to fit into their family or group. The core emotions that are met with negative reactions then remain unacknowledged, unexpressed, and unresolved.

Similar trajectories occur with the cumulative experiences of unjust or prejudicial treatment in which children (and adults) may suppress their emotional authenticity to prevent further mistreatment of themselves or their loved ones. For many historically marginalized communities, the need to suppress core emotion was the result of the coercive control and physical violence of genocide, colonization, or enslavement. Moreover, emotional patterns of irritability, pessimism, mistrust, apathy, bitterness, hostility, or other emotions may develop (Harrell & Sloan-Pena, 2006). These emotional styles as well as suppression of core emotion "represent adaptations to living in the context of racism and their ultimate function is protective" (Harrell & Sloan-Pena, 2006, p. 399). Emotional defenses, no matter their source, are an effort to reduce the likelihood that the person will be the target of negative affect, action, or even abuse.

From traumatic and nontraumatic interactions with significant others and later with society at large, children form internal working models (Bowlby, 1969/1982, 1973, 1988) about self, others, and the world. These are encoded in procedural memory and become automatic strategies of affect regulation (Schore, 1994) and relational expectations. These models, with their predictions, beliefs, emotions, and physical patterns, are affected by consecutive experience, and thus are not static. Working models and their procedural patterns are a testament to the adaptability of the brain and body. They reveal human capacity to interpret and synthesize information and anticipate the effect of our actions.

We develop different kinds of relationships to different people and different groups. Bowlby (1969/1982) wrote that individuals often operate with more than one working model of both attachment figures and the self (as well as of other people and the world). Because the "self" is an emergent, associative process "arising out of a hard-wired disposition to relate to another" (Wilkinson, 2006, p. 155), different parts of the self may adhere to different working models that each have their own island of conflicting truth and expectations. The degree, intensity, and duration of trauma and relational stress will result in different degrees and kinds of contradictions, and thus integrative failure.

All of us experience minor integrative failure, because all caregivers renounce parts of their children, often unwittingly. Bromberg clarifies:

> A person's core self—the self that is shaped by early attachment patterns—is defined by who the parental object both perceives him to be and denies him to be. That is, through relating to their child as though he is "such and such" and ignoring other aspects of him as if they don't exist, the parents "disconfirm" the relational existence of those aspects of the child's self that they perceptually dissociate. . . . The main point is that "disconfirmation" . . . is relationally nonnegotiable. (2006, p. 57)

Children will reject the aspects of themselves that caregivers and significant others disavow. Thus, two or more working models of attachment figures, others, and the self can be formed, one related to aspects that are welcomed, and the other to aspects that are denied. And as aspects of marginalized people are collectively disavowed through forms of psychological, political, material, and structural oppression, particular working models might form that pertain to society. Each working model is vitalized through patterns of thinking, feeling, and action, and each is incorporated into a part of the self. Each part of the self, as Bromberg asserts, "holds a relatively non-negotiable affective 'truth' that is supported by its self-selected array of 'evidence' designed to bolster its own insulated version of reality" (2012, p. 15). Contradictory working models and self-states that do not communicate well with one another ensue.

As parts are disconfirmed by people important to them, children will automatically ignore and override the voices and needs of these parts. "Not-me" states develop that relate to the parts that are disconfirmed, and their working models contradict the working model of the parts of the self that are confirmed. Forming not-me self-states ensures that expectations are met, whether they are implicit or explicit, individual or societal, and thus protects the child from negative responses. For example, a working model dictating that acceptance is earned by compliance can override a creative not-me part that wants to follow a unique path that may not please others. Or the part of the self that feels confident and successful may deny a not-me part that feels insufficient or inadequate.

Although non-traumatized clients will experience self-states like these that have contradictory goals, traumatized clients may experience profoundly different, often oppositional, parts of the self, one or more of which will have survival as its main agenda. Disconfirmation is extreme in relational trauma, resulting in severe integrative failure in which several dissociative parts may exist, each with its own fixed sense of self and working model that can be markedly different from those of other parts. Understanding two general categories of psychobiological action systems—those of daily life and those of instinctive survival defenses—can help untangle the complexity of trauma-related parts of the self.

Daily life systems, which call for engagement with other people and the world, stimulate us to form close attachment relationships, explore, play, participate in social relationships, regulate energy, reproduce, and care for others (Bowlby, 1969/1982; Cassidy & Shaver, 1999; Fanselow & Lester, 1988; Lichtenberg, 1990; Lichtenberg & Kindler, 1994; Marvin & Britner, 1999; Ogden et al., 2006; Panksepp, 1998; Van der Hart et al., 2006). These daily life systems all require the neuroception of safety, and thus activation of the social engagement system. As stated, survival defenses (cry-for-help, fight, flight, freeze, and feigned death) emerge when danger and life threat are neurocepted. The goals of these instinctive defenses (to protect and ensure survival) conflict with the goals of daily life systems (to engage with others and the world). Contradictory arousal states, emotions, thoughts, and physical actions accompany these two systems, and thus they tend to mutually inhibit one another. The defensive systems must be deactivated to respond to the daily life systems. However, inhibiting defensive systems to carry on with daily life priorities can be problematic for traumatized people. And it may be challenging and even ill-advised for marginalized populations to deactivate defensive systems when daily life priorities require interactions with society at large because they must be prepared to contend with oppression, lack of safety, and the ongoing possibility of physical trauma perpetrated by those prejudiced against them.

Traumatized parts can be conceptualized as organized along the lines of daily life action systems and instinctive defensive systems. Each dissociative part of traumatized individuals is mediated by one or more action systems, and parts of the self may not be aware of or in control of the thoughts, emotions, and actions of other parts. Each has its own first-person perspective, or its own sense of self, which is different from the other part(s) (Nijenhuis & Van der Hart, 2011). Although each part has its own working model and sense of self, the individual does not have different selves, but rather the parts have different senses of self that exist within the whole (Steele & Van der Hart, 2013). No part of the self is completely sequestered from other parts because there are at least a few permeable boundaries between parts, with overlapping functions and goals.

In cases of both distressing (not-traumatic) relational interactions and relational trauma, a sense of not-me is experienced. For clients with nontraumatic relational issues, the self-states usually tend to be more ego-syntonic. But clients with trauma-related dissociation often suffer from discordant intrusions of parts that usurp daily functioning. Trauma-related dissociation is often accompanied by symptoms that reflect activity of parts, such as hearing voices, amnesia for behaviors, and so forth, and at least a rudimentary first-person sense of self in the dissociative part (Kathy Steele, personal communication, June 17, 2013). Trauma-related dissociation explains the behavior of many clients who are thought to be resistant, ambivalent, or continually relapsing when they demonstrate behavior that reflects internal conflicts between parts of the self.

Clients come to therapy struggling with the conflicting goals of daily life parts and survival defense parts, as well as with the disavowed aspects related to inadequacies in relationship with significant others. When we understand parts of the self and recognize each one's purpose and goals, we can better conceptualize and appreciate the difficulties of our clients and their treatment. Contradictory physical actions, emotions, and beliefs can be understood, in part, as conflicts between goals of different action systems, and/or between disconfirmed and affirmed parts of the self.

TREATMENT

The effects of relational strife and trauma interface, and one will stimulate the other. Therefore, appropriate therapeutic approach and interventions are a matter of relative priority. Differentiating between top-down and bottom-up interventions can be useful in conceptualizing the clinical emphasis in the treatment of each category of injury. MacLean's (1985) triune brain model divides the human brain into three parts, each with predominant functions: the neocortex, responsible for thought and cognition; the mammalian, responsible for subjective emotions; and the reptilian, the seat of survival instincts. MacLean's theory helps clarify top-down and bottom-up processing, and thus informs related therapeutic interventions.

In the treatment of trauma, Sensorimotor Psychotherapy prioritizes bottom-up interventions by directly targeting the body's movement and sensation, thus directly impacting the instinctive defensive movements and dysregulated arousal. The symptoms of trauma are resistant to top-down intervention, such as insight and rational thought, because they have their root in the body—in dysregulated arousal, over- or underactive survival defenses, and vehement emotions related to these defenses. Because trauma first and foremost affects the body and nervous system, and trauma-related vehement emotions are not resolved by their expression, bottom-up interventions are paramount. Addressing the effects of trauma emphasizes working with sensation, movement, and the slow progressive process of stimulating dysregulation and reregulating it with somatic resources and physical action, thus building regulatory capacity. The cognitive distortions that are often spurred by the events and subsequent dysregulated arousal, such as "I am never safe," "It was all my fault," or "I am worthless and unlovable," are explored and revised as arousal is regulated and survival defenses are addressed. The vehement emotions designed to fuel instinctive physical defenses naturally abate and resolve as these defenses are attended to somatically.

The symptoms of pervasive unresolved relational misattunements and misrecognitions include patterned emotions, cognitive distortions about self, others, and the world, and physical patterns that limit full expression and hold in place the limiting beliefs. Thus, the treatment of relational stress calls for an integration of top-down (cognitive and emotional) and bottom-up (physical) interventions. Top-down approaches target insight and meaning making, uncovering unconscious limiting beliefs and patterned emotions. The way in which these beliefs and emotions are reflected in the body's posture and movement is explored and changed. When the client's window of tolerance is wide enough, expression of intense core emotions related to misrecognitions of attachment figures, other significant relationships, and groups becomes possible as well. In the case of individuals who have been targeted by oppression, the integration of bottom-up and top-down interventions creates space to process dysregulated arousal, allows the identification and dismantling of beliefs projected onto them due to historical and ongoing oppression, and facilitates restoration of authentic emotional expression—all of which strengthen resilience as well as the capacity to resist and take appropriate action in the face of oppression.

Cognition, emotion, and the body are all viable avenues for therapeutic intervention. In practice, the therapist notices the client's patterns in each of these three interconnected yet distinct arenas, and then applies specific techniques that facilitate processing at the level thought to best support therapeutic goals. If arousal is dysregulated, the first intervention might be to find somatic resources to support regulation. If the window of tolerance is sufficiently wide, strong emotions related to past or current hurts may be targeted. If the shoulders are slumped, resources to align the spine or interventions such as exaggerating the pattern to discover related meanings, emotions, beliefs, and memories are considered, depending on integrative capacity. The most effective intervention will not only affect the target, whether it is cognition, emotion, or the body, but also will impact the other two levels. For example, expressing a disconfirmed core emotion, such as anger, can change beliefs and affect the body; working with challenging a belief, such as "I have no right to express my anger" can affect emotions and the body. New actions related to anger, such as pushing away, can impact emotions and help shift cognitive distortions. Any of these targets would potentially have a positive therapeutic effect.

Therapy with Jamie, a 35-year-old African American woman, will illustrate this interplay (Ogden, 2020). Raised by a single mother in a neighborhood disproportionately impacted by criminal activity, Jamie was single, cisgender, had a heterosexual sexual orientation, and was a college graduate. She had suffered ongoing racial trauma, oppression, discrimination, and prejudice throughout her life, including being ostracized by white children, called demeaning racial slurs, being threatened due to her race, and witnessing acts of brutality toward people of color in the media and in her community. At age 13, she was forced by a white boy to perform oral sex at knifepoint, and during that same year was sexually abused by her mother's boyfriend, also white. The effects of trauma and the complications of privilege/oppression dynamics that are inevitable in any therapy are amplified in a cross-racial dyad. Racism should be considered a risk factor, and it is essential that therapists "listen for and adequately assess a client's history of racism experiences, the client's perceptions and attitudes about racism, degree of internal-ized racism, the racism-related dynamics of current contexts, and the styles and behavioral strategies that have been developed to cope with racism" (Harrell & Sloan-Pena, 2006, p. 400). Jamie's therapist was a 52-year-old, white, college-educated, cisgender woman of middle-class socioeconomic status. Treatment began with an open discussion about belonging to a marginalized minority group and the racism that was a part of her traumatic history. Jamie said she felt safer (words that were accompanied by a deeper breath) when her therapist acknowledged her own privilege, particularly that of not being the victim of systemic racism and oppression, inherent with being a member of the privileged culture.

Jamie's initial presenting difficulties were related to the effects of past trauma, including vehement emotions of instinctive defenses, so mapping internal parts was an important first step. Jamie and her therapist discovered several parts rooted in defense: tension in her jaw, arms, and hands that pertained to a fight part; panic in the chest that Jamie felt when her boyfriend was upset with her spoke to a cry-for-help part; addictions, particularly to alcohol, related to a flight part, which was noticed in a jittery feeling, especially in her legs; overall constriction and high anxiety indicated a freeze part; and finally the numbness, collapsed posture, self-loathing, and shame pertained to a shut-down, feigned death part. Identifying these physical signals alerted Jamie to the emergence of the various parts whose goals were survival.

The first task at the onset of therapy was to develop resources to stabilize dysregulated arousal. Her therapist asked Jamie if she could recall a time when she felt good in some way or at least less bad, which led to two significant bottom-up, somatic resources. Jamie recalled having brought homemade cookies to a party at work, which elicited praise from her boss. As Jamie remembered this incident, she smiled, her spine lengthened slightly, and she felt calmer. However, Jamie reported that the more upright posture made her feel exposed and a bit anxious in her belly, reporting that all her life she had tried to be invisible to avoid abuse and racial harassment. Certain actions, like sitting taller, can be adversarial or threatening to other parts of the self, so it is important to find actions that increase communication between parts, rather than overriding one of them. Jamie found another resource to calm the anxiety—self-touch to her belly—which she said offered some protection and made her feel less exposed. With that touch, she could maintain the upright posture representative of a part that felt more calm and confident, and simultaneously soothe and protect the anxious part.

Another bottom-up resource for the effects of trauma was found when Jamie reported that she felt stuck and hopeless because her boyfriend had withdrawn from her. The pain of being abandoned led her to drink alcohol to feel better, which she had previously identified as associated with the part of her that wanted to get away: her flight part. Her therapist suggested that they walk together around the room and notice that their legs could carry them away from certain things in the room and toward other things. This movement intervention countered the immobility Jamie felt during past trauma, as it directly elicited the physical action of the flight part. When asked if the part that felt abandoned and stuck could feel her capacity to move, Jamie replied that it could. She liked the feeling of her legs being strong and able to move, and she realized that when she felt helpless and alone, she turned to drink to prevent the feeling of shutdown and depression. Familiarizing herself with the action of a flight defense in this way helped mitigate the hopelessness and risk of shutting down that were precipitating factors to drinking alcohol. Finding resources such as these helped Jamie regulate arousal and quiet some of the vehement emotions associated with past trauma.

After several months of learning resources to regulate, Jamie and her therapist shifted focus to addressing relational stress. A repeated theme in Jamie's therapy was feeling alone, isolated, and not able to obtain the support she felt she needed, which would lead to a familiar feeling of hopeless despair. Jamie expressed that she had been alone during past traumatic events, with no support, and that it was the same in her life now. Since her window of tolerance had widened, and she had acquired regulatory skills to stabilize arousal, her therapist suggested that they might work with the part of her that felt so alone, knowing that core emotions related to early lack of support were likely to arise. She noted that Jamie's posture slumped and invited her to be aware of that collapse, even exaggerate it slightly, and see what she could learn about it. Jamie recalled a pivotal memory that had a strong impact: As a 7-year-old, she had asked her mom for a hug after a bad day at school, and her mom told her she was too big for hugs, and Jamie felt rejected and alone at that time.

It should be noted here that such messaging may also be conceptualized as a kind of socialization process that African American children go through as a result of the historical (and ongoing) trauma their community has faced in the United States, a process that helps the child develop the strength and resilience needed to navigate ongoing marginalization and oppression. In a context of ongoing racism, it is not unusual for Black children to be encouraged to develop strategies of resistance that amount to little more than emotional armoring (Watson & Hunter, 2016; Woods-Giscombé, 2010). Specifically, Black girls are often socialized to exude a veneer of impenetrable strength, toughness, and self-sufficiency (Beauboeuf-Lafontant, 2005; Thomas & King, 2007).

Jamie realized the caring purpose of her mother's words, and at the same time, the personal internalized message was emotionally painful for her. With the help of her empathically attuned therapist, Jamie began to cry, an expression that was different from her usual pattern of hopeless, helpless, numbing despair. As the tears subsided, Jamie realized that she had formed the belief "I don't deserve support," but that of course every child should have the support she needs. Her therapist asked her if in her imagination, she could envision the child that she was, and suggested that both she and Jamie tell this child part of her, "You deserve support." Together, the therapist and the adult Jamie were able to communicate with the vulnerable and hurt child state. With this act of recognition of the part of her that she had pushed aside—the vulnerable child—Jamie cried more softly. When asked what kind of tears they were, Jamie softly said, "These are tears of grief—I should have had support."

Communication between the child part and adult Jamie was then facilitated by finding the right degree of alignment that included both the collapsed part (the child) and the upright posture of a resourced adult. Jamie experimented between the collapsed and erect postures until she found a posture in between these polarities that included both parts, so that the collapsed child part was not somatically overridden. In this way, Jamie could literally hold the child state in her body as well as her mind. Note that in this example of resolving past relational strife, the beliefs and the body were both addressed, and strong core emotion was expressed.

Working with the memory above provided Jamie with the relational resources she needed to move forward into work with traumatic memory. These resources included both the internal support of communication between parts of herself and her increased ability to sense support from her therapist. Jamie now was ready to address the traumatic memory of sexual assault at knifepoint when she was 13. In preparation for approaching this memory, contextualizing Jamie's trauma within a larger historical and sociocultural context was imperative, given that an element of her experience was also racialized gender violence (the boy using a racial slur). Jamie and her therapist identified and acknowledged the history of sexual violence that has been part of the experience of many young African American girls in the United States, and discussed its direct link to the processes of psychological, physical, and mental domination and exploitation of Black people. Naming this helped Jamie feel more resourced and seen by her therapist, as the impact of such historical violence has often remained unacknowledged, bypassed, or minimized.

In working with attachment-related memory, the core emotion is expressed and linked to beliefs and the body, as in the previous excerpt. However, work with traumatic memory is conducted more cautiously, in a stepwise manner, pausing to work bottom-up when arousal becomes dysregulated or when physical impulses or changes emerge as the memory is recalled.

As she began to think about the assault, Jamie's body began to tremble, and she reported feeling the terror she had felt then. Expressing vehement emotions, like terror, can increase dysregulation without resolution, and at best only helps clients feel better momentarily. These emotions need to be addressed bottom-up. Her therapist asked Jamie if she could put the terror aside and just follow the sensation of the trembling and notice what happened in her body. Disregarding the vehement emotion prevented arousal from escalating so that Jamie could focus exclusively on the somatic components gave her a task that she could fulfill. She reported that the sensation moved up into her shoulders, then progressed into her arms and out her fingertips. When Jamie described how the sensation sequenced in her body, she observed that the trembling quieted and her arousal calmed. In this way, Jamie increased her confidence in interrupting her escalating arousal by noticing signs of dysregulation (the trembling) and utilizing a bottom-up intervention of following her sensation as it moved through her body until it settled.

Jamie was plagued by the memory of the boy calling her the racial slur, and she could clearly hear the contempt in his voice. She reported shame, as if the assault were her fault, and again experienced terror, a vehement emotion indicating a bottom-up approach was called for. Her therapist directed her mindful attention to a sliver of memory—the boy's voice and words—rather than to the emotion, and asked her to be aware of her body. Jamie reported that her body felt tense. Since tension is usually a precursor to action, her therapist asked if there was an action her body wanted to make. This instruction helped Jamie identify the physical signal of a defensive action that she could not employ at the time of the event. She said she had wanted to protect herself, and her fingers lifted slightly in a preparatory movement of protection. Note that the impulses such as these that emerge, even when catalyzed by a specific incident, do not relate to only one event, but to the pattern itself that has developed from cumulative traumatic events. In this case, the catalyst that evoked the impulse was the boy's voice, but the action itself countered her overall immobility, a default pattern developed through many events, not only the immobility she had experienced during that particular trauma. The impulse to defend came forth not as an idea or concept but from Jamie's awareness of her body. The therapist asked Jamie to focus on this impulse and put aside the emotion, image, and other content of the memory, which mitigated apprehension of the possible negative effects of executing a defensive action in relationship to a specific incident and facilitated executing a protective action. Jamie slowly and mindfully pushed against a pillow held by her therapist, which completed the action of a fight defense. With this action, Jamie felt power, a good feeling, instead of terror.

In a subsequent session, Jamie again brought up feeling disconnected from everyone, including the therapist. Suggesting that perhaps they could explore what happened if the therapist sought connection with Jamie through a proximity seeking gesture, the therapist reached out her hand toward Jamie, and asked her to notice her internal reactions. At first, Jamie became still and shut down, reporting in a flat voice that she felt nothing. Initially unresponsive to her therapist's questions, she finally stated that she didn't know what was going on. After a time, Jamie said that everyone, especially white people, wanted something from her. Her therapist recognized that it made sense that Jamie would feel that way, and upon reflection acknowledged that she too had wanted something: for Jamie to respond when she reached out. With this acknowledgment, Jamie looked at her therapist for the first time, and a conversation ensued about her history of being abused by people in power, and the privilege/oppression dynamics in cross-racial interactions, including theirs. In this way, an enactment that could have sabotaged the relationship and the therapy itself was successfully negotiated. The therapist's acknowledgment of her own part and validation of Jamie's experience in the moment rather than denying or bypassing it created enough space for a repair of the relational exploitation that Jamie had experienced to take place in their relationship.

Eventually, they decided to repeat the experiment of the therapist reaching out toward Jamie. This time, Jamie reported that her heart beat faster, her body pulled in, and that she could still hear the words inside herself, "What do you want from me?" This suspicion was acknowledged as a protector part left over from past trauma, including experiences of white people's lack of boundaries with Black bodies like hers. Her therapist then asked if there were thoughts, images, or emotions that went along with the pulling in. Jamie reported a memory of telling her mom that her mom's boyfriend had raped her. Her mom had admonished her for being disrespectful instead of offering support. Jamie, crying, said that whenever she told something important, people used it to hurt her. She felt her body tighten and curl up as she remembered this incident, and her therapist asked her if there were words that went along with the tightening. Jamie said that she learned that her only value was to serve others. With empathic contact from her therapist, Jamie's sobs increased, then subsided, and her body then relaxed. She had developed a sufficiently wide window of tolerance to express these intense emotions without undue dysregulation or dissociation. As Jamie's emotions settled, a conversation ensued about the sexual violence and abuse African American women have survived over generations at the hands of white men, and the survival function of the victims' silence, which shifted Jamie's perception of her mother's response. She was able to acknowledge the relational failure, and experience a felt sense of connection to her mother and other women in her family, as she realized they had possibly suffered in similar ways.

With relational injuries like these, it is important not only to express the unregulated emotions from the past but to change beliefs, so the therapist asked what the experience in the moment, with the therapist, would communicate to the child. Jamie said that maybe she did have some value. When the therapist then extended her hand again in a reaching gesture, Jamie had a different experience—it was comforting. Jamie was able to make eye contact, and she felt connected to her therapist rather than manipulated.

CONCLUSION

At every moment of the therapy session, clinician and client together determine whether to address primarily the effects of trauma (hyper- and hypoarousal, vehement emotion, traumatic memory, survival defensive responses, dissociative parts) or of relational stress (limiting beliefs, relationship issues, strong emotions, memories of relational interactions, physical patterns that reflect relational dynamics, and the dynamics within the therapeutic relationship). In addressing the effects of trauma, the first task is to develop resources to regulate dys-regulated arousal from past and sometimes current trauma. For those suffering ongoing trauma of any kind—oppression, vicarious trauma, racism, domestic violence, and the like—finding resources to help arousal return to a window of tolerance when triggered by current events is essential and builds resilience. Once regulatory resources are learned, the incomplete actions related to truncated over-active defensive responses can be discovered and completed, and the nervous system can be recalibrated so that arousal can better remain in a window of tolerance, all of which mitigate vehement emotions.

Understanding relational patterns as they are reflected in movement and posture helps to unveil the meaning of previously unconscious limiting beliefs formed in relationships. Resolving these issues often involves expressing strong emotion associated with relational misrecognition and stress in the context of an attuned therapeutic relationship. Eventually, as painful emotions are expressed, limiting beliefs can shift toward expansive options that are supported by changes in the body's posture and movement. For example, the belief, "I do not deserve support" is replaced by "I do deserve support," and reaching out to others and receiving their support becomes more possible.

The overall goal of working with both trauma and relational stress is integration—of parts of the self, of not-me self-states, of body and mind, of the body itself, and so forth. For marginalized people, contextualizing the events within a larger sociopolitical context supports integration and helps to heal the effects of transgenerational trauma and relational imprints. Since both types of injuries—traumatic and relational—are present in our clients, we move back and forth in emphasis depending on what emerges at any given moment during a session, and what will support therapeutic goals, always remaining aware of the interplay between the effects of trauma and relational stress on individual and societal levels.

Discovering implicit patterns that hold in place the legacy of trauma and relational stress cannot be accomplished through insight alone. These patterns are brought to light in the therapy hour and interrupted. Empowering actions that have not been previously executed are explored. With the goals of resilience and integration, new connections are made on cognitive, emotional, and bodily levels, created by new experiences rather than insight alone. The pain of misrecognition, whether on an individual level or a societal level, whether traumatic or less severe by comparison, is soothed, and parts of the self that need to be recognized are finally seen and validated. As Taylor (1992, p. 26) states, misrecognition "can inflict a grievous wound, saddling its victims with a crippling self-hatred. Due recognition is not just a courtesy we owe people. It is a vital human need." With this need at least partially met in therapy, expectations of the future change so that visions of what were previously only a distant possibility become a reality.

REFERENCES

Ainsworth, M. (1963). The development of infant-mother interaction among the Ganda. In B. Foss (Ed.), *Determinants of infant behavior* (pp. 67–104). New York: Wiley

Beauboeuf-Lafontant, T. (2005). Keeping up appearances, getting fed up: The embodiment of strength among African American women. *Meridians, 5*(2), 104–123.

Beebe, B. (2006). Co-constructing mother-infant distress in face-to-face interactions: Contributions of microanalysis. *Infant Observation, 9*(2), 151–164.

Bowlby, J. (1973). *Attachment and loss. Vol. 2. Separation: Anxiety and anger.* New York: Basic Books.

Bowlby, J. (1980). *Attachment and loss. Vol. 3. Loss: Sadness and depression.* New York: Basic Books.

Bowlby, J. (1982). *Attachment* (Vol. 1, 2nd ed.). New York: Basic Books. (Original work published 1969)

Bowlby, J. (1988). *A secure base: Parent–child attachment and healthy human development.* New York, NY: Basic Books.

Brave Heart, M. Y. (2003). The historical trauma response among natives and its relationship with substance abuse: A Lakota illustration. *Journal of Psychoactive Drugs, 35*(1), 7–13.

Brazelton, T. (1989). *The earliest relationship.* Reading, MA: Addison-Wesley.

Bromberg, P. M. (2006). *Awakening the dreamer: Clinical journeys.* Mahwah, NJ: Analytic Press.

Bromberg, P. M. (2012). Credo. *Psychoanalytic Dialogues, 22*(3), 273–278.

Bryant-Davis, T. (2019). The cultural context of trauma recovery: Considering the posttraumatic stress disorder practice guideline and intersectionality. *Psychotherapy, 56*(3), 400–408. https://doi.org/10.1037/pst0000241

Bucci, W. (2011). The role of embodied communication in therapeutic change: A multiple code perspective. In W. Tschacher & C. Bergomi (Eds.), *The implications of embodiment: Cognition and communication* (pp. 209–228). Exeter, UK: Imprint Academic.

Cassidy, J., & Shaver, P. R. (1999). *Handbook of attachment: Theory, research, and clinical implications.* New York: Guilford Press.

DeGruy, J. (2005/2017). *Post traumatic slave syndrome: America's legacy of enduring injury and healing.* Milwaukie, Oregon: Uptone Press.

DeGruy, J. (2017). *Post traumatic slave syndrome: America's legacy of enduring injury and healing.* Milwaukie, OR: Uptone Press.

Dokoupil, T. (2012, December 3). A new theory of PTSD and veterans: Moral injury. *Newsweek.* https://www.newsweek.com/new-theory-ptsd-and-veterans-moral-injury-63539

Duran, E., Duran, B., Brave Heart, M. Y., & Horse-Davis, S. Y. (1998). Healing the American Indian soul wound. In Y. Danieli (Ed.), *International handbook of multigenerational legacies of trauma* (pp. 341–354). Boston: Springer.

Dutton, D. G. (1995). Trauma symptoms and PTSD-like profiles in perpetrators of intimate abuse. *Journal of Traumatic Stress, 8*(2), 299–316.

Edelman, M. W. (2018). Moving between identities: Embodied code-switching. In C. Caldwell & L. B. Leighton (Eds.), *Oppression and the body: Roots, resistance and resolution* (pp. 181–204). Berkeley, CA: North Atlantic Books.

Fanselow, M., & Lester, L. (1988). A functional behavioristic approach to aversively motivated behavior: Predatory imminence as a determinant of the topography of defensive behavior. In R. Bolles & M. Beecher (Eds.), *Evolution and learning* (pp. 185–212). Hillsdale, NJ: Erlbaum.

Fosha, D. (2000). *The transforming power of affect: A model for accelerated change.* New York: Basic Books.

Freire, P. (2007). *Pedagogy of the oppressed.* New York: Continuum.

Frijda, N. (1986). *The emotions.* Cambridge, UK: Cambridge University Press.

Grigsby, J., & Stevens, D. (2000). *Neurodynamics of personality.* New York: Guilford.

Harrell, S. P. (2020). *Understanding racial trauma and traumatization.* Unpublished paper.

Harrell, S. P. & Sloan-Pena, G. (2006). *Racism and discrimination.* In Y. Jackson (Ed.), Encyclopedia of multicultural psychology (pp. 396–402). Thousand Oaks, CA: Sage.

Hobson, J. (1994). *The chemistry of conscious states.* New York: Back Bay.

Janet, P. (1909). Problèmes psychologiques de l'émotion. *Revue Neurologique, 17,* 1551–1687.

Johnson, R. (2015). Grasping and transforming the embodied experience of oppression. *International Body Psychotherapy Journal, 14*(1), 80–95.

Kar, H. (2018). Acknowledging the victim to perpetrator trajectory: Integrating a mental health focused trauma-based approach into global violence programs. *Aggression and Violent Behavior, 47.* 10.1016/j.avb.2018.10.004.

Kirmayer, L. J., Gone, J. P., & Moses, J. (2014). Rethinking historical trauma. *Transcultural Psychiatry, 51*(3), 299–319.

Lichtenberg, J. D. (1990). On motivational systems. *Journal of the American Psychoanalytic Association, 38*(2), 517–518.

Lichtenberg, J. D., & Kindler, A. R. (1994). A motivational systems approach to the clinical experience. *Journal of the American Psychoanalytic Association, 42,* 405–420.

Lyons-Ruth, K. (1998). Implicit relational knowing: Its role in development and psychoanalytic treatment. *Infant Mental Health Journal, 19,* 282–289.

Lyons-Ruth, K., & Jacobvitz, D. (1999). Attachment disorganization: Unresolved loss, relational violence, and lapses in behavioral and attentional strategies. In J. Cassidy & P. R. Shaver (Eds.), *Handbook of attachment: Theory, research and clinical implications* (pp. 520–554). New York: Guilford.

MacLean, P. D. (1985). Brain evolution relating to family, play, and the separation call. *Archives of General Psychiatry, 42*(4), 405–417.

Marvin, R., & Britner, P. (1999). Normative development: The ontogeny of attachment. In J. Cassidy & P. Shaver (Eds.), *Handbook of attachment: Theory, research, and clinical applications* (pp. 44–67). New York: Guilford.

Menakem, R. (2017). *My grandmother's hands: Racialized trauma and the pathway to mending our hearts and bodies.* Las Vegas, NV: Central Recovery Press.

Misslin, R. (2003). The defense system of fear: Behavior and neurocircuitry. *Clinical Neurophysiology, 33*(2), 55–66.

Nijenhuis, E. R. S., & Van der Hart, O. (2011). Dissociation in trauma: A new definition and comparison with previous formulations. *Journal of Trauma and Dissociation, 12,* 416–445.

Ogden, P. (2009a). Emotion, mindfulness, and movement: Expanding the regulatory boundaries of the window of tolerance. In D. Fosha, D. Siegel, & M. Solomon (Eds.), *The healing power of emotion: Perspectives from affective neuroscience and clinical practice* (pp. 204–231). New York: Norton.

Ogden, P. (2009b). Sensorimotor psychotherapy for complex trauma. In C. Courtois & J. Ford (Eds.), *Treating complex traumatic stress disorders*. New York: Guilford.

Ogden, P. (2020). Sensorimotor psychotherapy for complex trauma. In Courtois, C. and J. Ford (Eds.), *Treating Complex Traumatic Stress Disorders*. New York: Guilford Press

Ogden, P., Minton, K., & Pain, C. (2006). *Trauma and the body: A sensorimotor approach to psychotherapy*. New York: Norton.

Panksepp, J. (1998). *Affective neuroscience: The foundations of human and animal emotions*. New York: Oxford University Press.

Porges, S. W. (1995). Orienting in a defensive world: Mammalian modifications of our evolutionary heritage—a polyvagal theory. *Psychophysiology, 32*(4), 301–318.

Porges, S. W. (2001). The polyvagal theory: Phylogenetic substrates of a social nervous system. *International Journal of Psychophysiology, 42*, 123–146.

Porges, S. W. (2004). Neuroception: A subconscious system for detecting threats and safety. *Zero to Three, 24*(5), 19–24. http://bbc.psych.uic.edu/pdf/Neuroception.pdf

Porges, S. W. (2005). The role of social engagement in attachment and bonding: A phylogenetic perspective. In C. S. Carte, L. Anhert, K. E. Grossman, H. B. Hrdy, M. E. Lamb, S. W. Porges, & N. Sahser (Eds.), *Attachment and bonding: A new synthesis* (pp. 33–54). Cambridge, MA: MIT Press.

Porges, S. W. (2009). Reciprocal influences between body and brain in the perception and expression of affect: A polyvagal perspective. In D. Fosha, D. Siegel, & M. Solomon (Eds.), *The healing power of emotion: Neurobiological understandings and therapeutic perspectives* (pp. 27–54). New York: Norton.

Porges, S. W. (2011). *The polyvagal theory: Neurophysiological foundations of emotions, attachment, communication, and self-regulation*. New York: Norton.

Ren, D., Wesselmann, E. D., & Williams, K. D. (2018). Hurt people hurt people: Ostracism and aggression. *Current Opinion in Psychology, 19*, 34–38.

Rivers, W. (1920). *Instinct and the unconscious: A contribution to a biological theory of the psycho-neuroses*. Cambridge, UK: Cambridge University Press.

Safran, J. D., & Greenberg, L. S. (Eds.). (1991). *Emotion, psychotherapy, and change*. New York: Guilford.

Schore, A. N. (1994). *Affect regulation and the origin of the self: The neurobiology of emotional development*. Hillsdale, NJ: Erlbaum.

Schore, A. N. (2003). *Affect dysregulation and disorders of the self*. New York: Norton.

Siegel, D. (1999). *The developing mind.* New York: Guilford.

Steele, K., & Van der Hart, O. (2013). Understanding attachment, trauma and dissociation in complex developmental trauma disorders. In A. N. Danquah & K. Berry (Eds.), *Attachment theory in adult mental health: A guide to clinical practice* (pp. 78–94). London: Routledge.

Steele, K., Van der Hart, O., & Nijenhuis, E. R. S. (2005). Phase-oriented treatment of structural dissociation in complex traumatization: Overcoming trauma-related phobias. *Journal of Trauma and Dissociation, 6,* 11–53.

Stern, D. (1985). *The interpersonal world of the infant: A view from psychoanalysis and developmental psychology.* New York: Basic Books.

Sue, D. W. (2010). *Microaggressions in everyday life: Race, gender, and sexual orientation.* Hoboken, NJ: Wiley.

Taylor, C. (1992). The politics of recognition. In A. Gutmann (Ed.), *Multiculturalism and the politics of recognition* (pp. 25–74). Princeton, NJ: Princeton University Press.

Thomas, A. J., & King, C. T. (2007). Gendered racial socialization of African American mothers and daughters. *Family Journal, 15*(2), 137–142.

Tronick, E. Z. (2007). *The neurobehavioral and social-emotional development of infants and children.* New York: Norton.

Van der Hart, O., Nijenhuis, E. R. S., & Steele, K. (2006). *The haunted self.* New York: Norton.

Van der Hart, O., & Rydberg, J. A. (2019). Vehement emotions and trauma-generated dissociation: A Janetial perspective on integrative failure. *European Journal of Trauma and Dissociation, 3*(3), 191–201.

Van der Kolk, B. A. (1987). *Psychological trauma.* Washington, DC: American Psychiatric Press.

Watson, N. N., & Hunter, C. D. (2016). "I had to be strong": Tensions in the strong black woman schema. *Journal of Black Psychology, 42*(5), 424–452.

Watts, R. J., Griffith, D. M., & Abdul-Adil, J. (1999). Sociopolitical development as an antidote for oppression—theory and action. *American Journal of Community Psychology, 27*(2), 255–271.

Wesselmann, E. D., Ren, D., & Williams, K. D. (2017). Ostracism and aggression. In B. J. Bushman (Ed.), *Frontiers of social psychology. Aggression and violence: A social psychological perspective* (pp. 155–168). New York: Routledge.

Wilkinson, M. (2006). *Coming into mind: The mind-brain relationship.* London: Routledge.

Woods-Giscombé, C. L. (2010). Superwoman schema: African American women's views on stress, strength, and health. *Qualitative Health Research, 20*(5), 668–683.

Chapter 3

THE IMPORTANCE OF THE BODY IN THE TREATMENT OF TRAUMA

> *You must always remember that the sociology, the history,*
> *the economics, the graphs, the charts, the regressions*
> *all land, with great violence, upon the body.*
>
> TA–NEHISI COATES

Clients with trauma in their history often complain of a baffling array of cognitive, emotional, and physical symptoms that leave them feeling powerless and out of control. Triggered by reminders of past trauma, an overwhelming cascade of dysregulated emotions, physical sensations, negative beliefs, and intrusive images typically replays endlessly in the theater of the body. Pierre Janet (1919, 1925) suggested long ago that traumatic memories are split off from conscious awareness, to be stored as sensory perceptions and behavioral reenactments. The individual remembers what happened through reliving these nonverbal iterations of the historical traumatic event, or through mysterious physical symptoms that seem to have no organic basis.

There are many sources of trauma inclusive of but not limited to accidents, sexual assault, physical abuse, domestic violence, medical trauma, natural disasters, transgenerational and historical trauma, the trauma of war, forced migrations, terrorism, and racism. For oppressed groups, triggers include various public reminders (symbols of historical traumatic events, stereotyped and pejorative media narratives of marginalized groups, and so forth), as well as personal encounters (microaggressions, discrimination, prejudice, bigotry, and the like). Mohatt, Thompson, Thai, and Tebes review many examples of these public and private triggers of historical trauma, noting, "Aboriginal reservations and decaying urban environments are examples of structural and physical contexts that can provide daily reminders of historic processes of loss, marginalization, discrimination, and trauma" (2014, p. 9). Another example is the perpetuation of stereotypes in the media and appropriation of Native American symbols, such as the iconography used by some American football teams (Fryberg et al., 2008) or the wearing of Native American or other indigenous regalia by non–Native Americans at music festivals.

Beyond these reminders, numerous researchers report that the sequelae of historical trauma may be associated with a range of negative health outcomes, including predisposition to PTSD, increased risk for anxiety and depression, and a number of health disparities (Mohatt et al., 2014). Historical trauma can also be seen in what Menakem (2017) calls "traumatic retentions": the intergenerational reflexive reenactments within and between groups, passed down from generation to generation. When these actions are unlinked from the original event, they lose their meaning and may be seen and criticized as part of the culture of a particular group. For example, drawing from historical and anthropological research, DeGruy (2017) and Patton (2017) conceptualize the use of corporal punishment for children in African American families as a possible trauma adaptation and residual of chattel slavery performed with an ambivalent yet protective intent ultimately meant to prepare the children for the harsh realities of racism.

The use of "talk therapy" alone falls short of accessing and resolving the manifold effects of trauma. Because traumatic memories are most often evident in nonverbal phenomena and are not encoded in autobiographical memory, the trauma therapist cannot depend upon the client's narrative to guide the therapeutic process toward resolution. Additionally, the capacity to verbalize internal somatic experience necessitates that clients attend to the body, which they have typically numbed or avoided in an attempt to minimize unpleasant or painful sensations. The recurring sense of impending danger, referred to as "speechless terror" (Siegel, 1999; Van der Kolk et al., 1996) also renders language unavailable.

Traumatized individuals are challenged by a nervous system that is unable to adaptively regulate arousal. Most experience too much arousal (hyperarousal) or too little arousal (hypoarousal), and often oscillate between these two extremes (Ogden et al., 2006; Post et al., 1997; Van der Hart et al., 2006; Van der Kolk et al., 1996). More than a century ago, Janet (1909) wrote that the vehement emotions accompanied by the hyperarousal evoked in trauma impair formulating the event into an explicit and cohesive narrative. Hypoaroused clients, as well, can find few words to describe their past because they experience a dearth of emotion and sensation—a numbing, a sense of deadness or emptiness, passivity, and immobilization (Bremner & Brett, 1997; Ogden et al., 2006; Spiegel, 1997; Van der Hart et al., 2004).

Using the talking cure to resolve these debilitating effects of trauma presents a major limitation when the words to describe what happened are inaccessible, yet therapists often do not know how to address the effects of trauma, if not through language. Sensorimotor Psychotherapy, developed by this author in the 1980s, offers an alternative to working with the verbal narrative by directly addressing the sensation and movement of the body itself to resolve the body-based, trauma-related symptoms, dysregulation, and patterns. This approach builds on traditional psychotherapeutic understanding, but addresses the body as central in the therapeutic field of awareness, using observational skills, theories, and interventions not usually practiced in psychodynamic psychotherapy (Ogden et al., 2006).

The premise of Sensorimotor Psychotherapy is that by directly addressing the body and related symptoms that so often complicate the treatment of traumatic stress disorders, traditionally trained therapists can improve the efficacy of their clinical work.

A primary task in the treatment of trauma is to modulate dysregulated arousal. The "window of tolerance" (Siegel, 1999) refers to a zone of autonomic and emotional arousal that is optimal for well-being and effective functioning. When arousal falls within this window, information received from both internal and external environments can be integrated.

In treatment, clients must first learn to modulate dysregulated arousal so that it returns to a window of tolerance. When autobiographical memory is available, discussing what happened can be important for clients, and can strengthen the therapeutic relationship. However, prioritizing guiding clients to mindfully track and observe the interplay of thoughts, feelings, and body experience related to the traumatic past will better support arousal regulation. Clients will begin to notice that a trauma-related sensation, such as increased heart rate, evokes a feeling of panic, which fuels a thought of current danger, thus escalating dysregulation. They learn to distinguish physical sensations from trauma-based emotions and habitual cognitive distortions and to mindfully track (follow in detail) the sequential physical sensations associated with dysregulated arousal. When clients cultivate awareness of sensations as they fluctuate in texture, quality, and intensity, they learn that the sensations themselves will gradually stabilize, and arousal will return to within the window of tolerance.

With all clients, the therapist supports them to recognize the signals of the body's needs and attend to these needs in an adaptive way, which can be as simple as to identify physical signs of tiredness and then to rest. This is particularly important for marginalized clients because oppression, racism, and structural trauma are directly associated with considerable costs to physical health (Williams et al., 2019). When clients face ongoing trauma of discrimination, oppression, domestic violence, living in a community disproportionately affected by criminal activity, and so forth, safety is compromised on a daily basis. Such threats cause the muscles of the body to naturally tense up, but they should relax when the threat is over. However, chronic threat can cause the muscles to be in a more or less constant state of tension. When muscles remain tight and taut for extended periods of time, this can contribute to and sometimes even cause stress-related conditions, such as chronic pain or insomnia. In these instances of daily vulnerability to threat, learning to regulate arousal, relax the body, and develop resilience is imperative. Thus, when the traumatic threats are not ongoing, the therapeutic intention changes from working to resolve the effects of a traumatic past to managing the natural reactions to current threat, such as tension and dysregulated arousal, while increasing clients' resilience and ability to respond in a measured rather than reactive way. Sensorimotor Psychotherapy supports these clients in focusing on physical sensations, as well as the associated thoughts and emotions, for the purpose of developing physical strategies, such as grounding or breathing, to return arousal to the window of tolerance when dysregulated, release tension, and discover somatic resources to remain more calm and alert.

Finally, therapists teach clients how to sequence (mindfully follow in detail their bodily sensations as they change and settle) to help metabolize the effects of current trauma, and "reset" (Levine, 1997) the nervous system to a more regulated arousal level. During threat, and when recalling past danger, adrenaline is released, which increases arousal and generates strong body sensations of tingling, shaking, increased heart rate, and so forth. Through the technique of "sensorimotor sequencing," clients observe these internal sensations associated with hyperarousal, and discover that the sensations are constantly changing. Gradually, clients learn that, through sensorimotor sequencing, the disturbing sensations related to hyperarousal gradually settle, the body relaxes, and the nervous system resets. This skill, and that of developing somatic resources, are valuable for all traumatized individuals, but it is particularly critical for those who are exposed to ongoing oppression or other forms of trauma because physical health is at risk when arousal remains dysregulated for long periods of time (McFarlane, 2010). When the physiological effects of current traumatic events are metabolized in a timely manner through sensorimotor sequencing, the vulnerability of the nervous system to unwarranted dysregulation is reduced and resilience is supported (Ogden & Minton, 2000).

Negative early attachment experiences as well as current and past trauma leave their imprint on the body's procedural memory system, contributing not only to dysregulated arousal, but shaping the posture, gestures, and movements of the body. Recognizing that mental disturbances were related to the awkwardness and irregularities in the posture and movement patterns of traumatized individuals, Janet posed the following question:

> Does it not seem likely enough that a transformation of movements by means of a process of education may have an effect upon the totality of the patient's activities, and thus prove competent to prevent or remove the mental troubles? (1925, p. 725)

Physical tendencies, such as a sunken chest, limp arms, and shallow breath, can reinforce chronic negative emotions and cognitive distortions and contribute to the trauma-related emotions of fear, rage, and shame. In therapy, clients learn to execute new physical actions that challenge these tendencies, so they do not reflexively repeat those habits when they are not adaptive in the present time. A client who was neglected as a child, for example, experienced the action of reaching out toward the therapist as both unfamiliar and hopeless, saying, "No one was ever there for me, and you won't be either." Exploring this action, along with its accompanying beliefs and emotions, served as an inroad to addressing early childhood attachment disturbances. Replacing the slumped posture and shallow breath with an aligned, erect but relaxed posture, and full breathing supported a positive sense of self.

It should be noted that if this client were from a racially marginalized group (e.g., Latinx, Asian American, African American, etc.) or a member of a group with a targeted identity (e.g., disabled, nonbinary, transgender, or undocumented), working with a therapist from the dominant group, such as white, cisgendered, and male, contextualizing the reaching-out action in a larger systemic perspective may be in order. For example, if the client is Latinx, several factors might contribute to a caregiver's unavailability: the deportation of one of the caregivers, family members or friends; the parents' own traumatic history including immigration trauma; the expectations of a Latinx collectivist culture that children, especially older children, help care for younger siblings; and so forth. All these factors will influence the experiment of reaching out in therapy. Power/oppression dynamics might be at play and need exploration as well, since reaching out to people in power, represented by the therapist, might evoke memories in which a client had been threatened or ridiculed in the past by those in power. In such a situation, for example, a client's hesitation to reach out might reflect an effort to avoid appearing vulnerable to someone in power or the need to protect oneself against microaggressions, rather than difficulty seeking connection or support.

Over the years, each person's body develops patterns of action and movement, some of which are easy or familiar, and some of which are not (Janet, 1925). In therapy, clients can learn to execute a variety of actions that might be unfamiliar to them in order to support adaptive behavior and a wide range of possibilities, including emotional possibilities. For example, adaptive anger can be supported by upright posture and pushing-away actions; joy by an uplifting of the spine and expansive movement; empathy by a softening of the face and chest and perhaps a gentle reaching out; play by a tilt of the head and spontaneous, rapid changes in movement (Ogden et al., 2006). When the available range of actions is expanded, the ability to adapt to different situations is increased. Often an exploration of how different situations and people call forth different physical actions and expressions is helpful. For example, a female client who explored an expansive movement of extending her arms wide and expanding her chest (which alleviated her chronic pain associated with tension of pulling in) expressed that this movement would cause her to feel unsafe in her neighborhood, where drug trade was "on every corner." The therapist suggested that the client imagine various contexts (at her job, in her neighborhood, at home, with a friend, in the park) and sense the degree of physical expansion that felt right to her in each situation. In another example, a American-born mixed-race client of immigrant parents (a German mother and an Uruguayan father) explored in therapy that social engagement required different physical actions depending on which parent or side of the family the client was relating to. The client had to learn how to move from a loud and quick-paced speech and movement interaction, with closer proximity and use of touch, with the father and his family, to a slower-paced speech and movement, with constrained and spatially distant relating with less touch with the mother and her family.

Janet wrote, "The patients who are affected by traumatic memories have not been able to perform any of the actions characteristic of the stage of triumph" (1925, p. 669). Individuals who have been subjected to overwhelming fear and danger may have had their attempts to defend themselves thwarted by overwhelming odds. These truncated or uncompleted actions of defense often subsequently manifest as chronic symptoms. As Herman states, "Each component of the ordinary response to danger, having lost its utility, tends to persist in an altered and exaggerated state long after the actual danger is over" (1992, p. 34).

If a person is endangered and experiences the instinctive impulse to cry-for-help, fight, or flee, but is unable to execute these actions, the previously activated but never completed sequence of possible defensive actions may persist in distorted or exaggerated forms, such as a constant lack of tone or sensation in a particular muscle group or increased tension in other muscle groups, chronically tight muscles, or heightened and unstable aggressive or flight impulses. For example, when the instinctive response to run persists in exaggerated form, it can be reflexively activated when African Americans are approached by police, causing the impulse and often the action of fleeing (Menakem, 2017). Many, if not most, traumatized patients come to therapy exhibiting chronic dysregulated survival defenses, ranging from physiological and psychological immobility to hyperactive but ineffective aggression. Mindfully executing actions of defense, such as pushing away or moving away, can mitigate the immobilizing defenses of freezing and feigned death and help to regulate overactive mobilizing defenses. This is more nuanced in the face of real danger or ongoing trauma that marginalized groups experience, when some of these chronic physical patterns and actions may be adaptive in specific situations and contexts. The automatism of traumatic reactions and defenses in the face of current threat can be challenged by helping clients resource themselves and learn to take more adaptive action in a way that maximizes safety.

Mark, a Jewish man in his 30s, was the grandson of Holocaust survivors. Sexually abused and called anti-Semitic slurs by an older neighbor for four years between ages 11 to 15, Mark felt he had never moved past the trauma. He was also triggered by exposure to media coverage of anti-Semitic violence and discrimination in the form of shootings and racial slurs. He came to therapy to process his past traumatic events and address his reaction to these current triggers. Mark worked as a sous chef but could not maintain a job for more than a few months at a time. He worked in small kitchen spaces, and he was often touched, sometimes accidentally and sometimes purposefully and inappropriately, by other men around him, which he described as "just how the kitchen culture is." These events triggered uncontrollable rage.

Mark remembered feeling confused and powerless during and after the abuse he had endured, and he berated himself for not resisting during his neighbor's sexual and racial assaults. It was important for him to understand that his physiological response of immobility was adaptive in that particular context; thus his therapist asked him what might have happened had he resisted, and he immediately realized that the neighbor would have become violent. This insight helped him accept his lack of defensive action as adaptive. Mark also discovered—from becoming aware of the tension in his back and arms and a feeling of energy in his legs—that his body's impulse was to fight the perpetrator and run. These physical impulses that he could not act upon at the time of the abuse appeared spontaneously as his therapist directed him to focus his attention on any physical sensations and impulses that emerged as he remembered the event. For example, when Mark reported a clear image of the salacious expression on his neighbor's face, he first felt frightened and helpless, and his eyes narrowed to focus on the threat. His therapist asked him to stay with that image of the face in his mind's eye and be aware of any physical urges. Mark sensed tension in his spine and legs, and reported an impulse to turn away and run, which were actions he could not execute at the time of the event. His therapist encouraged him to sense and follow these physical impulses, allowing his body to guide him as to the actions that wanted to happen. Mark stood up and slowly followed the impulse he felt in his spine to twist away. He reported "so much energy" in his legs, and decided to run in place in the therapy room, which felt good to him.

The lost impulses to resist and get away had become encoded not only in the praxis of submission, but also as a belief: "I don't deserve to defend myself." Sensorimotor Psychotherapy addresses the incomplete defensive responses, which, when completed (in this case by twisting the spine and running in place) foster a sense of mastery and triumph that then facilitates the execution of more adaptive mental actions, changing the cognitive distortions. Mark said his body felt strong after completing the actions of turning and running; his breath deepened and his spine lengthened, his peripheral vision returned, and he no longer felt helpless. When his therapist asked him if there were words that went along with these new feelings in his body, Mark said, "I don't have to just take it [the abuse]. I can do something."

Mark's therapist had supported him in mindfully observing his body—his movements, sensations, impulses, posture, and gestures—and noticing the interplay of these with cognitions, emotions, and perceptions. Through mindful awareness, Mark could shift from being caught up in the story and upset about his reactions to becoming curious and interested in his experience. In this way, clients like Mark discover the difference between having an experience and exploring procedural tendencies in the here and now, days or weeks or years after the event itself.

As a grandson of Holocaust survivors, Mark experienced anxiety triggered by television news coverage of violence toward an establishment owned by a Jewish family. He also reported feeling anxious upon seeing two tall, white, blond men talking together on the street corner. The men reminded him of the racial prototype idealized by the Nazi regime, a transgenerational trigger for him. In both cases, Mark felt afraid, his heart rate increased, his arousal escalated, he started to tremble, but he felt frozen. Recalling these events in therapy produced the same uncomfortable sensations and impulses. With his therapist's help, Mark was able to put aside the images, emotions, and thoughts about these triggers, and direct his mindful attention exclusively to the sensations in his body. Using sensorimotor sequencing, Mark was able to track and describe the sequence of these sensations as they progressed, or sequenced, through his body until the shaking subsided and his heart rate returned to normal. Once his arousal settled, he was also able to use his resources (breathing deeply, expanding his vision, and lengthening his spine). He also reminded himself that he was no longer trapped, as he had been during the neighbor's abuse, and sensed the capacity to move in his legs. Through learning sensorimotor sequencing and using these resources, Mark developed more resilience, and he could return his arousal more quickly to a window of tolerance, whereas previously he did not have the tools to do so. At the end of treatment, Mark had been happily working at the same restaurant for several months and enjoyed a new empowering capacity to speak up, set boundaries with coworkers, or report disrespectful behaviors at work to his supervisors as needed.

If, as Janet (1907) suggests, traumatization is a failure of integrative capacity, then the first priority in the treatment of trauma must be to restore clients' capacity to tolerate and integrate their own inner experience (thoughts, emotions, images, movements, and bodily sensations) to bear witness to their own experience, and to be able to process significant life events, past and present, painful and pleasurable, nontraumatic and traumatic, without arousal greatly exceeding their window of tolerance. Of equal importance, especially for marginalized clients who experience ongoing threats, is to learn new resources to develop resilience and return arousal more expeditiously to a regulated level.

Mindfulness can help to restore and promote these capacities. Mindfulness, as it is generally taught in Western countries, is considered a state of awareness that is receptive to whatever elements of experience arise in the mind's eye (Kabat-Zinn, 2005). However, when mindfulness is open-ended, clients may find themselves at the mercy of dysregulated arousal and other disturbing internal experiences that appear most vividly in the forefront of consciousness. Because of this, many people with a history of trauma find it challenging to turn their awareness toward their internal experience. Thus, mindfulness in Sensorimotor Psychotherapy is used in a very specific way: instead of allowing clients' attention to drift randomly toward whatever emotions, memories, or thoughts might emerge, "directed mindfulness" (Ogden, 2007, 2009) interventions guide the client's awareness toward particular elements of present-moment experience that are thought to support therapeutic goals. Directing mindfulness toward selected movements, sensations, and gestures, as illustrated in the case described above, makes it possible to utilize precise interventions targeted toward nonverbal symptoms.

Janet (1919, 1925) referred to a process of "realization"—"the formulation of a belief about what happened (the trauma), when it happened (in the past), and to whom it happened (to self). The trauma becomes personalized, relegated to the past, and takes on symbolic, rather than sensorimotor properties" (Van der Hart et al., 1993, p. 171). Janet (1919, 1925) emphasized that realization requires a change both in mental action—the way the person thinks and talks about the trauma—and in physical actions—movement, arousal, and sensation. Through Sensorimotor Psychotherapy, instead of only addressing the verbal narrative, clients learn to cultivate mindfulness of their bodies, discover physical actions that modulate arousal, develop resilience in the face of ongoing societal or interpersonal threats, mitigate dissociation, reinstate flexible adaptive defensive responses, and achieve a somatic sense of competency and mastery.

REFERENCES

Bremner, J. D., & Brett, E. (1997). Trauma-related dissociative states and long-term psychopathology in posttraumatic stress disorder. *Journal of Traumatic Stress, 10,* 37–49.

DeGruy, J. (2017). *Post traumatic slave syndrome: America's legacy of enduring injury and healing.* Milwaukie, OR: Uptone Press.

Fryberg, S. A., Markus, H. R., Oyserman, D., & Stone, J. M. (2008). Of warrior chiefs and Indian princesses: The psychological consequences of American Indian mascots. *Basic and Applied Social Psychology, 30*(3), 208–218.

Herman, J. (1992). *Trauma and recovery.* New York: Basic Books.

Janet, P. (1907). *The major symptoms of hysteria.* London: Macmillan.

Janet, P. (1909). *Les névroses.* Paris: E. Flammarion.

Janet, P. (1919). *Psychological healing.* New York: Macmillan.

Janet, P. (1925). *Principles of psychotherapy.* London: George Allen and Unwin.

Kabat-Zinn, J. (2005). Coming to our senses: Healing ourselves and the world through mindfulness. New York: Hyperion.

McFarlane A. C. (2010). The long-term costs of traumatic stress: intertwined physical and psychological consequences. *World Psychiatry: Official Journal of the World Psychiatric Association* (WPA), 9(1), 3–10. https://doi.org/10.1002/j.2051-5545.2010.tb00254.x

Menakem, R. (2017). *My grandmother's hands: Racialized trauma and the pathway to mending our hearts and bodies.* Las Vegas, NV: Central Recovery Press.

Mohatt, N. V., Thompson, A. B., Thai, N. D., & Tebes, J. K. (2014). Historical trauma as public narrative: A conceptual review of how history impacts present-day health. *Social Science and Medicine, 106,* 128–136. doi:10.1016/j.socscimed.2014.01.043

Ogden, P. (2007). *Beneath the words: A clinical map for using mindfulness of the body and the organization of experience in trauma treatment.* Paper presented at Mindfulness and Psychotherapy Conference, UCLA/Lifespan Learning Institute, Los Angeles.

Ogden, P. (2009). Emotion, mindfulness and movement: Expanding the regulatory boundaries of the window of affect tolerance. In D. Fosha, M. Solomon, & D. Siegel (Eds.), *The healing power of emotion: Perspectives from affective neuroscience and clinical practice* (pp. 204–231). New York: Norton.

Ogden, P., & Minton, K. (2000). Sensorimotor psychotherapy: One method for processing trauma. *Traumatology,* 6(3). www.fse.edu/-trauma/v6i3a3.html

Ogden, P., Minton, K., & Pain, C. (2006). *Trauma and the body: A sensorimotor approach to psychotherapy.* New York: Norton.

Patton, S. (2017, April). Corporal punishment in black communities: Not an intrinsic cultural tradition but racial trauma. *CYF News.* https://www.apa.org/pi/families/resources/newsletter/2017/04/racial-trauma

Patton, S. (2017). *Spare the kids: Why whupping children won't save Black America.* Boston: Beacon.

Post, R., Weiss, S., Smith, M., Li, H., & McCann, U. (1997). Kindling versus quenching: Implications for the evolution and treatment of posttraumatic stress disorder. In R. Yehuda & A. C. McFarlane (Eds.), *Psy-*

chobiology of posttraumatic stress disorder (pp. 285–295). New York: New York Academy of Sciences.

Siegel, D. (1999). *The developing mind: Toward a neurobiology of interpersonal experience.* New York: Guilford.

Spiegel, D. (1997). Trauma, dissociation, and memory. *Annals of the New York Academy of Sciences, 821,* 225–237.

Van der Hart, O., Nijenhuis, E., & Steele, K. (2006). *The haunted self.* New York: Norton.

Van der Hart, O., Nijenhuis, E., Steele, K., & Brown, D. (2004). Trauma-related dissociation: Conceptual clarity lost and found. *Australian and New Zealand Journal of Psychiatry, 38,* 906–914.

Van der Hart, O., Steele, K., Boon, S., & Brown, P. (1993). The treatment of traumatic memories: Synthesis, realization, and integration. *Dissociation, 2/3,* 162–180.

Van der Kolk, B., van der Hart, O., & Marmar, C. (1996). Dissociation and information processing in posttraumatic stress disorder. In B. Van der Kolk, A. McFarlane, & L. Weisaeth (Eds.), *Traumatic stress: The effects of overwhelming experience on mind, body, and society* (pp. 303–327). New York: Guilford.

Williams, D. R., Lawrence, J. A., & Davis, B. A. (2019). Racism and health: Evidence and needed research. *Annual Review of Public Health, 40,* 105–125.

Chapter 4

EMBEDDED RELATIONAL
MINDFULNESS

The work for the client in self discovery. Not problem
solving. Not counseling. Not curing diseases. This work
is the same internal search that is the work of all spiritual
disciplines. It tackles the question: "Who am I?"

RON KURTZ

Trauma of all kinds (interpersonal trauma, the trauma of oppression, racism, and historical trauma) as well as relational stress (in significant relationships and in society at large) strongly influences unconscious processes that underlie explicit content in the therapy hour. Implicit processes—visibly reflected in nonverbal behaviors of gesture, posture, prosody, facial expressions, eye gaze, and affect—persist in spite of attempts to regulate or change them with top-down executive control. Clients with unresolved trauma often feel at the mercy of an overwhelming cascade of dysregulated emotions, upsetting physical sensations, intrusive images, pain, smells, constriction, and numbing. These in turn influence cognitive distortions such as, "I am damaged," "I am a bad person," or "I cannot protect myself." Clients with unresolved relational issues also feel at the mercy of tenacious patterns that repeat in current relationships, including emotional habits, postural and movement habits, and cognitive distortions such as,

"I am not lovable," "Others do not support me," or "I will never be accepted."

These unconscious processes speak to the dominance of what Schore (2009) calls the nonverbal, affective, and bodily based "implicit self" over the verbal, linguistic "explicit self." A therapist's exclusive reliance on the talking cure to resolve symptoms of trauma as well as the effects of relational stress does not directly address implicit processing dynamics and can limit clinical efficacy. Memories, especially traumatic or early childhood ones, are often not explicitly encoded. Instead, the past is "remembered as a series of *unconscious expectations*" (Cortina & Liotti, 2007, p. 205, italics added), which are all the more potent precisely because memories of the events that shaped them are not available for reflection and revision. Memories may be dissociated—split off from conscious awareness—and many trauma survivors remember only isolated affective, sensory, or motor aspects of traumatic experience. During trauma, functioning of the prefrontal cortex or executive brain, responsible for clear thinking and decision making, and of the hippocampus, involved in the consolidation of emotional and verbal memory, is selectively impaired and enhanced in ways that increase emotional processes and their encoding while decreasing conceptual processes and their encoding (Arnsten, 2009; Schwabe et al., 2012). Attempting to describe the processes that precipitate implicit remembering only leads to failure and frustration or, worse, to reliving. Additionally, the preverbal relational interactions that initially taught us which emotions and behaviors are acceptable or capable of producing the desired outcome, and which are not, are also unavailable to verbal recall.

In historical or transgenerational trauma, the specific memories are absent but the effects of such trauma are often experienced profoundly nonetheless. Transgenerational trauma is defined as communal trauma that affects generations, that is, traumatic symptoms and expectations are transmitted from one generation to the next.

Clients present with implicit memories without links to any specific event that they have personally experienced in their lifetime. For example, the terror an African American mother felt at the possibility of her grown daughter moving away from home was related to the historical trauma of the family's enslaved ancestors, who endured the separation of parents and children that was used to break attachment bonds and support the institution of slavery.

Thus, the raw ingredients of therapeutic change lie not in what is explicitly spoken, but in the constantly changing experiential context that remains generally unsymbolized in ordinary verbal exchange (Bromberg, 2006). A paradigm shift is indicated that privileges mindful awareness of the moment-by-moment experience of implicit patterns over formulating a cohesive narrative, engaging in conversation, or "talking about" (Kurtz, 1990; Ogden & Fisher, 2015; Ogden & Minton, 2000; Ogden et al., 2006). This chapter offers a practical overview of a clinical map for using mindfulness embedded within what transpires between therapist and client, and delineates interventions from Sensorimotor Psychotherapy (Ogden et al., 2006) that directly address the in-the-moment experience of implicit processes.

APPROPRIATION OF MINDFULNESS

Mindfulness practices, like all contemplative practices, "provide opportunities for enhancement of experiential and critical self-other-world awareness, expansion of consciousness, and, ultimately, transformation of how we live in the world" (Harrell, 2018, pl. 12). Mindfulness has emerged as the prominent contemplative practice in psychology, although every culture has its meditative traditions: prayer, chanting, yoga, praise, mantra, worship, music, poetry, or something else. Mindfulness meditation had already been examined for its psychotherapeutic effects in the 1800s. It resurfaced in the 1960s and 1970s as a prominent focus of Western interest and research, in part due to popular culture figures of the times who promoted meditation (Surmitis et al., 2018). Since then, mindfulness interventions and programs, touted as universally beneficial to individual mental health, have been appropriated and adapted in many secular fields, including psychology.

Appropriation can be defined as the taking or adapting "of a group's symbols, rituals, images, or sacred philosophies by another group that has access to greater resources" (Surmitis et al., 2018, p. 7). Although mindfulness practices are found in Christianity, Islam, and Judaism (Trousselard et al., 2014), the industry that has been built around mindfulness has been described as capitalizing on Buddhist exoticism, benefiting primarily Western culture and values (Purser et al., 2016). With such appropriation, mindfulness practices have been decontextualized from their original cultural meaning, ethics, and spiritual practices of their place of origin, including Buddhism (Kirmayer, 2015). Although medical benefits have been attributed to mindfulness meditation, as Purser, Forbes, and Burke point out, the "medicalization" of mindfulness "has reinforced the notion that disease (including psychosomatic symptoms such as chronic stress, depression, and anxiety), along with interventions for enhancing health and well-being, is a matter for autonomous individuals" (2016, p. viii). This viewpoint ignores the effects of context, including systemic societal and interpersonal racism and oppression, on mental health. However, many argue that mindfulness as adapted in the West could include moral views aligned with social justice needs by incorporating systemic views. For instance, Cannon (2016) advocates for embracing mindfulness as a social justice practice rather than as a "technology of compliance," while Magee (2016) reclaims social justice concerns and ethical commitments inherent in secular Buddhist practices. When migrating practices from other cultures, as mindfulness from Buddhism, it is not only important to name and acknowledge the origin and the sociopolitical context in which those practices came to be, but also how those practices shift and change in their meaning and purpose when transplanted into another context for different purposes.

DEFINITIONS OF MINDFULNESS IN WESTERN CONTEXTS

Definitions of mindfulness as used in Western contexts vary. Williams and colleagues describe mindfulness as "the awareness that emerges through paying attention on purpose, in the present moment, and non-judgmentally to things as they are," a perspective that takes into account internal experience as well as "those aspects of life that we most take for granted or ignore" (Williams et al., 2007, p. 47). Included in most descriptions is an attitude of openness and receptivity to whatever arises, as a "quality of attention which notices without choosing, without preference" (Goldstein & Kornfield, 1987, p. 19). Many mindfulness practices encourage such unrestricted receptivity, while others, described as "concentration practices," promote focusing attention upon particular elements of either internal experience (such as the breath, body sensation, or a mantra) or the external environment (such as a candle flame or sound). Several psychotherapeutic methods have been developed that teach mindfulness through structured exercises, practices, and sets of skills for the specific purpose of supporting mental health. For example, in Linehan's (1993) model, developed out of her practice in the Zen Buddhist tradition, clients are taught mindfulness "what" skills of observing, describing, and participating, as well as "how" skills of focusing on one thing at a time and being effective (Robins, 2002).

Kurtz, as a student of Buddhist traditions, describes the essence of mindfulness as follows:

to be fully present to our experience, whatever it is: our thoughts, images, memories, breath, body sensations, the

sounds and smells and tastes, moods and feelings and the quality of our whole experience as well as of the various parts.
Mindfulness is not our notions about our experience, but even
noticing the notions. (2004, p. 39)

Influenced by Kurtz, mindfulness in Sensorimotor Psychotherapy
is not limited to interventions to reduce stress or other difficulties,
but is defined as being aware of the here-and-now internal experience of body sensation, movements, five-sense perception, emotions, and thoughts. Hence, mindfulness is not a practice to achieve
a specific state but a capacity and ability developed in session to discover and then interrupt automatic, procedural learnings. Through
mindfulness, attention is focused on the ebb and flow of present-
moment internal phenomena. It is not taught through structured
exercises or practices but is integrated with and embedded within
what transpires moment-to-moment between therapist and client,
including how the dynamics of the sociocultural and historical contexts play out between them.

THE ORGANIZATION OF EXPERIENCE

Sensorimotor Psychotherapy uses mindfulness to discover and
change habits of organizing experience, as over time we form habits of responding to both internal and external stimuli. As these
response habits and their meaning become incorporated into who
we are, they become automatic and procedural. Thus we do not
examine them, and often are not aware of them, but they powerfully influence the quality and even the content of our lives. They
become default reactions that may usurp more adaptive responses to
current stimuli. A first step to changing these habits is to discover
how we automatically organize experience—for example, how our
thoughts, emotions, and bodily experience change when we are
exposed to significant stimuli, like threats, criticism, appreciation,

challenges, and so forth. Mindfulness thus is an inquiry into the direct moment-by-moment internal experience of the effects of the past that impinge on our response options to current stimuli. We endeavor to bring these unconscious, unknown habits into awareness so that we can understand them and learn new options.

Noticing and studying the organization of experience represents a paradigm shift away from conversation and content toward mindful awareness of how internal experience is constructed in the here and now. It is founded on the premise that the quality of our experience is based on its internal construction, and our habits of construction strongly shape the content and meaning of our lives. Critically, the use of mindful awareness includes awareness of the effects of privilege, racism, and oppression as well as resilience and resources on how we organize experience. By engaging mindfulness, we access and can change the metalevel of organization, shaped by the past, that underlies the content of our lives, including the implicit ways we organize around privilege/oppression dynamics and the habits that emerge in the face of racism, discrimination, and other injustices. Because mindfulness supports the discovery of how experience is organized, it is favored over advice, interpretation, or conversation in Sensorimotor Psychotherapy practice. Therapists and clients mindfully attend to clients' internal experience long enough so that salient, novel, and previously unconscious elements are revealed, which in turn can prompt a natural reorganization.

A MAP FOR THE USE OF MINDFULNESS IN CLINICAL PRACTICE

In Sensorimotor Psychotherapy, the clinician maintains a dual focus: One is following the client's verbal narrative or story. The other, more important focus is tracking the five "building blocks" of present-moment internal experience—emotions, thoughts, five-sense perception, movements, and body sensations—that emerge spontaneously in the therapy hour. Sensorimotor Psychotherapy employs a specific clinical map using these five building blocks as the focal points of mindful exploration and transformation of the organization of experience (cf. Ogden et al., 2006). These building blocks are elaborated in Figure 4.1.

Reflecting implicit processes, these five elements constitute the present-moment internal experience of every waking moment; even though they often occur outside awareness, they strongly influence the quality of our experience. They change in response to themselves, with thoughts affecting emotions, which then associatively evoke internal perceptions, sensations, and so on. They also change in response to external stimuli. The building blocks are dramatically impacted by both internal and external traumatic reminders as well as reminders of relational stress that bring the past abruptly into the experiential present. When triggered by

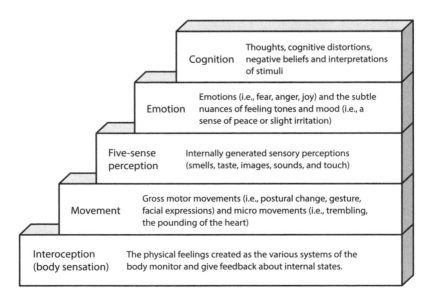

Figure 4.1: 5 Building Blocks of Moment-by-Moment Experience: Here-and-Now Internal Experience   *Graphic by Anne Westcott*

such reminders, traumatized clients report disturbing body sensations, movements, intrusive images, smells or sounds, fear, shame, panic or rage, and thoughts—even while realizing cognitively that these reactions do not match current reality. As one client put it, "I know I'm safe, but my body is running amok. I shake, I panic, I see my father's face, and I feel like I will die." Reminders of relational strife elicit similar, less intense, responses.

Rather than conversation, the focus of therapy becomes the spontaneous fluctuations of these five elements. The therapist is on the lookout for specific building blocks that point to internal experience indicative of unresolved trauma and relational issues, as well as those that reflect self-regulatory resources, positive affect, competency, and mastery. Together, therapist and client interrupt the automaticity of these building blocks by becoming mindful of them. In this way, the client can identify and observe, rather than identify with, the effects of the past, and to explore more adaptive actions, as well as discover internal resources. (cf. Ogden et al., 2006).

While tracking the client's present-moment experience is prioritized, therapists at times are also gently aware of their own five building blocks and how they dialogue and respond in relation to the client's present-moment experience. However, as Beebe states, "Our ability to sense and *not to inhibit* our own bodily arousal, attention patterns, affective reactions, orientation shifts, and touch patterns is key" (2014, p. 143). Because mindfulness is a dual state of consciousness that encompasses both an observer and that which is observed, the therapist's mindfulness of their own internal experience can distract them from being fully participatory in the dyadic dance. Presence, on the other hand, is a unified state of consciousness rather than a dual state. As therapists, our presence, as a participatory state of being-with rather than observing, of engaging rather than noticing, is constant in the therapy hour, and is integrated with occasional mindful awareness of our own building blocks.

DIRECTED MINDFULNESS

Mindfulness in Sensorimotor Psychotherapy is "motivated by curiosity" (Kurtz, 1990, p. 111), and thus "'allow[s]' difficult thoughts and feelings [and images, body sensations, and movements] simply to be there . . . to adopt toward them a more 'welcome' than a 'need to solve' stance" (Segal et al., 2002, p. 55). The therapist, by example and encouragement, helps clients cultivate an attitude of curiosity and receptivity toward their internal experience. However, unrestricted mindfulness toward any and all of the five building blocks can be disturbing and overwhelming, especially for people with PTSD, and thus can be met with dismay, judgment, self-criticism, and further dysregulation. To help prevent this, a Sensorimotor Psychotherapy approach employs mindfulness in a very specific way, termed "directed mindfulness," which entails carefully and firmly directing the client's mindful attention toward one or more of the five building blocks considered important to therapeutic goals (Ogden, 2007, 2009). For example, if an internal image of past trauma or an external traumatic reminder, such as an image of police brutality perpetrated toward a client's group of belonging that is shown in the media, causes hyperarousal, a therapist might first direct a client to become aware of the sensation in their legs to promote grounding and a sense of present-moment safety, rather than aware of the violent image, so that arousal might become regulated. Directing mindfulness toward any positive building block can support regulation. For example, if a thought such as, "I am safe right now" emerges, the therapist might direct the client to be mindful of physical impulses, images, or emotions that accompany the thought to become aware of, savor, and strengthen the components of feeling safe.

Mindfulness can also be directed to somatic indicators of resilience. Although marginalized clients often experience oppression, racism, or microaggressions on a daily basis, these experiences can also build resilience. As Harrell and Sloan-Pena (2006, p. 400) state, through adversity, "characteristics such as endurance, perseverance, passion, expressiveness, optimism, gratefulness, creativity, compassion, collectivism, spirituality, and faith can emerge." The somatic indicators of resilience, such as a lift of the chin or a compassionate gesture toward oneself (a hand placed over the heart, for example), can be brought to awareness and explored further. Doing so can deepen the embodiment "of inner strength and resilience in the face of the ongoing negative messages about one's value and worth" (Harrell & Sloan-Pena, 2006, p. 400). Mindful attention to the resources of the body such as these can be used to quickly bring extremes of arousal into a regulated zone in the face of ongoing present-time threat cues and triggers. Doing so prevents prolonged dysregulation and builds resilience.

SAFETY, DANGER, AND MINDFULNESS IN THE THERAPEUTIC RELATIONSHIP

Critically, mindfulness in Sensorimotor Psychotherapy is not a solitary activity, but is firmly embedded in what occurs within the therapeutic dyad. It is imperative that mindfulness is employed in a way that increases clients' experience of relational safety and fosters their ability to connect to and engage with the therapist. However, maintaining the moment-by-moment therapeutic alliance is precarious, especially with trauma survivors, because both external reminders of trauma and internal reminders (images, thoughts, emotions, impulses, and sensations) are implicitly triggering, which elicit instinctive defenses and dysregulated arousal. The emotional valence and intensity of dysregulation may be heightened and further complicated when client and therapist have different social locations, especially if these are reminiscent of past trauma. For example, an Indigenous Peruvian client who had emigrated to the United States became dysregulated with their Spanish therapist due to the difference in their accents that implicitly reminded the client of the historical trauma of the Spaniards colonizing Peru.

Danger that is (implicitly or explicitly) detected produces dysregulated arousal and either mobilization or immobilization defenses. Mobilization behaviors (cry-for-help, fight or flight) are accompanied by hyperarousal and tense muscles that prepare for calling or reaching for help, or for defensive fight or flight behaviors. Immobilization behaviors include both the freeze response (accompanied by alert senses and tense muscles) and the feigned death response (accompanied by hypoarousal, shutdown, and muscular flaccidity). The Peruvian client exhibited signs of feigned death as their posture slumped and their face became expressionless. Social behaviors, and therapy, can continue only if these defenses can be inhibited sufficiently so that the client can experience some degree of relational safety.

Porges (2004, 2011) introduced the term "neuroception," distinguished from "perception," to emphasize the brain's automatic detection of environmental features that are safe, dangerous, and life threatening. This detection is usually implicit—though not immune to social and cultural priming—and strongly affects one's physiological state to produce active defensive, or immobilizing ones. When safety is neurocepted, levels of autonomic arousal fluctuate within a "window of tolerance" (Siegel, 1999) in which behaviors typical of engagement with others can take place. In therapy, clients must automatically detect or neurocept some degree of safety in order to remain engaged with the therapist; otherwise therapy cannot take place. However, as stated, traumatized clients are often unable, based on prior conditioning, to detect accurately whether the environment is safe or another person is trustworthy. As well, the legacy of unresolved relational stress primes us to expect negative outcomes in relationships, causing us to interpret another's action or behavior as congruent with those expectations, and thus leaving us feeling unsafe or unsupported. These difficulties are exacerbated in therapy as the client's memories of trauma and relational stress are deliberately stimulated, which they must be in order to resolve the effects of the past. The therapist intends to bring the client's experience of the past into the therapy hour, but this can cause the client to implicitly neurocept danger, which activates the brain's fear circuitry, stimulates the nervous system to mobilize some degree of crying-for-help, fight, flight, freeze, or shutdown behaviors.

It is important to note that the client's neuroception of the environment as safe or dangerous occurs implicitly, triggering defensive or social behaviors usually without any conscious awareness. As Porges states, "Even though we may not be aware of danger on a cognitive level, on a neurophysiological level, our body has already started a sequence of neural processes that would facilitate adaptive defense behaviors such as [crying-for-help], fight, flight, [freeze], or [shutdown]" (2004, p. 20). Clients and therapists alike are often baffled by the client's unexpected change from social to defensive behaviors. The stimulus that provoked the change is typically not conscious for either party. When the therapist has privileged locations and the client has marginalized locations, the stimulus may pertain to the therapist's words or expressions that reflect bias or privilege/oppression dynamics, as illustrated in the Peruvian/Spanish therapy dyad. In another example, a gay, Middle Eastern male client implicitly neurocepted danger in response to his white male heterosexual therapist's unconscious distasteful facial expression as the client spoke of his lover.

Therapists must pay exquisite attention to the nonverbal signals that suggest state changes from regulated arousal (the client's neuroception of safety) to dysregulated arousal and defensive responses (the client's neuroception of danger and life threat) and take steps to help clients inhibit defensive systems sufficiently so that social engagement can continue or be re-established. Taking place within an attuned dyad, mindfulness can be used to activate not only clients' experience of trauma and dysregulated arousal but also to ensure that their social engagement is intact. In other words, the client must detect safety and danger simultaneously. Detecting only safety would preclude addressing past trauma or relational stress, and detecting only danger would lead to reliving the trauma or relational stress. The simultaneous evocation of both implicit relational or trauma-related dysregulating processes and safe social engagement can result in a depth of intersubjectivity and connectedness that exceeds that which ensues from conversation alone. For this to occur, mindfulness must be relational rather than solitary.

EMBEDDED RELATIONAL MINDFULNESS SKILLS

In Sensorimotor Psychotherapy, a specific set of essential relational mindfulness interventions is privileged over ordinary conversation, discussion, or "talking about" (Kurtz, 1990; Ogden et al., 2006), and over solitary mindfulness exercises or practices. These skills are described below, in a particular sequence that supports both social engagement between therapist and client and the discovery of the client's organization of experience.

Track

In Sensorimotor Psychotherapy, the first skill for therapists is to closely and unobtrusively track the client's unfolding experience of body sensations, movements, five-sense perceptions, emotions, and thoughts in response to a meaningful stimuli. The catalyst might be a description of past trauma, current difficulty, relational dynamics, or the therapist's words, manner, or action, all of which can elicit changes in present experience of the building blocks. The therapist is on the lookout for changes in sensation (like flushing in lighter skin or shine to the skin in darker skin), shifts in movement (in facial expression, posture, or gesture), internally generated perceptions (reports of images, smells, tastes, sounds, touch), emerging emotions (in moist eyes, facial expression, or prosody), or beliefs and cognitive distortions that emerge from the client's narrative. In addition, connections among the building blocks are noted, for example, the thought "It's my fault," expressed as the client reports the image of their caregiver's unwelcoming face when they turned to the caregiver for comfort, that emerges as their posture slumps and their facial expression reflects sadness.

Contact

These tracked elements of present-moment experience typically remain unnoticed by the client until the therapist brings attention to them through a contact statement that describes what has been noticed, such as, "As you see your caregiver's face, it looks like your posture slumps," or "You seem to feel hopeless right now." Therapists of all persuasions are skillful at reflective statements that convey their understanding of the narrative ("That must have been so painful for you." "You were devastated by that experience." "This has been happening for so many generations"). Although it is important for the client to know that the therapist is following and understanding the narrative details, it is essential to contact present-moment experience to facilitate mindfulness. If therapists only verbalize their understanding of the verbal narrative, clients will assume that the narrative, rather than present experience, is of greater import, inciting them to continue the conversation. Contacting present experience teaches clients to notice and track their own here-and-now internal experience, as verbal contact repeatedly shifts the client's attention "to the various things going on outside of the flow of conversation, to experiences" (Kurtz, 2004, p. 40) that can then be further explored through mindful awareness.

Contact statements should convey empathic understanding of the client's present experience (Kurtz, 1990; Ogden et al., 2006). Thus it is not only the words that therapists say, but also their nonverbal body language, affect, and prosody that modulate clients' fear circuitry and stimulate an experience of safety and social engagement. These contact statements spontaneously emerge from the clinician's own implicit processing while "the therapist resonates with the client's internal state of arousal dysregulation, modulates it, communicates it back prosodically in a more regulated form, and then verbally labels his/her state experiences" (Schore, 2003, p. 30). Such resonance followed by "labeling" or naming through a contact statement allows clients to become aware of here-and-now experience and paves the way for mindful exploration of that experience.

Contact statements contain "qualifiers," or "a sense of subtle questioning, a tone that implies an invitation for revision by the client" (Ogden et al., 2006). These qualifiers are adjunct clauses included in the contact statement (such as, "sounds like," "seems as if," "looks like," or "huh"), which leaves them open-ended, which invites revision and collaboration. If a therapist tracks tension in the client and states, "You seem to be getting tense, huh," the qualifiers ("seem to" and "huh") encourage the client to modify the statement if it is not accurate in their experience. Using qualifiers verbally scaffolds clients' experience, spurs collaboration, bolsters social engagement, and validates the client as the authority on their inner experience.

Frame

The therapist and client collaborate to determine a starting place, or frame, which becomes the focus or target of mindful exploration. This decision constitutes a commitment to a certain direction for the session in general—whether to start by exploring the present-moment effects of trauma, such as an intrusive image, cognitive distortions, disturbing sensations, or physical constriction indicative of instinctive defenses; the effect of relational strife, such as strong emotion, beliefs, or images related to such adversity; or instead to address something that points to resources, like relaxation, a sense of joy, a positive cognition, or a peaceful image.

What is framed depends on factors such as therapeutic goals, phase of treatment, the client's regulatory capacity, and the width of their window of tolerance. For example, reports of past trauma cause dysregulation, or if attachment failures cause dysregulating emotion, framing a resource, such as, "Let's stay with your breath for a moment" can support regulation. On the other hand, if the client's regulatory capacity is sufficient, and their window wide enough, a strong emotion might be framed ("How about we stay with the anger you're feeling") or an image related to trauma ("Let's focus on the sound of the gunshot for a moment"). Additionally, the therapist may have tracked and contacted shifts in experience as the client talks about a positive memory ("It seems your shoulders let go when you talk about this memory" or "Your breathing deepens, huh") and may frame by suggesting, "Let's find out more about this relaxation that occurs when you think about the memory." If the client agrees, the relaxation becomes the stimulus for mindful study.

For several reasons, this collaborative moment, inherent in the intervention of framing (as well as in the qualifiers mentioned earlier), is significant for historically marginalized individuals whose experiences include the trauma of oppression. The invitation to collaborate with the therapist (the person in power) is often experienced as new and potentially empowering in and of itself. Additionally, for such clients, their trauma histories are often disproportionately emphasized in therapy, so it is not unusual for these individuals to assume that the effects of trauma will be the most significant and/or exclusive focus of the treatment. To be presented with a collaborative option of attending to positive elements and resources can be quite meaningful. Moreover, the idea that their increased capacity for pleasure and joy is of therapeutic interest and seemed an important path to trauma recovery is highly compelling and nourishing because very often these are the experiences that have been targeted by forms of oppression. For instance, when a group of Black women were enjoying themselves on a train ride, they were escorted off the train due to their "offensive laughter," and police were called. To stay safe, marginalized people may need to curtail their joy in predominantly white spaces. Because joy and pleasure can thus become risky or dangerous to express in such contexts, attending to and deepening these feelings in therapy can be a small step in healing the impact of such injustices.

Mindfulness Questions

The above skills set the stage for mindfulness questions because they guide the client's attention gently toward their here-and-now internal experience. Only after tracking, contacting, and framing an element of present experience to explore does the therapist ask directed mindfulness questions. For example, if the thought "I know I'm okay" is framed, the induction to mindfulness might include a directive like, "Stay with that thought, 'I know I'm okay,'" followed by a question, such as "What images or emotions come up? What do you notice in your body as you have this thought? Does your sensation change when you focus on this thought? What movement does your body want to make?" In this way, new information is revealed that expands and deepens whatever is framed, in this case, the positive thought.

Mindfulness questions build upon the building block that was framed. If tension was framed and agreed upon, follow-up questions might include, "As you sense that tension, what can you learn about it? Is it the same in both shoulders and arms?" A "menu" is often articulated to further support the client to observe the tension and discover more about it, such as, "How it is pulling? What kind of tension is it—achy, sharp, diffuse, or . . . ? What are its parameters? Is there an impulse, image, or emotion that goes with it?" and so forth. If a numb feeling has been framed, a menu could include, "What does 'numb' feel like? . . .Tight, empty, spacey, nothingness—or maybe something else." Offering a menu of words that serve as descriptive suggestions for present experience can help clients become more aware of the nuances of internal awareness.

Mindfulness questions discourage discussion, conversation, and ruminating about past or future experiences and instead encourage clients to report what they notice, right here, right now. In order to answer mindfulness questions, clients must attend to the building blocks of their present-moment experience. To deter them from talking about what happened in the past or what will happen in the future and instead report on their present-moment experience, ask questions that draw attention to "right now," such as, "Are you feeling that *right now*?" "Are you seeing the image of that memory *right now*?" "Can you sense that tension *right now*?" Adding "right now" supports clients to notice their internal experience as it occurs in the here-and-now moment of the therapy.

Therapeutic Experiments

Therapeutic experiments are a specific version of mindfulness questions conducted to discover what changes in the building blocks of present experience when a client's attention is directed toward a specific stimulus. Experiments can be physical or verbal (Kurtz, 1990; Ogden et al., 2006), and are prefaced by the words, "What happens when . . ." For example, a verbal experiment might be, "What happens when you repeat those words, 'I know I'm OK'?" Or if the intention is to deepen awareness of a painful belief, "What happens when you say those words out loud, 'I'm just not good enough'?" In another variant of verbal experiment, the therapist might say a phrase, such as, "What happens when you hear me say, 'You have a right to your grief'?" The clause "what happens when" directs the client to observe the effect of the experiment—how the building blocks change as a result of the experiment—in this case, to saying the words.

For physical experiments, either the client performs an action, such as pushing against a pillow held by the therapist ("What happens when you push out with your arms?") or changes their position ("What do you notice when you curl up?). Actions of the therapist can also become a physical experiment ("What happens when I avert my gaze away from you?" or "What happens when I reach out toward you?").

The variety of experiments is endless, but obviously the stimulus should relate to the client's presenting problem and therapeutic goals. With that in mind, any building block can be the target for an experiment ("What happens when: You see that image of your mother's face? feel that tingling?; recall the smell of the apple blossoms?; hear the sound of the yelling?; remember cuddling your daughter?," and so forth). An experimental attitude invites exploration and discovery without an investment in a specific outcome. Thus there is no right or wrong response to experiments; they are simply conducted to explore how experience is organized in relation to a significant stimulus. Spontaneous discoveries arise unprompted from mindful experiments; often therapist and client alike are surprised by the unanticipated results.

CASE ILLUSTRATION

Sensorimotor Psychotherapy is conducted within a phase-oriented treatment approach, identified by Janet (1898) as consisting of three phases: symptom reduction and stabilization, treatment of trauma (or relational stress), and personality integration and rehabilitation. Omar's treatment will illustrate how the clinical map and therapeutic skills for mindfulness are utilized at each phase of treatment.

Omar was a 27-year-old, cisgender, heterosexual male, the child of immigrant Lebanese parents, and thus the first generation born in America. He was an only child of a single father, as his mother died from complications of his birth. His therapist was a cisgender heterosexual male who was an immigrant himself and white presenting (e.g., he appeared white to the client). Omar came to therapy to address the extreme anxiety he experienced in relationships, which was related to his excessive ruminating worry about being alone. Early in treatment, Omar discussed his history of being emotionally abused by his father since he was a toddler, and later being bullied by other kids after 9/11 because of his dark skin and Middle Eastern appearance. As he spoke, the therapist tracked his rapid breathing, his darting eye contact, constricted smile, and tense shoulders that were accompanied by an impulse to back away from the therapist. Omar reported vivid images of being bullied by his neighbors, only to face his alcoholic father when he arrived home. The therapist's contact statements brought Omar's attention to various building blocks ("Your body seems to be tightening up"; "Remembering is upsetting, huh"; "The images of that abuse are still with you, huh"), which not only helped Omar feel understood by his therapist, but also helped him to begin to be aware of his present-moment experience.

The thread of cognitive distortions was disclosed in the self-deprecating words he used—"Nobody will ever love me," spoken in a flat voice accompanied by a helpless shrug of his shoulders. Naming the specific elements of Omar's present experience ("Your breathing seems very fast as you speak about being bullied") was followed by Omar's report that he felt anxious, numb in his legs, and slightly nauseous. Clearly, his arousal was escalating. The therapist collaborated with him to determine an initial frame, deciding together to focus on the legs and feet, in the hope that Omar could learn to ground himself and bring his arousal into a window of tolerance. Thus, the numb feeling in the legs became the stimulus for exploration and the target of directed mindfulness questions: "What impulses emerge as you sense that numbness? Can you describe that sensation of numbness in your legs? Do you feel it equally in both legs?" In directing his attention solely to the body rather than the anxiety, Omar felt less fearful and was able to tolerate the discomfort of numbness in his legs. Note that these directed mindfulness questions are different from general mindfulness questions, such as, "What do you notice right now?"

In Sensorimotor Psychotherapy, mindfulness includes the client's labeling of internal experience using language, which engages the prefrontal cortex (Siegel, 2007). As Omar described the numbness, his therapist suggested he experiment with pressing his feet into the floor, an action intended to facilitate grounding (Ogden et al., 2006), and notice what happened in his body. This action became the second stimulus for mindful awareness, and Omar reported less nausea, and that his spine straightened, which he described as "solidity." His arousal returned within a window of tolerance, meeting Phase 1's goal of stabilizing arousal.

The therapist tracked that Omar lowered his eyes, despite his report of feeling more solid and sensing an aligned posture. The therapist contacted this ("It seems difficult to make eye contact") and framed it by suggesting they explore his downward gaze. Omar agreed, and his therapist asked him to continue to look downward and notice if any words or feelings accompanied this action. Quietly, Omar said, "I feel disgusting when you look at me" and reported feeling shame. For a moment, Omar glanced at his therapist, but quickly looked away, and reported that the nausea returned, and his body became tense again. The therapist wondered aloud whether these responses could be activated by his own white presentation, and Omar responded affirmatively, and reported that he always felt like a second-class citizen in this country, similar to his father's experience as well. His body relaxed with this acknowledgment, and again the nausea decreased. Discussing this with his therapist alleviated some of the tension, although Omar said that he often "lost himself" around white people, meaning that he felt that he had no protection, as if anything they said or did would "go right in."

The therapist suggested that they explore boundaries, and when Omar agreed, directed him to place a rope around himself to create a visible separation and boundary between them. Using mindful experiments, they explored what changed in Omar's internal experience when he had the rope boundary around himself and when he did not. When not using the rope as a boundary, he felt tense, anxious, and hypervigilant about the therapist's movement and facial expression. In contrast, Omar's breath deepened and his spine lengthened slightly when he used the rope and was able to see and sense his boundary. He said he felt safer, but immediately was overwhelmed by intense feelings of loneliness and separation. As his therapist contacted his experience ("It seems if you have a boundary, you feel alone. . . . It's painful, huh."), Omar reported an image of himself as an isolated boy, longing for connection, but afraid to approach his father or other children. Processing the ensuing emotions helped to resolve the early relational imprints of what was expected with others—that he had to sacrifice his safety and his own boundary to be in relationship. Afterward, as he repeated the experiment of placing the rope boundary around himself, Omar felt that he could both maintain his boundary and feel connected to his therapist.

Omar was able to notice how his activation increased and decreased with variations of the grounding and boundary experiments. He learned to mindfully apply these resources so that his arousal could return to the window of tolerance, in accord with the stabilization goal of Phase 1 of trauma treatment. Outside therapy, Omar practiced grounding by bringing awareness to his legs and feet and pressing his feet into the floor. He also practiced the effects of the rope exercise—deep breathing and lengthening his spine slightly—both of which helped him sense himself and his own boundary while in connection with others.

In Phase 2 treatment, Omar discovered his forgotten, dormant defensive impulse to protect himself. As he remembered how he became frozen when he recalled being beaten by neighborhood bullies, his arms and shoulders visibly tensed, which his therapist tracked and contacted, saying, "It looks like your shoulders are tensing up as you talk about the beating." The therapist selected the tension because he hypothesized that the tension was a preparatory movement of raising his arms in protection and/or pushing away—both instinctual defensive responses that Omar had refrained from executing at the time of the beating, because active protection or resistance would only have made the bullies more aggressive. Omar was not aware of the tension until the therapist contacted it. The therapist framed the tension, saying, "This tension seems important—let's stay with it," and Omar agreed. Thus, the tension became the framed stimulus to study in mindfulness.

To illustrate becoming mindful of a stimulus, Kurtz (2004) used the metaphor of tossing a pebble in a pond and watching the ripples. The quieter and more still the pond is, the more the ripples are visible. To support a sense of calm, the therapist asked Omar to take all the time he needed to gently become aware of the tension and to put the memory content aside. After a moment, he asked, "What happens when you sense this tension? Is the tension in both arms equally? How is it pulling?" This was a turning point in the session, because the focus shifted from conversation about his physical abuse to mindful study of a specific here-and-now physical response that emerged unbidden while talking about the incident with the bullies—the tension. This telling elicits implicit processing, reflected in present-moment alterations in the internal experience of the five building blocks, as illustrated in Figure 4.2.

As Omar became mindful, he first reported feeling "frozen," but his fingers started to curl slightly while the tension of his right arm increased, which the therapist tracked and contacted. Omar was surprised and curious about these small shifts, and the therapist asked, "As you sense the curling of your fingers, what does your body want to do?," directing Omar to take his time to sense the impulse from his body itself, not his idea of the impulse. He reported, "My right arm wants to protect my head, but I also want to punch out." At this moment in the session, Omar shifted from the memory of the bullies and recalled a single incident when his father had been drinking and raised a threatening hand to Omar, whose impulse was to strike back. Omar said, "That's scary. I can't do it—he is a sick and alone

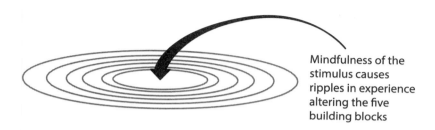

Mindfulness of the
stimulus causes
ripples in experience
altering the five
building blocks

Implicit processing is made explicit as the patient
mindfully studies and reports how the building
blocks change in response to the stimulus.

Figure 4.2: Directed Mindfulness: Eliciting and Discovering Implicit
Processing

man." The therapist acknowledged Omar's fear and compassion
toward his father, whose own traumatic history included experiences of racism in the United States, but firmly directed Omar's
mindful attention back to his body: "Let's just sense your body. Put
the fear and the compassion aside for now. Let's just follow what
your body wants to do."

The exclusive focus on physical sensation and impulses enabled
Omar to execute an "act of triumph" (Janet, 1925) by pushing
against a pillow that the therapist held with his right arm. The
execution of this empowering defensive response, which was an
active mobilizing defense rather than the more passive one of
using his arm to cover his head, elicited a feeling of satisfaction
and pleasure. Omar reported, "I feel less tense! This feels new,
good. . . ." Through directing mindful attention to his body
rather than to the image of his father, the instinctive impulses to
fight back to protect himself—which Omar could not act upon at

the time—developed into an action that led to the discovery of his lost physical ability to actively defend himself. It should also be noted that emotions of grief for himself and his dad followed the action, and Omar's therapist supported this emotional processing with empathic and attuned contact statements ("So much grief, huh?" "You wish it could have been different." "You seem sad for your dad's suffering, too."), facial expression, and prosody. The connection between the therapist and the client deepened as this long-dormant, empowering action emerged spontaneously, was executed and deeply experienced by Omar, and was seen as something he was entitled to do, and as grief was expressed. After Omar was able to execute his act of triumph, he said it was easier to maintain eye contact, with less feelings of anxiety. Experimenting with both boundaries and defensive actions supported his sense of self and feeling of safety, and enabled more relational contact.

Over many sessions, with the stabilizing skills gained in Phase 1 treatment, and the working through of several traumatic memories in Phase 2, Omar was ready to address more fully the Phase 3 treatment goals of increasing his capacity for intimacy and self-worth and challenging his "implicit relational knowing" (Lyons-Ruth, 1998). While Omar longed for a romantic partner, his fears of intimacy were reflected in his anxiety, physical tension, and a sense of wanting to run away in his legs that emerged when dating. These habits became the focus in Phase 3 treatment.

Proximity-seeking actions, such as reaching out to or moving toward another person, are hallmarks of close relationships, but they are abandoned or distorted when they are persistently ineffective in producing the desired outcome from caregivers or other important people. Such actions can become the targets of mindful exploration in Phase 3 treatment. The therapist asked Omar if he would be interested in noticing what happened if he reached out with his arm or arms toward the therapist. Omar agreed, and as he reached out, the part of him that had inhibited that action came forward, and Omar reported feeling "disgusting," which was accompanied by a pulling-away movement. At the same time, he felt an "obligation" to move toward his therapist, which he discovered was associated with "parenting" his father. When he was younger, he had translated for his dad, who could not speak English, and also took care of his father when he was intoxicated. Omar also remembered that his father sometimes berated him, including calling him "disgusting," and told him that he would never find a good wife. Omar reported that his father had experienced numerous rejections when he was dating American women, and he thought his father also felt unworthy. Omar cited other instances in which he tried to be an overly "nice Middle Eastern boy," to try to keep himself safe from the bullies at school, who had called him a "terrorist" after 9/11.

Exploring actions that are alternatives to habitual tendencies can bring forward parts of the client that are "inhospitable and even adversarial, sequestered from one another as islands of 'truth,' each functioning as an insulated version of reality" (Bromberg, 2010, p. 21). Omar became more fearful as he reached out, saying, "Thought comes up, 'I'm going to get hurt and humiliated,' 'I have to take care of you,' and 'I have to prove that I am worthy even though I am disgusting.' " He avoided eye contact, and images emerged of his father's angry face, alternating with his needy face, and of a teacher who stood by and did nothing to protect him from the bullies. These images were accompanied by hurt and sadness, which he had up to now held in check, but which Omar was able to express in the empathic presence of his therapist.

Eventually, Omar discovered new actions that supported reaching out: Using the grounding with the legs developed in Phase 1, he placed his hand in the middle of his chest, which helped him reach out to reassure the part of himself that felt disgusting. Omar then reached toward the therapist with the other arm. He reported that with this dual action he felt calm and strong, and able to take care of the part of him that felt disgusting, and even to convey a message that this part was likeable. Omar could sense himself and his body while reaching out to his therapist. His spine straightened, and he was able to maintain eye contact with the therapist without the anxiety or constricted smile. The therapist wondered if these gestures could be translated into words, and Omar replied, "I can support myself and connect with others at the same time." Remembering the words and the action helped Omar feel safe enough to begin to venture out into new social situations that he had previously avoided, including taking the risk of dating.

CONCLUSION

Mindfulness develops "the skill of seeing [the] internal world, and . . . shapes it toward integrative functioning" (Siegel, 2010, p. 223). It focuses attention on interrupting outdated implicit processing and creating new experiences: "the brain changes physically in response to experience, and new mental skills can be acquired with intentional effort with focused awareness and concentration" (Siegel, 2010, p. 84). In Sensorimotor Psychotherapy, mindfulness—specifically mindfulness embedded in the moment-to-moment interaction between therapist and client—is privileged over conversation. The therapist repeats directed mindfulness skills throughout the clinical hour, as illustrated in Figure 4.3.

The verbal narrative, while essential in clinical practice, cannot provide the same in-the-moment revelations about the habitual ways clients organize their experience that mindfulness can, nor can it directly facilitate a change in these habits. Even when the content that shaped patterns of organizing experience remains

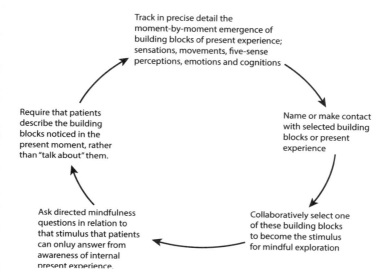

Figure 4.3: Clinical Map for Using Directed Mindfulness in Psychotherapy

unarticulated, or even unremembered, mindful to attention the building blocks reveals the here-and-now effects of past trauma and relational stress. Embedded relational mindfulness provides maps and tools to discover the implicit habits that were adaptive in the past but are restrictive in the present, so that they can be changed and new options can be explored.

REFERENCES

Arnsten, A. F. T. (2009). Stress signaling pathways that impair prefrontal cortex structure and function. *Nature Reviews Neuroscience, 10,* 410–422.

Beebe, B & Lachman, F. M. (2014). *The origins of attachment: Infant research and adult treatment.* New York, NY: Routledge.

Bromberg, P. M. (2006). *Awakening the dreamer: Clinical journeys.* Mahwah, NJ: Analytic Press.

Bromberg, P. M. (2010). Minding the dissociative gap. *Contemporary Psychoanalysis, 46*(1), 19–31.

Cannon, J. (2016). Education as a practice of freedom: A social justice proposal for mindfulness educators. In R. E. Purser, D. Forbes, & A. Burke (Eds.), *Handbook of mindfulness: Culture, context and social engagement* (pp. 397–410). New York: Springer.

Cortina, M., & Liotti, G. (2007). New approaches to understanding unconscious processes: Implicit and explicit memory systems. *International Forum of Psychoanalysis, 16*, 204–212.

Goldstein, J., & Kornfield, J. (1987). *Seeking the heart of wisdom: The path of insight meditation.* Boston, MA: Shambhala.

Harrell, S. P. (2000). A multidimensional conceptualization of racism-related stress: Implications for the well-being of people of color. *American Journal of Orthopsychiatry, 70*(1), 42–57.

Harrell, S. P. (2018). Being human together: Positive relationships in the context of diversity, culture, and collective well-being. In M. A. Warren & S. I. Donaldson. *Toward a positive psychology of relationships: New directions in theory and research* (pp. 247–284). Westport, CT: Praeger Publishing.

Harrell, S. P. & Sloan-Pena, G (2006). Racism and discrimination. In Y. Jackson (Ed.), *Encyclopedia of multicultural psychology* (pp. 396–402). Thousand Oaks CA: Sage.

Janet, P. (1898). *Neuroses et idées fixe.* Paris: Félix Alcan.

Janet, P. (1925). *Principles of psychotherapy.* London: George Allen and Unwin.

Kirmayer, L. J. (2015). Mindfulness in cultural context. *Transcultural Psychiatry, 52*(4), 447–469.

Kurtz, R. (1990). *Body-centered psychotherapy: The Hakomi method: The integrated use of mindfulness, nonviolence, and the body.* Mendocino, CA: LifeRhythm.

Kurtz, R. (2004). *Level 1 handbook for the refined Hakomi method.* Ron Kurtz Hakomi Educational Materials. http://hakomi.com/resources

Kurtz, R. (2010, January). *Readings in the Hakomi method of mindfulness-based assisted self-study.* Ron Kurtz Hakomi Educational Materials. http://hakomi.com/wp-content/uploads/2009/12/Readings-January-2010.pdf

Linehan, M. M. (1993). *Skills training manual for treating borderline personality disorder.* New York: Guilford.

Lyons-Ruth, K. (1998). Implicit relational knowing: Its role in development and psychoanalytic treatment. *Infant Mental Health Journal, 19,* 282–289.

Magee, R. V. (2016). Community-engaged mindfulness and social justice: An inquiry and call to action. In R. E. Purser, D. Forbes, & A. Burke (Eds.), *Handbook of mindfulness: Culture, context and social engagement* (pp. 425–440). New York: Springer.

Ogden, P. (2007). *Beyond words: A clinical map for using mindfulness of the body and the organization of experience in trauma treatment.* Paper presented at Mindfulness and Psychotherapy Conference, UCLA/Lifespan Learning Institute, Los Angeles.

Ogden, P. (2009). Emotion, mindfulness and movement: Expanding the regulatory boundaries of the window of affect tolerance. In D. Fosha, D. Siegel, & M. Solomon (Eds.), *The healing power of emotion: Perspectives from affective neuroscience and clinical practice* (pp. 204–231). New York: Norton.

Ogden, P. & Fisher, J. (2015). *Sensorimotor psychotherapy: interventions for trauma and attachment.* New York, NY: Norton.

Ogden, P., & Minton, K. (2000). Sensorimotor psychotherapy: One method for processing traumatic memory. *Traumatology, 6,* 1–20.

Ogden, P., Minton, K., & Pain, C. (2006). *Trauma and the body: A sensorimotor approach to psychotherapy.* New York: Norton.

Porges, S. W. (2004). Neuroception: A subconscious system for detecting threats and safety. *Zero to Three, 24*(5), 19–24. https://stephenporges .com/images/neuroception.pdf

Porges, S. W. (2011). *The polyvagal theory: Neurophysiological foundations of emotions, attachment, communication, and self-regulation.* New York: Norton.

Purser, R. E., Forbes, D., & Burke, A. (Eds.) (2016). *Handbook of mindfulness: Culture, context and social engagement.* New York: Springer.

Robins, C. J. (2002). Zen principles and mindfulness practice in dialectical behavior therapy. *Cognitive and Behavioral Practice, 9*(1), 50–57.

Schore, A. (2003). *Affect regulation and the repair of the self.* New York: Norton.

Schore, A. N. (2009). Right-brain affect regulation: An essential mechanism of development, trauma, dissociation, and psychotherapy. In D. Fosha, D. Siegel, & M. Solomon (Eds.), *The healing power of emotion: Affective neuroscience, development and clinical practice* (pp. 112–144). New York: Norton.

Schwabe, L., Joels, M., Roozendaal, B., Wolf, O. T., & Oitzl, M. S. (2012). Stress effects on memory: An update and integration. *Neuroscience and Biobehavioral Reviews, 36,* 1740–1749.

Segal, Z., Teasdale, J., & Williams, M. (2002). *Mindfulness-based cognitive therapy for depression.* New York: Guilford.

Siegel, D. (1999). *The developing mind: Toward a neurobiology of interpersonal experience.* New York: Guilford.

Siegel, D. (2007). *The mindful brain: Reflection and attunement in the cultivation of well-being.* New York: Norton.

Siegel, D. (2010). *The mindful therapist: A clinician's guide to mindsight and neural integration.* New York: Norton.

Surmitis, K. A., Fox, J., & Gutierrez, D. (2018). Meditation and appropria-
    tion: Best practices for counselors who utilize meditation. *Counseling
    and Values*, 63(1), 4–16. https://doi.org/10.1002/cvj.12069
Trousselard, M., Steiler, D., Claverie, D., & Canini, F. (2014). The history
    of mindfulness put to the test of current scientific data: Unresolved
    questions. *L'Encéphale: Revue de Psychiatrie Clinique Biologique et Thera-
    peutique, 40*(6), 474–480.
Williams, M., Teasdale, J., Segal, Z., & Kabat-Zinn, J. (2007). *The mind-
    ful way through depression: Freeing yourself from chronic unhappiness.* New
    York: Guilford.

Chapter 5

OPPRESSION, DEPRESSION, AND HYPOAROUSAL

Oppression is not simply understood in the mind—
—it is felt in the body in myriad ways.

PATRICIA HILL COLLINS

So many clients with trauma in their history complain of feeling sad, disinterested in life, unable to enjoy themselves, and challenged by normal daily activities. Causes of depression are complex, but unresolved and ongoing trauma is a significant determinant. In addition to physical, sexual, and emotional trauma, oppression and racism are shown to be convincing underlying factors contributing to depression (Banks & Kohn-Wood, 2007). Clinicians may fail to recognize the impact of systemic oppression on the depressive symptoms of their clients, compromising treatment outcomes. Along with ongoing societal racism, cissexism, transphobia, and so forth, healing from depression is further complicated by the transmission of transgenerational trauma when bodies and identities have historically been subjected to genocide, colonization, and enslavement, or otherwise dehumanized. The fact that these individuals must continue to live within the very structures and systems that seek to oppress them can impede resolution. Regardless of the cause, trauma-related depression often manifests as a perpetual physiological state of low arousal, which is characterized by a lack of emotion, motivation, and movement and sustained by a debilitating cycle of interaction between body and mind. These symptoms of depression prove difficult to treat, and therapists and clients alike may feel discouraged, perplexed, or defeated when therapeutic interventions fail to achieve the desired results again and again.

This chapter introduces three elements of Sensorimotor Psychotherapy that can help uplift the spirit so clients with trauma-related depression might reengage more fully in life: the "window of tolerance" map to assess dysregulated hypoarousal and regulated arousal; movement to discover and alter procedural patterns that contribute to depression; and embedded relational mindfulness to direct attention to specific elements of internal experience hypothesized to be helpful in alleviating depression. Interventions will be illustrated through describing a genderqueer client whose depression stems from the effects of cissexism and lack of support for their gender expression.

MODULATION: THE WINDOW OF TOLERANCE

The "window of tolerance" (Siegel, 1999) refers to a zone of autonomic and emotional arousal that is optimal for well-being and effective functioning. Falling between extremes of hyper- and hypoarousal, this is a zone within which "various intensities of emotional and physiological arousal can be processed without disrupting the functioning of the system" (Siegel, 1999, p. 253). When arousal falls within this window, information received from both internal and external environments can be integrated.

Most traumatized clients experience too much arousal (hyperarousal), and/or too little arousal (hypoarousal), and often oscillate between these two extremes (Ogden et al., 2006; Post et al., 1997; Van der Hart et al., 2006; Van der Kolk et al., 1996). Hyperaroused clients are typically hypervigilant and anxious, and suffer from intrusive images and dysregulated emotions. But hypoaroused clients endure another kind of torment stemming from a dearth of emotion and sensation—numbing, a sense of deadness or emptiness, passivity, and immobilization (Bremner & Brett, 1997; Ogden et al., 2006; Spiegel, 1997; Van der Hart et al., 2004). Prolonged shut-down states of hypoarousal are thought to contribute to depressive states.

The field of psychology has a long tradition of viewing particular behaviors as evidence of individual pathology. However, such behaviors can also be seen as adaptive strategies that have grown over time in response to oppression (Watts et al., 1999), as reasonable and coherent reactions. For example, historical trauma can result in depression due to "incomplete mourning" of transgenerational losses, such as language, tradition, and status (Duran et al., 1999). A transgender or genderqueer person may engage passive

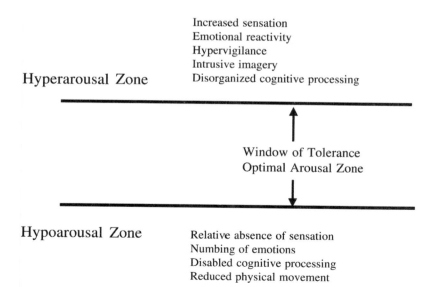

Figure 5.1: The Window of Tolerance

avoidance in the face of cissexism, transphobia, and lack of support for gender identity, which can contribute to depression. Sanders Thompson (2006) found that emotional numbing and behavioral inhibition were associated with avoidance when confronted with discrimination. Hoggard, Byrd, and Sellers (2012) discovered that although African American college students utilize active strategies under generalized stress, they use passive ones in the face of race- and oppression-related stress. Over time, excessive use of passive strategies for stress management, such as acceptance and resignation, may lead to increased feelings of isolation and lack of agency and may prove more detrimental than active strategies such as reaching out for support or working to solve the problem (Utsey et al., 2000). Moreover, "passive approaches to coping with racial discrimination such as keeping it to yourself or accepting it as a fact of life may exacerbate the effects of the resulting stress and promote harmful adaptations such as those exhibited in dissociative symptoms" (Polanco-Roman et al., 2016, p. 3). These findings support the hypothesis that discrimination and oppression may contribute to depression and shut-down states. At the same time, it should be reiterated that in the context of systemic historical and present-day oppression, passive strategies can prove to be the most adaptive, and should not be seen as only detrimental or as the equivalent to giving up. They occur when "social forces in the form of prejudice and discrimination are seen as too powerful to combat at that particular time" (Sue et al., 2019, p. 114).

In treatment, clients learn to recognize and assess their coping strategies as well as to identify the bodily signals of autonomic dysregulation (both hyper- and hypoarousal), and to develop a repertoire of resources to bring arousal into a window of tolerance. Those for whom traumatic events occurred in the past, who are now living in safe environments, can learn to stabilize arousal, resolving the dysregulation of past trauma. However, people who are living in oppressive circumstances, (e.g., societal cissexism, transphobia, racism, or poverty) are exposed to daily triggers. Traumatic events cannot be relegated to the past since they are occurring in the present time, which compromises the person's capacity for consistent stabilization. In these instances, learning resources to quickly regulate hypoarousal so that arousal returns to a window of tolerance can prevent protracted states of low arousal that may contribute to depression.

Bromberg (2006) states that therapy should occur in a climate that is "safe but not too safe." Addressing trauma or relational strife naturally evokes dyregulated arousal, even as the client feels safe with the therapist. This is desirable so clients can learn new resources that expand their ability to regulate. If arousal always remains within an optimal zone—"too safe"—new capacities to return dysregulated arousal to the window will not be learned. Navigating the effects of relational and traumatic stress challenges clients to increase their regulatory capacity, with the result of widening their window. On the other hand, if arousal is too dysregulated and greatly exceeds the window, the client is not "safe enough," and experience cannot be integrated.

Therapist and client must continuously evaluate the client's capacity to process at the regulatory boundaries of the window to ensure that arousal is dysregulated to a manageable degree so that the zone of optimal arousal can be expanded, but not so extreme as to sacrifice integration. Once arousal is at the regulatory boundary—in the case of depression at the hypoarousal boundary—it is imperative to avoid stimulating additional emotional or physiological hypoarousal or executing physical actions that cause further dysregulation at the expense of integration, and to work instead at the boundary with intention toward integration. The oppressive forces of cissexism, transphobia, sexism and so forth can result in shutdown, hypoarousal states that, when prolonged for extended periods of time, can feel like or possibly even induce depression. Address-

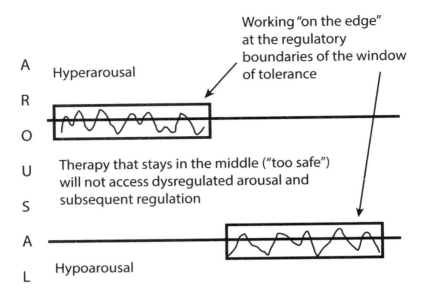

Figure 5.2: "Safe, but Not Too Safe"

ing the effects of past and ongoing oppression as well as other traumas, expressing painful emotions, and executing new resourcing and empowering actions might provide an antidote to depression, and serve to expand affect array and even increase the client's capacity for positive affect.

MOVEMENT: CHALLENGING PROCEDURAL MEMORIES

Most human behavior is driven by procedural memory, the memory for physical processes—the "how" rather than the "what" or "why." Consistently negative attachment experiences and unresolved trauma, including the relational trauma of systemic oppression such as being attacked or rejected for one's gender identity, all

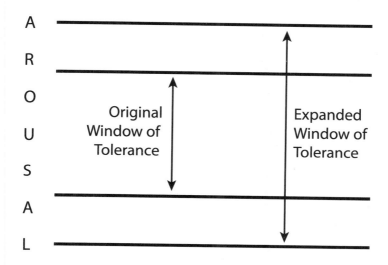

Figure 5.3: Expand the Regulatory Boundaries of the Window of Tolerance to Integrate Previously Dissociated Emotions, Expand Affect Array and Intensity

leave their imprint on procedural memory, shaping the posture and movements habits of the body. Some physical patterns that develop, such as a sunken chest, limp arms, and shallow breath, can reinforce chronic negative emotions and cognitive distortions and constrict affect array. Powerful determinants of current behavior, enduring procedural patterns are formed by repeated iterations of physical movements.

Characterized by automatic, reflexive performance, procedural learning becomes an even more potent influence because its relative lack of verbal articulation renders most procedural behavior unavailable for thoughtful reflection. Even when stressful conditions have changed, we remain in a state of readiness to perform the procedurally learned actions adaptive in the past. And many oppressive societal conditions have not changed: for example, cissexism continues to create a lack of safety for those who identify with a different gender than assigned at birth.

In therapy, clients learn to execute new physical actions that challenge their procedural tendencies and develop the somatic resources to support resilience in the face of ongoing discrimination and other stressors. As clients identify their triggers and the initial physical signals indicating that their arousal is becoming dysregulated, they can intervene with physical action to quickly return arousal to a window of tolerance. Replacing a slumped posture and shallow breath with an aligned, erect but relaxed posture, full breathing, and supple tonicity can mitigate trauma-related hypoarousal, and additionally may support a positive sense of self, increase resilience, and alleviate depression. Learning actions of boundaries and defense, such as pushing away, can mitigate the immobilizing defenses of freezing and feigned death that often accompany trauma-related depression. Clients can also learn a variety of actions that engage a wide range of emotions, including positive affect. For example, adaptive anger is supported by increased alignment of the spine, a degree of physical tension, and the capacity to push away or strike out; joy by an uplifting of the spine and expansive movement; empathy by a softening of the face and chest, and perhaps a gentle reaching out; play by a tilt of the head, and spontaneous, rapid changes in movement. Executing these movements and experiencing the accompanying emotions can mitigate passive strategies and shut-down states, and help to expand the regulatory boundaries of the window of tolerance.

EMBEDDED RELATIONAL MINDFULNESS: DIRECTING ATTENTION

In therapy, clients are taught to mindfully observe their procedural tendencies—the movements, sensations, impulses, posture, and gesture—and to notice the interplay of these tendencies with cognitions, emotions, and perceptions. Therapist and client together "study what is going on, not as disease or something to be rid of, but in an effort to help the client become conscious of how experience is managed and how the capacity for experience can be expanded" (Kurtz, 1990, p. 111). Through mindfulness, clients shift from being caught up in the story and upset about their reactions to becoming curious and interested in their internal experience. They discover the difference between having an experience and exploring their procedural tendencies here and now, in reaction to ongoing as well as long-ago traumatic events, and how these tendencies influence their responses to current challenges.

In the Western conceptualization (cf. Chapter 4, this volume), mindfulness is generally thought of as a state of awareness that is receptive to whatever elements of experience arise in the mind's eye. However, when mindfulness is used in therapy with open-ended interventions, clients may find themselves at the mercy of dysregulated arousal and internal experiences that appear most vividly in the forefront of consciousness, which can perpetuate hypoarousal-fueled depression. Instead of allowing the client's attention to drift randomly toward whatever emotions, memories, or thoughts might emerge, "directed mindfulness" (Ogden, 2007) interventions guide the client's awareness toward particular elements of present-moment experience that are thought to support therapeutic goals.

THE CLIENT

A single white genderqueer person in their late 30s, Blake (who used the pronoun "they") had recently discontinued their previous therapy because the therapist consistently misgendered them, which conveys a lack of respect and denial of self-designated identity (Galupo et al., 2020; Mizock & Lundquist, 2016). Misgendering is correlated with depression, gender dysphoria, anxiety, and stress

(Galupo et al., 2020). When misgendering or other cissexist micro-aggressions occur in therapy, past attachment ruptures are triggered, calling for intentional, gender-affirming repair that is often unavailable (Lindsay Elin, personal communication February 6, 2021). Blake faced such interpersonal and structural cissexism daily, both in public—at work, at school, on the bus—and in private in a family that sanctioned cissexism, and thus were unable to support their gender expression. Blake was haunted by memories of these offenses and of early sexual abuse. Although they maintained a high level of functioning as a network administrator, they reported few close friends, social isolation, an inability to enjoy life, and a yearning for a romantic partner.

Blake appeared depressed. As they walked into the office, the therapist noted their posture was slumped and they walked with a heavy and plodding gait, and sat quite still on the sofa, head down. Blake's curly, dark hair was cut in a short modern style, and they came to sessions often dressed in baggy jeans, T-shirt, and sneakers. Internally the therapist felt a sense of numbness in Blake's presence, as if something about their general presentation lacked aliveness. There was visible tension across their hunched shoulders, and a lack of movement throughout the body. Blake's speech was flat, punctuated by sighs, and lacked vitality and enthusiasm.

Blake and their therapist determined that they would begin with physical interventions targeted at their slumped posture. This intervention was chosen in the hope of evoking a more positive outlook. It has been found that "adopting an upright seated posture in the face of stress can maintain self-esteem, reduce negative mood, and increase positive mood compared to a slumped posture" (Nair et al., 2015, p. 632). The therapist suggested that positioning their legs and feet squarely under the body and aligning their spine so that the head could sit centered over their shoulders would support an ergonomic posture and might also lead to more vitality and confidence. First, the therapist asked Blake to explore their lack of alignment by standing and slightly exaggerating their head jutting forward, tail tucked under, shoulders hunched, and spine curved. As Blake mindfully observed the emotions and thoughts that spontaneously emerged while they exaggerated the habitual posture, they discovered that the purpose of this posture was to keep themselves small and safe, in the hope of remaining unnoticed. The slumped posture went hand in hand with feelings of inferiority, helplessness, and passivity that they had felt even as a child. Gender-creative children like Blake growing up in homes that do not recognize gender expressions outside of the binaries of male and female face significant psychological distress when their self-designated identity is not validated or accepted (Ehrensaft, 2012, 2014).

Blake's therapist guided them to imagine being lifted upward by the crown of their head while sensing their feet firmly planted on the ground and allowing the spine to straighten and the chest to lift. This posture enhanced their breathing and permitted their head to rest squarely on their shoulders. Blake reported that indeed, this new posture "felt better" and raised their arousal level. Blake's thoughts correspondingly started to become less negative and their emotions more buoyant.

Although this somatic resource did not resolve Blake's underlying depression, it did alleviate their tendency to slump and provided them with a tangible practice (they called it "standing tall") that they could use to feel better. Standing tall countered Blake's usual feeling that they could take no action in the face of feeling helpless and inferior. While the new posture felt awkward initially, Blake agreed to practice it daily, and gradually it became increasingly more natural and comfortable.

Blake had reported multiple experiences in social situations where they felt at risk of physical harm as a genderqueer person, and in these situations they felt safer in a slumped posture. So they found comfort in the fact that an upright posture could also be practiced discreetly, which allowed them both to feel empowered in their body and to preserve their sense of safety, especially in unfamiliar social groups. Blake learned to sense the physical support of their spine even within a slightly slumped posture, take deeper, regular breaths, sense their feet firmly on the ground, and differentiate their painful experiences as a gender-expansive child without gender-affirming caregiver support from their experience as a competent adult who could take positive action to modulate their excessively low arousal.

After a few months of treatment with a primary focus on developing somatic resources like the alignment described above, Blake began to discuss a longing for more ease in social situations. Their desire for increased social engagement also signaled to the therapist that Blake's window was expanding, which increased their capacity for pleasurable experience. Abused by their father throughout childhood, taunted by peers for their nonconforming gender expressions, and with no support from family members or teachers for their gender identity, Blake said their body was always tense in childhood. Eventually they withdrew as much as possible from family and shunned play dates with other kids. As an adult, this muscular tension remained, and although Blake desperately longed for a romantic partner and meaningful friendships, the tension and accompanying fear were exacerbated at the thought of social contact. Blake's childhood experiences of cissexism and transphobia were often replicated when they were in social situations. Blake said that people stared at them, constantly misgendered them, and asked intrusive and inappropriate questions about their gender expression such as, "So, are you a man or . . . ?" Blake said that when they thought of being with others, their first impulse was to withdraw and shut down, a familiar strategy they had used over decades when facing discrimination and microaggressions.

Their therapist suggested experimenting with the physical distance between the two of them with the intention of first exploring and appreciating the protective intent of Blake's passive coping strategy, and then discovering an active alternative to shutting down in the face of relational challenges. Blake and the therapist stood at opposite ends of the office, and Blake slowly walked toward the therapist while mindfully noticing their physical reactions. This exercise was intended to stimulate Blake's procedural tendencies related to social contact, and indeed, Blake reported that the tension in their body increased as they reached a distance of about six feet from the therapist. Blake felt a constriction of breath and tension in their viscera, and expressed feeling increasingly uncomfortable as the proximity increased. Soon, they felt themselves shutting down. The ensuing tension, emotional numbing, and physical prepared-ness to move away and withdraw felt familiar to them. Blake said they were afraid of what the therapist would want from them if they sought to be close. Memories emerged about being forced to submit to unwanted contact, often abusive, in relationship to their father.

Blake's tension and numbing were also linked to devastating childhood experiences of shaming by others and their subsequent attempts to suppress their gender identity. They said that safety in their childhood was found through conforming to gender norms. As a child, Blake reported that they were made to wear dresses, play with dolls, and otherwise conform to stereotypical female behavior, clothing, postures, and so forth. Blake realized that as a child they wondered if their non-stereotypical gender expression was the rea-son their father abused them. These realizations were accompanied by reexperiencing the pain and despair that Blake had felt as a child, this time with the empathic support of their therapist.

Blake's window of tolerance expanded through processing of these painful early experiences over many therapy sessions, and practicing new actions. They and their therapist continued to exper-iment with proximity between them, and Blake eventually learned to consciously refrain from tightening their body, to take a deep breath, and sense their spine. Blake also tried compatible mental actions—such as repeating to themselves that they were no longer a child and that they did not have to do anything they did not want to do. These strategies, practiced first with their therapist, were also applied when in social situations, with positive results for Blake.

Eventually, Blake was ready to directly address memories of the sexual abuse by their father. When traumatized clients first turn their attention to traumatic memories, they typically become aware of disempowering, immobilizing defenses rather than triumphant actions, and Blake was no exception. As they first talked about the abuse, Blake became aware of increased physical tension, but then reported spacing out and feeling "nothing," signs of hypoarousal, a dissociative response in the face of childhood trauma that contributed to their passive coping strategies of withdrawal as an adult. The therapist directed them to be mindful of their body and see if there was anything that came to their attention. Blake noticed a very slight tightening in the jaw and throat, indicative of a possible active defense, since tension is a precursor to action. As they stayed with the constriction, and the therapist asked if there were words that went along with the tension, Blake said they wanted to shout, "Stop." This was an impulse they may have had during childhood, but wisely refrained from expressing because such assertive action most likely would have made their father angry. Blake and their therapist decided that on the count of three they would shout the word "Stop" together. Their therapist shouting along with Blake conveyed relational support for assertion and the right to defend themselves, which they had not experienced from others in childhood. Blake reported that it felt good that someone was on their side, saying they felt empowered and more energetic.

In Sensorimotor Psychotherapy, clients are helped to rediscover their truncated physical defensive impulses to push away, strike out, or run away that were not executed during abuse or other traumatic situations. Discovering and physically enacting these empowering active defenses in therapy can be effective in mitigating present-day patterns of passive coping, hypoarousal, and depression. As Blake remembered a particularly disturbing abusive event, they reported a small movement of their fists, a curling that seemed to be indicative of a larger aggressive movement. The therapist asked Blake to sense their fist curling and notice any action their body might want to make, directing them to allow any impulse to emerge from their awareness of their body. Blake became aware of a physical impulse to strike out, and slowly executed this motion against a pillow held by the therapist. Being able to be mindful of how their body wanted to respond enabled awareness of the previously halted physical urge to not only punch their father but also run away, reflected in a tightening and feeling of energy in their legs. Note that these physical actions did not emerge from thinking about what action to make; they appeared without conscious prompting as Blake mindfully sensed the physical sensations and impulses that emerged spontaneously as they recalled the abuse. After executing the action of the fighting by pushing against the pillow and of fleeing by running in place, Blake again reported feeling empowered, and said that their body was "coming alive."

Later in therapy, Blake's hands spontaneously came up in a protective gesture as they remembered their father coming into their bedroom. As their therapist asked Blake to notice this movement, they expressed being ashamed, and said they wanted to curl up and hide. As they followed the impulse to curl up, Blake tearfully said that as a child they thought they deserved this abuse—that they were being punished for their gender expression. As the shame was processed, Blake began to believe that the abuse was not their fault—they were only a little child when it happened, and their gender identity should have been supported and celebrated. With these realizations, Blake reported a tension in their arms and a feeling of anger—contrary to the usual pattern of helplessness, shame, and fear, all of which were associated with hypoarousal-related depression.

In previous therapy, Blake had repeatedly expressed shame and helplessness, but their propensity to first dissolve into tears and then shut down contributed to their depression and feelings of being unable to take action. These patterns prevented the emotional and physical responses, such as anger and assertive action, that helped to alleviate their depression. Once Blake recovered their anger at what had happened and was able to execute protective physical actions, such as pushing away, they reported a core feeling of empowerment and strength. This was reflected in an effortless upright posture and deeper breath, and from this stance, the future looked more promising to Blake. Together, they and their therapist shared deep appreciation for these gains, and Blake began to cry softly. They expressed a depth of grief at the loss of the innocent trust in their father that they had treasured as a very young child. Blake also expressed profound grief at the injustice they and children like them face as gender-creative kids living in cissexist families and communities that do not support them. The therapist's ongoing empathic contact with the pain of such injustice and celebration of Blake's identity helped them differentiate their world today from their abusive childhood. Their very powerful emotion of grief was accompanied by a surge of energizing arousal, challenging the upper regulatory boundaries of Blake's window of tolerance, which they were able to experience without extreme dysregulation. Afterward, Blake reported feeling a new sense of energy, along with a softening in their body. The depression was beginning to lift.

Over time, Blake's wish for a romantic partner came to the fore. Their therapist encouraged them to be mindful of their body as they felt their desire for a partner, and Blake experienced a softening in their entire body. They said that they felt less defensive and more vulnerable as the body softened, and then said they could also feel the longing for connection in their heart. Blake and their therapist explored sensing the longing in the heart and initiating a reaching-out movement from the core of their body through the arms. Blake first said that the thought of reaching out made them uncomfortable. When they did eventually reach out, their arm was stiff, the movement was awkward, and their body tightened again. Blake said the gesture felt unfamiliar, and that they felt more vulnerable, again afraid of having to meet the other's needs and suppress their true gender expression. Blake became sad, and their old belief emerged again as they said, "Others will use and hurt me if I reach out." Giving way once again to strong feelings of anger and hurt about the past helped to soften Blake's aversion to intimacy as well as to relax their body.

Blake first practiced actions of reaching out merely as a somatic exercise, attending only to the physical action itself—noticing the muscles that were engaged, experimenting with palm open or facing down, with the angle of the elbow, the degree of alignment in their spine, and so forth—with no psychological content until these actions were comfortable. Blake gradually became physically accustomed to maintaining a relaxed upright posture while reaching with palm up and their elbow bent slightly. Then they added eye contact as they practiced reaching out in this way to their therapist, which brought up a long-forgotten childhood longing for their mother's approval and her protection from abuse and misrecognition, and Blake again wept with grief. Naturally, these new motor actions were accompanied by new meanings: Blake began to express the conviction that perhaps it would be safe to reach out in their current life, that they knew everyone was not like their father, not every situation was going to be a repeat of the misrecognition of their past, and that they could now choose social situations that would welcome them and their gender expression, and they could walk away from those that did not. Eventually, Blake began spontaneously reaching out to others instead of isolating and shutting down, which had been their tendency for so long. One new and nourishing way that Blake began reaching out was through exploring community groups that organized and advocated for the LGBTQ+ community.

Blake also verbalized a desire to be more playful. Their history of abuse, misattunement, and misrecognition truncated playfulness, which is challenged in the shadow of threat and danger, a fact that can carry far-ranging consequences characteristic of the plight of traumatized individuals. During the course of therapy, Blake and their therapist practiced other movements that facilitated playfulness and lightness of spirit, such as exchanging their plodding gait for a bouncy, head-up walk, and their hunched shoulders and rounded spine for an upright, shoulders-down posture that encouraged eye contact and engagement with others. They and their therapist giggled, as together they exaggerated the bounce and talked about what life would be like if they sustained this playful bounce. Over time, with continued practice, Blake's new upright posture and movements became more natural, and their enjoyment of social interactions increased. Blake's ability to use somatic resources to recover quickly when they felt their arousal approaching hypoarousal due to ongoing oppression they faced in daily life became more effortless.

CONCLUSION

We cannot change what happened in the past, and the work to change systemic oppression such as the cissexism that Blake experiences is ongoing. However, we can help clients change the procedural tendencies and hypoarousal patterns that they may have formed in response to past and ongoing trauma that contribute to depression. Therapeutic change is supported by mindfully challenging and changing procedural tendencies that sustain hypoarousal and depression resulting from personal and systemic trauma.

Sensorimotor Psychotherapy interventions that directly challenge procedural habits and regulate hypoarousal help clients to feel empowered even in the face of ongoing stress of systemic oppression. Clients can be engaged in mindful observation of the interplay of their perceptions, emotions, movements, sensations, impulses, and thoughts to discover procedural tendencies, and then to change them. Innate physical regulatory capacities, or somatic resources, become spontaneously available or can be evoked by the therapist: resources such as taking a breath, adjusting the spine, making a movement, and orienting perceptually and physically to the environment—all of which can help arousal quickly return to a window of tolerance in the face of ongoing societal oppression. Through mindful attention to the body, clients become aware of the previously aborted physical impulses that they did not and could not act upon in the past, often because they would not have been capable at that time of producing a desirable outcome. As clients discover these truncated movements—from defensive actions such as pushing, striking out, kicking, or running, to actions that support relationships, such as reaching out, making eye contact, opening up, or letting go—passive strategies are exchanged for active ones, and action replaces shutting down.

Oppression takes many forms, from the unfair or cruel use of authority and control to being emotionally dominated, mistreated, or bullied, to being deprived of professional, financial, or personal opportunity. Cissexism, transphobia and transmisogyny profoundly impact a person in unique ways. In childhood, the safety of early attachment relationships is profoundly compromised when caregivers subtly convey that the child is not the person they want them to be, engage in overt transphobia and "conversion" attempts, or fail to provide needed support and advocacy, all of which can shame a child or threaten a child's sense of safety and protection (Lindsay Elin, personal communication, February 4, 2021). These early relationships, along with living in a society that enforces a cisgender norm, impacts posture and movement, as we have seen. While words are necessary in the treatment of such traumas, they cannot take the place of the thoughtful therapeutic facilitation of the client's actual experience of empowering, adaptive, physical actions, and choosing to respond in a self-affirming manner (which can include not responding) to current acts of oppression. The satisfaction and pleasure of finally being able to know and perform direct physical actions such as those described above alter the somatic sense of self in a way that talking alone does not. Knowing, feeling, and doing—and thus experiencing—these physical actions helps to reorganize the way in which clients consciously and unconsciously hold and organize their understanding of past and current traumas, and may prove effective in the treatment of depression. As clients change their more passive procedural tendencies through movement, along with addressing emotions and beliefs, they change the way they respond to the stresses of their current life and the way they envision the future.

REFERENCES

Banks, K., & Kohn-Wood, L. (2007). The influence of racial identity profiles on the relationship between racial discrimination and depressive symptoms. *Journal of Black Psychology, 33,* 331–354. doi:10.1177/0095798407302540

Bremner, J. D., & Brett, E. (1997). Trauma-related dissociative states and long-term psychopathology in posttraumatic stress disorder. *Journal of Traumatic Stress, 10,* 37–49.

Bromberg, P. M. (2006). *Awakening the dreamer: Clinical journeys.* Mahwah, NJ: Analytic Press.

Duran, B., Duran, E., & Brave Heart, M. Y. H. (1999). Native Americans and the trauma of history. In R. Thornton (Ed.), *Studying Native America: Problems and prospects* (pp. 60–76). Madison: University of Wisconsin Press.

Ehrensaft, D. (2012). From gender identity disorder to gender identity creativity: True gender self child therapy. *Journal of Homosexuality, 59*(3), 337–356.

Ehrensaft, D. (2014). Listening and learning from gender-nonconforming children. *Psychoanalytic Study of the Child, 68,* 28–56.

Galupo, M. P., Pulice-Farrow, L., & Lindley, L. (2020). "Every time I get gendered male, I feel a pain in my chest": Understanding the social context for gender dysphoria. *Stigma and Health, 5*(2), 199–208. https://doi.org/10.1037/sah0000189

Hoggard, L. S., Byrd, C. M., & Sellers, R. M. (2012). Comparison of African American college students' coping with racially and nonracially stressful events. *Cultural Diversity and Ethnic Minority Psychology, 18*(4), 329.

Kurtz, R. (1990). *Body-centered psychotherapy: The Hakomi method: The integrated use of mindfulness, nonviolence, and the body.* Mendocino, CA: LifeRhythm.

Mizock, L., & Lundquist, C. (2016). Missteps in psychotherapy with transgender clients: Promoting gender sensitivity in counseling and psychological practice. *Psychology of Sexual Orientation and Gender Diversity, 3*(2), 148.

Nair, S., Sagar, M., Sollers, J., III, Consedine, N., & Broadbent, E. (2015). Do slumped and upright postures affect stress responses? A randomized trial. *Health Psychology, 34*(6), 632–641. https://doi.org/10.1037/hea0000146

Ogden, P. (2007). *Beneath the words: A clinical map for using mindfulness of the body and the organization of experience in trauma treatment.* Paper presented at Mindfulness and Psychotherapy Conference, UCLA/Lifespan Learning Institute, Los Angeles.

Ogden, P., Minton, K., & Pain, C. (2006). *Trauma and the body: A sensorimotor approach to psychotherapy.* New York: Norton.

Polanco-Roman, L., Danies, A., & Anglin, D. (2016). Racial discrimination as race-based trauma, coping strategies, and dissociative symptoms among emerging adults. *Psychological Trauma: Theory, Research, Practice, and Policy, 8*(5), 609–617.

Post, R., Weiss, S., Smith, M., Li, H., & McCann, U. (1997). Kindling versus quenching: Implications for the evolution and treatment of posttraumatic stress disorder. In R. Yehuda & A. C. McFarlane (Eds.), *Psychobiology of posttraumatic stress disorder* (pp. 285–295). New York: New York Academy of Sciences.

Sanders Thompson, V. L. (2006). Coping responses and the experience of discrimination. *Journal of Applied Social Psychology, 36*(5), 1198–1214.

Siegel, D. (1999). *The developing mind: Toward a neurobiology of interpersonal experience.* New York: Guilford.

Spiegel, D. (1997). Trauma, dissociation, and memory. *Annals of the New York Academy of Sciences, 821,* 225–237.

Sue, D. W., Sue, D., Neville, H. A., & Smith, L. (2019). *Counseling the culturally diverse: Theory and practice.* Hoboken, NJ: Wiley and Sons.

Utsey, S. O., Ponterotto, J. G., Reynolds, A. L., & Cancelli, A. A. (2000). Racial discrimination, coping, life satisfaction, and self-esteem among African Americans. *Journal of Counseling & Development, 78*(1), 72–80. https://doi.org/10.1002/j.1556-6676.2000.tb02562.x

Van der Hart, O., Nijenhuis, E., & Steele, K. (2006). *The haunted self.* New York: Norton.

Van der Hart, O., Nijenhuis, E., Steele, K., & Brown, D. (2004). Trauma-related dissociation: Conceptual clarity lost and found. *Australia and New Zealand Journal of Psychiatry, 38,* 906–914.

Van der Kolk, B., van der Hart, O., & Marmar, C. (1996). Dissociation and information processing in posttraumatic stress disorder. In B. van der Kolk, A. McFarlane, & L. Weisaeth (Eds.), *Traumatic stress: The effects of overwhelming experience on mind, body, and society* (pp. 303–327). New York: Guilford.

Watts, R. J., Griffith, D. M., & Abdul-Adil, J. (1999). Sociopolitical development as an antidote for oppression—theory and action. *American Journal of Community Psychology, 27*(2), 255–271.

Chapter 6

A SENSORIMOTOR PSYCHOTHERAPY APPROACH TO COMPLEX TRAUMA

with Clare Pain and Janina Fisher

> *But if one observes, one will see that the body has its own intelligence; it requires a great deal of intelligence to observe the intelligence of the body.*
>
> KRISHNAMURTI

Psychotherapists who work with survivors of psychological trauma recognize the almost inevitable clinical complexity of trauma-related disorders. Traumatized individuals do not just suffer from memories of tragic and horrifying experiences: They demonstrate a number of complicated and debilitating signs, symptoms, and difficulties including, importantly, bodily responses to dysregulated affects. These often have no clear subjective connection to their fragments of narrative memory (North et al., 1999), a disconnection that is even more pervasive in cases of historical trauma, when the effects of cumulative emotional and psychological trauma are carried across generations. Additionally, most traumatized individuals meet criteria for a number of coexisting diagnoses, which usually include mood disorders, anxiety disorders, substance abuse and dependence disorders, eating disorders, somatoform disorders, personality disorders, and medically unexplained symptoms (Courtois & Ford, 2009;

Davidson et al., 1991; Faustman & White, 1989; Kulka et al., 1990). With differences between the *DSM-5* and the *ICD-11*, the diagnosis of PTSD according to the *DSM-5* requires the person to have suffered or witnessed a traumatic experience as defined in criterion A, as well as endorsing symptoms from different clusters' criteria: intrusion and reexperiencing; persistent avoidance; negative alterations in cognitions and mood; and marked alterations in arousal and reactivity, with a duration of more than 1 month, and demonstrating clinically significant distress and impairment, and the disturbance cannot be attributed to the physiological effects of a substance or another medical condition (American Psychological Association, 2013).

The episodic alternation between avoidance and reliving symptoms is the result of traumatic events, both current and historical, that are "distanced and dissociated from usual conscious awareness in the numbing phase, only to return in the intrusive phase" (Chu, 1998). Triggered by stimuli reminiscent of the trauma, these relived dissociated fragments of past experience return unbidden in the form of both psychological symptoms (amnesia, cognitive distortions, feelings of badness or worthlessness, intrusive images, dysregulated emotions) and somatoform symptoms in any of the five sensory systems of smell, hearing, sight, touch, or taste as well as physical pain, physical numbing, intrusive sensations, and dysregulated autonomic arousal (Brewin et al., 1996).

Moreover, PTSD diagnostic criterion A fails to explicitly include collective experiences of systemic oppression, despite evidence documenting their impact (Holmes et al., 2016). Not only do marginalized populations experience a disproportionate occurrence of traumatic and invalidating events due to discrimination and social violence, but their symptoms are often exacerbated by other vulnerabilities, such as poverty, poor access to and quality of health care, and structural racism (Brave Heart & DeBruyn, 1998; Holmes et al., 2016; SAMHSA, 2014), which may lead to chronic somatization of symptoms. If the trauma of oppression were to be included in criterion A, as Holmes et al. (2016) advocate, we would most likely see many more cases of PTSD. However, even when the collective experiences of trauma and systemic oppression are acknowledged, the diagnosis focuses on individual pathology, and these systemic causes are unrecognized, which disproportionately impacts already marginalized individuals and their communities.

Despite the central involvement of the bodily experience and expression of unresolved trauma, the autonomic and somatic/sensory components of trauma-related disorders have been relatively neglected in both the understanding and treatment of these disorders (Van der Kolk, 1994, 2015). Although the body is receiving increased attention in treatment, especially by highlighting exercise or yoga-related modalities, which are beneficial, few therapeutic modalities attend directly to the movement, posture, and physiology of the body to resolve the effects of trauma.

TALK THERAPIES AND EXPOSURE THERAPY

Although there is evidence to suggest that treatments targeting the various psychological symptoms and problems of trauma-related disorders can promote significant improvement in some clients, full remediation of these disorders is elusive (Bradley et al., 2005; Ursano et al., 2004). These traditional talk therapy approaches, which include any method that depends on the words of the client as the primary entry point of therapy, address the explicit, verbally accessible memory of trauma. They emphasize the role of narrative, emotional expression, and meaning making (Brewin & Holmes, 2003; Herman, 1992). However, because avoidance and withdrawal help the client avoid triggering the reexperiencing of psychologically distressing PTSD symptoms, exposure has been seen as a necessary component to the evidence-based treatment of PTSD. Prolonged exposure (Powers et al., 2010), one of the first evidence-based exposure therapies, has two exposure components. Imaginal exposure to the potent elements of the client's trauma experience, during which the client is helped to speak of what happened, followed by behavioral desensitization to the feared and avoided stimuli as homework. A sizable number of clients do drop out of exposure therapy, perhaps because they are not sufficiently stable to manage the exposure without the threat of retraumatization (Swift, & Greenberg, 2014).

In addition to prolonged exposure, various other trauma-focused therapies are now recognized as evidence based for the treatment of PTSD, such as trauma-focused cognitive-behavior therapy (TF-CBT), EMDR, cognitive processing therapy, narrative exposure therapy (NET), and more (American Psychological Association, 2017). In a 2014 meta-analysis of trauma-focused versus non-trauma-focused therapy, the former were found to be more helpful than non-trauma-focused therapies (Ehring et al., 2014). However, there are traumatized populations where evidence is lacking for the effectiveness of exposure techniques and their necessity in all PTSD therapies. Markowitz and colleagues (2015) have found that interpersonal therapy is an effective treatment for PTSD despite the fact that it does not include an exposure component.

Populations who are still undergoing targeted violence, such as people caught up in war, or people living with systemic oppression where they are repeatedly confronted by societal triggers, discrimination, and the threat of assault, may not be well served by exposure therapy. Similarly, refugees who have fled from their country following torture and systemic violence do not require exposure therapies to recover (Kanagaratnam et al., 2017). For clients who experience ongoing trauma and violence, for refugees, and for complex clients who are not adequately stable, interventions that promote emotional and physiological regulation are advised. A focus on emotional literacy, where the client is encouraged to recognize, name, feel, and welcome their embodied emotions as sources of important information can assist affect regulation. Identifying the triggers and physical signs of dysregulation and then learning resources to return arousal to the window of tolerance quickly will prevent prolonged dysregulation. For example, recognizing the need to set boundaries and limit current exposure to traumas such as restricting watching TV reports of police violence, violent movies, and so forth can help prevent a client from feeling overwhelmed and supports a sense of mastery to keep arousal within their window of tolerance. In the next section, more advanced sensorimotor techniques with regard to the window of tolerance are discussed.

Clients who are easily overwhelmed by trauma memories when triggered by present stimuli often find the implicit somatosensory components of their memory are activated by their narrative (explicit memory), frequently leading to a reexperiencing of somatoform symptoms, which can include autonomic dysregulation, dissociative defenses associated with hyper- and hypoarousal states, intrusive sensory experiences, and involuntary impulses and movements. This debilitating, repetitive cycle of mind-body triggering can thwart desensitizing regimes and keep past trauma alive, prolonging rather than resolving trauma-related disorders (Kepner, 1987; LeDoux, 1996; Rothschild, 2000; Siegel, 1999; Van der Hart & Steele, 1999; Van der Kolk, McFarlane, et al., 1996). Similarly, collective institutionalized historical trauma narratives can trigger implicit somatosensory responses in individuals, families, and groups, especially when resiliency factors are not included in the retelling of the stories (Brave Heart & DeBruyn, 1998; Kellerman, 2001; Mohatt et al., 2014).

TOP-DOWN AND BOTTOM-UP THERAPIES

It is the sensorimotor symptoms and the autonomic dysregulation of chronic traumatic reexperiencing and avoidance that prove difficult to ameliorate, even with relatively straightforward PTSD clients who have single-incident traumatic experience as adults. To address these body-based symptoms of trauma as well as the psychological components, a different approach to treatment may be helpful. We propose weaving sensorimotor understandings and techniques into existing psychodynamic or cognitive-behavioral models of therapy, including exposure treatments (Chefetz, 2004). The working premise in most approaches to psychotherapy, less so with exposure techniques, is that change occurs in a top-down direction. That is, a significant change in a client's thought processes (either through insight or cognitive restructuring), in conjunction with remembering or therapeutic reexperiencing of the event, will resolve the problematic emotions, behaviors, and physical symptoms of the client. Although top-down therapy is effective and necessary in helping clients with many important therapeutic tasks, the addition of bottom-up approaches that directly address the effects of traumatic experience on the body may be equally necessary to resolve the symptoms of trauma-related disorders.

Sensorimotor Psychotherapy (Ogden & Fisher, 2015; Ogden & Minton, 2000; Ogden, et al., 2006) is an approach developed specifically to address the symptoms of chronic trauma and relational strife. This method supports clients to develop somatic resources to promote resilience and the ability to return physiological arousal to a window of tolerance, necessary skills for those suffering from ongoing trauma and traumatic triggers, including oppressed and marginalized people. In Sensorimotor Psychotherapy for the treatment of trauma, bodily experience becomes the primary entry point for intervention, while emotional expression and meaning making often arise out of the subsequent somatic reorganization of habitual trauma-related responses. That is, sensorimotor approaches work primarily from the bottom up rather than the top down in the treatment of trauma. By attending to the client's body experience directly, the more primitive, automatic, and involuntary functions of the brain and body that underlie traumatic and posttraumatic experiences are addressed.

Sensorimotor Psychotherapy is founded on the premise that "the brain functions as an integrated whole but is composed of systems that are hierarchically organized. The 'higher level' [cognitive] integrative functions evolved from and are dependent on the integrity of 'lower-level' [limbic and reptilian] structures and on sensorimotor experience" (Fisher et al., 1991, p. 16). The capacity of human beings for self-awareness, interpretation, abstract thought, meaning making, and feeling exists within this developmental and hierarchically organized relationship to the instinctual and non-conscious responses of the body. These hierarchically organized, interconnected responses range from instinctual arousal and defenses, mammalian feelings, and affective expression through to thoughts, reflective self-awareness, and meaning making. In neuropsychology, MacLean (1985) has conceptualized this hierarchy as the "triune brain," or a "brain with a brain within a brain." Although the model is simplified and thus sometimes inaccurate in depicting the structure, patterns of evolution, and brain functionality (Cory, 2002; Smith, 2010), it efficiently explains symptoms and interventions related to top-down and bottom-up processes. We draw upon the triune brain as a metaphor to illustrate how the synergistic relationship among these three "brains" can be chronically impaired by unresolved trauma.

First to develop in the human infant is the brain stem and cerebellum or reptilian brain, which controls the body's vital functions such as heart rate, breathing, body temperature, balance, and instinctual behaviors involved in aggression, dominance, territoriality, and ritual displays. As a primary regulator of arousal, it is the basis of sensorimotor experience. The second brain is the "paleomammalian brain" or limbic system found in all mammals, which anatomically surrounds the reptilian brain and serves to regulate somatosensory experience, emotion, memory, some social behavior, and learning (Cozolino, 2002). Last to develop phylogenetically is the neocortex, which enables verbal language, cognitive information processing, self-awareness, executive functioning, and conceptual thinking (MacLean, 1985).

This hierarchical organization facilitates two bidirectional information processes, top-down and bottom-up, and the reciprocal relationship between them has critical significance for therapy with those who suffer from trauma (LeDoux, 2002). In nontraumatic circumstances, "higher cortical areas" act as "control centers," such that the orbital frontal cortex dominates subcortical activity with "veto power" over limbic responses (LeDoux, 2002). Thus, top-down processing enables us, for example, to outline plans, determine what to accomplish for the day, and then structure time to meet particular goals. Emotions and sensations, such as feelings of frustration, fatigue, or physical discomfort, may be overridden in order to accomplish these goals. It is as though, most of the time, we hover just above our somatic and sensory experience, not allowing it to be the primary determinant of our actions without conscious decision making. For the traumatized individual, however, the intensity of trauma-related emotions and sensorimotor reactions often disorganizes the individual's cognitive capacities, interfering with the ability for executive and top-down regulation. This phenomenon has been described as "bottom-up hijacking" (Ogden, et al., 2006) and as previously noted is a frequent source of problems for trauma survivors (LeDoux, 2002).

When bottom-up hijacking occurs, dysregulated autonomic arousal generates strong waves of body sensations and emotion, interpreted as data that confirm the cognitive conviction of threat. For example, if a body sensation, such as rapid heart rate (physiological), is interpreted as fear or panic (emotions), each of those aspects of the experience inflate and compound the other. If together they are interpreted as meaning, "I am not safe," both physical sensation and emotion will further intensify, and arousal can quickly escalate beyond the person's tolerance or integrative capacity. Adaptive top-down regulation is temporarily lost, leaving the individual at the mercy of bottom-up hijacking.

The idea that what we think directs how we feel is a fundamentally important development of Cartesian theory, which has informed the influential therapies of the Western world. However, if traumatic memories largely consist of reactivated nonverbal implicit-type memories and habitual procedural responses with limited explicit memory components, then such memories may not be transformed adequately by insight alone (Grigsby & Stevens, 2000; Siegel, 1999; Sykes, 2004; Van der Kolk, 2015). We propose that sensorimotor interventions that directly target the body can work to process relevant implicit memories, challenge procedural learning, and help regulate autonomic arousal.

In Sensorimotor Psychotherapy, the client is encouraged to engage mindful observation of the interplay of perception, emotion, movement, sensation, impulse, and cognition (Kurtz, 1990), a function of the prefrontal cortex. In the act of noticing body experience, innate somatic regulatory capacities, or resources, become spontaneously available or can be evoked by the therapist. Such resources include taking a breath, altering the position of the spine, making a movement, sensing the legs, orienting perceptually and physically to the environment, and so forth. As clients learn to become aware of their internal experience—their in-the-moment thoughts, emotions, images, and particularly their bodily experience—and use somatic resources, they can better adapt to challenging sociocultural contexts. For example, a lesbian client can notice that she begins to hold her breath, tighten her shoulders, lose her upright posture, and feel fearful when asking her openly antigay boss for a raise. With this awareness, she chooses to use the resources of breathing more deeply, relaxing her shoulders, and maintaining an upright posture, which help her to feel less fearful. Using resources like these is especially important because the implicit reminders of past and current trauma will shift depending on how the client's social location and intersecting identities interplay with those around them. For instance, clients of color or of a minority religion may learn in therapy to develop somatic resources, such as using the awareness of breathing to center themselves, which can help them be less reactive when among people whom they fear may reject or discriminate against them. Moreover, they can use other resources for connection and intimacy, like reaching out and taking up more space physically when they are in their faith community or with people they trust.

With the help of somatically oriented interventions, Patricia, a 45-year-old cisgender female living in the U.S. and originally from Honduras, realized that the perpetual slump in her spine had served to maintain her feelings of inferiority and disempowerment. She reported that those feelings had increased in the decade she had lived in the U.S. As this component of her early abusive experiences in Honduras was addressed somatically, over time, her posture gradually became more vertical, transforming from a physical liability to a physical resource that supported a newly found sense of well-being and competency. Her thoughts correspondingly started to become more positive, her negative emotions became less fearsome, and positive emotions became more available. As the therapist worked with her somatically, Patricia's body gradually became her ally rather than her enemy. Patricia was also able to notice how the somatic resources she built in therapy supported her inner sense of agency and self-worth in different sociocultural contexts and with people of the dominant culture. For example, when interacting at work with white coworkers and supervisors, she experienced different microaggressions (i.e., "But you speak so well" or "You are from Honduras? But you are so pretty!"). Patricia was able to draw upon her somatic resources during those incidents, which maintained her arousal within a window of tolerance. She reported that she could remain centered during these offenses and could then calmly decide whether she wanted to address them or not. Such somatic changes alone can oftentimes in and of themselves help to resolve habitual trauma-related responses, or sometimes provide enough stability so that arousal can stay within the window of tolerance, providing a sense of resilience rather than fragility.

BOTTOM-UP DYSREGULATION AND THE WINDOW OF TOLERANCE

The characteristic components of the trauma response—a low tolerance for stress and arousal with consequent affect dysregulation—render traumatized individuals either hyperaroused, experiencing too much activation, or hypoaroused, experiencing too little (Van der Kolk et al., 1996). In neither state can information be processed effectively. Top-down regulation and clear thinking are lost when the client experiences hyperarousal, strong emotions like terror and panic are paramount, and meaning making becomes biased by the subjective experience of danger. In contrast, a hypoaroused state can be accompanied by motor weakness, paralysis, ataxia, and numbing of inner body sensation, as well as cognitive abnormalities, such as amnesia, fugue states, and confusional states (Van der Hart et al., 2004). Although hyperarousal symptoms and intrusive reexperiencing are commonly considered the hallmark symptoms of trauma, not all trauma clients respond to trauma reminders with hyperarousal. In one study, 30% of subjects responded with hypoarousal and emotional symptoms when hearing their trauma scripts read to them (Lanius et al., 2002). Moreover, although both hyperarousal and hypoarousal have often been considered discrete states, there is some evidence that there can be secondary dissociation and hypoarousal patterns in hyperarousal states (Pain et al., 2011).

In order to process the effects of past traumatic events, experience new states of mind and body, and integrate past and present, it is necessary that the client's autonomic arousal remain neither extremely overactivated nor extremely underactivated. The optimal zone between the two extreme physiological states of hyper- and hypoarousal has been described by Siegel (1999) as the window of tolerance, the range of activation within which the individual can experience psychophysiological arousal as tolerable or manageable and compatible with reflection and recognition of the accompanying emotions. In this zone, the client can integrate old and new information on cognitive, emotional, and sensorimotor levels. All of the interventions characteristic of Sensorimotor Psychotherapy either seek to develop or rely upon the client's achievement of a stable and generous window of tolerance.

By explaining to the client that these extremes of autonomic arousal were adaptive in the past at the moment of danger when there was no help available, they become normalized and destigmatized, which assists the client to feel safer to move forward in therapy. At the same time, these autonomic extremes can create a therapeutic impasse when the client cannot maintain arousal within the window of tolerance (Chefetz, 2000). When a threat is first detected, an instinctive mind-body chain reaction is set in motion, involving cascades of neurochemicals that mobilize the sympathetic nervous system and prepare the individual for cry-for-help, flight, fight, and freeze defenses. When adaptive responses are successful, the body utilizes and metabolizes the neurochemicals, and arousal may gradually return to an optimal zone when the threatening stimulus has receded or disappeared. However, in the wake of an unresolved or ongoing traumatic threat, this return to baseline does not always occur. Especially in cases of extreme or prolonged trauma, in the context of subsequent inadequacies in soothing and relational responsiveness and support, or in ongoing experiences of oppression and systemic violence, the individual may have difficulty recalibrating autonomic arousal (Cloitre et al., 2004; Herman, 1995; Nemeroff, 2004; Ogden & Fisher, 2015; Van der Kolk et al, 1996).

Chronic hyperarousal creates a vicious cycle: A hyperaroused nervous system increases vulnerability to state-dependent memory retrieval triggered by trauma-related stimuli, which then results in "increased access to traumatic memories and involuntary intrusions of the trauma, which lead in turn to even more arousal" (van der Kolk et al., 1996, p. 305). Hypoarousal can also become chronic: When mobilizing defenses fueled by hyperarousal are ineffective and the dorsal vagal system is recruited, dorsal vagal hypoarousal can become the default response. Additionally, arousal may vacillate between these two extremes; and any of these patterns can worsen as time goes on. Because repeated traumatic responses can result in kindling of survival-related neural pathways, traumatized people tend to become increasingly vulnerable to progressively minor triggers (Post et al., 1995). This occurs not only when traumatic events are in the past, but also in the presence of ongoing trauma such as systemic oppression. For instance, racist microaggressions, witnessing racial violence, or racist portrayals in the media can serve as triggers as well as becoming a new traumatic event for the client, increasing vulnerability to triggering by future events.

Clients can remain autonomically on guard against danger (either hyperaroused and hypervigilant or hypoaroused and numb). When the trauma occurred in the past, clients typically fail to notice or integrate new data from the present that tells them that the danger is over. Even when in a safe environment, the resources that could be used to recalibrate extremes of arousal are not available, have not been learned, and environmental ones may not be called upon. When trauma is ongoing, default patterns that have developed over time in response to danger are automatically catalyzed, and may interfere with being able to respond flexibly to current threats.

People with trauma-related disorders have difficulties adapting to current contexts or knowing how to make use of resources that might be available in these contexts; they lose their somatic connection to present reality even in the face of objective safety and respond reflexively to traumatic reminders as repetitions and reenactments of the past.

In Sensorimotor Psychotherapy, connection to the present is maintained through attention to present-moment experience through the use of mindfulness-based interventions. In addition, the voice of the therapist can be an important part of helping the client keep present and also feel psychologically supported. Treatment is focused on the client's here-and-now somatic experience by mindfully noticing the unresolved effects of a traumatic past when they are triggered in present time as they manifest in changes in heart rate, breathing, posture, and muscle tone. The client is encouraged to experience being here, now, in the therapy hour, while acknowledging the "there and then" effects of traumatic experiences.

DEFENSIVE SUBSYSTEMS

In the context of threat, hyper- and hypoarousal states are accompanied by two general types of defensive responses: either mobilizing defenses (such as cry-for-help, fight, or flight), or immobilizing defenses (such as freeze and feigned death), or both. No one defensive response is better than another: all are potentially adaptive and effective at diminishing threat, depending on the situation and the capabilities of the individual. We propose that inflexibility among these defensive subsystems, and their overactivity in the absence of threat, involves chronic dysregulated arousal and contributes to the traumatized person's continued distress after the traumatic event is over. In the face of ongoing societal or individual threat, the inflexibility or necessary overactivity of defenses may prevent people from bringing arousal into a window of tolerance and building resilience. The mobilizing defenses of cry-for-help, fight, and flight are characterized by arousal of the sympathetic nervous system and the corresponding neurochemically mediated physical reactions. An infant's first defense is to cry out, called the "separation cry" (Panksepp, 1998; Van der Kolk, 1987), "attachment cry" (Steele et al., 2005), or simply "cry-for-help" (Ogden & Fisher, 2015). This defense is designed to secure the nearness of attachment figures for help and protection.

As motor capacities develop, flight is probably the most common response to threat when successful escape is probable (Nijenhuis, 1999), which when activated readies the large muscles to flee and diminishes awareness of any pain or injury. Flight can be understood not only as running away from danger but also as running toward safety (Bowlby, 1988). Versions of the flight response can be observed in clients in a variety of additional, less obvious behaviors, such as twisting, turning, or backing away from a perceived source of danger. If the chance of escape is remote and the threat closes in, the potential victim's attempts at flight may become increasingly frantic. When flight becomes impossible, fighting may provide the alternative self-defense (Nijenhuis & Van der Hart, 1999). The fight response is often provoked when the victim feels trapped, when one's offspring are threatened, or whenever aggression might effectively secure safety.

Mobilizing defenses also include innumerable patterns of skilled responses that are both learned and spontaneous and are enacted automatically in the course of safely performing physical activities. For example, the ability to drive or operate machinery requires the incorporation of complex movements that, through repetition, become procedural actions that can be executed without thought, such as putting on the brakes and turning the steering wheel to prevent an accident. Such defensive actions anticipate and correct for possible difficulties without invoking flight/fight systems, and include such motor acts as engaging the righting reflexes during a near fall, raising an arm for protection from a falling object, avoiding a rock in a downhill ski run, and so on.

The mobilizing defenses give way to immobilizing responses when the former are ineffective or cannot ensure survival (Misslin, 2003; Nijenhuis & Van der Hart, 1999; Ogden & Fisher, 2015; Ogden, et al., 2006; Porges, 2011). A cry-for-help response is not employed when the caregiver is the perpetrator, and no one is available to protect the child. As Nijenhuis and Van der Hart (1999) state, a child who is being sexually or physically abused by a caregiver is obviously not in a psychological or physical position to fight back. In some situations, running or fighting (mobilizing defenses) would worsen the situation for the child who is being physically or sexually abused or who witnesses violence, increasing the danger and provoking more violence. Defensive responses can also worsen the situation in the face of oppression and racist dynamics. For instance, if the upper body tenses in a held-back or frozen fight response (Bovin, Ratchford, & Marx, 2014), it may be misinterpreted as threatening. If an African American, Muslim, or other marginalized person, primed by multiple exposures to racism and police brutality, freezes when approached by a police officer, there may be a risk that their tension will be interpreted as a preparation for fight (or flight), which can trigger a disproportionately violent response from the police officer (Menakem, 2017).

We identify the following immobilizing defenses, some of which are driven by the sympathetic nervous system, and one of which is driven by the dorsal vagal system. Clients who have experienced immobility powered by sympathetic nervous system arousal frequently report that they were hyperaware of the environment, especially of threat cues, potential escape routes, or protective impulses, and felt energized and tense, ready and able to run if needed (Ogden et al., 2006). Misslin (2003, p. 58) described this response as "alert immobility," where there is complete cessation of movement except for respiration and movement of the eyes. This response appears to involve a highly engaged sympathetic system in which "muscle tone, heart rate, sensory acuity, and alertness are all high" (Lewis et al., 2004). The individual may be waiting to assess more data from the threat before taking action; thus this type of immobility can be a preparation for mobilization (Bovin et al., 2014; Ogden et al 2006).

Another version of a freeze state occurs when the predator is still at a distance and immobility may prevent detection. This kind of freezing occurs as a preventive measure in nature, as when fawns are left camouflaged in tall grass while the mother deer is away foraging for food. For children growing up in traumatogenic environments, similar behavior often accompanies hiding from threat, for example, in the closet, behind a chair, or under the stairs. Freezing promotes safety in these instances, because the child is still and quiet, which increases the likelihood that they will remain unnoticed.

A third type of freezing, perhaps most significant in PTSD, is accompanied by feeling terrifyingly incapable of moving and unable to breathe. This version is associated with a sense of being trapped. Also known as "tonic immobility," this variant of freeze involves a high level of arousal, combined with an inability to take action (Levine, 1997; Siegel, 1999). Both the sympathetic and the parasympathetic systems are aroused simultaneously, which produces muscular constriction paired with a feeling of being unable to move (Siegel 1999). Bovin, Ratchford, and Marx (2014) postulate that this third type of freeze shares many relevant commonalities and co-occurrence with peritraumatic dissociation, increasing the likelihood of the development of psychopathology in the long term.

Other immobilizing defenses of feigning death, shutdown, flagging energy, and/or fainting are powered by the parasympathetic dorsal branch of the vagus nerve (Porges, 1995). These defensive variants (feigning death, shutdown, flagging energy, or fainting) of this immobilizing defense response are apparent states of passivity that involve the person's muscles becoming flaccid rather than tense, and the breathing shallow (Holman & Silver, 1998; Levine, 1997; Scaer, 2001). Clients often describe this condition as feeling trancelike or dreamlike, and it is accompanied by a reduced capacity to attend to the external environment or to internal phenomena. The feigned death response can maximize survival in the short term, but may have long-term or chronic consequences that can impede recovery

from traumatic states. Anesthesia, analgesia, and the slowing of mus-
culoskeletal responses (Levine, 1997; Nijenhuis, 1999; Van der Hart
et al., 2000) often co-occur in this group of responses as well.

Submissive behaviors (such as crouching, avoiding eye contact,
and generally appearing physically smaller and therefore nonthreatening) are also common among traumatized individuals. Submissive
behaviors serve a protective and preventive function, as they "aim
at preventing or interrupting aggressive reactions" (Misslin, 2003,
p. 59). Body language in these circumstances is characterized by
nonaggressive movements, automatic obedience, and compliance,
in which the eyes are lowered and the back is bowed before the
perpetrator. Elements of the submissive behavior, such as downward
flexion (head ducking), appear to be part of the fixed action patterns
of fear. As a result of chronic abuse, it is not uncommon for clients
to characteristically respond to threat cues with mechanistic compliance or resigned submission, which may be wrongly understood
as collusion or agreement. This can be seen, for example, in the client who perfunctorily allowed a male relative into her apartment,
despite knowing he would rape her as he had done in the past.

A version of this condition, described as "robotization," has been
noted in Nazi concentration camp survivors; it includes mechanical
behavior and automatic obedience, without question or thought,
to the demands of others (Krystal, 1988). Such mechanical submission is a survival behavior that reduces the emotional terror when
death is felt to be inescapable and can be learned both individually (e.g., when kidnapped, held hostage, abused in childhood, or
in any other inescapable trauma) and collectively (e.g., when systemic violence is directed toward an entire community, as in Nazi
concentration camps, American Indian residential schools, and so
forth). Such behaviors can be transmitted behaviorally from generation to generation by means of socialization or modeling behaviors (Kellermann, 2001). Internalized racism can also be another
mechanism that can perpetuate submissive behaviors. For instance,

Tull et al. (2005) found positive correlations between chronic physical submissive responses to social stressors, health problems, and higher internalized racism for African Caribbean women on the island of Dominica. Predatory or abusive individuals often seek to evoke these behaviors in others, taking advantage of the instinctive defensive response to elicit automatic compliance with the abuse (Herman, 1992).

INCOMPLETE MOBILIZING DEFENSES

In Sensorimotor Psychotherapy theory we postulate that when the cascade of mobilizing and immobilizing defensive actions is evoked, some of the actions, in particular the mobilizing ones, that might have enabled escape or the warding off of danger have been rendered ineffective or interrupted and left incomplete. An automobile accident victim might have felt the impulse to turn the steering wheel but was unable to execute the action before they hit the oncoming car. The sexual abuse survivor might have wanted to fight the perpetrator but was overpowered and unable to follow through. These incomplete defensive actions may subsequently manifest as chronic symptoms. As Herman (1992, p. 34) states, "Each component of the ordinary response to danger, having lost its utility, tends to persist in an altered and exaggerated state long after the actual danger is over." Incomplete defensive actions also occur in transgenerational trauma, persisting long after the initial historical traumatic events, through modeling family and community behaviors as well as ongoing exposure to events that trigger traumatic reminders of that history (Kellermann, 2001; Menakem, 2017).

If a person, when endangered, experiences the instinct to cry-for-help, fight back, or flee but is rendered unable to execute these actions, this incomplete sequence of possible defensive actions may recur in distorted forms. The individual may experience the cry-for-help defense as a frantic need to reach for another person and an inability to feel safe when alone, or conversely may abandon the hope of help ever being available, resulting in habitual flaccidity of the muscles associated with reaching. The fight response may persist in chronically tight muscles related to fighting back (jaw, arms, shoulders, hands) or a chronic lack of tone or sensation in those muscle groups. Increased tension or flaccidity in the muscles related to the flight defense—legs, feet, and muscles that engage in turning away or pulling back—may also persist. As well, many if not most clients come to therapy exhibiting chronic immobilizing defensive tendencies in their body, exhibited by the tension of the freeze response or the flaccidity of the feigned death response. All the physical and physiological manifestations of incomplete defenses, in turn, profoundly influence emotions and cognitions (Ogden et al., 2006).

In Sensorimotor Psychotherapy, these clients are helped to rediscover their truncated mobilizing defensive impulses through tracking their bodily movements and sensations that emerge during the therapy session. For example, a cisgender female client was subjected to her mother's physical disciplinary tactics as a child. The mother, who had been imprisoned in Russia where she herself was forced to submit to torture, had fled to the U.S. soon after her release. The mother often reflexively struck her daughter when the girl showed a particular stance, such as standing tall or placing her hands on her hips. These postures were a trigger for the mother, left over from her own unresolved trauma. Her aggressive and reflexive reaction reflected both her identification with her torturers, who hit her if she showed any defiance, and her unconscious attempt to protect the daughter, because such a posture had incited more violence from her own perpetrators. Such complex patterns are common in the intergenerational transmission of trauma.

In therapy, the daughter experientially discovered the physical impulse to stand tall, to push away, and to flee that she had not acted upon. As she mindfully sensed how her body automatically became immobile under her mother's physical reprimands, she noticed a tightening in her jaw, a tension that traveled from the jaw down her neck and into her right shoulder and arm. As the therapist encouraged her to continue studying her tension, the tightening increased, and her right hand spontaneously lifted off her lap in a palm-out position. The memory itself was the catalyst that elicited the forgotten defenses, and, being able to observe and attend to the signals of how her body wanted to respond, she became aware of the previously aborted physical urge to not only stop her mother's hands but also run away, reflected in a tightening and feeling of energy in her legs. These physical impulses that she did not and could not act upon at the time of the physical abuse appeared spontaneously as she became meticulously aware of her physical sensations and impulses when she recalled the abuse in therapy. She subsequently discovered the truncated, lost impulses to resist that had become encoded not only in the praxis of submission, but also as beliefs or automatic assumptions of "I don't deserve to defend myself" and "It is dangerous to defend myself."

Sensorimotor Psychotherapy thus addresses the failed processing of the old trauma directly as it is discovered in the present moment in the embodied experience of the client. The sensorimotor-informed therapist carefully observes moment by moment with the client how the impulses to engage mobilizing defenses are automatically inhibited and immobilizing defenses activated: that is,, they freeze or become hypoaroused and "floppy," as Lewis et al. (2004) describes the immobilizing defense of feigning death. Bromberg (2006) notes that retelling the trauma is reexperiencing it to some degree. By recalling the traumatic event in the session, the physical impulses that "wanted to happen" are evoked, and the therapist can then help the client reexperience and then transform immobilizing defenses into mobilizing ones.

It should be noted that therapist and client work to maintain arousal at the edge of the window of tolerance during such memory processing so that it does not greatly exceed the window. The client can with the therapist's guidance fully execute the defensive action with arousal at the edge of or within the window of tolerance, completing that action instead of repeatedly reexperiencing a dysregulated mobilizing defense or the frozen or feigned death immobilizing responses. Prior to treatment, habitual immobilizing defenses insidiously predict the client's future before the future has happened. The future has been prescribed as hopeless by the past. Until the abused client can experience the possibility of executing their active defensive actions fully, the future seems to hold only further abuse and disappointment, without the likelihood of defending themselves. As clients consciously execute their mobilizing physical defensive actions rather than only the inflexible immobilizing ones of their original trauma, their new actions can become intentional and available to them, and as a result the future hold more promise. Rather than insight alone, it is the actual experience of mobilizing action (which had been abandoned for good reason during the original trauma) executed with conscious intention and awareness, while simultaneously addressing the cognitive distortions and emotional reactions, that help effect such change.

SENSORIMOTOR TREATMENT: BOTTOM-UP INTERVENTIONS

Thus, instead of focusing on the verbal description of traumatic events, Sensorimotor Psychotherapy treatment focuses on the reactivation of autonomic hyper- or hypoarousal and defensive action tendencies as these occur within the therapy hour. In a bottom-up approach, the narrative becomes a vehicle for stimulating these physiological responses and movements so that they can be studied and ultimately transformed or reorganized. The therapist and client have an opportunity to work with the implicit elements of traumatic memories by directing the client's awareness away from the verbal components of memory to the nonverbal residue of the trauma. Somatic bottom-up interventions that address the repetitive, unbidden, physical sensations of hyperarousal and hypoarousal, together with exploring movement, can then be integrated with more traditional top-down interventions that help to transform the narrative of the trauma and facilitate the development of a reorganized somatic sense of self. The sense of self is represented not only in top-down beliefs and emotional responses, but also in bottom-up physical organization, postural habits, and movements of the body. An integrated approach to soma and psyche helps these clients regulate their physiology and learn new actions so that their corresponding sense of self feels grounded, resourced, and oriented toward present experience.

Sensorimotor Psychotherapy builds on and adds to traditional, widely accepted psychotherapeutic understandings and principles. For instance, Sensorimotor Psychotherapy, along with talk therapies (regardless of theoretical model), recognizes the necessity of a good therapeutic alliance between therapist and client. However, the alliance in a sensorimotor treatment is built from the bottom up, as the therapist takes on the role of an "auxiliary cortex" for the client (Diamond et al., 1963) and "affect regulator of the client's dysregulated states in order to provide a growth-facilitating environment for the client's immature [or traumatized] affect-regulating structures" (Schore, 2001, p. 17). That is, as therapists track the client's bodily experience, they notice the physiological signs of dysregulation and introduce the appropriate interventions so that arousal can settle or increase as needed: adjusting voice tone, energy level, pacing, choice of vocabulary, mindfulness questions, and movement, and attending to the amount of emotional or cognitive content elicited. Additionally, the therapist needs to be aware of power/oppression dynamics by paying special attention to the nonverbal cues of the interaction, and sometimes name and discuss these dynamics, since they might play a role in the arousal of the client in the therapy room.

The therapist's sensitivity to, knowledge of, and comfort in discussing social dynamics will strengthen the therapeutic alliance. As the client experiences the calm and relief that accompanies a return of arousal to their window of tolerance, the therapeutic alliance is also strengthened. With an increase in the sense of safety in the relationship and when arousal is within the window, the client's exploration system becomes less inhibited; as fear subsides, they find themselves more able to explore their inner and outer world.

For the traumatized client, chronically activated instinctive defenses and their corresponding emotions of fear, rage, or helplessness tend to override and inhibit the exploratory system, also a wired-in motivational or action system, which is accompanied by emotions of curiosity and interest (Panksepp, 1998; Ogden, et al., 2006; Van der Hart et al., 2006). Panksepp (1998, p. 145) maintains that the exploration system "drives and energizes many mental complexities that humans experience as persistent feelings of interest, curiosity, sensation seeking, and, in the presence of a sufficiently complex cortex, the search for higher meaning." Evoking the client's exploration system in therapy stimulates curiosity about how they can combat and/or inhibit habitual fear-based survival responses. At the moment of threat, survival defenses take precedence over cognitive functions. Long after the traumatic events are over, activation of the prefrontal cortices and cognitive functions can be intermittently inhibited in response to trauma-related stimuli (Van der Kolk, 2015; Van der Kolk et al., 1996), hindering the capacity for successful self-observation, exploration, and new learning. In the face of ongoing trauma, reactive instinctive and learned defensive responses can take precedence over other more adaptive behaviors, as subcortical reactions intermittently inhibit cortical functions in response to trauma-related stimuli.

The therapist's job is to "wake up" the exploratory system by promoting a somatic and psychological sense of safety and cultivating the capacity for curiosity, observation, and mindfulness in the client. Observation of the present moment experience engages the executive and observing functions of the prefrontal cortex, and the capacity to maintain this observing focus prevents clients from becoming overwhelmed by the reactivation of a traumatic event.

For example, as Ally discusses a traumatic motor vehicle accident in therapy, she is asked by her therapist to become interested in how she is organizing the experience—what is happening inside her—as she begins to talk and think about her accident. The therapist gently and empathically interrupts the story to direct Ally's awareness away from her verbal dialogue to her inner-body sensations, movement impulses, and sensory experience as well as thoughts and emotions. In a state of mindful observation, Ally notices that, as she talks about the accident, she has the thought that she is going to die. Next, she observes her body tensing in response to the thought and notes a feeling of panic. Rather than reliving this experience, as she might have if the therapist had not carefully directed her attention to the present-moment experience of recalling it, she metaphorically steps back, observes it with curiosity, and reports how it is manifesting internally now. The panic subsides, her heart rate returns to normal, and she knows at a body level that she did not die; she survived. With this somatic differentiation of having an experience and exploring how she has organized it, the traumatic event is relegated to the past. It no longer causes her to reexperience the effects of the past trauma; rather, Ally experiences the felt sense that it is over: "I thought I was going to die, but I didn't."

Often, just by uncoupling trauma-related emotion from body sensation and attending exclusively to the physical sensations of the arousal (without attributing meaning or connecting emotion to it), the physiological responses diminish and settle. This conveys at a bodily level that the danger is past, and all is now safe (Levine, 1997). These transformations at the sensorimotor level result in improved emotional and cognitive processing: emotions can be better tolerated, and cognitive reprocessing reflects the incorporation of information from the body.

Martin, a male veteran, came to therapy to "get rid of" nightmares and feelings of being chronically emotionally overwhelmed. In the course of Sensorimotor Psychotherapy, Martin learned to track his physiological arousal as he experienced it in his body. He learned to pay active attention to his rapid heart rate and the shaking and trembling that occurred after the original combat, and which he had subsequently reexperienced intermittently over the years. Over the course of several therapy sessions, he learned to describe his inner body sensations, noting the tingling in his arms that preceded the shaking, the slightly accelerated heart rate, and the increase of tension in his legs. As his capacity to observe and describe bodily sensations developed, he learned to accept these sensations without trying to inhibit them. The therapist instructed him to track these sensations as they moved, changed, or "sequenced." Martin noticed that, as he tracked the sequence of sensations progressing through his body, the shaking gradually became quiet, his heart rate returned to baseline, and the tension in his legs diminished. Martin's body relaxed and his arousal quieted, he felt less afraid and hopeless, and he experienced a somatic feeling he described as "calm" and "safe."

In another example, a young adult cisgender woman, Audra, had suffered from a severe bone disease since she was 11 years old, which resulted in an above-the-knee amputation of her right leg. For years, she had endured the constant pain and discomfort of phantom limb syndrome. She felt overwhelmed by her condition and unable to manage the pain, and reported that she was "too much" of a burden for her parents. In therapy, Audra learned to track the sensation of physiological arousal in her body as she remembered the treatments and surgeries she had endured on her leg over many years. She learned to observe and describe her sensations without becoming unduly dysregulated. Over time, Audra began to identify sensations of itching and throbbing, rather than only pain, in her missing right leg, which resulted in a significant reduction of phantom limb pain. Eventually, as she became increasingly able to identify sensations that were more neutral than painful, Audra could recall the trauma of her surgeries with minimal discomfort.

Thus, in Sensorimotor Psychotherapy, top-down, cortically mediated functions are harnessed to observe and facilitate sensorimotor processing. Clients are encouraged to observe and report (both of which are cognitive functions) the interplay of physical sensations, movements, and impulses and notice their internal reactions. They also learn to observe the effects of their thoughts and emotions on their body; noticing in which part of the body they feel the impact of a particular thought or how the body organizes a particular emotion.

Meaning-making emerges from the observing and subsequent transformation of habitual responses. For example, as Martin's body experienced the completion of the trembling and shaking evoked by a memory of combat, he finally achieved the somatic experience of "peacetime" decades after the end of the Vietnam War. He could physically experience and then cognitively recognize that feelings of calm and safety meant that the events which had continued to torment him were in the past. When the daughter of the physically abusive mother was able to finally execute mobilizing defensive responses, the meaning that emerged was, "I can protect myself now." Integrated meaning-making is possible for clients when they experience a transformation of sensorimotor, emotional, and cognitive responses to their persistent traumatic reactions rather than to the memory of the trauma itself. Integrated meaning making will also be crucial for transgenerational trauma in which the meaning making does not happen only at the individual level, but at the collective level. The narratives of historical abuse as well as of ongoing oppression can reflect new meanings of resilience and strength (Denham, 2008), for instance "We survived," or "We are strong and resilient."

Along with body sensation, impulses, posture, and movement,

thoughts and emotions are also viable targets of intervention that can support resolution of the traumatic experience. Top-down approaches that attempt to regulate arousal, emotions, and cognitions are a necessary part of trauma therapy, but if such interventions overmanage, ignore, or suppress body processes, traumatic responses may not be resolved. Similarly, bottom-up interventions that reinforce bottom-up hijacking, or that fail to include cognitive and emotional processing as well, can sabotage integration and may lead to endless repetitive flashbacks, hypoarousal states, or chronic post-traumatic kindling.

We believe that if the use of insight, understanding, and somatically informed top-down management of symptoms is thoughtfully balanced with bottom-up processing of trauma-related sensations, arousal, movement, and emotions, the complex effects of trauma are more likely to respond to treatment. Effective treatments for trauma involve evoking the fragmented, cognitive, emotional, and sensorimotor responses within the client's window of tolerance and facilitating new, adaptive responses that can lead to the integration of past and present, belief and body, emotion and meaning.

REFERENCES

American Psychiatric Association. (2013). *Diagnostic and statistical manual of mental disorders* (5th ed.). https://doi.org/10.1176/appi.books.9780890425596

American Psychological Association. (2017, February 24). Guideline Development Panel for the Treatment of Posttraumatic Stress Disorder in Adults Adopted as APA Policy.

Aposhyan, S. (2004). *Body-mind psychotherapy: Principles, techniques, and practical applications.* New York: Norton.

Bovin, M. J., Ratchford, E., & Marx, B. P. (2014). Peritraumatic dissociation and tonic immobility: Clinical findings. In U. F. Lanius, S. L. Paulsen, & F. M. Corrigan (Eds.), *Neurobiology and treatment of traumatic dissociation: Toward an embodied self* (pp. 51–67). New York: Springer.

Bowlby, J. (1988). *A secure base: Parent-child attachment and healthy human development.* New York: Basic Books.

Bradley, R., Greene, J., Russ, E., Dutra, M. A., & Westen, D. (2005). A multidimensional meta-analysis of psychotherapy for PTSD. *American Journal of Psychiatry, 162*(2), 214–227.

Brave Heart, M., & DeBruyn, L. M. (1998). The American Indian Holocaust: Healing historical unresolved grief. *American Indian and Alaska Native Mental Health Research, 8*(2), 56–78.

Brewin, C. R., Dalgleish, T., & Joseph, S. (1996). A dual representation theory of post traumatic stress disorder. *Psychological Review, 103*(4), 670–686.

Brewin, C. R., & Holmes, E. A. (2003). Psychological theories of posttraumatic stress disorder. *Clinical Psychology Review, 23*(3), 339–376.

Bromberg, P. M. (2006). *Awakening the dreamer: Clinical journeys.* Mahwah, NJ: Analytic Press.

Burnstein, A. (1986). Treatment noncompliance in clients with posttraumatic stress disorder. *Psychosomatics, 27,* 37–40.

Chefetz, R. A. (2000). Affect dysregulation as a way of life. *Journal of the American Academy of Psychoanalysis, 28*(2), 289–303.

Chefetz, R. A. (2004). The paradox of "detachment disorders": Binding-disruptions of dissociative process. *Psychiatry, 67*(3), 246–255.

Chu, J. A. (1998). *Rebuilding shattered lives: The responsible treatment of complex post-traumatic and dissociative disorders.* New York: John Wiley and Sons.

Cloitre, M. K., Stovall-McClough, M. R., & Chemtob, C. (2004). Therapeutic alliance, negative mood regulation and treatment outcome in child abuse-related posttraumatic stress disorder. *Journal of Consulting and Clinical Psychology, 72*(3), 411–416.

Cory, G. A. (2002). Reappraising MacLean's triune brain concept. In G. A. Cory and R. Gardner (Eds.), *The evolutionary neuroethology of Paul MacLean: Convergences and frontiers* (pp. 9–27). Westport, CT: Praeger.

Courtois, C., & Ford, J. (2009). *Treating complex traumatic stress disorders: An evidence-based guide.* New York: Guilford.

Cozolino, L. (2002). *The neuroscience of psychotherapy: Building and rebuilding the human brain.* New York: Norton.

Davidson, J. R., Hughes, D., Blazer, D. G., & George, L. K. (1991). Posttraumatic stress disorder in the community: An epidemiological study. *Psychological Medicine, 21,* 713–721.

Denham, A. R. (2008). Rethinking historical trauma: Narratives of resilience. *Transcultural Psychiatry, 45*(3), 391–414.

Diamond, S., Balvin, R., & Diamond, F. (1963). *Inhibition and choice.* New York: Harper and Row.

Ehring, T., Welboren, R., Morina, N., Wicherts, J. M., Freitag, J., & Emmelkamp, P. M. G. (2014). Meta-analysis of psychological treatments for posttraumatic stress disorder in adult survivors of childhood abuse. *Clinical Psychology Review, 34,* 645–657.

Faustman, W. O., & White, P. A. (1989). Diagnostic and psychopharmacological treatment characteristics of 536 inpatients with posttraumatic stress disorder. *Journal of Nervous and Mental Disease, 177,* 154–159.

Fisher, A., Murray, E., & Bundy, A. (1991). *Sensory integration: Theory and practice.* Philadelphia: F. A. Davis.

Grigsby, J., & Stevens, D. (2000). *Neurodynamics of personality.* New York: Guilford.

Herman, J. (1992). *Trauma and recovery.* New York: Basic Books.

Herman, J. L. (1995). *Complex PTSD: A syndrome in survivors of prolonged and repeated trauma in psychotraumatology.* New York: Plenum.

Holman, E. A., & Silver, R. C. (1998). Getting "stuck" in the past: Temporal orientation and coping with trauma. *Journal of Personality and Social Psychology, 74*(5), 1146–1163.

Holmes, S. C., Facemire, V. C., & DaFonseca, A. M. (2016). Expanding criterion A for posttraumatic stress disorder: Considering the deleterious impact of oppression. *Traumatology, 22*(4), 314–321. https://doi .org/10.1037/trm0000104

Kanagaratnam, P., Pain, C., McKenzie, K., Ratnalingam, N., & Toner, B. (2017). Recommendations for Canadian mental health practitioners working with war-exposed immigrants and refugees. *Canadian Journal of Community Mental Health, 36*(2), 107–119.

Kellerman, N. P. F. (2001). Transmission of Holocaust trauma: An integrative view. *Psychiatry, 64*(3), 256–267.

Kepner, J. (1987). *Body process: A gestalt approach to working with the body in psychotherapy.* New York: Gestalt Institute of Cleveland Press.

Krystal, H. (1988). *Integration and self-healing: Affect, trauma, alexithymia.* New York: Routledge.

Kulka, R. A., Schlenger, W. E., Fairbank, J. A., Hough, R. L., Jordan, B. K., Marmar, C. R., Weiss, D. S., & Grady, D. A. (1990). *Trauma and the Vietnam War generation: Report of findings from the National Vietnam Veterans Readjustment Study.* New York: Brunner/Mazel.

Kurtz, R. (1990). *Body-centered psychotherapy: The Hakomi method: The integrated use of mindfulness, nonviolence, and the body.* Mendocino, CA: LifeRhythm.

Lanius, R. A., Bluhm, R. L., Lanius, U., & Pain, C. (2006). A review of neuroimaging studies of hyperarousal and dissociation in PTSD: Heterogeneity of response to symptom provocation. *Journal of Psychiatric Research, 40*(8), 709–729.

Lanius, R. A., Williamson, P. C., Boksman, K., Densmore, M., Gupta, M., Neufeld, R. W., Gati, J. S., & Menon, R. S. (2002). Brain activation during script-driven imagery induced dissociative responses in PTSD: A functional magnetic resonance imaging investigation. *Biological Psychiatry, 52,* 305–311.

LeDoux, J. (1996). *The emotional brain: The mysterious underpinnings of emotional life.* New York: Simon and Schuster.

LeDoux, J. (2002). *Synaptic self: How our brains become who we are.* New York: Penguin.

Levine, P. (1997). *Waking the tiger: Healing trauma.* Berkeley, CA: North Atlantic.

Lewis, L., Kelly, K., & Allen, J. (2004). *Restoring hope and trust: An illustrated guide to mastering trauma.* Baltimore, MD: Sidran Institute Press.

MacLean, P. D. (1985). Brain evolution relating to family, play, and the separation call. *Archives of General Psychiatry, 42,* 405–417.

Markowitz, J. C., Petkova, E., Neria, Y., Van Meter, P. E., Zhao, Y., Hembree, E., Lovell, K., Biyanova, T., & Marshall, R. D. (2015). Is exposure necessary? A randomized controlled trial of interpersonal psychotherapy for PTSD. *American Journal of Psychiatry, 172,* 1–11.

Menakem, R. (2017). *My grandmother's hands: Racialized trauma and the pathway to mending our hearts and bodies.* Las Vegas, NV: Central Recovery Press.

Misslin, R. (2003). The defense system of fear: Behavior and neurocircuitry. Le système défensif de la peur: Comportement of neurocircuiterie. *Neurophysiologie-clinique, 33*(2), 3355–3366.

Mohatt, N. V., Thompson, A. B., Thai, N. D., & Tebes, J. K. (2014). Historical trauma as public narrative: A conceptual review of how history impacts present-day health. *Social Science and Medicine, 106,* 128–136. doi:10.1016/j.socscimed.2014.01.043

Nemeroff, C. B. (2004). Neurobiological consequences of childhood trauma. *Journal of Clinical Psychiatry, 65*(Suppl. I), 18–28.

Nijenhuis, E. R. S. (1999). *Somatoform dissociation: Phenomena, measurement, and theoretical issues.* Amsterdam: Van Gorcum.

Nijenhuis, E. R. S., & Van der Hart, O. (1999). Forgetting and reexperiencing trauma: From anesthesia to pain. In J. Goodwin & R. Attias (Eds.), *Splintered reflections: Images of the body in trauma* (pp. 39–66). New York: Basic Books.

North, C. S., Nixon, S. J., Shariat, S., Mallonee, S., McMillen, J. C.,

Spitznagel, E. L., & Smith, E. M. (1999). Psychiatric disorders among survivors of the Oklahoma City bombing. *Journal of the American Medical Association, 282*(8), 755–762.

Ogden, P., & Fisher, J. (2015). *Sensorimotor psychotherapy: Interventions for trauma and attachment.* New York: Norton.

Ogden, P., & Minton, K. (2000). Sensorimotor psychotherapy: One method for processing traumatic memory. *Traumatology, 6*(3), 149–173.

Ogden, P., Minton, K., & Pain, C. (2006). *Trauma and the body: A sensorimotor approach to psychotherapy.* New York: Norton.

Orr, S., McNally, R. J., Rosen, G. M., & Shalev, A. Y. (2004). Psychophysiological reactivity: Implications for conceptualizing PTSD. In G. M. Rosen (Ed.), *Posttraumatic stress disorder: Issues and controversies.* Chichester, UK: John Wiley & Sons.

Pain, C., Bluhm, R. L., & Lanius, R. A. (2011). Dissociation in patients with chronic PTSD: Hyperactivation and hypoactivation patterns, clinical and neuroimaging perspectives. In P. F. Dell & J. A. O'Neil (Eds.), *Dissociation and the Dissociative Disorders: DSM-V and Beyond* (pp. 373–380). New York: Routledge.

Panksepp, J. (1998). *Affective neuroscience: The foundations of human and animal emotions.* New York: Oxford University Press.

Pitman, R. K., Altman, B., Greenwald, E., Longpre, R. E., Macklin, M. L., Poiré, R. E., & Steketee, G. S. (1991). Psychiatric complications during flooding therapy for posttraumatic stress disorder. *Journal of Consulting and Clinical Psychology, 52*(1),17–20.

Porges, S. W. (1995). Orienting in a defensive world: Mammalian modifications of our evolutionary heritage. A polyvagal theory. *Psychophysiology, 32*(4), 301–318.

Porges, S. W. (2011). *The polyvagal theory: Neurophysiological foundations of emotions, attachment, communication, and self-regulation.* New York: Norton.

Post, R. M., Weiss, S. R. B., & Smith, M. A. (1995). Sensitization and kindling: Implication for the evolving neural substrates of post-traumatic stress disorder. In M. J. Friedman, D. S. Charney, & A. Y. Deutch (Eds.), *Neurobiological and clinical consequences of stress: From normal adaptation to PTSD.* Philadelphia: Lippincott-Raven.

Powers, M. B., Halpern, J. M., Ferenschak, M. P., & Gillihan, S. J. (2010). A meta-analytic review of prolonged exposure for posttraumatic stress disorder. *Clinical Psychology Review 30*(6), 635–641.

Resick, P. A., & Schnicke, M. K. (1993). *Cognitive processing therapy for rape victims: A treatment manual.* Newbury Park, CA: Sage.

Rosen, G. M. (Ed.). (2004). *Posttraumatic stress disorder: Issues and controversies.* Chichester, UK: John Wiley & Sons.

Rothschild, B. (2000). *The body remembers: The psychophysiology of trauma and trauma treatment.* New York: Norton.

SAMHSA. (2014). *Trauma-informed care in behavioral health services.* Treatment Improvement Protocol (TIP) Series 57. HHS Publication No. (SMA) 13-4801. Rockville, MD: Substance Abuse and Mental Health Services Administration.

Scaer, R. C. (2001). The neurophysiology of dissociation and chronic disease. *Applied Psychophysiology and Biofeedback, 26*(1), 73–91.

Schore, A. (2001). The effects of early relational trauma on right brain development, affect regulation, and infant mental health. *Infant Mental Health Journal, 22,* 201–269.

Schore, A. N. (2002). Dysregulation of the right brain: A fundamental mechanism of traumatic attachment and the psychopathogenesis of posttraumatic stress disorder. *Australian and New Zealand Journal of Psychiatry, 36*(1), 9–30.

Siegel, D. (1999). *The developing mind: Toward a neurobiology of interpersonal experience.* New York: Guilford.

Smith, C. U. (2010). "The triune brain in antiquity: Plato, Aristotle, Erasistratus." *Journal of the History of Neuroscience, 19*(1), 1–14. doi:10.1080/09647040802601605

Steele, K., van der Hart, O., & Nijenhuis, E. R. S. (2005). Phase-oriented treatment of structural dissociation in complex traumatization: Overcoming trauma-related phobias. *Journal of Trauma and Dissociation, 6,* 11–53.

Swift, J. K., & Greenberg, R. P. (2014). A treatment by disorder meta-analysis of dropout from psychotherapy. *Journal of Psychotherapy Integration, 24*(3), 193–207.

Sykes, W. M. (2004). The limits of talk: Bessel van der Kolk wants to transform the treatment of trauma. *Psychotherapy Networker, 28*(1), 30–41.

Tull, E. S., Sheu, Y. T., Butler, C., & Cornelious, K. (2005). Relationships between perceived stress, coping behavior and cortisol secretion in women with high and low levels of internalized racism. *Journal of the National Medical Association, 97*(2), 206–212.

Ursano, R. J., Bell, C., Eth, S., Friedman, M., Norwood, A., Pfefferbaum, B., Pynoos, R. S., Zatzick, D. F., & Benedek, D. M. (2004). Practice guideline for the treatment of clients with acute stress disorder and posttraumatic stress disorder. *American Journal of Psychiatry, 161,* 3–31.

Van der Hart, O., Nijenhuis, E., Steele, K., & Brown, D. (2004). Trauma-related dissociation: Conceptual clarity lost and found. *Australian and New Zealand Journal of Psychiatry, 38,* 906–914.

Van der Hart, O., Nijenhuis, E. R. S., & Steele, K. (2006). *The haunted self.* New York, NY: Norton.

Van der Hart, O., & Steele, K. (1999). Relieving or reliving childhood trauma? A commentary on Miltenburg and Singer. *Theory and Psychology, 9,* 533–540.

Van der Hart, O., van Dijke, A., van Son, M., & Steele, K. (2000). Somatoform dissociation in traumatized World War I combat soldiers: A neglected clinical heritage. *Journal of Trauma and Dissociation, 1*(4), 33–66.

Van der Kolk, B. A. (1987). *Psychological trauma.* Washington, DC: American Psychiatric Press

Van der Kolk, B. A. (1994). The body keeps the score: Memory and the emerging psychobiology of post traumatic stress. *Harvard Review of Psychiatry, 1,* 253–265.

Van der Kolk, B. A. (2015). *The body keeps the score: Brain, mind and body in the treatment of trauma.* New York: Viking.

Van der Kolk, B., McFarlane, A. C., & Weisaeth, L. (Eds.). (1996). *Traumatic stress: The effects of overwhelming experience on mind, body, and society.* New York: Guilford.

Wilber, K. (1996). *A brief history of everything.* Boston: Shambhala Publications.

Chapter 7

INTEGRATING BODY AND MIND*

with Janina Fisher

> *Knowledge is only a rumor until it lives in the muscle.*
>
> PAPUA NEW GUINEA PROVERB

Trauma-related disorders have long been characterized by intrusive reliving of past trauma accompanied by dysregulated autonomic arousal and instinctive survival defenses, as well as by numb avoidance of traumatic reminders accompanied by constriction, loss of energy, and diminished pleasure (Chu, 1988; Van der Hart et al., 2006; Van der Kolk et al., 1996). Sometimes there is a vacillation between these two extremes. Both symptom clusters reflect the body's efforts to survive and adapt to a threatening environment. In such contexts, these alternations between instinctive defensive reactions and avoidance symptoms allow people to organize adaptive behavior to meet the ever-changing demands they face daily. In a traumatic environment, activities of daily life must be interrupted as the person prepares to respond to danger or life threat. However, when the threat is over, the ability to resume daily life functioning and refocus on work, family, and community is also crucial

---

★ The authors wish to thank Onno van der Hart, PhD, and Kathy Steele, MN, CS, for their contributions to this chapter.

for adaptation and survival. In order to "go back to normal," the traumatized individual attempts to avoid both external reminders and internal triggers (i.e., thoughts, emotions, and body experience) connected to the trauma. Long after the danger is over, reliving of traumatic experience occurs as subcortical survival responses—instinctive defenses of cry-for-help, fight, flight, freeze, and feigned death—continue to be repeatedly ignited by exposure to stimuli directly or indirectly related to past trauma. However, biphasic alternations between reexperiencing (i.e., preparing to defend) and avoiding traumatic reminders in order to engage in daily life result in the encoding of self-states that hold procedurally learned tendencies: particular constellations of autonomic, affective, cognitive, perceptual, and motor responses.

The collective effects of community historical and ongoing trauma can encompass both group patterns of avoiding to acknowledge and address these events to get on with daily life, and group patterns of dysregulation and dissociation that disrupt daily functioning. These patterns are resistant to integration in part because they can be adaptive because the systemic oppressive forces are often experienced as insurmountable for an individual or group. As Bloom (para. 2) asserts, there is a clear relationship between the occurrence of violence toward marginalized groups and the sociocultural conditions that support such traumatizing behaviors; thus comprehensive sociocultural change is required to resolve systemic oppression and violence.

The patterns of reliving and avoidance occur in entire communities, especially when the transgenerational effects of trauma in which historically traumatic and violent events are not mourned, processed, and healed by both the communities who were perpetrated against and by those communities whose role was that of perpetrator. For some, current reminders of historical traumatic events that happened in the past contribute to revictimization, as triggers such as witnessing current violence, discrimination and oppression and its aftermath, hearing narratives, and watching media reports of trauma perpetrated on one's community or on individual members of one's group of belonging, and so forth, are encountered (Hamby et al., 2019). Such transgenerational and vicarious retraumatization occurs in addition to current challenges, oppression, and violence that marginalized populations face. And impacts perpetrators and their progeny as well. Mohamed (2015, p. 1215) states that while it can be difficult "to recognize the suffering of a person who seems to deserve no such recognition," acknowledging the relational nature of oppression, and that both parties can suffer, fosters the understanding that the targets of interpersonal violence often become the perpetrators themselves (Friere, 2007; Kar, 2018). The dysregulation that perseveres after traumatic events can contribute to a cycle of trauma and oppression. Hyperarousal and anger can lead to violence, and conversely, numbing and detachment can prevent empathy for the pain and suffering of others. To challenge this cycle, a shift is required, as Mohamed (2015, p. 1206) states: "perpetrator trauma demands to be recognized not only as real, but also as profoundly affecting the future of societies riven by violence." All-inclusive treatment that involves perpetrators and their targets, as well as the systems that perpetuate oppression, is needed.

In this chapter, we focus on the relationship between dissociative parts of the self and discrete psychobiological behavioral or action systems that are aroused in response to conflicting demands to both defend one's life and go on with normal life. We present approaches from Sensorimotor Psychotherapy that highlight the use of controlled actions to help overcome traumatic repetitions and fixed patterns of cry-for-help, flight, fight, freeze, and feign death defenses, integrate parts of the self, promote more flexibility of response, and support integration of body and mind. Although the case presented in this chapter is of a white middle-aged woman working with a white female clinician, we include reflections and suggestions on how Sensorimotor Psychotherapy can address the effects of ongoing systemic oppression in clinical practice.

PSYCHOBIOLOGICAL ACTION SYSTEMS AND DISSOCIATION

Understanding psychobiological systems that organize responses to both internal and environmental stimuli can help unravel the complexity of trauma-related dissociation. In Sensorimotor Psychotherapy, we draw upon the theory of structural dissociation of the personality developed by Van der Hart, Nijenhuis, and Steele (2006), a theoretical construct that conceptualizes traumatic dissociation as an integrative failure of psychobiological subsystems. These systems are epigenetically hard-wired, self-organizing, self-stabilizing, open to classical conditioning, and adaptive in nature (Cassidy & Shaver, 1999; Nijenhuis et al., 2002; Panksepp, 1998; Van der Hart et al., 2006). They can be categorized into two general types: the instinctive defense systems stimulated by danger and life threat, and the daily life systems stimulated by nonthreatening environmental demands of work, learning, family, and community responsibilities (Van der Hart et al., 2006). A variety of terms describe similar concepts: behavioral systems (Bowlby, 1982); motivational systems (Gould, 1982; Lichtenberg & Kindler, 1994); functional systems (Fanselow & Lester, 1988); or emotional operating systems (Panksepp, 1998). Van der Hart, Nijenhuis, and Steele (2006) call these systems *action systems,* and we have chosen to follow their lead because each system's goals are supported by particular physical (behavioral and physiological) and mental (emotional and cognitive) actions.

Daily life action systems motivate us to engage in a variety of adaptive activities in a safe environment: form close relationships, explore the environment, play, participate in social relationships, regulate energy (e.g., eat, sleep, etc.), reproduce, and care for others (Bowlby,

1982; Cassidy & Shaver, 1999; Fanselow & Lester, 1988; Lichten-berg, 1990; Lichtenberg & Kindler, 1994; Marvin & Britner, 1999; Panksepp, 1998; Van der Hart et al., 2006). Whereas daily life systems emerge in a context of environmental safety, defensive systems are catalyzed under dangerous or life-threatening conditions. Under threat, an infant's first instinct is the attachment cry or cry-for-help, designed to elicit the help and protection of someone stronger (distinguished from attachment-related behavior that is designed to secure and maintain enduring close relationships). Additional instinctive defenses that mobilize the body to flee or fight become available as the infant's motor capacities mature. Yet another instinctive defense is to freeze, which immobilizes the body and heightens the senses to detect additional information. The last line of defense is the immobility response of feigned death—to shut down and endure whatever harm is to follow.

Specific physical actions that serve the purpose of each system are stimulated when a system is aroused. For example, when separation from the caregiver exceeds a child's comfort zone, in terms of either time or distance, the attachment action system is stimulated. This system organizes proximity-seeking behaviors: reaching out, holding on, facial expressions such as smiling, eye contact, shaping (Stern, 1985), that is, conforming to the caregiver's body, and so forth (Ainsworth, 1963; Bowlby, 1988; Lyons-Ruth & Jacobvitz, 1999; Schore, 1994). These actions, as well as infant participation with caregivers, family, and community members in game playing and imitation of verbal prosody, pitch, and sounds, induces social and attachment-related behavioral sequelae in contexts of safety.

Each daily life action system is characterized not only by specific behaviors but also by emotions typical of that system. The curiosity of the exploration system fuels orienting and seeking movements that enable the investigation of novelty: learning opportunities, challenges at work, the tasks of parenting. The play system, characterized by laughter, can involve a variety of movement patterns: tilting of the head, relaxed, open posture, nonstereotyped movements that change quickly (Bekoff & Allen, 1998; Bekoff & Byers, 1998; Caldwell, 2003; Donaldson, 1993). The caregiving system, often stimulated by empathy, can manifest in "subtle, warm, and soft" (Panksepp, 1998, p. 247) behavior when the caregiver attunes voice, behavior, and touch to the needs of the person being cared for. A wide variety of emotions and behaviors that include gestures, facial and bodily expressions, and vocalizations accompany social interaction. The reproductive system, accompanied by feelings of lust and attraction, incorporates specific movement sequences characteristic not only of sexual behavior, but also of courtship and flirting: eye contact, smiling, vocalizations that are both of a higher pitch and augmented volume, and exaggerated gestures (Cassidy & Shaver, 1999). It is important to note that various systems may be aroused simultaneously, complicating both behaviors and emotions.

When threat is detected, defensive actions that appear to best serve survival are stimulated. Defensive subsystems manifest in a variety of movements and emotions consistent with particular survival demands. The cry-for-help may be the best option, usually accompanied by feelings of desperation and exaggerated proximity-seeking actions such as reaching and clinging movements. In Western individualistic cultures, this response is usually directed toward a few primary caregivers, when available. In collectivist communities, the child is also encouraged to call upon others, such as grandparents, siblings, relatives, and older peers, who also perform the role of "alloparenting" (Keller, 2013). While the cry-for-help behaviors themselves may be the same in both instances, they may target a wider range of people in a collectivist culture instead of a few primary caregivers in an individualistic culture.

If escape seems possible, flight may be the instinctive defense of choice, sometimes in addition to the cry-for-help defense. A flight defense might be accompanied by feelings of fear, physical postures of pulling back, tension and impulses to flee in the legs and feet, a heightened arousal and awareness of exit routes, a sense of feeling trapped, and thoughts of escape. When aggression appears likely to be effective, or when the victim feels trapped, the fight response may be provoked, accompanied by tension in the jaw, shoulders, and arms, and readiness to lash out, heightened arousal, anger, and an aggressive manner. When these mobilizing defenses prove ineffective or provocative, such as in instances when a fight response might incite more violence from the perpetrator or when the perpetrator and attachment figure are one and the same, immobilization behaviors are the only survival strategies remaining (Allen, 2001; Misslin, 2003; Nijenhuis et al., 1999; Ogden et al., 2006; Schore & Schore, 2007). The freeze immobility response is distinguished by muscular contraction and stiffening coupled with high anxiety and hyperalert senses. During one version of freeze, the person is still able to move. Another version, called tonic immobility, is characterized by motionless rigidity, leading to an inability to move. The feigned death response is a shut down immobility, also called "floppy immobility" (Allen 2001), indicated by numbness, flaccid muscles, flat affect, and reduced cognitive capacity.

The emotional demands of each action system and the physical actions that serve its needs are associated with particular patterns of sensory perception. When sympathetically mediated defensive systems are aroused, perceptions become heightened to threat cues. When the attachment system is stimulated, perceptions become attuned to the proximity of the caregiver or another individual who is close to the person can be relied upon. If exploration is aroused, the senses become heightened to novel, interesting stimuli. Different contexts will evoke different perceptual organization: for instance, the exploration of a research topic requires a different perceptual and motor organization from the exploration of a new part of town.

The habits of an individual's response to the arousal of any action system are developed early in childhood, primed by culture, and adjusted to the behaviors of early key relationships. For example, if caregivers are limited in number and unreliable, proximity-seeking behaviors may become anxious and hyperactive. If caregivers are neglectful or unavailable, or punishing in the face of need or vulnerability, proximity-seeking behaviors may cease or be replaced with approach-avoidance patterns of response (Liotti, 1999). If caregivers are restrictive or overly cautious, the impulse to explore may be hindered.

In traumatogenic environments where caregivers are abusive and/or neglectful, full engagement in daily life action systems is disrupted by frequent arousal of emergency stress responses and instinctive defenses. In communities disproportionately exposed to violence and systemic oppression in all its forms, participating freely in certain daily life activities may be challenging when traumatic reminders are triggered. As well, those who adhere to xenophobic, racist, white supremacist viewpoints may have difficulty participating in activities or with people that stimulate those views and their associated strong emotional and bodily responses. Normal life is disrupted by hyperarousal and mobilizing defenses in both the oppressor (who may react with violence) and the oppressed (who may remain hyperalert). Hypoarousal and immobilizing defenses may also be present, for example when individuals employ passive strategies such as accommodating or placating in the face of a systemic oppression and discrimination that is too pervasive to overcome by direct action (Sue et al., 2019). Hypoarousal, avoidance, and numbing may also be present for the oppressor or person embodying the privileged identity, for example when individuals fail to recognize or ignore the potent impact of their ideology on others or withdraw into the refuge of their privilege. Keep in mind as well that defensive responses are subject to sociocultural priming; thus different cultures may favor different defensive responses. For example, in "honor cultures" where members interpret threats as damaging to the family reputation, fight defenses are more prominent than immobilizing behaviors, but in other cultures when threat is not interpreted as such, compliant behaviors may be more prevalent (Günsoy et al., 2015).

The goals of action systems "extend over long periods of time, with the behavior needed to achieve [them] being adjusted flexibly, in a non-random fashion, to a wide range of environments and to the development of the individual" (George & Solomon, 1999, p. 651). For example, the goals of the exploration system remain relatively constant throughout the life span, even though the behavior required to accomplish these goals is modified and developed as the individual matures and as the environment changes. However, increasing maturity and/or environmental safety and stability may not markedly change patterns developed in a traumatogenic environment. Additionally, patterns may not have the opportunity to be revised in the face of ongoing oppression and the absence of societal protection, which may affect one's ability to respond to action systems of daily life. When marginalized people are continually vulnerable to violent attacks, the curiosity and openness needed to activate the exploration system when interacting with the larger society may be inhibited.

Stimulated by threat, the goals of the defensive system—to defend and protect—conflict with the goals of daily life action systems: to engage with other people and the environment. Each system provokes contradictory emotions, thoughts, and physical actions. For traumatized individuals, responding to the arousal of daily life systems—the needs of one's children, the demands of work, or the sexual needs of one's partner—requires keeping emotions, thoughts, and actions of defensive systems at bay. However, this is accomplished with varying degrees of success. Reactivating stimuli and ongoing triggers repeatedly evoke defensive action systems, which encroach upon and interrupt the tasks of daily life systems. The ability to perform at one's job may be compromised by instinctive defense-related insomnia; experiences of play and laughter may evoke fear or shame followed by avoidance; sexual relations might arouse a cry-for-help or immobilizing defense; when a marginalized person participates in certain sectors of the larger society, the need to be alert to cues of potential threat may interfere with social interactions. Thus, defensive actions can become default behaviors that inhibit actions suitable to daily life unrelated to threat.

Therapists may be baffled or confused when the conflict between defensive and daily life action systems emerges in the therapy hour. Most clients come for treatment with a wish to sleep better, regulate their moods better, feel better about themselves, and have less troubled relationships, yet they instinctively continue to be dominated by their survival defense systems and dysregulated arousal. It can also be confusing for the therapist because the different action systems can involve the alternation of different dissociated parts. For instance, a female client experiences a defensive response of wanting to run when her eyes meet her male therapist's eyes. Her accelerated heart rate and the tension in her legs and feet fuel trauma-related emotions of fear and dread, reactions that sabotage her ability to accurately appraise current reality and interact with her therapist. Feeling trapped and unable to physically leave the therapy office, her arousal plummets as her body resorts to a version of the feigned-death response; she looks away and becomes unresponsive for the remainder of the session. In another example, a gay cisgender male client who has not yet come out experiences a defensive response of wanting to hide when discussing his hopes and dreams for his life. His widening eyes, shallow breath, and the sinking of his shoulders fuel trauma-related emotions of shame and fear, which impede his capacity to stay present with his male therapist. Feeling like he is failing even at therapy, he starts to associate these feelings with negative messages about his sexuality. Suddenly, his upper body and jaw become tight, and he makes comments about his friends being "too gay" and referring to their mannerisms, indicating a displaced fight defense and an internalized homophobia. Both these examples illustrate the emergence of different parts of the self in the therapy hour, which can complicate the therapeutic relationship and the therapy itself.

If a traumatized person repetitively and persistently experiences biphasic alternations between defensive and daily life systems, the result will be increased compartmentalization rather than integration. Janet (1889, 1907) noted this division of the personality when he wrote about the successive alternation of two parts or "psychological existences" in traumatized individuals: "In one [condition], he has sensations, remembrances, movements, which he has not in the other, and consequently he presents, in a manner more or less clear . . . two characters, and in some sort two personalities" (p. 491). What began as a necessary defense in the face of a real past or historical threat becomes a pervasive, unrelenting reaction to the anticipation of threat, with all the concomitant changes in physiology and physical tendencies (Ogden et al., 2006; Ogden & Fisher, 2015). The alternation of reexperiencing with numbing and avoidance becomes habitual and anticipatory. As Steele, Van der Hart, and Nijenhuis state:

> Metaphorically speaking, fault lines occur between action systems of daily life and those of defense, because they naturally tend to mutually inhibit each other. For example, one does not stay focused on cleaning the house or reading when imminent danger is perceived; instead one becomes hypervigilant and prepares for defense. Then, when danger has passed, one should naturally return to normal activities rather than continuing to be in a defensive mode. Integration between these two types of action systems will more likely fail during or following traumatic stress. (2004, p. 17)

In such situations, one part of the self remains fixated in defense against threat, while the other part is dedicated to carrying out the activities of the daily life action systems: attachment, energy regulation, exploration, play, sociability, reproduction, and care-taking. The instinctive defense parts, triggered by exposure to unintegrated fragments of the traumatic memories, remains fixated on the trauma and on surviving it, repetitively rekindling the defensive action system. Note that the language of "parts" is not intended to imply an actual division of the self into discrete, separate entities, but rather to describe the compartmentalization of the relationships between encapsulated action tendencies. Dissociative parts, each mediated by an action system, are not completely separated or split, but rather have some degree of overlap and permeable boundaries in most traumatized clients, with the exception of some who have dissociative identity disorder or DID. "Parts" of the personality are used as "metaphoric descriptive labels of mental [and somatic action] systems that have failed to integrate" (Steele et al., 2004).

DISSOCIATION AND THE NERVOUS SYSTEM

When a person or group is driven by dissociative parts, accurate appraisal of environmental stimuli is compromised at a basic neural level. Porges (2004) coined the term "neuroception" to highlight a neural process that discriminates degrees of environmental safety, danger, and life threat. According to Porges, "the nervous system evaluates risk in the environment and regulates the expression of adaptive behavior to match the neuroception of an environment that is safe, dangerous, or life-threatening" (2011, p. 17). Neuroception occurs unconsciously and automatically when subcortical areas of the brain stimulate neural circuits (Porges, 2011). When a person's environment is "safe enough" for that person, the social engagement system is online, and the action systems of daily living predominate. In this case, neuroception of danger will not be biased by a chronically dysregulated nervous system. However, neuroception is affected by experience-dependent anticipation, as illustrated by the tendency to neurocept danger in the presence of cues associated with previous experiences of threat. Note that such cues can be associated with past trauma of the individual, as well as with the historical trauma of their community of belonging.

Engagement with daily life action systems requires the participation of the ventral vagal complex, or "social engagement system," governed by the ventral branch of the vagus nerve, the myelinated vagus. This complex facilitates responding to daily life action systems in two ways: one, by maintaining arousal within a window of tolerance (Siegel, 1999) such that affect and arousal are well regulated; and, two, by governing areas of the body that are utilized in social and environmental interaction. Porges clarifies:

> The social engagement system has a control component in the cortex (i.e., upper motor neurons) that regulates brain stem nuclei (i.e., lower motor neurons) to control eyelid opening (e.g., looking), facial muscles (e.g., emotional expression), middle ear muscles (e.g., extracting human voice from background noise), muscle of mastication (e.g., ingestion), laryngeal and pharyngeal muscles (e.g., prosody), and head tilting and turning muscles (e.g., social gesture and orientation). (2005, p. 35)

Available to the full-term infant, this neural regulation of facial muscles serves to increase proximity and facilitate the attuned interaction between infant and caregivers that ensures the infant's survival. The social engagement system is further developed via attuned interactions built upon a series of face-to-face, brain-to-brain, body-to-body nonverbal communications with attachment figures that effectively regulate the child's autonomic and emotional arousal.

In order to respond to daily life action systems and thus to adaptively engage with others and the environment in a nonthreatening context, one must neurocept some degree of safety via the ventral vagal complex. The social engagement system is overridden, however, under threat and when reminders of past trauma arouse the defensive system. If danger is neurocepted, the sympathetically mediated instinctive defenses of cry-for-help, fight, and flight are aroused to ensure survival. Note that the cry-for-help response, which occurs in response to neuroception of danger, is quite different from social engagement system–related attachment behaviors that emerge in the context of the neuroception of safety. Cry-for-help responses are accompanied by autonomic hyperarousal, anxious proximity seeking, and sensitivity to rejection. "Alert immobility" (Misslin, 2003, p. 58), a variant of the freeze response, also involves a highly engaged sympathetic system in which "muscle tone, heart rate, sensory acuity, and alertness are all high" (Lewis et al., 2004) to help the person appraise the situation more fully before taking action; note that in this case, action is still possible. Tonic immobility, another variant of freeze, involves activation of both sympathetic and parasympathetic systems leading to rigid immobility; in this case, the individual feels unable to move.

Although hyperarousal has commonly been considered the hallmark of PTSD, not all traumatized individuals respond to trauma reminders with hyperarousal. In a script-driven provocation study, 30% of subjects responded with hypoarousal in response to hearing their trauma scripts read (Lanius et al., 2002). This finding might be attributed to the failure of both the social engagement system and the sympathetically mediated defensive responses to ensure safety. Parasympathetic nervous system activity via the dorsal vagal complex becomes the next and best line of defense. The neuroception of inescapable threat (as contrasted with the neuroception of danger when survival still appears to be possible) stimulates the dorsal vagal system to enable survival-related immobilization: feigning death, behavioral shutdown, and syncope. The dorsal branch of the vagus nerve, the unmyelinated vagus, is the most primitive of these systems and is available at birth (Porges, 2011).

When this system is aroused, sympathetic arousal quickly changes "from interactive regulatory modes into long-enduring less complex [dorsal vagal] autoregulatory modes" (Schore, 2009, p. 8). In these hypoaroused states, observed even in newborns (Bergman et al., 2004), the person is nonresponsive to interactive regulation (Schore, 2009). Many functions of the body begin to slow down, leading to "a relative decrease in heart rate and respiration and . . . a sense of 'numbness,' 'shutting down within the mind,' and separation from the sense of self" (Siegel, 1999, p. 254). When action is not feasible, extreme dorsal vagal arousal can result in fainting, vomiting, or loss of control of the rectal sphincter (Frijda, 1986). This final defensive response is sometimes called "total submission" (Van der Hart et al., 2006).

The hierarchical relationships between ventral vagal parasympathetic (social engagement), sympathetic, and dorsal vagal parasympathetic systems are established early in life, resulting in enduring arousal tendencies, reactions under stress, and even vulnerability to psychiatric disorders (Cozolino, 2002; Lyons-Ruth & Jacobvitz, 1999; Porges, 2011; Schore, 2001, p. 209; Sroufe, 1997; Van IJzendoorn et al., 1999). Early trauma, especially repeated trauma, "functionally retunes neuroception to conservatively detect risk when there is no risk" (Porges, 2011, p. 253). And historical trauma functions as a secondary trauma for some members of marginalized groups when exposed to triggers of their history. For instance, skeletons hanging by the neck from a tree at Halloween may be a traumatic reminder of lynchings of African Americans. Trauma, both direct and secondary, compromises the ability to accurately assess whether other people or the environment are safe, trustworthy, or dangerous, and thus results in the development of "faulty" or biased neuroception (Porges, 2011). In addition, structurally dissociated individuals may find that some trauma-related parts of the self are biased toward hypovigilance or decreased ability to detect threat while other parts of the self are driven by heightened threat detection and the activation of instinctive defenses, both sympathetic and dorsal vagal responses.

In either case, engagement with daily life action systems, which require a neuroception of safety, is hampered or prevented. Janet (1907, p. 332) pointed out a century ago that individuals with complex trauma-related disorders develop "a tendency to the dissociation and emancipation of the systems of ideas and functions that constitute personality." In individuals and in groups, neuroception of safety, danger, or life threat can become compartmentalized. When hyperarousal (neuroception of danger) and hypoarousal (neuroception of impending life threat) become extreme and enduring, responses and processes that are normally unified and integrated may become chronically dissociated. While some authors (Perry et al., 1995) state that only hypoaroused conditions are dissociative, Janet's (1898, 1907) description of dissociation as a failure of integrative capacity applies to both hypoaroused and hyperaroused states (Allen, 2001; Krystal et al., 1998; Van der Hart et al., 2004). An example of this is seen in a female client whose dissociative hypoaroused state of "not being there," associated with a feigned death defense, endured sexual abuse as an adult from a family member without complaint or resistance. However, her dissociative hyperaroused state correlated with an unintegrated fight defense that manifested as explosive aggression, which led her to physically abuse her children when they disobeyed her in minor ways. She profoundly regretted both of these behaviors when she "came back to herself" and to the parts able to neurocept safety and engage in daily life action systems.

When traumatic reminders stimulate these extreme arousal states, neuroception that is biased toward danger or life threat evokes instinctive defensive responses. It is important to note that even when arousal is within the window of tolerance, individuals may still have trauma-related parts that neurocept danger and life threat dissociatively, and remain compartmentalized and unintegrated with parts that can neurocept safety. Under these circumstances, the individual's ability to process and integrate trauma-related information is compromised even when arousal is within the window of tolerance. In the same environmental situation, one dissociative part of the individual may neurocept safety, while other dissociative parts rooted in defense may neurocept danger or life threat. Thus, in dissociative disorders, the individual is dissociated not only when hyper- and hypoaroused, but also when arousal is within the window.

For individuals with trauma-related disorders, it is profoundly challenging to integrate the markedly different states of consciousness, memory, identity, and action tendencies connected to different parts of the self, each governed by different action systems, combinations of action systems, and nervous system arousal. Integration can occur over time, in therapeutic dyads, through the collective process of metabolizing trauma, and in different contexts outside of the therapy room. It is an extended process that includes both physical and mental actions that facilitate a unified sense of self (and community) and help the client assimilate their traumatic past (Steele et al., 2009). The concept of structural dissociation points to a number of important features crucial to an understanding and treatment of dissociative disorders through Sensorimotor Psychotherapy: the inherent conflict between action systems of defense and those of normal daily life; the way in which physical and mental action tendencies related to each action system become encapsulated into parts of the self; the essential role of the therapeutic relationship, the client's capacity for mental integrative and integrated physical action.

SENSORIMOTOR PSYCHOTHERAPY TREATMENT

The failure to integrate defensive action systems with those of daily life manifests physically, not just psychologically. Preconscious somatic patterns of muscle tension, posture, gaze, facial expression, and other behavioral tendencies based on past and historical events, triggered by both reminders and current traumatic events, continually influence conscious perceptions and predictions. As previously discussed, each action system is associated with particular patterns of physical action tendencies unique to that system. And the specific action systems that mediate various parts also constrain them, leading to somewhat fixed and inflexible actions (Steele et al., 2009). Physical actions of diverse parts of the self can vary widely, depending on the action system that most influences the part. Since action systems are inherently physical in nature, the lack of integration among parts can be clearly perceived in the lack of integration in a dissociative client's movements, and thus addressing the body directly can be a powerful avenue of integration.

In Sensorimotor Psychotherapy individual treatment, therapists and clients together study clients' somatic and mental patterns of response to the arousal of action systems. Developing accurate neuroception and fostering more adaptive, integrated actions related to daily (nonthreatening) life activities, as well as adaptive flexibility of defensive responses to threatening situations, require that both categories of action systems be explored simultaneously, and purposefully evoked in therapy. The therapist's social engagement system facilitates the social engagement system of the client in order to maintain the presence of at least one part of the client that neurocepts a degree of safety, and also to develop a therapeutic relationship that can serve as a secure base for discovering habitual reactions to the arousal of each of the action systems, including defensive ones, and exploring new responses.

It is important to note that the identities and social locations of both therapist and client may play out dissociated aspects of culture. Identifying physical actions and patterns in both parties and bringing awareness to how they participate in unconscious dialogue with each other may help the therapist and client negotiate enactments, which can soften the inflexibility of the automatic responses of dissociation (see Chapter 10, this volume). Additionally, therapy is more complicated when trauma such as oppression is ongoing, rather than in the past. In the face of current discrimination, racial profiling, denial of resources, and other acts of systemic oppression, clients can learn to recognize the early bodily signals of dysregulated arousal and develop strategies and resources that can return arousal expeditiously to a window of tolerance, thus preventing prolonged distress and dysregulation. Because systemic oppression is ongoing, and related triggers will be faced in the future, the client and the therapist may identify additional resources for responding to these threat cues in a more adaptive and nuanced way. Clients can develop a variety of somatic resources that can be called upon in different situations— for instance grounding and regulating in one situation in which they are triggered, moving away in a different circumstance, or stating a boundary in another.

In the following case illustration, client and therapist share similar locations, but even in those similar locations there are nuances of differences. In cross-cultural dyads, the differences are more obvious and profound. The reactions of the different parts of the client involve a combination of past traumas, relational failures, and privilege/oppression dynamics; hence, interactions in the therapy room are a potential opportunity to explore and bring to awareness such dynamics at both the individual and systemic/structural level.

CLINICAL EXAMPLE

Julie is a married 58-year-old white, cisgender client with a heterosexual sexual orientation and middle socioeconomic status. She suffered neglect and sexual abuse from infancy through adolescence and reported that her older sister remembered that Julie was often kept in a closed drawer as a baby. Although Julie had no recall of her first three years, she did remember spending hours hiding in her closet as a child, hoping that her father would not find her. In her current life, dysregulated arousal frequently disrupted daily life action systems associated with marriage, work, play, and child rearing, despite Julie's best attempts to avoid reminders of past trauma in an effort to prevent her arousal from exceeding a window of tolerance. Even when her arousal was within the window, her traumatic experience was not integrated but avoided and thus remained dissociated. The parts engaged in daily life action systems steered clear of traumatic reminders.

Julie reported symptoms of terror, panic, hyperalertness, and impulses to run, alternating with feelings of shame and self-disgust, shutdown, and motor weakness. She described hypoarousal episodes that occurred frequently, even during her previous therapy, for which she was often amnesic. In the hypoaroused condition, she often experienced time loss and time distortions and said she sometimes felt so "dead" that she wanted someone to hit her so that she could "come back." At other times, when she was able to avoid traumatic reminders, she reported engaging in a detached way to communicate with her husband, raise her child, and go to work as a psychotherapist—all activities related to daily life action systems. Her arousal was within a window of tolerance during these times, indicating that this part of her neurocepted some degree of safety, although she reported often feeling emotionally "flat," "just going through the motions," and a sense of distrust despite her apparent ease in talking with others. At other times, reminders of the trauma caused Julie to neurocept danger or imminent life threat, driving arousal past the edges of her window of tolerance and disrupting her daily life functioning. Unable to avoid traumatic reminders in her daily life, she expressed great difficulty functioning in social situations and was constantly triggered by her clients' stories. For Julie, and for others with trauma-related disorders, going on with normal life required remaining dissociatively compartmentalized and distanced from the parts of her holding the trauma-related arousal, affects, and defensive responses.

Julie was frustrated that she felt like a different person in each of these states and wondered why she could not seem to "just live" her life. She was internally aware of the "going on with daily life" part and the shut-down part, as well as other parts of herself that had a different "consciousness, memory, identity, or perception of the environment" (American Psychiatric Association, 2000, p. 519) and markedly different symptoms. For example, the part of Julie that was compliant neurocepted threat unless she was sure that people close to her were pleased, and she tried hard to satisfy them. The part of her that engaged the defensive response of flight was activated when people were displeased, and then she searched her surroundings for ways of escape. During the periods when she succeeded at maintaining regulated arousal and focus on day-to-day life, Julie contended with the fear of losing control over the hyper- and hypoarousal states that threatened at any moment to usurp her ability to carry out daily life activities. She did her best to prevent this from happening by avoiding trauma-related cues, achieved at the cost of continued dissociation.

Julie sought Sensorimotor Psychotherapy with the first author (Pat Ogden) of this chapter because, after years of talk therapy, she still could not live her life as she wanted. She was baffled by her radical fluctuations in mood, and her subjective experience was one of separation, fragmentation, memory lapses, and unpredictable intrusions. Julie initially was frightened to work somatically because her body alternately felt numb or agitated, making it anxiety provoking to be in touch with bodily sensations and movements. She did not understand how somatic work could benefit her and had only come to Sensorimotor Psychotherapy because a previous therapist had recommended it.

PHASE 1 TREATMENT: BODY AWARENESS AND STABILIZATION

A primary intention of initial contact and intake, along with assessment and formulating a beginning plan for treatment, is to establish a trusting therapeutic relationship, which is supported by the therapist's understanding of the client's difficulties and presenting problems, and the confidence that these can be effectively addressed. Especially when the client has marginalized locations, the beginning of therapy requires establishing the therapist's credibility as one who understands issues of oppression, discrimination, immigration, and so forth. As mentioned in Chapter 1, this includes radical openness and cultural humility, demonstrated when discussing privilege/oppression dynamics, talking about the historical and sociopolitical context of the client's presenting issues, or making overt the locations of the therapist and how they differ from the client's. However, these explorations depend upon both the client's receptivity and the strength of the therapeutic relationship. The timing of these discussions needs to be geared to the client, not the therapist. That said, broaching these issues early in the therapy can help the client feel welcome to bring them up themselves as the treatment continues.

Julie's first session included psychoeducation relevant to her concerns. Like many clients, Julie was distressed and ashamed of her "unreasonable" bodily reactions. Ongoing psychoeducation helped her both make sense of and normalize her symptoms and gave her hope for resolution. Learning about how a history of trauma and attachment failure impacts posture, movement, and physiology also helped her appreciate the potential value of sensorimotor interventions. In the first phase of therapy, it was important that Julie understand the nature of dissociation and instinctive defense-driven parts of the self. Reassurance that her disturbing symptoms were purposeful, protective, and expected, that they reflected the alternation between defensive systems and daily life systems, and that a senso-rimotor approach could help her meet her goal of increased enjoy-ment of her life were important elements of Julie's psychoeducation.

Planning mutually agreeable somatic interventions with clear goals sets the stage for success. Clients often benefit from being asked how they "would behave differently or what they would like to be able to do after [therapy] that they cannot currently do" (Bundy, 2002, p. 212). When I asked Julie to imagine how she would like her experience to be different, she replied, "I would like to feel competent and be able to enjoy my life without get-ting so weird." In other words, she wanted to be able to respond adaptively to daily life action systems without her defensive systems being activated. Despite the different goals of parts driven by defen-sive subsystems, this overarching wish was the impetus that encour-aged Julie to explore the body-oriented interventions she needed to achieve her goal. The initial phase of therapy, phase 1 stabiliza-tion, focused on assessing her faulty neuroception and quieting her defensive subsystems.

Building Relational Resources: Different
Parts Have Different Reactions

It is of utmost importance that the therapist be aware of the poten-tial subsystems or parts of the self in clients like Julie rather than assuming that she is well integrated based on her ability to function. Therapist and client together seek to understand the entire disso-ciative system of the client and to improve cooperation and com-munication among all parts. The client's body reveals observable cues that pertain to various parts, as we shall see in Julie's work. For example, during one of our early sessions, as she mentioned her childhood, Julie's eyes locked onto mine as if her life depended on maintaining eye contact. Her terrified gaze spoke of the danger she neurocepted when telling the secret of her abuse and seemed to reflect a cry-for-help part. I asked her to be aware of what happened when my eyes met hers, and she reported feeling safer and able to take a deeper breath. Julie resonated with my explanation that eye contact between us could be a relational resource, something we could use consciously to help her to stay engaged with me and feel safer.

Different parts will typically have different reactions to a given intervention, as well as different transferences to the therapist, and an intervention that is helpful for one part may not be so for another. Julie's eyes locking onto mine represented the desperate action of a part seeking protection, but it was evident that another part frightened by connection and proximity also needed attention. I carefully tracked Julie's responses to my eye contact and physical proximity in the initial stage of treatment. I noticed that when our eyes met, her body pulled back; when I took a step toward her, she consistently took a little step back; when I leaned forward in my chair, she moved back in hers. She also frequently glanced at the door. All of these reactions appeared to belong to a flight part that, alarmed by eye contact and proximity, wanted to escape.

When I brought her attention to her body pulling away, Julie, speaking from the part influenced by daily life systems of attachment and sociability (and thus neurocepting some degree of safety), stated that it was "fine" with her that we were near to one another. However, the signals of her body had already disclosed a part of her that neurocepted danger and prepared for flight when the proximity between us increased. With the intention of integrating these parts and their physical action tendencies, I suggested that we explore what might be an optimal distance for both parts of her. This collaboration between us increased her social engagement and strengthened the parts of her that functioned in daily life. Social engagement helped Julie to stay present in the here and now and to regulate her arousal within the window of tolerance, which in turn lowered the reactivity of the parts that were driven by defensive action systems.

As I asked Julie to sense what was the "right" distance between us, she again repeated that where I sat was "fine." Recognizing that this was the perspective of only one part connected to daily life systems, I said, "I wonder which position feels better to you?" Slowly, I moved my chair further away from her, and then moved it closer, asking Julie if she noticed any difference in her reactions. Julie recognized that she felt better when I moved away; her body relaxed, but her clinging eyes expressed fear. By increasing the distance between us, I had met the needs of the part of her that was frightened of proximity, left over from the abuse proximity brought her in her childhood, but the cry-for-help part desperately needed me close as a safe haven and seemed to fear that I had "left her" when I moved away.

As I returned Julie's unfaltering eye contact, I asked her to notice if she could sense if I was with her or leaving her energetically. She reported that she could see I was still with her. I asked her if the fearful part of her could make eye contact with me and also see that energetically I was still with her. Next, I asked her to notice what my eyes told this fearful part of her. She reported that my eyes looked engaged, and she could see that I had not abandoned her. With this, the fearful, cry-for-help part of her was reassured, and Julie's eyes lost much of their fear.

Different goals of various action systems manifested in the above excerpt, creating a multitude of conflicting thoughts, feelings, and actions in Julie. The flight part attempted to increase distance, while the cry-for-help part aimed to increase proximity. And another part simply wanted to participate in the present moment without the interference of defensive subsystems, so reported being "fine." Julie and I were faced with the complicated task of fostering integration by attending to the goals of all these systems simultaneously. As these three parts of the self—influenced by various action systems—were held in awareness, communication among the parts was facilitated.

Physical experiments such as those illustrated above can be more nuanced or have varying implications depending on the identities and social locations of therapist and client—race, socioeconomic status, gender, age, religion, sexual orientation, ability, education, language, geographic location, immigration status, and the like. Therapists need to recognize the differences in identities and sometimes address them, which "requires seeing the differences, seeking a contextualized understanding of the differences, and examining one's own identity statuses and social locations in relationship to the differences" (Harrell & Bond, 2006, p. 374). Without awareness, for example, a white therapist might compensate by being overly friendly with a client who belongs to a different race, not wanting to be perceived as racist by the client. On the other hand in another example, a male therapist who is cognizant of the privilege and impact of his male identity will be aware that the signals of defensive systems of a client like Julie, such as the widening of her eyes and the pulling back of the body, are likely influenced not only by past trauma but by sexism and constructions of heteronormative gender roles. These dynamics, linked to centuries of patriarchy and the oppression of women's bodies, might be important to explore, especially if they were also implicated in the client's personal history of abuse. If the therapist were dark complexioned, Julie's reaction might be primed by racial bias that she may be unaware of, such as the dominant culture's portrayal of dark-complexioned men as dangerous or untrustworthy. If the therapist is not aware of and able to address such dynamics, therapy will be compromised, if not explicitly, then implicitly.

The advantage of a somatic approach is that the therapist is alert to the client's physical signals that might indicate dynamics related to the different social locations of therapist and client and can bring them to the client's attention and explore their meaning. In this way, bias can be uncovered and challenged in the context of therapy. When signs of defensive systems emerge as client and therapist experiment with distance between them, they can explore the underpinnings, which may be related to the differences in their identities. For example, the uneasiness a white female client experienced as she and her Black female therapist experimented with proximity was partially influenced by the client's implicit bias and stereotype that Black women are easily angered. Because the therapist tracked the client's averted eye contact and tension in her body, and named these indicators of defensive systems, their meaning could be discovered. In this way, the client's bias, revealed in bodily signals, was made conscious, providing the opportunity to challenge and revise the inaccurate racial bias. In this way, with a culturally sensitive therapist, clients might have more opportunities to track their bodily signals of defensive parts and explore possible underlying bias in relationship to the different social locations of therapist and client. This can support clients in their capacity to regulate in the presence of others of different locations and be receptive to more accurate data about what is safe and unsafe in others that is not based on bias and stereotypes.

It is imperative to maintain social engagement between client and therapist, to track when it is in jeopardy, and to reestablish it. The activation of the social engagement system keeps the client "right here, right now," maintains arousal within the window of tolerance, and stimulates parts involved in daily life action systems of exploration, sociability, and even play. If the client's social engagement diminishes or is lost, which occurs automatically as defensive parts emerge and may occur when privilege/oppression dynamics and differing identities are at play as illustrated above, when traumatic reminders are present, or when the client feels misattuned to, the therapist must focus on what will enable the client to reengage. In the above example with Julie, I tracked for signs of flight and cry-for-help parts, and then we were able to discover what those parts needed to prevent further dysregulation. It is crucial that the therapist and client be on the alert for signals of defensive responses, and explore their cause, whether they emerge in relation to the therapist, to their differing identities, to recalling past trauma that is now over, to reminders of past or historical trauma, or in reaction to current oppression and threat. From an open and collaborative assessment, therapist and client can better determine how to quiet these defenses when they are not needed or, if threats are current, to learn how to return arousal quickly to a window of tolerance once safety is reestablished. Without a present orientation and regulated arousal, traumatic triggers—which occur in the therapy hour as we saw above—can result in the unfettered emergence of parts rooted in defensive subsystems, usurping therapeutic gains and exacerbating dissociative tendencies.

Mapping Parts of the Self

Julie was perplexed and distressed by her discordant behaviors, thoughts, and feelings. Additional psychoeducation helped her understand the dramatic shifts she experienced as reflections of the roles of different parts in managing the effects of trauma. I clarified that the use of parts language did not indicate an actual split of the self but referred to the functions of action systems of defense and daily life. She resonated with the parts terminology and was relieved to hear that the internal conflicts were logical, and that it was possible to work toward integrating them. I suggested we might map her internal system by identifying the behaviors, thoughts, emotions, memories, and especially physical components associated with each part, and writing or drawing a representation of each one on paper. The purpose of this exercise is to identify parts that are correlated with both defensive and daily life action systems regulation and integration (Fisher, 2017; Ogden 2020; Ogden & Fisher, 2015).

First, we mapped parts associated with daily life action systems. Julie said that the part of her that wanted to please was connected to daily life, and although she realized that this part also was trying to appease others to stay safe, she also genuinely took pleasure in contributing to the happiness of those close to her, particularly her daughter. She also identified a capable part that could go to work and be sociable. She reported that a signal of the pleasing part (when the part did not usurp her own wishes) was a smile and relaxed eye contact, while the capable part was experienced in a lift of her chest, a sense of her back, and a slight lengthening of her spine.

After psychoeducation about the various defensive subsystems, Julie reported that she had no fight part, but she had no insight into why. However, we were able to identify various other defensive subsystems and make a list of their somatic signs: the widening and clinging of her eyes, a fear of being left, and "feeling like a child" indicated the cry-for-help part; impulses to move back and look at the door signaled the flight part; and an overall feeling of numbness, slumped posture, a downward turn of her head, a spacey feeling, and lack of body sensation were the characteristics of the collapsed part to whom "nothing mattered." She was frequently amnesic for those periods of time when she was severely hypoaroused, which appeared to be related to a feigned-death defense and increased dorsal vagal tone. Of course, this extreme hypoarousal profoundly disrupted her ability to function in her life. Julie routinely submitted to emotional abuse from her boss. Sexual advances from her husband often precipitated Julie "leaving" her body, and at times she did not remember their sexual contact. She expressed shame and dislike for these shut-down, submissive tendencies.

It is essential to understand that each part of the self has an important function. Julie and I discussed how her survival resource of hypoarousal, compliance, and shutdown minimized the severity of the abuse when she was a child, whereas trying to fight or flee her father would have been ill-advised. Her mobilizing flight and fight responses were abandoned in favor of the more adaptive (in that situation) immobilizing defenses. Julie began to relinquish some of her harsh self-judgment in favor of curiosity. Together we explored questions like, "How is this part helping you? How can we understand your body's language? What is this slumped posture and spacey feeling telling us? How did you best protect yourself and survive when you were little? How can we appreciate these parts that helped you survive?"

If clients are receptive to exploring topics of gender, class, race, or other social locations, the psychoeducation and mapping of the different parts might include exploring oppression of women, of LGBTQ+ people, of darker-complexioned people, of refugees, and so forth, and whether the client has internalized these oppression dynamics. For example, a dark-skinned Indian woman living in the U.S. presented with eating-disordered behaviors that turned out to be about challenges of multiracial identity. Therapy addressed not only the eating disorder but also the dynamics of oppression internalized as negative messages about her body (e.g., that dark skin is undesirable and kinky hair is ugly) that she had received from her external environment. It was not until the impact of these detrimental messages was realized that the symptoms of the eating disorder started to abate. Considering sociocultural influences and different role models can allow some clients to develop more understanding and acceptance of the parts of themselves that internalized oppression. For example, a white female client who was physically abused throughout childhood discovered that she had internalized the messages of the media (through advertising, movies and TV shows, and the like) that the role of a woman was to please others, be compliant and tolerant, and be amenable to the demands of male authority figures. The client and her therapist acknowledged the adaptive function of this stance in a patriarchal society and family, considering the repercussions of not adhering to these messages.

Initial Goals: Strengthening Daily Life Functioning and Regulating Hypoarousal

Drawing upon our list of somatic signs, Julie and I were able to strengthen the parts connected to daily life, observe the emergence of defensive parts, particularly the hypoaroused part, during the course of therapy, and foster awareness of present-focused internal communication among these parts. One of our first goals was to bolster the capable part, so we explored the lift in her chest and length in her spine, finding words ("I can do it") and feelings ("determination") that went along with these physical indicators. For several weeks early in therapy, Julie practiced embodying the lift in her chest and length in her spine between sessions, consciously building up the part of her that was capable of engaging in daily life.

Another initial goal was to develop resources that Julie could implement when she became immobilized and hypoaroused. We decided to focus on her sexual relationship with her husband because we thought that by doing so, Julie might begin to experience some of the somatic signs of hypoarousal that we had previously identified. From her present-moment experience of these symptoms in the therapy hour, we hoped to discover the specific somatic resources she needed. As Julie began to think about this topic, and tried to talk about it, she reported a trapped feeling, which quickly led to some of the symptoms we had listed: feeling numb and spacey, a slumping of her spine, and loss of sensation in her body. I suggested that we stand and walk together to notice that our legs could carry us away from certain objects in the room and closer to others. Julie soon said she felt more present and observed that it felt good to notice her legs. The experience of mobility was a simple action that helped alleviate Julie's numb, spacey feeling. Her social engagement system enabled her to stay in relationship with me as we consciously executed the physical action of the flight response through locomotion to mitigate the immobilization of the collapsed part.

Throughout therapy with clients with dissociative disorders, every intervention is intended to support integration, providing ways for parts to communicate somatically, not just verbally. After we sat down, I asked Julie to take this newfound felt awareness of her ability to use her legs to escape back to the hypoaroused part of her. She reported that the collapsed child, whom she saw vividly as a child lying passively on her father's bed, felt supported by sensing her legs and the capacity to get out, an action that she could not have safely accomplished at that time. It was also important to communicate to this child part of her that the past was over, she was no longer trapped, and she could safely use different, more empowering, actions in her current life. Julie's body relaxed during this exploration, and she reported a new ability to sense her entire body, whereas previously she was only able to feel parts of it at a time. Again, throughout, the part of Julie that could engage in daily life and with me was encouraged to stay present, aware, and in charge, rather than allowing parts rooted in instinctive defenses to take over.

When working with those who perpetrate trauma on others, identifying parts that committed the actions and other parts that can help regulate aggressive actions is critical. For a white male client who was repeatedly violent with his wife and children, recognizing the signals of his hyperarousal and dysregulated fight defense (rush of energy upward, and tension in his jaw, eyes, and fists) was the first step in his treatment. Discovering somatic resources (taking a breath, opening his fists, and placing his hands on his torso) when he experienced these signals became the tools he needed to curtail his impulsive violent outbursts. As he practiced these actions over and over, he became less reactive and developed more confidence in his regulatory capacity, which prepared him for addressing his own traumatic memories of a violent father.

Clients occupy both marginalized and privileged locations, and intersectionality and social location will always impact therapy and the relationship. Julie, for example, benefits from white skin privilege while her gender locates her on the downside of power. In society, most positions of power are filled by individuals who represent privileged locations, for example, in the United States by upper-middle-class heterosexual white cisgender men. In Julie's family, her father also occupied the position of power and authority, and that, combined with the abuse she suffered, left Julie feeling generally unsafe around men. She learned to identify resources—a deeper breath and discreet self-hug—that reassured the frightened part of her when she was in mixed social situations. She also learned to acknowledge and use the resources that she had acquired (aligned spine and upper chest, with more capacity for voice) that could help her to be more active when expressing her views or defending her rights as a woman. It can be helpful for clients who occupy marginalized locations (in Julie's case, of being female) to expand their referential images and reclaim role models and historical narratives that had been hidden by the predominant culture, as well as to integrate a narrative of resilience that can support clients. For example, Julie might benefit from finding alternative role models in other women, both in this lifetime and across history, that challenge the images and messages about women that she has received and introjected, and embody these new resources and ideas. Julie might also find inspiration in other women of her own ancestral and cultural lineages and in her present community that demonstrate resilience. Such explorations can help the client find resources for and integrate parts of themselves that have been or are oppressed or have marginalized locations.

Use of Embedded Relational Mindfulness

Through the use of embedded relational mindfulness (cf. Chapter 4, this volume), Julie and I together were able to notice her present-moment experience, including the physical tendencies of various dissociative parts. She could also be mindful of how different actions altered her here-and-now emotions and thoughts, and of which actions facilitated communication between parts. Embedded relational mindfulness engages the prefrontal cortex in studying the present-moment internal experience of dissociative parts, rather than enacting them, and includes labeling and describing experience (Kurtz, 1990; Ogden et al., 2006; Siegel, 2006). Because mindfulness is "motivated by curiosity" (Kurtz, 1990, p. 111), it activates the exploration system and facilitates a nonjudgmental acceptance of internal experience, allowing emotions, thoughts, and sensations "simply to be there, to bring to them a kindly awareness, to adopt toward them a more 'welcome' than a 'need to solve' stance" (Segal et al., 2002, p. 55).

A Western description of mindfulness typically refers to being open and receptive to "whatever arises within the mind's eye" (Siegel, 2006) without preference. The use of "directed mindfulness" (Ogden, 2007, 2009) helps the client be precisely aware of particular elements of present-moment experience considered important to therapeutic goals. In the initial phase of Julie's therapy, I directed her mindfulness specifically to increase her awareness of resources that helped her stabilize, asking questions like, "Can you say what happens in your body right now as you sense your legs carrying you through space?" When clients' mindfulness is not directed (as in open-ended questions like, "What are you feeling in your body?"), they are often confused by the conflicting feelings they experience that represent conflicting perspectives of their dissociative parts.

Directed mindfulness was instrumental in helping Julie further develop length in her posture, which supported her to assert herself appropriately in her environment. Julie had great difficulty setting boundaries and saying "no," a submissive tendency that belonged to the hypoaroused part of her and the slumped posture and spaciness that characterized that part. We challenged her compliance by changing her posture. I first demonstrated a more assertive posture by extending my spine to stand more erect and then tactfully contrasted this movement with an imitation of Julie's slumped posture so that she could notice and describe the differences she observed. Next, Julie tried out both options, and together we explored moving back and forth between these two extremes with the purpose of Julie discovering for herself a posture between these two polarities that felt most integrative. In the initial phase of treatment, length in the spine was practiced as a somatic resource that strengthened

Julie's capability to engage in daily life. But at this point in her treatment, an integrative function of this posture was explored. It was essential that Julie not override the collapsed part of herself by compliantly imitating my assertive posture but instead mindfully experiment by practicing different postures, noticing each part's reaction, and finding a stance that felt both assertive and inclusive of the collapsed part of her, and was acceptable to both parts.

Because both therapist and client are representative of larger societal groups, the location of each can be important to consider in relationship to practicing postures and actions. For example, a client like Julie might mindfully experiment with the degree of length in her spine, inclusive of the collapsed part, while making eye contact with her therapist, or while she imagines facing a person with a different location, such as a male authority figure. A refugee might visualize immigration authorities, while a domestic violence survivor might visualize their abuser. As discussed, the social location of the therapist can also be identified and explored, as when a female client notices what happens as she executes a boundary action toward her male therapist, while the therapist's gender presentation is directly named. In mindful experiments such as these, new resources may be added; for example, one client discovered that taking a breath and lifting their chin as they executed a boundary action while visualizing their boss helped them relax their shoulders, and supported social engagement rather than withdrawal. Mindful explorations such as these can support clients' ability to generalize the resources and actions they are learning in therapy to a variety of situations outside the therapy room.

Somatic Indicators of Additional Parts

Over several sessions during which Julie and I worked with new posture, she became mindful of three parts: one that was afraid of assertion, one with persecutory voices that judged her for not having asserted herself previously, and yet another part that feared punishment if she were to be assertive. Each had characteristic physical concomitants that contributed to Julie's feeling of fragmentation. The judgment was held in her lifted chin, disgusted look, and narrowed eyes; the fear of punishment was held in her hiked shoulders and rounded back, while the fear of assertion manifested in a general pulling in and immobility of her body, representing a newly discovered freeze part associated with the instinctive defense of tense immobility. These parts were added to the map of internal parts that Julie and I had initially created. All had to be addressed, their function acknowledged and appreciated, their resistance to each other explored, and their discordant action tendencies integrated in such a way that no part was overridden.

As we together embodied each part, we began to ask questions that facilitated understanding about the function and motivation of each part. As we took on the judgmental part by lifting our chins and narrowing our eyes, we asked, "What might this part be saying with this lifted chin and narrowed eyes?" to which Julie first replied, "It's disgusted because I didn't defend myself." As we stayed with the physical embodiment of this part to find a deeper meaning and salubrious function, Julie said, "It's trying to tell me that I have a right to be angry and assertive." We also realized as together we took on the fear of assertion by pulling in and becoming immobile that this frozen part was trying to keep her from getting hurt even more. We tracked the changes in Julie's body as the physical movements helped parts exchange information, and Julie began to sense her body as less fragmented. Her empathy for and understanding of the functions of these parts was elucidated as well, contributing to her acceptance of each part. Eventually, we discovered and practiced a new posture in which she felt the collapsed part of her was being protected by a more assertive part. Gradually, over time, her new posture began to feel more comfortable and solid, and she grew increasingly capable of saying "no" in a way that felt integrative and inclusive of the collapsed part, as well as respectful of the parts that were judgmental or afraid of assertion or fearful of punishment.

Parts and their somatic indicators can also be associated with societal messages connected to cultural norms and myths that the client has internalized. For example, a white person of privilege may be fearful of a person with Middle Eastern features, and experience tension and thoughts such as "I am afraid you will hurt me," which can activate defensive parts. In another example, parts might be signaling introjected racism: A Latinx client told of an internal bully that said, "I'm so lazy," which brought forward different internal parts of both the bully (rooted in societal messages) and the part that was bullied. If the therapeutic alliance is strong and the therapist is culturally aware, these internalized myths can be explored with curiosity that can mitigate defensiveness or shame. Psychoeducation provided at the beginning of therapy, as well as discussing the societal messages that might be related to parts of the self throughout therapy, can support the client in naming and unveiling parts that belong to a larger cultural narrative, which may emerge in many forms, such as submission, fear, shame, defiance, self-judgment, or entitlement.

Tracking the moment-to-moment somatic shifts, the therapist and the client are attentive to the dialogue and information coming from all these parts, and their deeper function, as well as their biases and costs. For example, an African American therapist and his female client explored lifting their chins, breathing deeply, and aligning their posture to embody her assertive part. The client, reacting from internalized biases toward darker skin, felt suspicious about the therapist's intentions and neurocepted danger, which manifested in tension, gaze aversion, and pulling away in her body, and a clipped, matter-of-fact speech. Because they had discussed the possibility of privilege/oppression dynamics showing up in their relationship at the onset of therapy, and because the therapist tracked and named these physical indicators in the therapy hour, the client became aware of her bias, which was discussed and challenged.

Afterward, the client could practice this new posture that incorporated her assertiveness with her therapist embodying the same posture, with a reaction based on his genuine support of her deep desire to be heard and respected, rather than on the societal messages she had internalized about darker skin indicating threat.

Appreciating and Challenging Parts

Acknowledging that every part of the self has a purpose, and discovering exactly what the purpose is, facilitates acceptance and eventual integration. The part of Julie that had collapsed and submitted in the face of life threat was not interpreted as negative but acknowledged as the best defense for that time and place, to be celebrated even as its survival responses were being transformed and integrated with other parts of the self. We repeatedly thanked this part (and other parts) for the service that had been so essential in the past, facilitating its integration as a life-preserving instinctive defense rather than a humiliating defeat. At the same time, we challenged this part of her in such a way that safe, assertive, relational action could be experienced as new alternatives to foster fuller participation in daily life. If this hypoarousal pattern had been understood and interpreted but gone unchallenged, Julie would have continued to experience the same survival-oriented defensive habits of collapse in response to the same cues in her daily life again and again. Instead, slowly, she experienced more stabilization, more ability for assertion, connection, and self-care, and fewer hypoaroused, amnesic episodes.

In working with perpetrators, the parts that oppress others or commit violence also need to be both acknowledged and challenged. Discovering these parts and their underlying function, regulating their actions, and challenging their beliefs are all important in healing. For example, one client who had repeatedly raped his girlfriend when she was intoxicated discovered in therapy that the part of him associated with those acts felt terribly inadequate and had desperately wanted approval from his father, who also had abused women. He first discovered the part that committed the acts, experienced as overall tension, a hardening of his heart, and a narrowing of his eyes, but underneath was a tender child part. Eventually, he could challenge the negative beliefs of the perpetrator part (that he had to assert dominance to earn respect) and of the child part (that he was completely worthless), and learn new actions to soothe the child part of him that felt "like scum" by taking a breath and placing his hands over his heart. Once this occurred, he began to express the remorse and shame he felt for his misguided violent actions.

Challenging somatic cues that stem from racism or patriarchy or any other power and oppression dynamic will require the readiness and willingness of both client and therapist to address these issues. Cultivating awareness of one's implicit bias requires a committed effort (cf. Chapter 1, this volume) and paves the way for transforming these attitudes. Helping clients to track somatic reactions more accurately in their daily life, recognizing when these reactions (e.g., held breath or loss of grounding) are connected to their own biases, and choosing another action (e.g., taking a breath, or sensing the legs and feet) can become a daily practice of challenging narratives that are not true, but are reinforced by social messaging.

Supporting Social Engagement

Julie learned that a change in the angle of her head facilitated social engagement and a neuroception of safety, strengthening the parts that were associated with daily life systems. During one session, we both practiced imitating a habitual downward turn of her head and mindfully studied its effects, noticing that recognizing and receiving signals from the environment from that head position was much more difficult. Slowly, we explored lifting our heads by lengthening our spines and bringing our shoulder blades slightly toward each other, and we both experienced more contact with each other and the environment. Again, to include all parts in treatment, we needed to explore the different reactions of various parts to this intervention and address those that were afraid of seeing and being seen, those who felt safer with her head down, those who judged her, and so on. As these parts were acknowledged and integrated actions were performed repeatedly, Julie's fears of lifting her head and connecting with others and the outside world lessened.

In another example of working with an older white woman who lived in a poor neighborhood of a large city disproportionately impacted by crime and illegal drug use, working with head position and social engagement was more nuanced. When we explored lifting her head, she felt exposed and in danger, and explained that in her neighborhood it was safer to have a posture and gait that did not attract attention: to keep her head down, her eyes to the ground, to move in a deliberate manner that was neither rushed nor slow, and to not engage. We acknowledged this as a survival resource, necessary given her place of residence, as well as the helpful function of this resource in her abusive childhood. Additionally, we imagined other contexts, such as Sunday morning at church, where she felt she could embody a more receptive, open posture and spontaneous movement. Exploring these two parts that emerged in different environments, contrasting and comparing the postures, movements, thoughts, and emotions that accompanied each, and validating their functions, was both resourcing and integrative for this client.

When expanding skills to support social engagement with clients who have suffered historical and ongoing collective trauma, the first daunting reality, as we have shared, is that the threats and danger are continuing. Safety on a societal level requires a sociocultural change process beyond the individual therapy room. Hence, for clients directly affected by past and current trauma and oppression, embodying the open posture appropriate for safe contexts may be more nuanced, as illustrated above. However, it is important to help the client develop the resources to not only manage, but also increase resilience in the face of ongoing trauma and stress, by recognizing their internal signals of dysregulated arousal and engaging a resource to expeditiously bring arousal into the window of tolerance.

In these instances it will also be relevant to help the client connect to family and community resources for support and possibly as a means to resist or take action against oppressive forces. For example, a strong racial identity can be supported by encouraging clients "to find alternative sources of pride, identify with same race role models, and seek affirming support systems" (Harrell & Sloan, 2006, p. 401). In relation to her gender socialization and the historical abuse of women, a female client was helped to identify female role models within her family, her life, or the public realm as resources to foster solidarity among women, and share the pain, challenges, and resilience to mitigate the sense of isolation. Such external resources may be carried through family or community storytelling and customs well. With the therapist's support, this client explored the felt sense in her body when recalling these resources and hearing narratives of strength and solidarity. She sensed a softening of a push forward, a strength in her back, and squared shoulders, all developed into somatic resources that she could call upon to recapture the sense of resonance with other women. Helping the client find words to go along with these somatic resources—for example, "I can face this; I am not alone; we are resilient and powerful as women together"— can further sustain the client when facing current reminders of gender socialization and sexism, witnessing ongoing violence against women, or hearing stories of victimization.

PHASE 2 TREATMENT: TRAUMATIC MEMORY

Once we had achieved some success with mitigating the interference of defenses, particularly feigned death and hypoarousal, with daily life activities, we progressed to working directly with memories of childhood abuse. Addressing traumatic memory presents a challenging paradox. First, success depends on the client's ability to neurocept safety, which maintains social engagement and engages those parts associated with daily life action systems. However, as clients begin to recount the trauma, defensive action systems and dysregulated arousal are stimulated, often resulting in a loss of social engagement and connection to the action systems of daily life. To keep the social engagement system and parts connected to daily life systems in charge, the therapist must help clients remain in the here and now rather than relive the past. The challenge is to process the past so that there is a steady integration of fragmented parts and fragmented body/emotional/cognitive experiences, which requires that the parts rooted in defense be evoked, but not so much that these dysregulated, dissociated parts usurp social engagement. Thus, the client must simultaneously access parts that neurocept danger, and sometimes life threat, without loss of mindful witnessing, social engagement, and some degree of a neuroception of safety.

In addressing the trauma of oppression, we must be aware that traumatic memory may extend further than the client's direct experience to encompass interrelated events across time, such as the trauma of ancestors. Descendants of perpetrators, as well as descendants of those they targeted, can be traumatized from historical oppression (e.g., colonization, enslavement, internment, genocide, and so forth) and other traumas (e.g., discrimination, microaggressions, poverty), which often continue in current time. The memories of historical oppression encompass the knowledge and other vestiges of the events, which, similar to preverbal memories, are not recalled directly, but implicitly in the symptoms, dysregulated arousal, and related behaviors of activated defensive action systems. Current internal and external triggers will stimulate the effects of these historical memories. By using a body-oriented approach, these effects can be targeted even when the specific content or direct experience of the traumatic events is unavailable to verbal recall.

Using Resources in Memory Work

In Sensorimotor Psychotherapy treatment, declarative memory narrative, when available, can be used to evoke the body responses, physical actions, and dysregulated arousal related to parts of the self. Thus, the narrative is used to address the effects of the past on clients' current life functioning, rather than only as a vehicle for formulating a cohesive narrative. As Julie recalled one particular memory of abuse, the related hyperarousal, shaking, panic, and terror became overwhelming. To help regulate her hyperarousal, I instructed her to disregard the emerging images of abuse, drop the content of the memory, focus exclusively on her body, and concentrate on lengthening her spine, sensing her feet on the ground, and staying in eye contact until she felt her arousal coming back into the window of tolerance. These physical resources, most of which we had already identified and practiced, prevented further dissociation and reengaged the parts of Julie that could stay in the present moment. When her arousal returned to the window, she was again able to simultaneously neurocept the sense of safety connected to the present and the sense of danger connected to the past.

As traumatic memories are addressed, new resources are cultivated, and the resources used long ago to cope with the traumatic event are discovered and strengthened. No matter how sudden or severe the traumatizing events are, peritraumatic resources are invariably utilized and can subsequently be brought to awareness in therapy. For example, as Julie began to recall a memory of her father angrily yanking her out of her hiding place in the closet, she reported that she did not resist and felt ashamed of the hypoaroused part of her that was so passive. However, as I asked her how her passivity affected her father, she said that he became less angry when she did not resist. Although we had acknowledged this hypoaroused part for its value earlier in therapy, in the context of working directly with state-specific processing of traumatic memory, reframing her acquiescence as an adaptive action that pacified her father deepened Julie's acceptance and even gratitude for her passivity at the time of her abuse.

I encouraged Julie to consider the sequence of events in this memory, not to relive them, but instead to notice what had supported her and how she had coped. She remembered that as her father led her to his room, her older sister watched helplessly from the hallway. Julie's eyes met her sister's, and she felt her sister's compassion, knowing that afterward, she and her sister would cuddle together in the bed they shared. While they never spoke of what happened, there was a wordless support that existed between them.

This was a particularly important recollection to Julie because, prior to this therapy session, she could not recall any positive experiences of her childhood. I noticed the change in her body when she talked about the comfort she experienced afterward with her sister. Wanting to help her capture the memory of neurocepting safety, I said, "Pause for a moment. Just remember cuddling with your sister. What happens?" Julie replied, "I take a little breath, and I know it's over for now." In an effort to help her translate what this moment meant to her, I said, "There is something very important about this moment for you. Just sense this experience. What might it tell you?" As Julie continued to focus on the memory of being together with her sister, her breathing deepened, and her shoulders lost their tension. She reported, "Her being there tells me I am not alone," and she began to softly cry, and her body relaxed. Even in the midst of a traumatic environment, which necessitated chronic activation of parts prepared for danger and life threat, Julie and her sister found moments of connection to sustain them.

When such moments of social engagement within a traumatic experience are remembered and embodied, the parts of the client engaged in daily life action systems are strengthened and integrated with the parts related to the defensive subsystem. Integration of past and present is facilitated when remembering of empowering or resourcing moments in the traumatic past is interwoven with remembering dangerous or overwhelming moments, and with the neuroception of safety now. This attention to parts representing daily life subsystems and defense also mitigates both the phobic avoidance of traumatic memory and the continual replaying of it in a fixed form. As Julie said after that session, "Now I won't just remember the abuse. I will also remember that my sister and I were in it together, and we had each other." In this manner, again, the part that neurocepts safety now could be integrated with the parts that neurocept danger and the part that could neurocept the safety shared with her sister. The somatic memory of cuddling with her sister could become a resource as well as a moment of integration. All parts could feel a physical and emotional sense of "It's over, and I'm not alone."

Completing Incomplete Actions

Janet (1919, 1925) refers to a variety of mental and physical actions that remain incomplete for people with trauma-related disorders. A Sensorimotor Psychotherapist helps the client to complete truncated actions and to integrate these actions through somatic communication with other parts of the self. Using state-specific processing focused on how the body has encoded the traumatic events, the parts associated with instinctive defenses are activated and their implicit memories processed, evoking new reactions that can now be integrated with the old reactions. In Sensorimotor Psychotherapy, a particular segment or sliver of a memory is selected that, when focused on, will activate an internal state reminiscent of the one experienced when the event occurred, without overly dysregulating the client. Remembering the sliver must have a significant enough impact on the client's present-moment experience to stimulate the body's responses. A variety of parts are often involved in a particular segment or sliver of memory that is selected to focus on, which prevents attending to the entire memory at once. It is important to choose a sliver that, when focused on, will activate an internal state similar to the one experienced when the event occurred, without overly dysregulating the client. However, the sliver must be potent enough to stimulate the client's felt sense of that state to the degree that their internal experience is clearly altered in the present moment. When memory is retrieved in small doses, or "slivers," and clients practice both dual awareness and the use of their resources, the immediate impact on their experience is not so dramatic that they become overly dysregulated—which would prevent integration of the effects of the memory—yet the sliver is potent enough to impact and change present-moment internal experience. These slivers hold the immobilizing defensive responses that did happen and those that hold empowering physical actions like fleeing or fighting back that "wanted to happen" but were truncated at the time of the original event. These actions, when executed in the therapy hour, mitigate feelings of helplessness and shame, give rise to moments of confidence and satisfaction, and facilitate integration (both somatic and mental) among parts and between past and present.

It should be noted that clients might also experience shame and defeat from dysregulated fight or flight defenses that are not only frozen or inactive but also that are chaotic and out of control. Julie could not at first find a fight part, but other clients may have overactive fight parts. One client was ashamed of the bouts of explosive rage he experienced, during which he lashed out at his family and broke household objects. As we addressed a sliver of an early traumatic memory—the moment when a gang of bullies had cruelly humiliated and taunted him just before they beat him up—he felt his body tense and said this was what happened in his body just before he went into a rage. I asked him to be mindful of his body sensation and tension and to find out what action his body wanted to make. He felt the impulse to suddenly strike out, an impulse originating from a dysregulated fight part. I directed him to sense this action in his body and execute it in slow motion, reporting to me what he experienced in his body. He followed this impulse in a slow and contained manner, pushing against a pillow I held. By executing the movements associated with his fight part in slow motion, he could experience the energy of his rage in a titrated dose. As he executed the pushing-away movement, he could mindfully report to me how he felt it first as a surge of energy, and then as an impulse that started in his back and moved slowly out through his hands. With many iterations of executing these aggressive actions in a mindful, deliberate fashion, the fight part of this client began to experience a sense of self-regulation. Other parts could appreciate its protective function when it was not destructive, and his aggressive outbursts diminished in his daily life.

The sociocultural locations of the therapist and the client are important to consider when completing incomplete defensive actions. If we think of the therapist as a migrant or a person of color working with a cisgender white male client, pushing directly against a pillow held by the therapist might be more complicated. Other options include pushing an object, like a physio ball, against the wall, can simplify potential transference and countertransference dynamics associated with differing social locations so that the focus can remain on completing the action. For example, a Latino male therapist's client was a white veteran that was deployed undercover in Latin America during the late 1960s. Once he was back in the United States and retired from military services, the client often got into fights, which had landed him in jail on several occasions. As a child, the client had endured physical abuse from his dad (also white), and this as well as the stories of victimization from his family contributed to an intense emotional pain that he fought out with his fists. When a memory emerged in which the client had committed what he called an "inhuman" crime against Latin American civilians, the therapist noted the tensing of the fists and supported the client in pushing slowly and mindfully against the wall to complete an aggressive action in a regulated manner. An image of his father emerged, and he realized that he was trying to push away his father, but had the sense of being too small and weak to fight his father. The impulse to fight and protect himself, he said, came forward toward anybody that he felt he could overpower. He also realized that he was pushing away the military training and the part of him that felt inhuman as a result of perpetrating violence against another person. The therapist tracked a shame part in the lowering of his head and the softening of the push. By naming that part, the client was able to connect to it, and looking with cry-for-help eyes to the Latino therapist, he said, "You must think I am a monster." The therapist guided the client to look mindfully into his eyes. The client shared that he saw compassion and pain in his therapist's eyes, which brought forth his anguish of having been in the position of a perpetrator of atrocities against Latinx civilians when deployed.

Signals of Mobilizing Defenses

Often, as clients first begin to address past trauma, instead of empowering defenses, they are aware of the immobilizing defenses that were the most effective defense at the time of the events. Simultaneously, though, parts driving empowering defenses, incipient and often unrecognized during the original trauma, often spontaneously emerge, ready to be further developed and integrated. These actions that were truncated or held back at the time of the original trauma present themselves physically in the form of preparatory movements: tension in the arms or jaw, lifting of the hands or fingers related to a flight defense; tension or movement in the legs indicative of a flight response; or sensations in the throat that might indicate an urge to speak or cry-for-help.

For example, as Julie talked about her sense that she had been abused as an infant, she noticed a tightening in her jaw, which developed into an impulse to bite. Of course, she had no explicit memory of such early abuse, but through awareness of her body's preparatory movement (the tension in her jaw), Julie could then make a biting motion, which lessened her helplessness. Recall that it is not necessary to have access to declarative memory to help the client become aware of preparatory movements and execute empowering defensive actions. Resolution of implicit memories can be effective without reference to declarative memory, which is relevant not only to preverbal memories such as Julie's but when addressing historical trauma in which a direct memory that the client can recall is absent.

A particularly devastating childhood memory emerged for Julie when her own daughter turned 11, the same age Julie was when she endured the most terrible time period of her abuse. As Julie observed her internal experience in reaction to her decision to work on this memory, she felt her arousal escalate, and noticed that trembling and shaking had already begun. Julie, like many clients, reported that she was frightened of her own hyperarousal and, as a result, sometimes felt revictimized by exposure to her own memories. She felt "electricity" in her arms and then impulses to curl up into a ball as she sensed the downward turn of her head and rounding of her shoulders. Instead of focusing on these impulses, I invited Julie to carefully notice the electricity in her arms and to sense if there was any action her body wanted to make. The language "Is there any action your body wants to make?" is important. Had I asked her, "Is there any action you want to make?," she might have begun to think instead of staying connected to the body response, or the question might be answered by a part afraid to move or a part carrying the belief that action is dangerous. She reported that she could feel her arms wanting to push away, and I suggested she notice what happened if she pushed against a pillow that I held.

It is important to note that Julie was able to stay mindful of her body's response as we talked about the memory, and when she felt the impulse to push, we turned our attention to executing that action. The impulse emerged from Julie's awareness of her body's response to the memory, not as an idea or concept. As she mobilized not only her arms but also her whole body in pushing, she began to sense a part of her that felt strong and powerful. Her anger, usually experienced with a sense of impotence, felt robust and exciting. As we contacted the angry part that was emerging through her body as she pushed, I asked Julie to notice the reactions of other parts to the anger and the pushing, and we took care to facilitate communication among various parts. One part, for example, was acutely afraid that the anger would escalate out of control and needed to know that executing the pushing action did not mean that the angry part would take over. This communication took place both mentally and somatically, as I asked Julie to find a way to push that reassured the fearful part. Julie noticed that when her arms were stiff and straight and her energy was in the front of her body, the fear escalated. But when her arms were bent and flexible, and she pushed very slowly, being mindful of her entire body and especially her back, the fear quieted. Making sure Julie's social engagement system was activated through our eye contact and my reassurance that she would not be punished for pushing away or being angry, as she might have been as a child, facilitated completion of the action and its integration with the trauma-related fears and beliefs held by other parts.

Impulses to cry-for-help, fight back, run, or otherwise defend emerge not only through memories of direct traumatic experiences, but of vicarious trauma, where an individual witnesses or hears stories about trauma inflicted on others, either in person or through the media. Examples include witnessing racialized violence, reports of hate crimes, discrimination, microaggressions, or other forms of oppression and harrassment. For example, a Black father of two young boys working with a white male therapist experienced dysregulated hyperarousal after watching news reports of a young Black man, Ahmaud Arbery, who was shot dead while jogging. The client's fear and anger, related to a protective fight defense, was accompanied by impulses to strike out.

In therapy, he completed this action by pushing strongly against a therapy ball held against the wall. His therapist helped him stay mindful of his internal experience, rather than "explode," and this helped him feel more "in control." By executing the strong protective impulse, his arousal was metabolized, and the pushing turned into a resource the client could use during vicarious experiences of racialized trauma in the future so that his arousal could more quickly become regulated.

Sensorimotor Sequencing

After Julie had executed the pushing action, we returned to the content of the same memory. Again, she reported that her arousal escalated, and her body trembled, although the sensations were less intense than before. At these moments in therapy when hyper-arousal is experienced as physical trembling, clients may be encouraged to find and execute empowering actions like pushing, as Julie had. Or they may be encouraged to follow or "just allow" the natural, spontaneous progression of the physical sensations, movements, and impulses through the body until the arousal has subsided, a technique called "sensorimotor sequencing."

To press for additional traumatic material when clients are already hyperaroused can promote an escalation of arousal and dissociation, leading to reenactment instead of integration. I asked Julie if she would be willing to be mindful only of her body sensation and to put the emotions and content of the memory aside: "Can you just focus on your body: Feel the panic as body sensation—what does it feel like in your body?" Julie was able to direct mindful attention to the sensations of trembling, and describe them using sensation vocabulary (tingling, traveling, shaking, calming down) rather than emotion vocabulary (scared, ashamed, panicked, anxious). I continued to ask Julie to follow the sensations as they moved through her body: "Stay with that sensation of trembling—what happens next in your body? How does the sensation change?" As Julie followed and described the progression of these sensations, she noticed that, gradually, the sensations settled, the trembling abated, and her arousal returned to her window of tolerance.

Although the narrative of Julie's memory provided the starting point for our work, the story is but the means to an end. It is a way to activate the implicit memories held in the body by specific parts and either sequence or execute truncated actions in current time. Because the collapsed part played such a crucial role in Julie's survival and in her current symptoms, we paid special attention to both immobilized parts and parts holding empowering mobilizing defenses, so that the physical defensive actions could be identified and completed in the context of therapy. After discovering the angry part, completing its assertive actions in therapy, addressing her hyperarousal by being mindful and sequencing the trembling of her body, and integrating parts over time, Julie noted that the habitual cringing and hypoaroused tendency was increasingly absent in her day-to-day life. The years of therapeutic work she had previously spent in retelling the events of her abuse had not succeeded in providing the bodily experience that protective and self-assertive actions were now safe action that could support adaptive and healthy defenses and boundaries as needed to the arousal of action systems.

Social narratives, implicit or explicit, can also play a role in activating the client's parts that are historically traumatized. This process is very similar to the one described with Julie, as the therapist will instruct the client to drop the narrative to focus on the body and help sequence the activation. This sequencing, when repeated a few times prompted by different images or collective narratives, can become a skill that the client can utilize outside the therapy hour to quickly metabolize hyperarousal experienced when confronted with ongoing triggers. In working with clients who, due to their marginalized location, experience ongoing trauma reminders, it will also be important to help them develop a template for recuperation after the metabolization, which might mean moving away from the trigger or setting a boundary with the triggers. For example, it may be helpful to refrain from watching media coverage of violence against people of color, or reports of sexual violence, and instead reach out to a friend to stimulate the social engagement system, and perhaps do something restorative such as a walk in nature.

The Legacy of Relationships

Areas of daily life that Julie had neglected began to surface once she learned skills to regulate arousal and had processed the effects of traumatic memories. With the somatic skills to regulate arousal already established and with many memories already addressed, Julie's confidence in the body as an ally instead of an enemy was growing, and we turned our attention to the ways in which her everyday life could be enriched.

We began to examine limiting beliefs, how body posture and movement enforce them, and navigate painful emotions associated with relational dynamics. Julie still felt overwhelmed and spaced out in groups of people, and she wanted to participate in different fun ways with her friends. A sliver of memory—in this case, a moment that was charged for her, full of unexpressed, painful emotion—was a moment when she felt deeply hurt the prior week when having coffee with four women friends. She said her friends ignored everything she said, as if she were not there, until she finally gave up and stopped talking completely. Such a significant moment of memory rife with emotional pain is revisited when the client has developed a sufficiently wide window of tolerance to express strong emotions without undue dysregulation.

We decided to focus on the image of this sliver, which included the sound of her friends talking and laughing. Julie's spine slumped, her shoulders curled inward, her head turned downward, and her eyes stared at her lap, but were unfocused. She said she felt sad and alone, and she was able to express her emotional pain without undue dysregulation or dissociation. Weeping softly, Julie said she felt like a misfit, unworthy of attention, and that no one would ever want to be with her.

Patterns of response are the focus in memory work, rather than specific events, although remembered events are used to catalyze these patterns and the emotional pain that accompanies them. When Julie's emotions subsided, I asked her to stay with her body's response, rather than the content, to learn more about this pattern. Julie reported the same image of herself as a child on her father's bed after the abuse that had previously emerged, but this time we focused on the meaning of that experience. Julie said that she felt like she "gave up" being a "real person" deserving of positive attention. This meaning had been superimposed on her current interactions with her friends. More tears accompanied this realization, tears of sadness and grief. Julie cried hard as she sensed that small child who felt like such a misfit, but could maintain her awareness of the here and now and receive my empathic support.

Once Julie's sobs subsided, I asked her if she was still in contact with that child part of her, and she nodded. I wondered aloud if this child could sense the two of us with her, that we were perhaps conveying a different message to this little girl. After a moment, Julie quietly said, "You are paying attention. She doesn't feel like a misfit right now." Experiments can be verbal as well as physical, and I asked Julie if I could talk to this part. With Julie's assent, I softly repeated Julie's words, "You are not a misfit—you deserve attention and I'm happy to give you attention," asking if anything changed in this little girl inside or in her body. Julie became tearful, saying, "I felt so hopeless," but reported that she could see hope in this little girl's eyes. She took a big breath, her spine became more erect, and her eyes met mine for the first time in this session. The experience, rather than insight alone, helped to finish the past for Julie and opened up the possibility of changing the meaning she had made of her abuse as a child.

In a subsequent session, we worked to embody a feeling of receptivity, symbolized by motions of reaching out and then bringing her arms toward her torso as if drawing something in toward her chest. I asked her to repeat that motion mindfully, exploring it for meaning and memories. Julie said that the movement felt connected to "taking in" and "receiving for myself" instead of only giving to and pleasing others. Again, she felt the lift in her chest, length in her spine, and a sense of her back that she had experienced before, which were connected to the sociability action system. These changes in her gesture and posture countered the belief "I don't deserve attention for myself" and helped to challenge its veracity. The experience finished some of the imprints of Julie's relational past, so that her social engagement improved, and she could remain in the conversation when she met with her friends.

CONCLUSION

In Sensorimotor Psychotherapy, integration of parts of the self is a process of repeated experiences of well-executed actions under cortical control, in social engagement with an attuned therapist. In this context, the client is supported to neurocept the necessary degree of safety to stay present in the here and now. Integration is fostered when present-moment connections—cognitive, emotional, and somatic—are made and experienced among dissociative parts. As integration among parts occurs, so does the connection between past and present, historical trauma and present-day experiences, and mind and body.

These connections between body and mind are a process rather than an endpoint and are cumulative over time. This process often starts with psychoeducation about parts of the self, defensive and daily life action systems, peritraumatic resources, and mapping dissociative parts and their physical indicators. Clients discover and practice somatic resources to return dysregulated arousal quickly to a window of tolerance when traumatic reminders are present, and when safety is restored after present-day threats. Completing truncated mobilizing defensive actions brings a sense of solidness and safety to the body and therefore to the parts holding experiences of fear, powerlessness, and collapse. Regulating out-of-control mobilizing defensive actions that are fueled by strong emotions, like rage, fosters a sense of self-agency. Addressing defensive actions through controlled movement encourages flexibility among and adaptive use of the instinctive defenses. Learning to track the sequence of the sensation of hyperarousal also leads to a new sense of resilience and trust in the body. Along with its focus on the body and sensorimotor processing, Sensorimotor Psychotherapy emphasizes the integration of emotions and cognitive distortions of various parts as well. As the parts and their physical tendencies become increasingly integrated, clients find that it is possible to experience and integrate strong emotions like grief, anger, and even joy without undue dysregulation and to resolve cognitive distortions.

Integration also includes somatic integration: helping the physical patterns that have developed over time in response to trauma and attachment failure develop into more adaptive actions. Instead of unintegrated actions that reflect the division of the individual into dissociative parts, such as simultaneously seeking both proximity and distance by reaching out for contact as the upper body pulls away, the body is congruent and purposeful in its movement and gesture. As Julie learned to lengthen and align her posture in a way that integrated dissociative parts, to lift her head in a way that included the part that angled it downward, to push outward instead of tighten inward, and so on, her physical structure and posture became increasingly integrated. Her body found more integrity, alignment, balance, and economical movement. Her actions became more purposeful instead of contradictory. For example, she could make eye contact without pulling back when she felt safe.

The integration of her structure and movement reflected and sustained the integration of dissociative parts.

Dissociation can occur both in perpetrators and victims, dominant and marginalized people, privileged and oppressed groups, and at the individual and societal level. For example, in considering society in its entirety, the privileged group could be conceptualized as the faction that is able to experience a general sense of safety in the world and engage freely in daily life action systems, as this group is not directly impacted by the trauma of oppression. The oppressed faction, however, does not experience consistent safety in the world, is not able to avoid the continued effects of past trauma and ongoing threat, and thus must draw upon defensive action systems on a regular basis for protection and survival in a dangerous world.

When extended to communities that experience collective trauma, the concept of dissociation may elucidate different tendencies within the group itself. Subgroups that reflect daily life action systems might encompass those factions of a community that avoid the trauma and try to assimilate to the dominant culture and go on with life. Other subgroups may reflect instinctive defensive action systems: A faction that holds the fight defenses can emerge as aggressive and defensive with the goal of protecting their individual and collective identity, possibly in street gangs or hate groups. Other subgroups might manifest in numbing and express their pain in symptoms, apathy, or somatization, or display compliant attitudes toward oppressive forces with the goal of survival. Flight defenses may appear in substance abuse or addictive behaviors. When these factions manifest collectively, they are often misunderstood and misconstrued as if they were characteristic of a specific community instead of logical responses to traumatogenic forces.

Although the trauma of oppression requires systemic change and cannot be resolved in clinical practice, Sensorimotor Psychotherapy can be helpful to explore and integrate parts of the self related to historical and ongoing trauma, both individual and collective.

Clients can discover resources to regulate arousal, practice actions that integrate parts of the self and foster flexibility among defensive responses, and learn sensorimotor sequencing to metabolize the dysregulation caused by triggers or actual threat. In turn, these resources and actions can support both a verbal and somatic narrative of resilience and empowerment. Through integrating body and mind and parts of the self, clients develop a new, cohesive sense of themselves, both linguistic and somatic, that is more flexible, adaptive, consistent over time and contexts, and capable of fuller engagement with life. Clients experience the body, and all parts of the body, as "me."

Similarly, when as a society we recognize the interconnection between oppressors and the oppressed, both aspects can be perceived as parts of the same whole. There can be no oppression without privilege; the same systems and forces that uplift and offer opportunities to privileged groups simultaneously oppress or marginalized other groups. When we realize we all participate in the whole, experience all parts of the whole as "us," recognize our differences represented in dissociative but interrelated factions, and understand the underlying suffering and function of each, we can begin to build bridges between aspects of ourselves and between various factions of society, and healing can begin.

REFERENCES

Ainsworth, M. (1963). The development of infant-mother interaction among the Ganda. In B. Foss (Ed.), *Determinants of infant behavior* (pp. 67–104). New York: John Wiley & Sons.

Allen, J. (2001). *Traumatic relationships and serious mental disorders.* Chichester, UK: John Wiley & Sons.

American Psychiatric Association. (2000). *Diagnostic and statistical manual of mental disorders* (4th ed.). Washington, DC: American Psychiatric Association.

Bekoff, M., & Allen, C. (1998). Intentional communication and social play: How and why animals negotiate and agree to play. In M. Bekoff

& J. Byers (Eds.), *Animal play: Evolutionary, comparative, and ecological perspectives* (pp. 97–114). New York: Cambridge University Press.

Bekoff, M., & Byers, J. (1998). *Animal play: Evolutionary, comparative, and ecological perspectives.* New York: Cambridge University Press.

Bergman, N. J., Linley, L. L., & Fawcus, S. R. (2004). Randomized controlled trial of skin-to-skin contact from birth versus conventional incubator for physiological stabilization in 1200- to 2199-gram newborns. *Acta Paediatrica, 93*(6), 779–785.

Blume, S. L. (1998). *The sanctuary model: Tramatogenic forces in society.* http://sanctuaryweb.com/PublicHealth/TraumatogenicForcesinSociety.aspx

Bowlby, J. (1982). *Attachment* (2nd ed., Vol. 1). New York: Basic Books.

Bowlby, J. (1988). *A secure base: Parent-child attachment and healthy human development.* New York: Basic Books.

Brown, D., & Fromm, E. (1986). *Hypnotherapy and hypnoanalysis.* Hillsdale, NJ: Lawrence Erlbaum.

Bundy, A. C. (2002). The process of planning and implementing intervention. In A. C. Bundy, S. J. Lane, & A. A. Murray (Eds.), *Sensory integration: Theory and practice* (pp. 211–225). Philadelphia: F. A. Davis.

Caldwell, C. (2003). Adult group play therapy. In C. Schaefer (Ed.), *Play therapy with adults* (pp. 301–316). Hoboken, NJ: John Wiley & Sons.

Cassidy, J., & Shaver, P. (1999). *Handbook of attachment: Theory, research, and clinical applications.* New York: Guilford.

Chu, J. (1988). Ten traps for therapists in the treatment of trauma survivors. *Dissociation, 1*(4), 24–32.

Cozolino, L. (2002). *The neuroscience of psychotherapy: Building and rebuilding the human brain.* New York: Norton.

Donaldson, F. (1993). *Playing by heart: The vision and practice of belonging.* Deerfield Beach, FL: Health Communications.

Fanselow, M., & Lester, L. (1988). A functional behavioristic approach to aversively motivated behavior: Predatory imminence as a determinant of the topography of defensive behavior. In R. Bolles & M. Beecher (Eds.), *Evolution and learning* (pp. 185–212). Hillsdale, NJ: Lawrence Erlbaum.

Fisher, J. (2017). *Healing the fragmented selves of trauma survivors: Overcoming internal self-alienation.* New York: Routledge.

Freire, P. (2007). *Pedagogy of the oppressed.* New York, NY: Continuum.

Frijda, N. (1986). *The emotions.* Cambridge, UK: Cambridge University Press.

George, C., & Solomon, J. (1999). Attachment and caregiving: The caregiving behavioral system. In J. Cassidy & P. Shaver (Eds.), *Handbook of attachment: Theory, research, and clinical applications* (pp. 649–670). New York: Guilford.

Gould, J. (1982). *Ethology: The mechanisms and evolution of behavior*. New York: Norton.

Günsoy, C., Cross, S. E., Uskul, A. K., Adams, G., & Gercek-Swing, B. (2015). Avoid or fight back? Cultural differences in responses to conflict and the role of collectivism, honor, and enemy perception. *Journal of Cross-Cultural Psychology, 46*, 1081–1102. doi.10.1177/0022022115594252

Hamby, S., Schultz, K., & Elm, J. (2019). Understanding the burden of trauma and victimization among American Indian and Alaska native elders: Historical trauma as an element of poly-victimization. *Journal of Trauma and Dissociation, 21*(2), 172–186. doi:10.1080/15299732.2020.1692408

Harrell, S., & Bond, M. (2006). Listening to diversity stories: Principles for practice in community research and action. *American Journal of Community Psychology, 37*, 365–376. doi:10.1007/s10464-006-9042-7

Harrell, S. P., & Sloan-Pena, G. (2006). Racism and discrimination. In Y. Jackson (Ed.), *Encyclopedia of multicultural psychology* (pp. 396–402). Thousand Oaks, CA: Sage.

Janet, P. (1889). *Névroses et idées fixes*. Paris: Félix Alcan.

Janet, P. (1907). *The major symptoms of hysteria*. London: Macmillan.

Janet, P. (1919). *Psychological healing*. New York: Macmillan.

Janet, P. (1925). *Principles of psychotherapy*. London: George Allen and Unwin.

Kar, H. (2018). Acknowledging the victim to perpetrator trajectory: Integrating a mental health focused trauma–based approach into global violence programs. *Aggression and Violent Behavior, 47*. 10.1016/j.avb.2018.10.004.

Keller, H. (2013). Attachment and culture. *Journal of Cross-Cultural Psychology, 44*(2), 175–194. https://doi.org/10.1177/0022022112472253

Krystal, J., Bremner, J. D., Southwick, S. M., & Charney, D. S. (1998). The emerging neurobiology of dissociation: Implications for treatment of posttraumatic stress disorder. In J. D. Bremner & C. Marmar (Eds.), *Trauma, memory and dissociation* (pp. 321–363). Washington, DC: American Psychiatric Press.

Kurtz, R. (1990). *Body-centered psychotherapy: The Hakomi method: The integrated use of mindfulness, nonviolence, and the body*. Mendocino, CA: LifeRhythm.

Lanius, R. A., Williamson, P. C., Boksman, K., Densmore, M., Gupta, M., Neufeld, R. W., Gati, J. S., & Menon, R. S. (2002). Brain activation during script-driven imagery induced dissociative responses in PTSD: A functional magnetic resonance imaging investigation. *Biological Psychiatry, 52*, 305–311.

Lewis, L., Kelly, K., & Allen, J. (2004). *Restoring hope and trust: An illustrated guide to mastering trauma*. Baltimore, MD: Sidran Institute.

Lichtenberg, J. D. (1990). On motivational systems. *Journal of the American Psychoanalytic Association, 38*(2), 517–518.

Lichtenberg, J. D., & Kindler, A. R. (1994). A motivational systems approach to the clinical experience. *Journal of the American Psychoanalytic Association, 42*(2), 405–420.

Liotti, G. (1999). Disorganization of attachment as a model for understanding dissociative psychopathology. In J. Solomon & C. George (Eds.), *Attachment disorganization* (pp. 291–317). New York: Guilford.

Lyons-Ruth, K., & Jacobvitz, D. (1999). Attachment disorganization: Unresolved loss, relational violence, and lapses in behavioral and attentional strategies. In J. Cassidy & P. Shaver (Eds.), *Handbook of attachment: Theory, research, and clinical applications* (pp. 520–554). New York: Guilford.

Marvin, R., & Britner, P. (1999). Normative development: The ontogeny of attachment. In J. Cassidy & P. Shaver (Eds.), *Handbook of attachment: Theory, research, and clinical applications* (pp. 44–67). New York: Guilford.

Misslin, R. (2003). The defense system of fear: Behavior and neurocircuitry. *Neurophysiologie clinique (Clinical neurophysiology), 33*(2), 55–66.

Mohamed, S. (2015). Of monsters and men: Perpetrator trauma and mass atrocity. *Columbia Law Review, 115*, 1157–1216.

Nijenhuis, E. R. S., Spinhoven, P., Van Dyck, R., Van Der Hart, O., & Vanderlinden, J. (1996). The development and psychometric characteristics of the Somatoform Dissociation Questionnaire (SDQ-20). *Journal of Nervous and Mental Disease, 184*(11), 688–694. https://doi.org/10.1097/00005053-199611000-00006

Nijenhuis, E. R. S., Van der Hart, O., & Steele, K. (2002). The emerging psychobiology of trauma-related dissociation and dissociative disorders. In H. D'Haenen, J. DenBoer, & P. Willner (Eds.), *Biological psychiatry* (pp. 1079–1098). London: John Wiley & Sons.

Ogden, P. (2009). Emotion, mindfulness, and movement: Expanding the regulatory boundaries of the window of tolerance. In D. Fosha, D. Siegel, & M. Solomon (Eds.), *The healing power of emotion: Perspectives from affective neuroscience and clinical practice* (pp. 204-231). New York, NY: Norton.

Ogden, P. (2020). Sensorimotor psychotherapy for complex trauma. In Courtois, C. and J. Ford (Eds.), *Treating Complex Traumatic Stress Disorders*. New York: Guilford Press

Ogden, P. & Fisher, J. (2015). *Sensorimotor psychotherapy: interventions for trauma and attachment.* New York, NY: Norton.

Ogden, P., Minton, K., & Pain, C. (2006). *Trauma and the body: A senso-rimotor approach to psychotherapy.* New York: Norton.

Panksepp, J. (1998). *Affective neuroscience: The foundations of human and instinctive emotions.* New York: Oxford University Press.

Perry, B., Pollard, R., Blakely, T., Baker, W., & Vigilante, D. (1995). Childhood trauma, the neurobiology of adaptation, and "use dependent" development of the brain: How "states" become "traits." *Infant Mental Health Journal, 16,* 271–291.

Porges, S. W. (2004). Neuroception: A subconscious system for detecting threats and safety. *Zero to Three.* Retrieved August 8, 2005, from http://bbc.psych.uic.edu/pdf/Neuroception.pdf

Porges, S. W. (2005). The role of social engagement in attachment and bonding: A phylogenetic perspective. In C. Carter, L. Ahnert, K. Grossman, S. Hrdy, M. Lamb, S. W. Porges, & N. Sachser (Eds.), *From the 92nd Dahlem Workshop report: Attachment and bonding: A new synthesis* (pp. 33–55). Cambridge, MA: MIT Press.

Porges, S. W. (2011). *The polyvagal theory: Neurophysiological foundations of emotions, attachment, communication, and self-regulation.* New York: Norton.

Porges, S. W. (2012). *The polyvagal theory: Neurophysiological foundations of emotions, attachment, communication, and self-regulation.* New York: Norton.

Schore, A. N. (1994). *Affect regulation and the origin of the self: The neurobiology of emotional development.* Hillsdale, NJ: Lawrence Erlbaum.

Schore, A. N. (2001). The effects of early relational trauma on right brain development, affect regulation, and infant mental health. *Infant Mental Health Journal, 22,* 201–269.

Schore, A. N. (2009). Right-brain affect regulation: An essential mechanism of development, trauma, dissociation, and psychotherapy. In D. Fosha, D. Siegel, & M. Solomon (Eds.), *The healing power of emotion: Affective neuroscience, development and clinical practice* (pp. 112–144). New York: Norton.

Schore, J. R., & Schore, A. N. (2008). Modern attachment theory: The central role of affect regulation in development and treatment. *Clinical Social Work, 36,* 9–20. http://link.springer.com/article/10.1007%2Fs10615-007-0111-7#page-1

Segal, Z., Teasdale, J., & Williams, M. (2002). *Mindfulness-based cognitive therapy for depression.* New York: Guilford.

Siegel, D. (1999). *The developing mind: Toward a neurobiology of interpersonal experience.* New York: Guilford.

Siegel, D. J. (2006). *The mindful brain: Reflection and attunement in the cultivation of well-being.* New York: Norton.

Sroufe, L. A. (1997). Psychopathology as an outcome of development. *Development and Psychopathology, 9*(2), 251–268.

Steele, K., Van der Hart, O., & Nijenhuis, E. R. S. (2004). Phasenorientierte behandlung komplexer dissoziativer störungen: Die bewältigung traumabezogener phobien [Phase oriented treatment of complex dissociative disorders: Overcoming trauma-related phobias]. In A. Eckhardt-Henn & S. Hoffman (Eds.), *Dissoziative bewusstseinsstörungen: Theorie, symptomatik, therapie [Dissociative disorders of consciousness: Theory, symptoms, therapy]* (pp. 357–394). Stuttgart: Schattauer.

Steele, K., Van der Hart, O., & Nijenhuis, E. (2005). Phase-oriented treatment of structural dissociation in complex traumatization: Overcoming trauma-related phobias. *Journal of Trauma and Dissociation, 6*(3), 11–53.

Steele, K., Van der Hart, O., & Nijenhuis, E. R. S. (2009). The theory of trauma-related structural dissociation of the personality. In P. F. Dell & J. O'Neill (Eds.), *Dissociation and the dissociative disorders: DSM-V and beyond* (pp. 239–259). New York: Routledge.

Stern, D. (1985). *The interpersonal world of the infant: A view from psychoanalysis and developmental psychology.* New York: Basic Books.

Stotzer, R. (2009). Violence against transgender people: A review of United States data. *Aggression and Violent Behavior, 14*, 170–179. doi:10.1016/j.avb.2009.01.006

Sue, D. W., Sue, D., Neville, H. A., & .Smith, L. (2019). *Counseling the culturally diverse: Theory and practice.* Hoboken, NJ. Wiley & Sons.

Van der Hart, O., Nijenhuis, E., & Steele, K. (2006). *The haunted self.* New York: Norton.

Van der Hart, O., Nijenhuis, E., Steele, K., & Brown, D. (2004). Trauma-related dissociation: Conceptual clarity lost and found. *Australia and New Zealand Journal of Psychiatry, 38,* 906–914.

Van der Kolk, B. A., McFarlane, A., & Weisaeth, L. (1996). *Traumatic stress: The effects of overwhelming experience on mind, body, and society.* New York: Guilford.

Van IJzendoorn, M., Schuengel, C., & Bakermans-Kranenburg, M. (1999). Disorganized attachment in early childhood: Meta-analysis of precursors, concomitants and sequelae. *Development and Psychopathology, 11,* 225–249.

Chapter 8

THE ROLE OF THE BODY IN FORECASTING THE FUTURE

> *Oppression spares no body. Injustices are both*
> *systemic and intimate, taking root in the flesh.*
> MARY WATKINS

Human beings are meaning makers. Every waking moment, we make meaning through a range of automatic, nonverbal capacities such as observing, inferring, and compiling data gleaned not only from environmental stimuli, but also from our own internal reactions. These data are compared to our past experience by brains capable of processing a colossal amount of information in a split second through operations that are so complex they elude the understanding of even the most brilliant neuroscientists. The most critical result of this comparison is movement: We make a physical action (Llinas, 2001). In a millisecond, we assimilate our internal sensations, images, thoughts, emotions, and memories, as well as the myriad sensory input from the external world, and compare that information to past experiences. At the same moment, we forecast the future, and act (even if by remaining still). The overarching purpose of this largely implicit process is to anticipate the future accurately enough so that the actions we make preserve our survival. But surviving is not the same as living. Bromberg clarifies:

> Through their anticipatory protective system, people are able to more or less survive. But many are also more or less unable to live, because full involvement in ongoing life is drained of meaning by the affective residue of developmental trauma that in adulthood serves as a perpetual reminder that stability of self cannot be taken for granted and requires that life be managed with vigilance rather than lived with spontaneity. (2010, p. 276)

Our clients come to therapy because they want to move beyond surviving, and to do so, the restrictive predictions of self-states that are rooted in the past must be revised to fit current reality.

The meaning we make of each moment precipitates our predictions of the future. Meaning making is typically thought of as a conscious and verbal process, but meaning is shaped and expressed through a wide variety of human capacities and phenomena. Tronick states:

> Meanings include anything from the linguistic, symbolic, abstract realms, which we easily think of as forms of *meaning*, to the bodily, physiologic, behavioral and emotional structures and processes, which we find more difficult to conceptualize as forms, acts, or actualizations of meaning. (2009, p. 88)

Meaning making is thus both explicit, described through symbols and language, and implicit, gleaned through a plethora of automatic processes. The non-conscious meaning makings that take place beneath the words are arguably more significant than the meaning we make with language. This chapter focuses on the nonverbal behaviors of gesture, posture, prosody, facial expressions, eye gaze, and movement habits that visibly reflect and sustain the meanings that fuel predictions. We also explore meaning making in its intrinsic relationship to the sociocultural context that inherently influences every experience. The somatic narrative, mediated by context, is a powerful determinant of behavior. It reveals implicit expectations that not only flavor the manner in which content is explicitly expressed but in part determine the content itself. Ever present in all human interactions, the somatic narrative is influenced by race, ethnicity, country of origin, gender, sexual orientation, and other social locations.

While we might view our behavior as logical and conscious, Schore (2011) asserts that it is the brain's right hemisphere, responsible for implicit emotional processing and communication, that dominates human behavior. Taking shape long before the more rational and linguistic neocortex and left brain are fully developed, the implicit self "represents the biological substrate of the human unconscious mind and is intimately involved in the processing of bodily based affective information associated with various motivational states" (Schore, 2009, p. 114). The implicit self absorbs unspoken messages from our families, significant people in our lives, and society as a whole. Implicit selves, or self-states, and their predictions are echoed in the movement patterns of the body. Our ability to forecast or imagine the effect of our actions is the most potent determinant of which actions we execute and how we execute them.

A prediction that particular actions, if executed, will lead to undesirable outcomes induces that action to be inhibited or modified. For example, if caregivers respond to our proximity-seeking actions (such as reaching out for contact or support) with abuse, criticism, rejection, and the like, we may cease reaching out. Similarly, when the circumstances around us are harsh, as in the case of poverty and marginalization, and we do not receive needed support or opportunity, we may stop trusting others and shut down, which affects the body as well. Or when we experience repeated racialized trauma and discrimination, we may become hypervigilant and sustain a defensive posture in anticipation of fending off future injustices, especially in white spaces—our bodies may be tense or our eyes may continually scan the environment searching for threat cues. If an erect, upright posture elicited unwanted attention, abuse, or shame in the context of our families or of society at large, we may slump and keep our heads down. These physical patterns may be chronic or may be related to specific contexts, and as such they could reflect predictions of the future in general, of the immediate future, or of the future with a particular person, group, or society. These physical habits can be explored not only through engaging in conversation, or "talking about," but through body-based mindfulness interventions embedded within the therapeutic relationship (Kurtz, 1990; Ogden, 2014; Ogden & Minton, 2000; Ogden et al., 2006).

As we grow, our repeated interactions with our caregivers, other significant people, and the larger society instill in us "implicit relational knowing" or, in other words, "how to do things with others" (Lyons-Ruth, 1998). Eluding conscious understanding and verbal description, implicit relational knowing powerfully predicts what vocalizations, expressions, and actions will be welcomed or rejected by others, in close interpersonal contexts and in the wider society. This knowing is typically shaped by memories that are organized on a primitive and fundamental level (Piaget, 1962), carrying with them forecasts of the future that live not in words but in action sequences brimming with unconscious meaning rather than in words.

Implicit relational knowing first of all depends upon the infant's attachment figures and other significant people's implicit, embodied mentalizing, which is crucial for developing the experience-dependent brain. Mentalizing is often described as an explicit process of making sense of our internal experience and that of others through conscious, deliberate, verbal reflection. However, most mentalizing is implicit, strongly determined by non-conscious sensations, emotions, meanings, and how we hold our bodies and execute actions. Embodied mentalizing is expressed through a somatic conversation made up of back-and-forth movements and expressions. Mentalizing occurs as caregivers "implicitly conceive, comprehend, and extrapolate the infant's mental states (such as wishes, desires, or preferences) from the infant's whole-body kinesthetic expressions, and adjust one's own kinesthetic patterns accordingly" (Shai & Belsky, 2011, p. 3). Mentalizing includes identifying, distinguishing, and predicting another person's actions at a visceral, affective, and motor level, and responding accordingly through movement, expression, gesture, posture, and so on. Infants develop affect-regulatory capacities when their attachment figures match, attune, and respond to their continually changing states (Beebe & Lachman, 1998).

The relational process that informs mentalizing occurs in a specific sociocultural context that surrounds primary caregiving relationships. Mentalizing between an infant and caregivers is impaired when the primary caregivers are unable to be fully present to the infant's needs due to conditions such as mental disorders and substance use, or due to external stressors such as poverty, war, or the threat of deportation. In communal societies where caregiving is distributed among multiple people within and outside of the immediate family, mentalizing is mediated by the larger community in which the infant is raised. A collectivist culture can mitigate some of the external factors that interfere with a primary caregiver's ability to mentalize, which supports the child's implicit relational knowing in ways that are not usually available in an individualistic culture. For example, a young Colombian male client from a working-class immigrant family was attached to multiple caregivers. He found comfort in and was supported by the extended family that were often present in the family home, given that his parents worked long hours and were frequently absent. The implicit relational knowing for this young boy was shaped by the mentalizing of multiple caregivers that actively participated in his daily care, rather than by a few primary caregivers.

The rapid, moment-by-moment nonverbal interactions with caregivers that shape infants' nonverbal physical tendencies expose their relational expectations. As Beebe asserts, "Infants form expectancies of how these interactions go, whether they are positive or negative, and these expectancies set a trajectory for development (which can nevertheless transform)" (2006, p. 160). In secure relationships, the infant's experience is by and large mentalized adequately, and thus responded to in an attuned manner by others, so that they develop generally positive expectations of interactions with others and become increasingly effective at nonverbal signaling, engaging, and responding to others (Brazelton, 1989; Schore, 1994; Siegel, 1999; Stern, 1985; Tronick, 2007).

An infant's predictions are unmistakable in Tronick's (2007) Still Face experiments, when an attachment figure is directed to be unresponsive to the infant. When the lack of response continues past a few moments, the infants exchange active proximity-seeking actions like eye contact, reaching, and crying for more passive postural collapse and autoregulatory behaviors like thumb sucking (Tronick, 2006). The meaning is plainly revealed in the procedural organization of these actions. Over time, infants will learn to repeat the expressions, postures, movements, and gestures that elicit a desired response from their attachment figures, or at least, in traumatogenic environments, minimize the effects of abuse and neglect. Similarly, as infants mature and venture into the larger world, they learn to repeat physical postures, gestures, and facial expressions as these are shaped by their social location, privilege/oppression dynamics, and the messages they receive from the world. These actions express their implicit relational knowing—their expectations of human interaction in personal and societal realms.

Repeated executions of particular movements shape the body itself; form is determined by function. As Todd claimed, "For every thought supported by feeling, there is a muscle change . . . [a person's] whole body records [their] emotional thinking" (1937/1975, p. 1).

Predictions and related emotions can be discovered from habitual affect-laden postures and movements when explored in therapy. Habitual tension in the upper body and a forward thrusting of the chest may reflect preparation to defend in the face of a threatening environment and may contribute to chronic anger. A sunken chest and downward-turning head may perpetuate long-drawn-out feelings of sadness and grief due to repeated misrecognition of caregivers or of society. When society at large misrecognizes a group, such as LGBTQ+ people, it can be a form of oppression and convey negative and even odious messages about that group (Taylor, 1992). If misrecognition induces the loss of the postural integrity seen in the slumped postures of Tronick's babies, over time that posture can become chronic, which in and of itself impacts emotions, meaning making, and movement forecasts, as well as movement potential. A slumped posture may both reflect and sustain feelings of helplessness, and in turn contributes implicitly to particular expectations and constraint actions. Hiked shoulders and a wide-eyed gaze may reflect chronic fear due to an environment where misrecognition, danger, and threat are commonplace. Since the spine is an axis around which movement can be made, a collapsed spine or a rigid one can render proximity-seeking actions, such as reaching out or pushing away, more difficult. Range of motion and even eye contact are more effortful with a slumped or a rigid spine that disrupts the position of the head and neck.

Sierra was a 13-year-old girl treated in private practice. Her working-class family made ends meet but struggled to make a living. Sierra's native ancestry was reflected in her dark skin and curly hair. As the third of four children born in the United States to first-generation immigrant parents, Sierra had few extended family members close by and very little contact with her extended family in her home country of Mexico. Additionally, her family had few community supports here in the United States. Her mother Rosa described being isolated, saying, "All I do is work and take care of my children. I don't have friends." As is the case with many first- and second-generation immigrant families, Rosa worked seven days a week from home and had little time to spare for her daughter. Her father, Juan, was unemployed and struggled with feeling emasculated due to his inability to procure work. Though Juan demonstrated love and caring for his children, he was also distant and disengaged from the day-to-day needs of the family. It was evident that the family was overburdened with survival needs that affected their ability to have meaningful attuned connection with Sierra on a consistent basis.

Rosa and Juan's first language was Spanish, and Juan had little mastery of English. Conversely, their U.S.-born children had little mastery of Spanish. Thus, family conversations and dynamics were limited by their language differences. It is often the case that children of immigrant families lose proficiency in their parents' language due to the considerable influence of the dominant culture through social media, television, radio, and everyday interactions in places like school. Furthermore, some immigrant families may perceive their children's proficiency in the dominant language of the country where they now reside as a sign of greater contact and assimilation, thus increasing the likelihood of their children's success.

Sierra's carriage was similar to that of Tronick's infants. Her body was constricted, her spine slumped, her neck pulled into her shoulders, her head held stiffly to one side, and her shoulders hunched. This carriage can reflect caregiver dynamics, in addition to reflecting social contextual factors impacting Sierra and her family. She vacillated between blank but unflinching eye contact and staring into space. Sierra had become increasingly isolated and nearly nonverbal in recent months. She would hide behind her long, thick hair, letting it fall in front of her face to avoid eye contact. Her school counselor requested that Sierra's hair be cut short to improve peer interactions, which needless to say, did nothing to solve the

difficulty. Sierra was referred to therapy because teachers were fearful that she might follow in the footsteps of a classmate who had
committed suicide. Unbeknownst to her parents, Sierra had hardly
spoken at school for nearly two years. Rosa reported that although
Sierra had not wanted to go to school and had refused peer activities, the family had believed that this was typical American teenager
behavior. Formerly an excellent student, Sierra's grades had plum-
meted in the last year.

At the time of commencing therapy, her mother had decided
on homeschooling because she felt that Sierra wasn't ready for
the stresses of public education. During the initial intake, Sierra
sat silently, head pulled down and to the left, avoiding eye contact, while Rosa did all the talking. Rosa and her daughter were
extremely close, which from a Western perspective could be perceived as enmeshed. However, through a larger sociocultural lens,
their relationship could be perceived as reflecting the values of collectivist cultures around maintaining close proximity and contact.
Rosa seemed confused by her daughter's behavior, claiming that she
had no idea until recently that there was a problem. She reported no
abuse, although Sierra exhibited typical symptoms of both trauma
and eating disorders: difficulties in her family, and as Courtois
describes, problems with "intimacy, shame, low self-esteem, mistrust of others, guilt, conflict and anxiety about sexuality, a negative
body image, the need to succeed, and powerlessness and depression"
(2010, pp. 559–560). Sierra had never been to therapy before.

In one-on-one therapy sessions, Sierra revealed that her problems began much earlier than her mother thought. Speaking
in a nearly inaudible whisper, Sierra attributed her difficulties to
repeated humiliating incidents at school where her classmates called
her names and made fun of her for her native features and darker
skin. Sierra had not conveyed to anyone the depth of her anguish,
nor had she ever sought help. Her solution was to remain quiet and
shut down, fearful of taking risks, implicitly predicting that doing

so would decrease the chances of ridicule and humiliation. She felt many things were out of her control, and her binging and purging behavior may have offered her some sense of control over her body.

Sierra's forecast that the future would hold only more humiliation influenced her actions and how she executed them—she sat very still and seemed to move as little as possible. The Nobel Prize winner Roger Sperry asserted that the primary purpose of the brain is to make our bodies move; all the other functions are secondary (in Van der Kolk, 2006, p. xviii). In order to want to move our bodies, we must predict a positive outcome for the immediate future should we take action. Siegel (1999) describes the brain as an "anticipation machine." Every single move we make, from reaching for an object to reaching for help, is the result of our anticipation of what will happen in the next moment. Although Sierra did not recall memories before age five or six years, her earliest experiences were remembered "as a series of unconscious expectations" (Cortina & Liotti, 2007, p. 205). These experiences are not available for reflection and revision, rendering implicit predictions all the more potent and influential. We know memories are constructive; each time we "remember" something, we can add new associations to the memory, changing how it is encoded in the brain. But when we do not remember what happened, the memories remain unchanged, yet shape subsymbolic processes that, as Bucci writes, "operate in sensory, motoric and somatic systems, as sounds, smells, feelings of many different sorts" (2011, p. 210). Sierra's constricted body, monotone voice quality, low volume, restrained movement, and lack of engagement coupled with pervasive emotions of shame and fear told the story of her unremembered past.

Bromberg asserts, "Trauma occurs in situations (explicitly or implicitly interpersonal) in which self-disconfirmation cannot be prevented or escaped, and from which there is no hope of protection, relief, or soothing through communication with another human being" (2012, p. 274). In one self-state, Sierra seemed to have given up on human comfort and become increasingly isolated, but in another, she talked in baby talk, "acted like a baby," and constantly sought "hugs and kisses" from her mother who (explicitly) found Sierra's neediness "too much" and wanted her to "grow up," be more assertive, and take more responsibility in the family. Rosa shared how at Sierra's age, back in her home country, she had to cook, clean, get herself ready for school, and keep up with her schoolwork because her parents were busy working long hours outside of the home. She wanted her daughter to "grow up," but at the same time, Rosa protected Sierra, homeschooling her and thus depriving her of her previous contact with school peers and friends, explaining that Sierra was not "ready" to be with her peers. Additionally, Rosa afforded her daughter little privacy, often entering her room suddenly and uninvited.

In therapy, Sierra complained that her mother wanted Sierra to "tell her everything." I asked Rosa if she could demonstrate with her movement and her words how she asked Sierra to tell her "everything." Rosa pulled her daughter's head to her chest, stroking her daughter's face and arms, saying, "I want you to tell me everything that's going on with you." Sierra responded, saying, "But I don't want to," in a childlike voice. In a later session when Rosa asked Sierra to stop "acting like a baby," Sierra expressed fear that her mother did not "accept" her and defended her behavior as "just having fun." It appeared that Rosa's seemingly conflicting behavior encouraged Sierra to remain dependent, while at the same time rejecting Sierra's "inappropriate" neediness. Sierra's needy self appeared in behaviors that served to push Rosa away rather than elicit the physical contact this self-state craved. At the same time, Sierra's more independent self requested more boundaries with her mother. Her relationship with her mother and her immediate family seemed to be ineffective in meeting her attachment needs, which were further unfulfilled by her feeling of disconnection from other sources of support and connection such as extended family or community networks.

Different self-states, both explicit and implicit, make different meanings and thus have different predictions. Bromberg (2006) clarifies how these different self-states come about, pointing out that caregivers will inevitably relate to their child in such a manner that certain aspects of the child are validated and accepted, while other aspects are ignored and rejected. In this way, the relational existence of some aspects of the child are negated or "disconfirmed" by the caregivers, and subsequently by the child. Since this disconfirmation is relationally non-negotiable, it remains irresolvable, and conflict ensues between an aspect that is accepted and one that is not, each of which makes its own meaning and has its own goals, needs, expectations and behaviors.

Sierra seemed to find it impossible to reconcile her needy young self with the demands of adolescence, and Rosa seemed conflicted in her interactions with each of her daughter's self-states. However, these dynamics were not the only source of stress for Rosa and Sierra. They both reported experiences of being belittled and discriminated against in public, which are societal disconfirmations that are also relationally nonnegotiable. Moreover, the struggles in these family dynamics were likely exacerbated by the clash between the individualistic values of the dominant culture of their new country and the collectivist values of their country of origin. The extensive contact and meaningful connections with a variety of relatives, neighbors, and community supports that would be available in their homeland would most likely mitigate these issues, at least in part. Because the "transgenerational transmission of family values and beliefs in upbringing children is performed [implicitly and] continuously from generation to generation" (Todorovic & Matejevic, 2014, p. 275), it would make sense that an implicit conflict between the values of a collectivist culture and those of their adopted country could be playing out in the family dynamics.

Making the meanings that fuel forecasts of the future is a complex endeavor that is not static. As Tronick asserts, "meaning is not one thing—one meaning. Meaning is a layered flow over time of the different meanings emerging from the multiple levels and processes that make meaning" (2009, p. 87). Sierra alternately described Rosa's behavior as "controlling" and as "caring," depending on her own self-state, while also showing apathy about drawing upon any other potential sources of support outside of her mother. Llinas asserts that when our brains compare present-moment data with past experience, "an 'upgrading' [occurs] of the internal image of what is to come to its actualization into the external world" (2001, p. 38). Yet, particular self-states in Sierra continued to hold forecasts fixed in the past situations, and her movements were both constrained and reinforced by these predictions.

Trauma and attachment experience, with their consequential neuropsychological deficits, often prevent "upgrading the forecast" because brains are conservative in taking the risk that outcomes of certain actions might be safe when they were once dangerous. The lack of upgrading, of course, serves survival functions (as the saying goes, "better to mistake a stick for a snake than a snake for a stick") but also can thwart adaptive action in favor of what has worked in past circumstances. One part of Sierra remained fearful and withdrawn, even in accepting environments, unwilling to undertake the risks typical of her peers in the United States, and reluctant to engage with other potentially supportive people or systems within the school or in the community, fearing that by doing so she would again become a target of ridicule. For Sierra taking action had stalled in many arenas.

Each self-state within Sierra had its own perspective of reality, which were not communicated to one another explicitly. As Bromberg confirms, "The felt otherness between one's *own states* becomes an alien 'thing' to be managed because it can no longer be contained as negotiable internal conflict that is mediated by self-other wholeness" (2012, p. 274). Sierra had great difficulty holding the incompatible truths of different self-states in her mind at the same time. Conflicting simultaneous or sequential nonverbal indicators often reveal signs of dissociative self-states and their opposing meanings and predictions. These indicators "comprise the language of eating disordered clients," who tend to act on rather than discuss their emotions (Petrucelli, 2008, p. 245). When Sierra wanted me to cease my questioning, instead of telling me so, her voice would become inaudible and her words slurred. Her outward compliance was evident in the ducking of her head, lack of eye contact, and hunched shoulders. Verbal and nonverbal messages often contradict each other, and can seek to hide certain self-states as well as make them known. Sierra giggled comfortably when she attempted to say "no" to her mother in therapy, saying that she felt bad pushing Rosa away and not telling her everything.

Sierra's conflicting self-states were clearly revealed when she expressed her aspirations of becoming an actress. But verbally, her body told a different story: Her lack of meaningful eye contact, slowed movement, and constricted stance exposed a fear of attention that she did not acknowledge. If the self-state who wanted to be an actress expected that risk taking would bring her happiness, if engagement with others had not been opposed by her "unconfident" self-state, and if communication had not been explicitly foreclosed between these two self-states, Sierra would be more likely to be curious about her environment and engage in approach behaviors that would bring her the recognition, attention, and connection she explicitly desired.

The conflict between these two self-states was apparent when she asked if I liked her new outfit, and I said I did. Sierra unconsciously turned her head to the side, stiffened, pressed back in her chair, seemed uneasy, and smiled uncomfortably, although the explicit wish of the self-state that wanted to be an actress was to be noticed as attractive. This part of her strove to be "thin and pretty" and wanted to wear skinny jeans like the girls at school she admired, but another part found it dangerous, implicitly predicting that looking attractive would draw attention that would only bring humiliation. Although Sierra was not obese, she was also not slender, and like many adolescents with eating disorders, she perceived herself as "fat and ugly" and feared being teased about her size and looks, and also about her darker skin (both of which had happened in the past). Sierra had fallen prey to damaging societal stereotypes around darker skin like hers, and the media's portrayal of ideal size and weight, combined with an appetite for junk food for which she criticized herself. She could provide little information about what happened during her binging and purging episodes, which presumably took place in a dissociated not-me self-state.

The somatic narrative not only reveals self-states to others, but also tells us about ourselves. Sierra's sense of self was greatly impacted by the non-conscious meaning of her body's chronic posture. The slump in her spine seemed to diminish her self-esteem and perpetuate and possibly even catalyze her feelings of shame, helplessness, and fear. A variety of studies demonstrate the impact of posture and other physical actions upon experience and self-perception. Subjects who received good news in slumped posture reported feeling less proud of themselves than subjects who received the same news in an upright posture (Stepper & Strack, 1993). Schnall and Laird (2003) found a correlation in subjects who practiced postures and facial expressions associated with sadness, happiness, or anger, with a tendency to recall past events that contained a similar emotional valence as that of the one they had rehearsed, even though they were no longer practicing the posture. Similarly, Dijkstra, Kaschak, and Zwaan (2007) showed that subjects embodying a particular posture tended to recall memories and emotions in which the posture had been operational.

Tronick states, "Some meanings [and some predictions] are

known and symbolizable, some are unknown, implicit but with 'work' can become known" (2009, p. 87). With keen attention to her physical pattern in therapy, Sierra was eventually able to shed the old meaning and thoughts of self-loathing that reflected the subjective truth of one of her self-states, and open communication with it. By directly addressing the predictions reflected in the body's indicators of implicit self-states, client and therapist can bring the relational experience of these indicators into the present moment.

I recognized Sierra's habitual holding of her head to the left, pulling it into her shoulder girdle and hunching her shoulders, as just such an indicator and asked Sierra to notice the way she held her head. She identified these physical habits as representing a part of her that lacked confidence. I wondered aloud what would happen if she explored aligning her head, and as she did so, the self-state that had learned to inhibit that action became frightened and anxious. Having made up its mind that the humiliation would be minimized if she made herself small and insignificant, this part of her believed aligning her head would only bring more shame. Every action has a purpose, and it made sense to both Sierra and me that it was no wonder she held her head to the side. New actions, like new words, can be viewed as threatening and adversarial by other self-states whose reality is challenged by such actions. Keep in mind that these actions are not simply physical exercises: They are rich with strong emotions and painful memories of what had happened when that action had been executed in the past. Processing these actions and related emotions can ultimately encourage self-states or parts to get to know one another and increase the ease of transitions between them.

As we explored her carriage, Sierra recounted a childhood experience when she was 8 years old in which she felt humiliated. In a quiet, hesitant voice, full of held-back pain, she said,

I wrote something—I wrote an essay, and I went up there [in front of her class at school]. I . . . I . . . I, like, I glitched a little bit. And then when I read it people laughed at me. And I kept reading. But I didn't say anything afterwards. I never told anyone that people were laughing. . . . And I'm wondering is . . . is anything I do worthwhile?

The self-state recounted in this painful experience was that part of her that completely lost her confidence and remained small and withdrawn. This part also seemed to be wounded by the lack of attuned responsiveness from the teacher who was present at the time of her presentation. When I asked Sierra what that 8-year-old part of her might want to know, she was able to explicitly communicate with this self-state whose need for comfort and acceptance she had not before addressed. "I guess I would tell you [the child part of her]) . . . you're up there. It's all about you. It's 7 minutes of fame, kind of, I guess. Don't worry about what people think. Think about yourself." Acknowledging her ability to communicate with and know what this younger part of her needed, I asked if in her imagination she could envision being with herself when she was 8 years old, and tell this child part of her, "It doesn't matter what they think. It's about you." In a moving moment of the therapy, I felt that together we were communicating with this particularly vulnerable and hurt self-state, recognizing its painful reality and offering understanding and support. With this act of recognition of the self-state she had pushed aside, Sierra began to cry softly, murmuring, "These are good tears."

Subsequently, we worked with somatic communication between these self-states as well. We discovered that if Sierra held her head straight on her shoulders, she felt anxious, but if she placed her hands on her belly where she felt the anxiety, the anxiety lessened, and she felt safe. Together, we had found actions that recognized and soothed the self-state that had felt humiliated, and Sierra was able then to take the risk of being seen by straightening the position of her head. Through these actions, she was able to hold both self-states literally in her body as well as in her mind.

This chapter would be disquietingly incomplete without high-lighting how the therapist's own nonverbal expressions and the self-states they represent have a strong impact on what takes place within the relationship. We therapists tend to invite and interact with the parts of the client they are most comfortable with, discon-necting from and ignoring the client's self-states we would rather not deal with (Bromberg, 2006). We are more prone to disconnect from or ignore aspects of the client's experience we experience as foreign, "other," and also in situations where we lack curiosity or fail to seek a deeper understanding of the client's lived experience contained within the particular self-state. For example, had I not met with Sierra's mother and gathered information about their fam-ily history and dynamics, immigration history, and current familial stressors, the paramount impact of these factors on Sierra and her family may have been missed. For example, therapists who do not recognize and understand the norms of a collectivist culture or hold value for interdependence might judge the family as being dysfunc-tionally enmeshed.

Additionally, we therapists tend to work with actions we are comfortable exploring. Physical actions that are familiar to us, are easy for us to execute, and do not challenge or stimulate not-me self-states in ourselves are the actions we are likely to explore with the client. We will unconsciously ignore or reject actions that would make us uncomfortable. For example, if we are uneasy with an aligned posture that reflects confidence, we will be unlikely to explore this action effectively with our clients. If we attempt to do so, we will probably be unable to demonstrate an emotionally and physically integrated and aligned posture, so the exploration will have little chance of being fruitful. But this is not cause for undue concern for those of us who are curious about our own contribution to the nonverbal aspects of what takes place in treatment, including the power and privilege differential and how it manifests in the therapeutic relationship. In fact, the mysterious power of relational growth often emerges from the unsymbolized bearing of therapist and client upon one another, which reflects the lived experiences, socialization, and relational histories of both parties. Knowing this, therapists might become curious about their own postures and actions that feel familiar, and those that do not, and explore their influences and meanings.

Therapy is always a dance of safety, uncertainty, and risky challenge. The atmosphere of the therapeutic relationship is described by Bromberg (2006) as "safe but not too safe." Too much safety indicates that arousal remains regulated in the middle of the window of tolerance, but if either hyper- or hypoarousal are extreme, clients may relive rather than rework the past, and be unable to integrate their experience. Thus, the effects of painful past traumatic and relational experiences must be evoked to a degree so that arousal reaches the regulatory boundaries of the window so that new affect regulation capacities can be developed, new meanings made, and the window of tolerance expanded.

Together, therapist and client must navigate the perilous terrain of working at their own regulatory boundaries. This is challenging for both parties, as unpredictable interactions between them elicits self-states from each that want something from the other that may not be obtainable at the time it is desired. Thus, while safety is essential to establish a context in which psychotherapy can begin, it is impossible to sustain. Therapist and client are both fortunate and compelled to negotiate the inescapable enactments fueled by these dissociated self-states—fortunate because through the intimate encounters of the enactment, higher levels of organization are attained by both parties, and compelled because this negotiation often takes place against the desire of some of their self-states that would rather not deal with not-me ones (cf. Chapter 10, this volume).

Each therapeutic relationship travels two paths. The explicit, conscious path represents what client and therapist believe they are doing together, supported by theory and technique. The explicit goals of Sierra, her mother, and myself were to help Sierra become more assertive and feel confident to live more fully. These goals reflect the values of this family's individualistic adopted culture and may contradict their implicitly familiar relational expectations and values of the collectivistic culture of their homeland. Explicit therapeutic goals may and often do belie implicit ones. For the explicit journey, body-oriented, embedded relational mindfulness interventions from Sensorimotor Psychotherapy (cf. Chapter 4, this volume) are employed to help Sierra's self-states find new physical actions that foster integration between explicit and implicit selves. In contrast, the implicit journey pertains to what is enacted beneath the words, beyond technique. Elusive and unconscious, this journey may feel vaguely familiar to one or both parties, but typically leads to outcomes that were neither intended nor predicted.

At the beginning of our work, I noticed that I mirrored Sierra's collapsed posture, empathically attuning nonverbally to her vulnerable self-states. As time went on, my posture became more erect, especially when we explored Sierra sitting tall and pushing away with her arms in a gesture of assertion and boundary setting. Sierra obediently explored these actions, but she sometimes seemed detached, and her voice reverted to its old monotone quality. I was disappointed in subsequent sessions that her posture had not changed. I did not understand what I was feeling and could not think about it with any clear meaning. Upon reflection, I realized her infantile self was aversive to one of my self-states, and the words of my own mother came back to me: "Where there's a will, there's a way; just tough it out." An implicit tête-à-tête was taking place between a part of me that wanted Sierra to become empowered and abandon her regressed self-state, evidenced in my aligned posture and assertive prosody, and a part of Sierra that could not authentically meet those expectations, reflected in her lackluster actions and compliance. The meaning of our relational dance belonged to both Sierra and me, and in subsequent sessions it would become our task to share our respective experiences both verbally and nonverbally to discover together the "safe surprises" (Bromberg, 2006) of relational negotiations that would emerge from our interaction.

The communication of the somatic narrative may be intentional or unintentional, conscious or unconscious, clear or confusing, and often represents contradictions among dissociated self-states of both therapist and client and the meanings that belong to each state. Reflecting the imprints of early attachment as well as the influences of the larger society, the implicit self reflects elements of social location and oppression/privilege dynamics fundamental to the identities of therapist and client alike. The heartbeat of the therapeutic dance is the somatic representation of self-states and the body-to-body dialogue between them. A wealth of nonverbal indicators rife with meaning that reflect and sustain implicit "me" and "not-me" self-states lie waiting under the surface and beneath the words, to be discovered in the relational context of therapy.

REFERENCES

Beebe, B. (2006). Co-constructing mother–infant distress in face-to-face interactions: Contributions of microanalysis. *Infant Observation, 9*(2), 151–164.

Beebe, B., & Lachmann, F. (1998). Co-constructing inner and relational processes: Self- and mutual regulation in infant research and adult treatment. *Psychoanalytic Psychology, 15*(4), 480–516.

Brazelton, T. (1989). *The earliest relationship.* Reading, MA: Addison-Wesley.

Bromberg, P. M. (2006). *Awakening the dreamer: Clinical journeys.* Mahwah, NJ: Analytic Press.

Bromberg, P. M. (2010). Minding the dissociative gap. *Contemporary Psychoanalysis, 46*(1), 19–31.

Bromberg, P. M. (2011). *The shadow of the tsunami and the growth of the relational mind.* New York: Routledge.

Bromberg, P. M. (2012). Credo. *Psychoanalytic Dialogues, 22*(3), 273–278.

Bucci, W. (2011). The role of embodied communication in therapeutic change: A multiple code perspective. In W. Tschacher & C. Bergomi (Eds.), *The implications of embodiment: Cognition and communication* (pp. 209–228). Exeter, UK: Imprint Academic.

Cortina, M., & Liotti, G. (2007). New approaches to understanding unconscious processes: Implicit and explicit memory systems. *International Forum of Psychoanalysis, 16,* 204–212.

Courtois, C. (2010). *Healing the incest wound: Adult survivors in therapy* (2nd ed.). New York: Norton.

Dijkstra, K., Kaschak, M. P., & Zwaan, R. A. (2007). Body posture facilitates retrieval of autobiographical memories. *Cognition, 102*(1), 139–149.

Kurtz, R. (1990). *Body-centered psychotherapy: The Hakomi method: The integrated use of mindfulness, nonviolence, and the body.* Mendocino, CA: LifeRhythm.

Llinas, R. (2001). *I of the vortex: From neurons to self.* Cambridge, MA: MIT Press.

Lyons-Ruth, K. (1998). Implicit relational knowing: Its role in development and psychoanalytic treatment. *Infant Mental Health Journal, 19,* 282–289.

Ogden, P. (2007). *Beyond words: A clinical map for using mindfulness of the body and the organization of experience in trauma treatment.* Paper presented at Mindfulness and Psychotherapy Conference, UCLA/Lifespan Learning Institute, Los Angeles.

Ogden, P. (2014). Beyond conversation in sensorimotor psychotherapy: Embedded relational mindfulness. In V. M. Follette, D. Rozelle, J. W. Hopper, D. I. Rome, & J. Briere (Eds.), *Mindfulness oriented interventions for trauma: Integrating contemplative practices* (pp. 227–242). New York: Guilford.

Ogden, P., & Minton, K. (2000). Sensorimotor psychotherapy: One method for processing traumatic memory. *Traumatology, 6*(3), 1–20.

Ogden, P., Minton, K., & Pain, C. (2006). *Trauma and the body: A sensorimotor approach to psychotherapy.* New York: Norton.

Petrucelli, J. (2008). When a body meets a body. In F. Anderson (Ed.), *Bodies in treatment: The unspoken dimension* (pp. 237–254). New York: Analytic Press.

Piaget, J. (1962). *Play, dreams, and imitation in childhood.* New York, NY: Norton.

Schnall, S., & Laird, J. D. (2003). Keep smiling: Enduring effects of facial expressions and postures on emotional experience and memory. *Cognition and Emotion, 17*(5), 787–797.

Schore, A. (1994). *Affect regulation and the origin of the self: The neurobiology of emotional development.* Hillsdale, NJ: Lawrence Erlbaum.

Schore, A. N. (2009). Right-brain affect regulation: An essential mechanism of development, trauma, dissociation, and psychotherapy. In D. Fosha, D. Siegel, & M. Solomon (Eds.), *The healing power of emotion: Affective neuroscience, development and clinical practice* (pp. 112–144). New York: Norton.

Schore, A. N. (2011). The right brain implicit self lies at the core of psychoanalysis. *Psychoanalytic Dialogues, 21*, 1–26.

Shai, D., & Belsky, J. (2011). When words just won't do: Introducing parental embodied mentalizing. *Child Development Perspectives, 5*(3), 173–180.

Siegel, D. (1999). *The developing mind: Toward a neurobiology of interpersonal experience.* New York: Guilford.

Stepper, S., & Strack, F. (1993). Proprioceptive determinants of emotional and nonemotional feelings. *Journal of Personality and Social Psychology, 64*(2), 211–220.

Stern, D. (1985). The interpersonal world of the infant: A view from psychoanalysis and developmental psychology. New York, NY: Basic Books.

Taylor, C. (1992). The politics of recognition. In A. Gutmann (Ed.), *Multiculturalism and the politics of recognition* (pp. 25—74). Princeton: Princeton University Press.

Todd, M. E. (1975). *The thinking body: A study of the balancing forces of dynamic man.* New York: Dance Horizons. (Original work published 1937)

Todorovic, J., & Matejevic, M. (2014). Transgenerational transmission of the beliefs of competent parenting. *Procedia: Social and Behavioral Sciences, 141*, 275–279. https://doi.org/10.1016/j.sbspro.2014.05.048

Tronick, E. Z. (2006). Self and dyadic expansion of consciousness, meaning-making, open systems, and the experience of pleasure. In G. B. La Sala, P. Fagandini, V. Lori, F. Monti, & I. Blickstein (Eds.), *Coming into the world: A dialogue between medical and human sciences* (pp. 13–24). Berlin: Walter de Gruyter.

Tronick, E. Z. (2007). *The neurobehavioral and social-emotional development of infants and children.* New York: Norton.

Tronick, E. Z. (2009). Multilevel meaning making and dyadic expansion of consciousness theory: The emotional and the polymorphic polysemic flow of meaning. In D. Fosha, D. Siegel, & M. Solomon (Eds.), *The healing power of emotion: Affective neuroscience, development and clinical practice* (pp. 86–110). New York: Norton.

Van der Kolk, B. (2006). Series editor's foreword. In P. Ogden, K. Minton, & C. Pain, *Trauma and the body: A sensorimotor approach to psychotherapy* (pp. xviii–xxvi). New York: Norton.

Chapter 9

BENEATH THE WORDS:
THE SOMATIC NARRATIVE

*To understand the role of the somatic dimension of
personhood, it would be important to explore the
cultural meanings of different parts of the body.*

SHELLY HARRELL

Unconscious processes and communication that take place beneath
the words during the therapy hour are arguably more significant
than content. These implicit processes, visibly reflected in nonverbal behaviors of gesture, posture, prosody, facial expressions, eye
gaze, movement habits, and affect, are the heartbeat of all relationships. Ethologists point out the significance of animal behaviors that
communicate an invitation for a specific activity, such as to play,
to be sexual, or to fight. Researchers who look at cross-cultural
exchanges emphasize that nonverbal interactions are shaped by and
reflect the history, values, and culture of specific groups of people
(Burgoon et al., 2016). Infant researchers highlight the body-based
communications between infants and attachment figures that generate affect regulation capacities, procedural memory, and so much
more. These nonverbal exchanges between infants and their caregivers, taking place within a present-day and historical sociocultural
context, shape the initial templates for future relational inter-

actions and strongly influence the functions and processes of the experience-dependent brain.

Schore states that a "paradigm shift" is taking place in psychology that privileges body-based, affective models over cognitive models of development, which takes into account the dominant influence of the nonverbal, right-brain "implicit self" over the verbal, left-brain "explicit self" (Schore, 2009; Schore & Schore, 2007). The left hemisphere, according to McGilchrist (2009) purposefully attends to details with an end point in view, and thus functions more mechanically than the right. The right hemisphere maintains a big-picture perspective that is more in touch with flow and the interconnectedness of things than the left, and thus is implicitly fundamental and influential. With the recognition of the critical role of the implicit processing of the right brain, a renewed interest in the unconscious is emerging in psychology, not only for the purpose of making it conscious, but also of inquiring into the role of the implicit self in clinical practice and how to restructure unconscious regulatory mechanisms through the process that takes place within the therapeutic dyad (Schore, 1994).

The implicit self is reflected and sustained in the nonverbal behavior reflecting the culture in which they were learned. As Dosamantes-Beaudry expresses: "The latent aspects of a culture are most readily revealed through non-verbal modes of expression— through the way members of a particular culture use their senses, gesture, move, organize themselves spatially, create interpersonal distances and create synchronous rhythms" (1999, p. 227). Therapeutic action is viewed as extending far beyond that of understanding and interpreting clients and their behavior to participating in and attending to what is being enacted beneath the words, visibly reflected in gesture, posture, prosody, facial expressions, eye gaze, and so forth that communicate both the legacy of caregiver/child interactions and the influence of sociocultural factors. The implicit dialogues experienced and enacted alongside the verbal dialogue during the therapy hour are receiving increased attention as an essential element of therapeutic change.

Usually beyond the grasp of the conscious mind, nonverbal phenomena—the "somatic narrative" of the implicit self—continuously anticipate the future and thus powerfully determine behavior. These implicit somatic cues express specific cultural identities and reproduce social dynamics, including power hierarchies and social norms such as establishing who speaks first, who takes more space, who holds gaze longer, and so forth. This chapter emphasizes the centrality of implicit processes in human behavior, the communicative role of nonverbal behavior to both self and other, and the significance of the somatic narrative in the therapy hour as a means to access and change implicit processes. Body-based embedded mindfulness interventions that directly target the visible physical indicators of the implicit self within the interpersonal context of the therapeutic dyad are illustrated as a way to alter the somatic narrative.

THE RIGHT-BRAIN IMPLICIT SELF

Developments in psychology that illuminate implicit processing underscore the importance of right-brain phenomena. The two lateralized right- and left-brain systems pertain to different memory organizations, emotions, and states of consciousness. Each has its own unique way of knowing the self and the other. The left hemisphere is primary for cognitive processing, verbal, conscious elaboration, reasoning, linguistic behaviors, and meaning making and represents a conscious, explicit self-system (Schore 2009). The right hemisphere is primary for emotional and body processing, implicit realms of communication, intersubjectivity, unconscious affect regulation, and responses to threat cues, and thus represents an unconscious, implicit self-system (Schore 2009). However, the primary difference, McGilchrist asserts, is not in what each does but how they do it—how each hemisphere engages with emotion, reasoning, and so forth. He states:

> the right hemisphere pays attention to the Other, whatever it is that exists apart from ourselves, with which it sees itself in profound relationship. It is deeply attracted to, and given life by, the relationship, the betweenness, that exists with this Other. By contrast, the left hemisphere pays attention to the virtual world that it has created, which is self-consistent, but self-contained, ultimately disconnected from the Other, making it more powerful, but ultimately only able to operate on, and to know, itself. (2009, p. 93)

From this perspective, the right hemisphere is fundamental, countering the popular perspective that the left brain is dominant in human behavior. In theory, and for the best outcome, the left hemisphere (more explicit) should be in service to the right (more implicit) (McGilchrist, 2009).

The experience-dependent implicit self develops through "right-brain to right-brain" (cf. Schore) affect-laden interactions with caregivers, relationships that are embedded since the beginning in a specific ethnocultural context (Fogel, 1993). If these interactions are sufficiently synchronized, "the organization of the infant's right brain shows increased coherence, as the flow of energy between the hierarchically organized higher right cortical and lower right subcortical components increase their connectivity, allowing the right brain to act as a self-regulating integrated whole, and therefore capable of increasing complexity" (Schore, 2001, p. 24). While we might view our behavior as well thought out and logical, governed by the left hemisphere, Schore asserts, "it is the emotion processing right hemisphere and its implicit homeostatic-survival and communication functions that is truly dominant in human existence" (2011).

Shaped by right-brain phenomena, the implicit self provides us with unconscious general knowledge of how to be in the world, how to interact with others, what to express, what to hold back, and what behavior is effective in producing desired results in the other—or in traumatogenic environments, including the trauma of systemic oppression—at least capable of minimizing abuse. As Schore states, "The right brain implicit self represents the biological substrate of the human unconscious mind and is intimately involved in the processing of bodily based affective information associated with various motivational states" (2009, p. 114). Taking shape long before the more rational and linguistic left brain and neocortex are fully developed and primed by culture, the implicit self is far reaching and enduring.

NONVERBAL EXCHANGES AND IMPLICIT RELATIONAL KNOWING

From the moment of inception, the fetus orients to sounds, cadence of movement, and rhythms of the culture around them (Fogel, 1993), so that after birth, the infant readily seeks proximity to those elements that feel familiar and thus safe. After birth, as caregivers match, attune, and respond to the infant's ever-changing arousal states, an infant's immature affect regulatory capacities are developed (Beebe & Lachmann, 1998). The interactions between caregiver and infant are also influenced by the way that child-rearing practices are understood in different sociocultural contexts (Fogel, 1993). Taking place within a community of belonging, these rapid, moment-by-moment nonverbal interactions shape the infant's nonverbal physical tendencies. Through the imitation of movements and gestures of others, children continue to develop their culturally embodied identities, even before they have a sense of self. They learn to repeat the actions that catalyze the desired response from their caregivers and other significant people in their community, and they become increasingly effective at nonverbally signaling, engaging, and responding to others (Brazelton, 1989; Schore, 1994; Siegel, 1999; Stern, 1985; Tronick, 2007).

Tronick (2007, 2011) has pointed out that movement and posture clearly denote the meaning infants make of interactions with attachment figures. One of his films shows a caregiver, in this case, the mother, and her infant son, who is pulling the mother's hair, eliciting a fleeting expression of anger from her. The infant responds by lifting his arms in front of his face in a gesture that appears protective, apparently interpreting the mother's angry expression as threatening. The mother's anger is momentary, and she swiftly seeks to repair the rupture in their connection, making every effort to reengage and play with her infant. Eventually the infant lowers his arms, relaxes his body, and smiles. In insecure attachment relationships, the infant may be left in prolonged dysregulated states with little or no interactive repair, or may be frightened, abused, and/or neglected by attachment figures, leading to disorganized attachment propensities (Lyons-Ruth et al., 1999). In these cases, affect regulatory mechanisms may fail to develop optimally, social engagement and nonverbal signaling and proximity-seeking behaviors may be compromised, and the infant's nonverbal cues may be unclear or contradictory.

Implicit relational knowing and movement habits are further refined in interaction with the larger society. Power and privilege are often communicated nonverbally, for example, as when a white person takes up more space in relation to a marginalized person, seeks more proximity, or uses touch more freely or even invasively. Repeated body-to-body interactions such as these "create largely unconscious reiterative actions in the body that subsequently form a social construction of either privilege or oppressed identities" (Bennett Leighton, 2018, p. 24). These identities are rife with implicit knowing about one another, accompanied by habitual physical movements and postures. For example, people that have been oppressed may restrict their movement, become hypervigilant for threat cues, or become numb when in dominant culture spaces. These tendencies reflect relational knowing, implicit or explicit, that speaks of the possibility of threat in dominant contexts.

Through both positive and negative affect-laden interactions with caregivers and society at large, the child acquires "implicit relational knowing"—that is, "how to do things with others" (Lyons-Ruth, 1998). This knowing evades explicit understanding, and thus cannot be described with words, but it powerfully informs us how to be in relationship; which vocalizations, expressions, or actions will be renounced, which ones will be or accepted or received gladly, and, moreover, what to expect in interactions with others. Lyons-Ruth points out that although implicit relational knowing is procedural, it is markedly different from what is commonly thought of as procedural knowledge (e.g., how to drive a car). The procedurally learned actions related to this relational knowing are accompanied by conscious or unconscious emotions and perceptions that are rooted in the person's early history (as well as imprints of the sociocultural context). They have a quality of being on autopilot—we no longer have to think about what we are doing, as when we drive the car or type these words—or when our posture, facial expressions, and gestures automatically change as we interact with our attachment figures and with others. For marginalized people, although words are unavailable to describe early or forgotten formative interactions with attachment figures, other significant relationships, or society at large, the impact of these is continually felt, and the somatic narrative tells their story.

One of the issues that brought Marley, a transwoman, to therapy was the trauma of being bullied for her more masculine appearance despite her efforts to appear more feminine. However, when Marley talked about being complimented by a friend on her new feminine outfit, Marley's spine slumped, her head lowered, her shoulders curled forward, and she scooted backward in her chair. Marley was unaware that these action sequences reflected the appraisal of her implicit self, and she was mystified as to why she suddenly felt fearful when the moment before she had felt fine. Studies show that people with post-traumatic stress disorder (PTSD) tend to respond to compliments negatively (Frewen et al., 2010), and Marley's reaction seemed to reflect the shame and fear she felt (but could not speak of and was not aware of) and the trauma she had experienced at the hands of transphobic bullies. At the same time, because in a binary society it is common to compliment women on appearance and men on their competencies, Kahalon, Schnabel, and Becker (2016) suggest that appearance compliments serve as a mechanism that might subtly perpetuate gender inequality and re-create sexist environments. Marley was also experiencing subtle ways in which she was now, after her gender affirmation, the target of sexism. She seemed to be feeling that she needed to express her gender in particular ways of moving and dressing.

Bromberg states, "When self-continuity seems threatened, the mind [and body] adaptationally extends its reach beyond the moment by turning the future into a version of past danger" (2006, p. 5). Marley unconsciously associated compliments with the bullying she had suffered since childhood, and with oppression of women, turning future interactions with her therapist into perilous ones characterized by shame for what had happened in the past. In Marley's case, the bullying was still occurring on a daily basis, and she experienced fearful apprehension for what she implicitly forecasted would happen in the future with her therapist. Action sequences like Marley's—slumped spine, lowered head, curved shoulders, and backward movement of the body—convey implicit predictions, expectations, intentions, attitudes, emotions, and meanings to others.

IMPLICIT KNOWING OF THE SELF

Our sense of self is determined both by the story we tell ourselves verbally and by the story we tell ourselves nonverbally through our affect-regulation capacities and other reflexive automatic behavior such as body posture and movement. A variety of studies demonstrate the impact of posture and other physical actions upon experience and self-perception (Dijkstra et al., 2006; Schnall & Laird, 2003; Stepper & Strack, 1993). Marley's slumped posture conveyed implicit meaning to her about herself. It seemed to diminish her self-esteem and contribute to, if not induce, feelings of shame, helplessness, and fear associated with both past and current situations. Even in the context of a safe therapeutic alliance, a client's behavior is alive in the present with action sequences associated with past threat and adversity, and for many like Marley, current threat in the forms of discrimination, bullying, and systemic oppression. Clearly, the implicit self is threatened by that which would challenge the perceived safety of familiar patterns of both relational knowing and self-knowing. These meanings of traumatic, negative relational experiences and oppression might show themselves in many ways, such as the constriction or collapse of the body, the shaking of a dysregulated nervous system, tension in the larynx and tightness in the voice reflecting a loss of social engagement, or in the avoidance of or locking in of eye contact. It is clear from such nonverbal behaviors that the implicit selves of our clients predict that the future will repeat the shame and peril that went before, no matter how strongly their explicit selves refute this position and describe the future as different from the past. And for marginalized clients like Marley, the accuracy of such predictions in relation to their current life and society must be validated and capacities that support resilience developed so that they can quickly recover from present-day threats.

FUNCTIONS OF NONVERBAL BEHAVIOR

Nonverbal interactions have specific and situational functions, while also reflecting patterns of behaviors across time that have meanings embedded in sociocultural contexts. Characteristic gestures, habitual postures, and action sequences reflect and sustain long-standing meanings and predictions at the individual, family, community, and society levels. They reveal, for instance, persistent emotional biases (e.g., a forward-thrusting chest and tension in the upper body may contribute to chronic anger, whereas a sunken chest and downward-turning head contribute to sadness or grief) and beliefs (e.g., overall tension, quick, focused movements, and erect posture all support working hard and may indicate a belief such as, "I have to be a high achiever to be accepted"). Nonverbal behaviors serve many functions in addition to anticipating the future, including affect regulation, emotional expression and communication, and signaling a readiness for or aversion to particular activities or interactions. These behaviors may be enduring action sequences, such as perpetually hunched shoulders, or fleeting expressions and gestures, such as a momentary narrowing of the eyes.

Nonverbal behaviors regulate here-and-now exchanges between people: The intonation of the voice or a thoughtful look away might indicate that the speaker has more to say; tensing the body and lifting the chin might impart a "stay away" message; lowering the head and bending the body slightly forward might signal compliance or submission. Verbal points can be strengthened or emphasized by physical cues, such as the deep sigh and downturned head of a client describing depression. Nonverbal behaviors might tone down a verbal message or make it more palatable, such as the disarming smile and forward leaning of a client when she told me how angry she was with me.

Nonverbal behaviors reflect not only early dynamics with significant others but also cultural values and norms. For instance, the differential use of space or level of emotional expression varies in individualistic and collectivistic cultures (Burgoon et al., 2016), as do the meanings of many gestures. Particularly significant are the messages conveyed by nonverbal communications that reflect power and sociopolitical status differentials between two or more people. These messages do not occur in a vacuum, hence the meaning changes depending on the context and the people involved. For instance, "high levels of gaze can show power and dominance (especially when someone gazes at others while speaking), but gaze can also communicate meekness and submission if someone is listening intently to a powerful person" (Burgoon et al., 2016, p. 343).

These implicit somatic communications may be designed to bring forth a particular behavior from the therapist. One client responded by narrowing his eyes, tightening his chest, frowning slightly, and looking away when his therapist asked about a relationship he did not want to discuss, effectively conveying his wish that the therapist drop the subject. Verbal and nonverbal messages might contradict each other as well, and can seek to hide aspects of internal experience as well as make them known. One client may say they feel fine as their shoulders roll inward and a furrow appears on their brow, whereas another smiles as they speak of their grief. We often see the signs of dissociative parts of the self in conflicting simultaneous or sequential nonverbal indicators, as when a client reached out to shake the therapist's hand while simultaneously leaning their upper body away.

Nonverbal communications can be intentional or unintentional, conscious or unconscious, clear or confusing. These cues may represent a unified implicit self or contradictions among dissociative parts of the self, as in the examples above. Body language may be different or may switch depending on the specific content and relational dynamics that are being enacted between the therapist's and client's social locations. If the content, such as discussing employment options, is relevant to similar locations (e.g., both parties are white, college educated, and middle socioeconomic status), the nonverbal communication may be relaxed and open. If the content, such as discussing sexual preference, is relevant to different social locations (e.g, the therapist is monogomous and heterosexual and the client is queer and polyamorous), the nonverbal communication may be more restricted and less open. The unconscious, unintentional, and involuntary cues are of most interest to psychotherapists because they tend to indicate that which is under the surface, beyond the words, visibly revealing elements of behavior that reflect and sustain the implicit self or selves and how these parts come forward in dialogue with the therapist. The dance that ensues within the relationship, including the therapist's unconscious responses (by their own implicit self) to the expressions of the client's implicit self, is the essence of therapy.

Bromberg states that the "road to the client's unconscious is always created nonlinearly by the [therapist's] own unconscious participation in its construction while he is consciously engaged in one way or another with a different part of the client's self" (2006, p. 43). Alongside the verbal narrative, unconscious encoding and decoding are taking place in a meaningful nonverbal conversation between the implicit selves of therapist and client, in their particular sociocultural context. Encoding "involves an ability to emit accurate nonverbal messages about one's needs, feelings, and thoughts," and decoding "involves an ability to detect, accurately perceive, understand and respond appropriately to another person's nonverbal expressions of needs, feelings, thoughts, and social roles" (Schachner et al., 2005, p. 148). As previously noted, meanings of nonverbal communications vary across sociocultural contexts; thus both encoding and decoding processes increase in complexity and can be misconstrued more easily when client and therapist do not share sociocultural locations. The ongoing interactive process of encoding and decoding shapes what happens within the relationship without conscious thought or intent. Note that the implicit selves of both client and therapist are engaged in this dance.

NONVERBAL INDICATORS IN TREATMENT

Kurtz states that psychotherapists ought to be on the lookout for nonverbal cues he called "indicators," which are "a piece of behavior or an element of style or anything that suggests . . . a connection to character, early memories, or particular [unconscious] emotions," especially those that reflect and sustain predictions that are "protective, over-generalized and outmoded" (2010, p. 110). Therefore, not every nonverbal cue or movement is an indicator. For example, reaching for a cup of tea or brushing one's hair out of the eyes are not usually indicators, but movements oriented to performing a task. Indicators are those nonverbal behaviors that help the therapist (implicitly and explicitly) "draw hypotheses about the client: what kind of implicit beliefs are being expressed and what kind of early life situations might have called for such patterns and beliefs" (Kurtz, 2010, p. 127). It is important to note that the therapist holds these hypotheses with curiosity and tentativeness, as the specific meaning for the client is not yet known. Additionally, therapists draw from their own experience to create a hypothesis, so it is strongly informed by the therapist's social locations and implicit selves.

Indicators encompass both the affect-laden cues reminiscent of early attachment and social interactions that shape the nonverbal habits (movements, postures, gestures, prosody, and facial expressions) of the child, and those that reflect dysregulated arousal and instinctive defenses elicited in the face of trauma. The therapist intends to bring the experience of these indicators into the present moment of the therapy hour. Therapy must "activate those deep subcortical recesses of our subconscious mind where affect resides, trauma has been stored, and preverbal, implicit attachment templates have been laid down" (Lapides, 2010, p. 9). Activating these elements requires right-brain to right-brain affective resonance and interaction rather than analytical, cognitive, or interpretive approaches (cf. Schore, 1994, 2003, 2009, 2012).

Indicators that register consciously for therapist or client (or that the client shares) can be explored explicitly, along with the associated affect, even while the content they represent remains unconscious. Grigsby and Stevens suggested that recognizing indicators and disrupting automatic behaviors hold more promise than conversing about what initially happened to shape them: "Talking about old events . . . or discussing ideas and information with a client . . . may at best be indirect means of perturbing those behaviors in which people routinely engage" (2000, p. 361). It may not be enough to gain insight without changing procedural action sequences. There are essentially two ways that implicit procedural learning can be addressed in therapy: "The first is . . . to observe, rather than interpret, what takes place, and repeatedly call attention to it. This in itself tends to disrupt the automaticity with which procedural learning ordinarily is expressed. The second therapeutic tactic is to engage in activities that directly disrupt what has been procedurally learned" (Grigsby & Stevens, 2000, p. 325).

Listening to the somatic narrative along with the verbal narrative naturally stimulates curiosity and awareness of nonverbal indicators. Therapist and client together interrupt the automaticity of these indicators when they become mindful of them, viewing them not as a symptom to eliminate or a problem to solved but with the intention to increase awareness of them, discover their function, and explore new options (Kurtz, 1990; Ogden et al., 2006; Ogden & Fisher, 2015). Note that the general notion of mindful attention as conceptualized in Western contexts (cf. Chapter 4, this volume)—being receptive to whatever elements emerge in the mind's eye—is different from mindful attention directed specifically toward nonverbal indicators. Instead of allowing clients' attention to drift randomly toward whatever emotions, memories, thoughts, or physical actions might emerge, Sensorimotor Psychotherapists use "directed mindfulness" to guide the client's awareness toward particular indicators that provide a jumping-off point for exploration of the implicit self (Ogden, 2007, 2009).

Mindfulness in Sensorimotor Psychotherapy is employed not as a solitary activity, conducted in the confines of one's own mind, but as embedded within the verbal and nonverbal dance between client and therapist (Ogden, 2014; see Chapter 5, this volume). Therapists track for nonverbal behaviors that might be indicators of significant implicit processes and ask clients to become aware of those selected indicators as they emerge in the present moment during the therapy hour. Therapists also pay attention to what transpires in the therapeutic relationship, as some of those indicators might be a result of relational dynamics and sociocultural differences. As clients become mindful of their nonverbal behaviors, they are asked to describe their internal landscape—emotions, thoughts, images, movements, sensations—verbally, as well. In this way, therapists are included in clients' internal journey, vicariously experiencing the varied scenery and sensing the many meanings. Through embedded relational mindfulness, awareness of the present moment is a shared, mutual experience that is regulated interactively.

The sections that follow depict some basic somatic indicators that might be significant in clinical practice and describe the use of embedded relational mindfulness to discover their nuances and elucidate ways to alter the somatic narrative within the therapeutic relationship. Indicators of the implicit self are noticed, outdated action sequences are interrupted, and new actions are initiated.

It is important for the reader to entertain the idea that specific interventions emerge spontaneously from what arises experientially and implicitly within the therapeutic dyad. Bromberg states that, most characteristically, he does not "plan" in advance what to do or say in the therapy hour, but rather "finds himself" doing or saying certain things that arise spontaneously from within the relationship (personal communication, December 21, 2010). His words and actions are not premeditated or generic techniques, but rather are emerging responses to what transpires in the here and now between himself and his client. In the description of my own work that follows here, my interventions similarly came to me unbidden, arising from what occurred in the moment within the relationship. Although I can and will explain the theoretical rationale behind these interventions, they were neither premeditated nor consciously thought out. Although they are techniques in principle, they are not generic. They never happen the same way twice, but come forth naturally and unexpectedly while both therapist and client are subjectively experiencing each other. In other words, they are communicating their affective and somatic responsiveness to an experience of what is taking place within their relationship that is not processed cognitively but is known implicitly.

It takes intention, experience, and practice for the therapist to know which of the clients' nonverbal cues might be indicators and which are not. This knowing is not cognitive; rather, therapists find themselves being drawn to a specific nonverbal cue, often without knowing why. Typically, later discoveries in the therapy hour reveal that the cue was a significant indicator of trauma and relational history, both individual and sociocultural, that reflects and sustains the implicit self. In addition to being aware of nonverbal cues, therapists are also aware of how their sociocultural location and specific privileged and marginalized intersectionalities might impact the relational and nonverbal dance with their clients. It requires intention, self-exploration, and commitment for therapists to identify potential indicators for attachment and sociocultural factors, including enactments, and to track the impact of their nonverbal communication on the client and vice versa (cf. Chapter 10, this volume).

The selected implicit indicators and examples of how to work with them in therapy explored in the following sections include prosody, eye contact, facial expression, preparatory movement of instinctive defense, arm movement, locomotion, posture, and proximity-seeking movement. Obviously, this list is not by any means exhaustive, and many potentially significant indicators of the implicit self have been omitted: the angle and movement in the pelvis; the tilt of the head and the way it sits on the neck and shoulders; the angle, pronation, or supination of the feet, and how they push off the ground when walking; the tension in the knees and other joints; the way the arms hang from the shoulder girdle; the range of motion of parts of the body; breathing patterns; and the involuntary trembling and shaking often experienced by people with PTSD, to name a few (cf. Ogden et al., 2006; Ogden & Fisher, 2015).

Prosody

Prosody refers to how something is said rather than to the content itself. It includes rhythm, intonation, pitch, inflection, volume, tone of voice, tempo (fast, slow), resonance, intensity, crescendos and decrescendos, and even vocal sounds that are not words, such as "um" and "uh-huh." The pauses, rushes, hesitancies, and vocal punctuations that accentuate or downplay what is being said are all part of prosody, as is affective tone: sarcastic, soothing, patronizing, energizing, joyful, threatening, and so on. Sentences that have identical sequences of words may have different meanings that are disambiguated through prosody (Nespor, 2010). Discourse depends on prosody; in fact, "aprosodic sequences of words are hard to understand. To say the least, communication would not be effective without prosody" (Nespor, 2010, p. 382).

Infants begin to learn prosody at birth (if not before), demonstrating exceptional sensitivity to prosodic melody. For example, newborns show a strong preference for their primary caregiver's voice (DeCasper & Fifer, 1980) and can distinguish the rhythmic distinctions of different languages (Nazzi et al., 1998). Prosody is shaped by interactions with caregivers as well as by sociocultural and power dynamics. Even an infant's melody when crying is formed by the inflection of their native language (Mampe et al., 2009). Because prosody varies between cultures and languages, decoding misunderstandings might occur when the therapist tries to hypothesize implicit messages about anger, strength, weakness, gentleness, and so forth in relation to prosody. For instance, certain cultures and subcultures are characterized by louder or more expressive speech than others. Accents and tone can also indicate otherness or foreignness, as well as hierarchy, power, and socioeconomic status between and within cultures. It is not unusual for a person with less status or power to assume patterns of prosody and vocalization of the person with more privilege. In a meta-analysis, Fuertes and colleagues (2012) confirm the negative impact of "non–standard-accented speakers" in the United States in comparison to standard American English speakers on interpersonal evaluations. Speakers who use a standard accent were rated more positively in a variety of variables (including knowledge, attractiveness, benevolence, and trustworthiness) than those using a nonstandard accent. The authors state that although "legislation has been drafted to prohibit discrimination on the basis of gender or race, it may be that use of language is as powerful a trigger in instigating negative evaluations of speakers, which may compound negative evaluations already experienced by minority group members, those members of society living in poverty, and citizens who speak with a non-standard accent such as immigrants" (Fuertes et al., 2012, p. 128). All of this indicates the presence of implicit biases expressed in prosody that may be present in, and unconsciously impact, cross–cultural therapeutic dyads.

Prosody is strongly affected by the neuroception of danger (Porges, 2011). The vagus nerve is neuroanatomically linked to the muscles of the face, the head, and the heart, which helps modulate both vocal prosody and facial expression to convey an individual's immediate physiological state to others. In contexts of safety, vocal prosody may be rich and modulated, while in contexts of danger, it

may be flat and the tone of the voice is lower. One of the first signals that the safety of social engagement is compromised is tension
around the larynx, heard as tension in the voice.

Prosody—the way the words are said—reveals volumes about
implicit realms and forecasts of the future. "I am so angry," said
in a weak, defeated tone indicates a very different prediction from
the same words said with vigor and emphasis. Prosody reflects the
explicit emotional state of the person in the moment, as well as
unconscious emotional states. Anger might be revealed through the
voice long before the person realizes they are angry; a tightening
around the larynx may cause a thinning or constriction of the voice,
and may be an early indicator of fear or anxiety.

Prosody may convey a command, request, plea, or question or
indicate submission or dominance. I once observed a therapy session with Ron Kurtz as the therapist with a white male-identified
client. The client's pitch rose at the end of every single sentence,
as if he were asking a question. Ron asked the client to focus on
his vocal pitch and even exaggerate its rise a bit as he spoke, and
the client almost immediately began to cry. He realized his prosody was beseechingly asking the question, "Do you understand
me?" The memories that emerged were about early emotionally
charged attachment interactions in which the client felt he was not
seen for who he was and could not "get through" to his parents.
Note that the meaning came from the client, not the therapist.
Meaning is discovered and becomes conscious through mindful
exploration of an indicator, rather than through the therapist's
interpretation, which unavoidably will be influenced by the therapist's own social location, understanding and experience of the
world. The client's own translation of the implicit meaning of the
indicator is elicited, a translation that emerges from their here and
now experience as the therapist guides them to mindfully explore
the indicator. Importantly, meaning emerges from experience, not
from cognitive analyses or interpretation.

In another example, a female-identified client had a voice that sounded childlike and dropped almost to a whisper as she reported that maybe she might be a little angry. "Cathy's" prosody was a potent indicator of a childhood filled with abuse and shutting down. I suggested that she might explore saying "I'm angry" in a louder voice, which at first felt threatening to her, and she became quieter—an old habit she had formed in an attempt to prevent drawing attention to herself. After we had explored volume and prosody, as well as childhood memories of unwanted attention and abuse, I asked Cathy to experiment with looking into my eyes, and saying, "I'm angry" in a loud voice. She felt more empowered and began to reclaim a healthy righteous anger that she had abandoned long ago because it had only made her father's abuse worse. It is significant that Cathy's childlike whisper, like all nonverbal behaviors, not only communicated a message of uncertainty to others, but also affected Cathy herself, leading her to feel disempowered and submissive.

In the therapeutic relationship, "right brain-to-right brain prosodic communications . . . act as an essential vehicle of implicit communications. . . . The right hemisphere is important in the processing of the 'music' behind our words" (Schore & Schore, 2007). Matching the client's prosody in terms of volume, tone, and pace is necessary to join and connect, and from there the therapist might slowly up- or downregulate arousal through the same mechanisms. Kurtz (1990) taught his students to speak in the simplest language possible to access early memories and process strong emotion. Lapides states that she knows to "keep [her] sentences simple as LH [left-hemisphere] processing is impaired at elevated levels of arousal and to rely on RH [right-hemisphere] nonverbal means to connect with [hyperaroused clients]" (2010, p. 9).

It bears repeating that all nonverbal indicators convey messages back and forth in the therapeutic dyad that are processed without conscious consideration. Imagine a male therapist who speaks to his female client in clipped, definitive statements and questions, without much affect. She implicitly interprets his prosody as indicative of his authority and superiority, which triggers compliance in her and prosody that sounds like a little girl who needs the protection and approval of an authority figure—a propensity shaped by both sociocultural norms and male authority figures in her childhood. Colluding together, the therapist feels protective and does not challenge his client, but is unaware of this. A collusion such as this can lead to an impasse in the therapy; an enactment typically ensues that challenges the therapist to "wake up" and realize that what is going on in the therapy hour pertains to each party's personal and sociocultural history and what is taking place between the two of them, instead of continuing to believe that what is going on between them pertains to the client and their history alone (Bromberg, 2006).

Eye Contact

The eyes can speak louder than words, as the saying goes. Prosodic communication can be confirmed or contradicted by downcast eyes, slow or rapid blinking, a flutter of the eyelashes, a look away and back. Intensity and orientation of eye contact, like all nonverbal indicators, are shaped by early caregiver relationships and culture and society. In some cultures, direct eye contact is a sign of respect and attentiveness, while in other cultures it is exactly the opposite: averting and lowering the eyes signals deference and respect (Burgoon et al., 2016). How long someone holds their gaze is another parameter to take into consideration. For instance, in the United States, too much eye contact can be interpreted as disrespectful and othering (e.g., objectifying women's bodies, or gazing at a person with physical disability) or arrogant or aggressive (e.g., a person of a marginalized racial identity holding sustained and direct eye contact with a white person), while too little eye contact could be interpreted as disrespectful and avoidant when it could have other meanings for the person averting their gaze. Hence, eye contact is a powerful and subtle factor in implicit communication, and the therapist must suspend any meaning they might hypothesize and instead track and explore the meaning in relationship and with the client.

Proximity is fine-tuned by eye contact, bringing us closer or creating more distance. Eyes can be intent, as the absorbed gaze of a baby with the caregiver, or blank and unseeing, like the vacant stare of a person in shock. One client's eyes locked onto their therapist as if their life depended on the eye contact. The terrified gaze of the client spoke of the huge risk they were taking in telling the secret of their abuse for the first time. Other clients scan the environment for potential threat cues, ever hypervigilant, and are unable to make eye contact for more than a fleeting second.

The eyes, like all nonverbal cues, change moment to moment in response to internal and environmental cues. A sudden tightening or narrowing of the eyes might indicate pain, aversion, disagreement, suspicion, or threat, whereas a widening of the eyes might signal excitement, surprise, or shock. Frequency, intensity, insistence on or aversion to eye contact, length of contact, and style (e.g., glancing, blinking, widening or shrouding, angling downward or upward and degree of pupil dilation) can all be important indicators of the implicit self.

Eye contact can be frightening for trauma survivors, and clients may be "beset by shame and anxiety and terrified by being judged and 'seen' by the therapist" (Courtois, 1999, p. 190). In the consulting room, therapist and client might experiment with making eye contact and averting gaze, with the client being mindful of what happens internally and what changes relationally when one or the other looks away or closes the eyes. Repeated patterns of using the eyes can also be explored. One young male client who frequently narrowed his eyes explored doing this voluntarily and mindfully and realized he always felt suspicious of his female therapist. He eventually traced this pattern back to emotionally charged memories of his unpredictable mother, experiences that had left him feeling guarded, insecure, and suspicious in relationships with women.

Another client, an Asian American male, Sook, came to therapy because of his difficulties navigating relationships at work. He expressed a high level of immobilizing anxiety when presenting his projects in front of his coworkers, the majority of whom were white Americans. He reported being preoccupied with negative interactions and conflict with others. In therapy, he consistently avoided eye contact with his white female therapist, especially when experiencing intense emotions. He only glanced at his therapist's face briefly after his emotions had subsided, and the therapist speculated that several factors could be impacting this dynamic: the difference between their two cultures in regard to emotional expression, her position of authority as the therapist, her being white and her client being Asian, or elements of the personal history of this client. In therapy, the therapist asked Sook to notice what happened internally when their eyes met, and he reported feeling uncomfortable and tense, and an impulse to avert his gaze. The therapist directed his awareness to the tension in his body, and he said that the tension went along with fear. As his therapist encouraged Sook to notice if there were words that accompanied the tension and the fear, he reported first that it was not OK to look directly into her eyes, and also that he was afraid the therapist would judge him. He reported several memories from the past that had a similar felt sense: instances in childhood in which he perceived disapproval in the eyes of his female relatives when his eyes met theirs, and memories of his "tough" friends at school who teased him for being "weak" when he showed emotion. Experimenting with eye contact became the jumping-off point, not only to work with eye contact itself, but to explore the imprint and emotional pain of these early memories.

Facial Expression

The human face has more highly refined and developed expressions than any other animal, which can make looking at faces extremely rewarding, demanding, and emotionally stimulating. The face is probably the first area of the body to reflect immediate emotions, often showing signs of emotion before we are aware of it. The ventral vagal complex governs the muscles of the face and is initially built upon a series of face-to-face interactions with an attachment figure who empathically regulates the infant's arousal. The "neural regulation of [facial] muscles that provide important elements of social cueing are available to facilitate the social interaction with the caregiver and function collectively as an integrated social engagement system" (Porges, 2005, p. 36).

Schore (1994) asserts that at around 8 weeks of age, the face-processing areas of the right hemisphere are activated, and face-to-face interactions remain an essential element of interactive regulation throughout the life span. However, adequate dyadic affect regulation does not mean that the caregiver's facial expressions consistently reflect attunement. Tronick and Cohn (1989) report that between 70% and 80% of face-to-face interactions between attachment figures and their infants can be mismatched. In the majority of cases, these mismatched moments are repaired expeditiously, and any dysregulation in the infant is alleviated (DiCorcia & Tronick, 2011). In an attuned interaction, each party rapidly and unconsciously adjusts their facial expression (as well as eye contact and prosody) in response to their own and their partner's affective expressions, and mismatches are quickly repaired.

Facial expression has been extensively studied across cultures, especially focusing, since Ekman's (1978, 2004) research, on the universality of basic emotions, with inconclusive results: "although people in different cultures are able to identify emotion in faces at a rate better than chance, the accuracy rate varies by culture. . . .

Overall, there has been mixed support for the universalistic perspective" (Burgoon et al., 2016, p. 300). There is an increasing recognition that facial expression and perception are strongly context-dependent (Aviezer et al., 2008; Barrett et al., 2019) and are culturally primed already in newborns (Dunham et al., 2008). Moreover, Aviezer and colleagues (2012) found that perception of facial expressions is strongly influenced by the posture and gesture of the body. Nonetheless, the face conveys a blend of information, emotional and otherwise, conscious and unconscious.

Though we can often be aware of our expression and what we are communicating to others, fleeting microexpressions can implicitly communicate emotional states without self-reflective consciousness. Thus, facial expressions can reveal both intended and unintended emotions. Microexpressions can be visible for as little as one-fifth of a second and can expose emotions that a person is not yet aware of or is trying to conceal. These expressions register implicitly, and "observers make inferences about intention, personality, and social relationship, and about objects in the environment" (Ekman, 2004, p. 412). Remember, the inference that therapists make is informed by the sociocultural lenses of their social locations. Their meaning runs the risk of being inaccurate in all therapeutic dyads, and that risk increases in cross-cultural ones. Microexpressions will be especially significant in terms of the implicit communication between client and therapist and may help to explain the frequent extreme sensitivity of some clients to the nuances of the therapist's emotional states.

The remnants of trauma are disclosed in the expressive facial indicators of unresolved shock: wide-open eyes, raised eyebrows, frozen movement, hypervigilance, or tension around the eyes. Increased dorsal vagal tone of the feigned-death defense shows clearly in faces that appear flat, with flaccid muscles that reveal little expression (Porges, 2011). In both shock and feigned death, facial expression can be greatly diminished, indicating a compromised social engagement system. Furthermore, clues to affective biases and the beliefs that go with them are etched into the face, visible in chronic wrinkles, lines, and patterns: a downturned mouth, lifted upper lip, furrowed brow, raised eyebrows, laugh lines, and so on.

John, a white cisgender heterosexual male, had a habit of frowning, and the parallel lines between his eyes were deeply etched, although he was only in his 20s. I found myself drawn to these furrows and noticed that they seemed to deepen as he talked about problems with his girlfriend. I asked him if he would be interested in exploring the frown. He experimented with exaggerating the frown and then relaxing his forehead, being mindful of the thoughts, emotions, and memories that emerged spontaneously as he did so. He saw an image of himself as a small boy hearing the sound of his father's hand striking against his mother's face as his parents argued. I asked him to notice if there were words that went with the frown, and he tearfully said, "What's going to happen to us?" These were the words of a small, helpless boy terrified at the violence in the next room, fearing that his world was coming to an end. John said that his reaction to his present-day conflict with his girlfriend traced back to these early memories, realizing that his current reaction was overblown since he and his girlfriend had a strong, secure relationship. Eventually, he experimented with discussing his current relationship while inhibiting the frown, and he felt calmer. His frown had implicitly communicated the terror of the past to him, which had little bearing on his current situation. Of interest also is that John reported that his girlfriend had interpreted his frown as criticism of her, which triggered her own defensiveness.

I could not have inferred the emotion or meaning from the frown in an abstract sense; the meaning emerged from the client's mindful exploration of the frown with my direction. I may have hypothesized that the frown was connected to sadness, and/or concern, fear, or another emotional state. But how John communicated his blend of emotions was uniquely connected to context and to his situational past, and was discovered through mindfulness. With a different client who exhibited such a frown with similar or dissimilar history and sociocultural location, the same process of curiosity and discovery of meaning for the client would be followed. The therapist's hypothesis about an indicator is only an assumption that may be accurate or inaccurate, and needs to be tested and contrasted with the experience of the client.

Preparatory Defensive Movement

Like fleeting microexpressions of the face, small movements of the body can be significant indicators. Anticipatory movements are evident in the minute physical gestures that are made in preparation for a larger movement. These involuntary movement adjustments occur just prior to a voluntary movement. Preparatory movements are reliable signs that predict actions that are about to happen because they are dependent upon the planned or voluntary movement for the form they take (Bouisset, 1991). For instance, the first indicators of instinctive defensive responses and proximity-seeking actions frequently show up in barely perceptible physical movements that antecede a larger movement. Visible prior to the execution of full gross motor actions, these micromovements take a variety of forms: a tiny crouch before a leap, a miniscule clenching of a fist before the strike, an nearly imperceptible opening of a hand before a reach, a slight leaning forward, a little arm movement toward the therapist. Such movements are reliable preparatory cues of action sequences that "wanted to happen" but may not have been fully executed in the original contexts.

Once the therapist catches a glimpse of such a movement, or the client reports what appears to be a preparatory cue, the therapist can direct the client to voluntarily execute the action "that wants to happen," slowly and mindfully. As Sergio, a Mexican American man, recalled the first combat he experienced in Afghanistan, his therapist noticed his fingers lifting slightly just as he reported the quiet atmosphere that he described as the "calm before the storm."

Sergio's eyes widened, he appeared frightened, and his arousal began to escalate. Rather than focus on the content, the therapist asked Sergio to momentarily put the memory aside in order to focus his attention exclusively on his hands and be aware of what "wants to happen" in his body. Sergio described a feeling that his arms wanted to lift upward. As his therapist encouraged him to allow the movement, he said that his arms wanted to move upward in a protective gesture. In staying with this movement, Sergio started to notice a slight change. Instead of covering his head with his arms and freezing, which he described as a habitual immobilizing defense, he said that he had a physical sense that his arms wanted to push away. Note that this feeling emerged from his awareness of his body, not as an idea or thought. His therapist encouraged the slow enactment of this mobilizing defense that was not possible at the time of previous trauma, holding a pillow against Sergio's hands for him to push against. It was important that Sergio temporarily disregard all memory and simply focus on his body and find a way to push that felt right. By executing an empowering defensive action, his arousal was downregulated and his terror subsided. Sergio's internal locus of control was strengthened because he was the one in charge of how much pressure his therapist used in resisting his pushing with the pillow, what position to be in, how long to push, and so on.

Sergio reported that it felt good to push against the pillow, and his therapist suggested doing it again. This time Sergio suddenly stopped the movement and averted his eyes from the therapist. Upon curiously inquiring about what had just happened, he mentioned with some guilt that he felt that he was in trouble, but he did not know why. He and his therapist decided to repeat this sequence of action in slow motion to see if they could discover more about Sergio's feelings. Sergio then recalled different instances of walking on the street in his hometown in the United States and feeling that police were watching him with suspicion, which felt similar to being targeted in Afghanistan, even though he was a U.S. citi-

328 THE POCKET GUIDE TO SENSORIMOTOR PSYCHOTHERAPY IN CONTEXT

zen. Sergio realized that the pushing action represented aggression, and that fighting with an authority, which he had projected onto the therapist at that moment, could put him in danger. With his therapist's support to address the feeling of the police watching him, Sergio discovered that his fingers lifted slightly in preparation for a different movement. Instead of pushing away, he raised his arms with his palms facing outward, as if setting a boundary so that the suspicious gaze of others could not affect him, which also helped him regulate hyperarousal.

Through awareness of these preparatory movements and following what the body wants to do, the possibility of new responses emerges, incipient during previous events, ready to be further developed into an action that is more flexible and empowering. The experience of these new actions—what they feel like, the sense of oneself as they are executed, what happens when the actions are supported by the therapist—typically lead to expanding the availability of these actions in clients' daily lives. Sergio, for example, reported that he felt more assertive instead of immobilized, and better able to regulate himself when he felt authorities were suspicious of him, signifying that he had integrated and internalized a felt sense of protection by executing the pushing and boundary actions.

Arm Movements

In addition to preparatory defensive actions, a variety of other positions and movements of the arms and hands can be significant indicators. Arms might be crossed over the chest, resting on the lap, or hanging limp at the side. Hands may be fidgeting, placed palm up or down, clenched or open, held still or moving expressively as the person talks, and so on. One of the most accessible indicators in this category is the simple act of reaching out, which can be executed in a variety of manners that reflect and sustain unsymbolized meaning: palm up, palm down, full arm extension or with bent elbow held close to the body, relaxed or rigid musculature, shoulders curved in or pulled back, and so forth. For example, if caregivers are neglect-ful, a child may cease reaching out to them and depend more upon autoregulation alone than interactive regulation with others. Aban-doning an integrated, purposeful action of reaching out to others is adaptive in such contexts, the result of an implicit prediction that no one will respond to proximity-seeking behavior. Keep in mind that caregiver unavailability can stem from individual factors (e.g., personal history of neglect or abuse, low self-esteem, illness, lack of parenting skills, focus on their own troubles, and so forth) as well as from societal factors, particularly the stress of a marginalized social location (e.g., poverty resulting in working two or three jobs, com-munity violence resulting in preoccupation with safety, the constant threat of deportation, and so forth).

Asking clients to simply reach out with one or both arms is a diagnostic experiment as well as an avenue for working through relational issues. One client reached out with a stiff arm, palm down, braced shoulders, and a rigid spine, whereas another client reached out weakly, shoulders rounded, keeping the elbow by the waist rather than fully extending the arm. Yet another, always pre-occupied with the therapist's availability, reached out eagerly, with intense need, leaning forward, both arms fully extended. All these movements reflect childhoods devoid of adequate care and support. Each person had abandoned an integrated reaching action because they did not expect others to empathically reach back.

Robert was a cisgender gay man from an affluent background, who came to therapy to work on his romantic relationships. During the course of therapy, I was drawn to the tension in Robert's arms and shoulders as he discussed his boyfriend's complaints that he was emo-tionally withdrawn. When I asked if he would be interested in notic-ing what happened as he reached out with his arm, as if to reach for another person, Robert said he immediately felt suspicious of the sug-gestion, but was willing to try it. As he reached out with his left arm, his body reflected his words in its tension, with a slight leaning back, stiff movement, locked elbow, and downward palm. His nonverbal message conveyed his discomfort and lack of expectation of attuned, empathic reception. Robert's affect transitioned from suspicion to defensiveness as he stayed with the gesture, saying angrily there was no point in reaching out: "Why bother?" Over time, together we explored his emotionally painful early memories of a father who could abide no weakness or need in his son. Robert learned to abandon this gesture simply because it evoked disgust and criticism from his father, both in early age and also as the father rejected his son's homosexuality. His course of therapy included learning to reach out in an integrated manner, arm relaxed, fully engaged, with eye contact, and intent to make real contact with the other—an action that was explored first with anger, but eventually with great sadness.

It should be noted that when asking the client to reach out, the social location of the therapist and client may impact the meaning and expectations that accompany the reach, especially in a cross-cultural therapeutic dyad. For example, a white therapist might suggest experimenting with a beckoning, proximity-seeking action to a client who expresses issues with proximity seeking and closeness. However, such an action has different meanings depending upon the client's culture. In a colonized country, oppressors may use a beckoning motion to call over a member of the oppressed group; thus the action can be interpreted as disrespectful or belittling not as inviting proximity (personal communication, Denise Gallagos, April 25, 2019). Also, clients may not have the capacity to speak to this or say "no" to the therapist, especially when the therapist holds privileged social locations in relation to the client.

In addition to reaching out, a variety of other arm movements can be vehicles for exploration (cf. Ogden, 2009; Ogden & Fisher, 2015; Ogden et al., 2006). Grasping, pulling, or gathering motions; hitting or striking actions, or circular motions that define one's personal boundary; expressive movements of opening the arms widely in gestures of anticipatory embrace or expansion; movements of self-touch, such as hugging oneself—all are significant, and the manner in which they are executed reflects the implicit self. Whereas reaching out, grasping, and pulling movements can be challenging for many clients, holding on and being unable to let go can be equally challenging (cf. Chapter 11, this volume).

Locomotion

Locomotion, the act of walking from one place to another, can be carried out with a variety of qualities: plodding, springy, tottering, hurried, slow, deliberate, and so on—all of which hold implicit meaning. The angle of the feet and how they come into contact with the ground; the swing of the arms; the movement of the pelvis forward and back and side to side while walking; the tension in the feet, knee, and hip joints; and the angle of the body (leaning forward or backward, to one side or the other) can all be significant avenues of exploration of the implicit self (cf. Ogden & Fisher, 2015). These traits are a unique movement "signature" of the individual, the most immediate and observable factor that can be captured in the blink of the eye, so obvious that we notice it without thinking about it (Moore & Yamamoto, 2012). We often can recognize a person in the distance, and perhaps surmise their social identity, by noticing the way they walk.

This movement signature, like all habitual actions, is shaped by the implicit self, developed in dialogue with the child's family and sociocultural environment. Children recognize the movement signatures of their caregivers and also absorb and internalize the subtleties of gait, expressions, gestures, and postures that might indicate sociocultural identities. Desmond states, "social identities are signaled, formed, negotiated through bodily movement" (1997, p. 34); thus the context defines what type of gait and other movements are appropriate by whom in what situations. For instance, people of color may code-switch speech, gait, and other movements when in predominantly white spaces. In a university classroom, a person of color may be inclined to use a white-sounding accent and contained movement rather than to the dialect and movement used when socializing with kin or intimate social groups.

While exploring gait in therapy, a white cisgender female client discovered a pattern of walking stiffly, with very little movement through her pelvis, a habit that originated in an attempt to conceal her femininity and sexuality in an abusive environment. In one session, she practiced swinging her hips as she walked, which initially elicited fear and increased hypervigilance, as well as shame of her sexuality. This movement eventually became pleasurable and fun as she learned to separate the present from the past, as well as to reject ideas of the body as something to control and not to enjoy, which is linked to historical Western denunciation of the body in favor of the intellect (Aposhyan, 1999).

A different client walked with a plodding, heavy gait and noticed that, with each step, her heel struck the ground forcefully, jarring her vertebrae. She hunched her shoulders and looked at the ground as she walked, limiting her vision and engagement with the environment. This pattern reflected and sustained her feelings of hopelessness that had no narrative or explicit content. In therapy, she became aware of her habitual walking style and experienced the negative repercussions both emotionally (hopelessness) and physically (pain, with the jarring effect of each moment of impact). Eventually, after processing the hopelessness, she began to practice a different, more empowered way of walking: pushing off from the balls of her feet to get a spring in each step. She also worked with having been taught as a child that girls should be passive. This gender socialization was typical of Western white woman ideals, which were encouraged and modeled by females in her family. She and her therapist compared her plodding gait with a bouncy, head-up walk, exchanging hunched shoulders and rounded spine for an upright, shoulders-down posture. Incompatible with passivity, this new gait supported an assertive attitude and engagement with others.

A child in a traumatogenic environment might experience an initial impulse to escape abuse, but these defensive actions are not executed in situations when escape is impossible. The active, mobilizing flight response may be abandoned in favor of the more adaptive (in that situation) immobilizing defenses of freeze or feigned death. Clients often report pervasive feelings of being trapped, which Lisa, a cisgender female client, experienced through a literal sense of heaviness and immobility in her legs, coupled with a foggy, spacey feeling. Her therapist suggested they stand and walk together to notice movements typical of a flight response: that their legs could carry them away from some objects in the room, and toward others. Lisa felt more present right away, and said it felt good to sense the movement in her legs. Simply being aware of her mobility became a resource that Lisa used often—it helped her feel less trapped and alleviated the foggy, spacey feeling.

Posture

Postural integrity involves the spine, which serves as an axis around which the limbs and head can move (cf. Ogden & Fisher, 2015). The spine is the physical core of the body; it provides support and stability to the entire physical structure and is grounded securely through the inside of the legs and feet. The first movements of an infant are initiated in the core of the body and radiate out to the periphery, then contract back inward toward the spine; such movements strengthen the core (Aposhyan, 2004; Cohen, 1993). Kurtz and Prestera note that the core also has a psychological meaning as the "place inside" to which we may "go for sustenance" (1976, p. 33).

Posture can be upright and aligned, or slumped, twisted, braced, frozen, collapsed, slouched, rigid, and so on. To assess postural alignment and integrity, a plumb line through the top of the head, middle of the ear, shoulder, hip joint, knee joint, and ankle can be imagined. A straight line passing through these points shows that each segment of the body supports the one above, and the body is in balance. Often this imaginary line is jagged or curvy, as parts of the body are displaced from alignment. Some bodies are bowed forward, others are bent backward; the head may jut forward, or the pelvis may be retracted. Without a strong and stable core, the spine may flex and droop, an indicator that might literally feel like "I can't hold myself up" and correspond with feelings of dependency, neediness, or passivity. Tronick's Still Face experiments often demonstrate the loss of postural integrity, as infants' spines slump and sag when their caregivers fail to respond to them. Many clients exhibit the same pattern. Postural integrity may also be compromised when the client experiences recurrent oppression and discrimination, either due to learned helplessness in the face of uncontrollable adverse conditions, or in an attempt to become less conspicuous or threatening. Other clients present with a rigid, tense, military posture, with head and shoulders pulled back and muscles tense, which may be developed as a readiness to fight or as a protection against vulnerability in the family, community, or society at large.

Janet (1925) pointed out that the therapist must be able to discern the action that the client is unable to execute, and then demonstrate the missing action. If the therapist's posture is slumped, or if the therapist does not have awareness of the range of action of the spine, they may not be able to demonstrate various postures or help the client develop alignment by modeling. The discovery of mirror neurons brings this point home by illustrating that the observation of another's movement stimulates corresponding neural networks in the observer, thus priming the observer for making the same action (Gallese et al., 1996).

Matthew, a transman client, came to therapy with a slumped spine, which became even more pronounced as he spoke of his wife. The therapist was interested in how his droopy posture related to the verbal narrative, and asked him to notice his stance. Matthew realized his posture had to do with feelings of inferiority and helplessness, familiar feelings in his marriage. He and his therapist explored early experiences of similar painful feelings in his family of origin, including memories of his body's development as a teenager, before he transitioned. Matthew said that at that time the slumped posture was an attempt to cover his developing breasts, which he rejected. After this exploration, both stood up to experiment with the difference between his habitual carriage and a posture that was aligned and erect, where his head sat centered over his shoulders, his chest rested over his body's lower half, his pelvis supported his torso, and his legs and feet were under his body. As he practiced an upright posture, Matthew's thoughts started to become less negative, and his feelings of helplessness transformed into a "can-do" (his words) attitude, while also expressing thoughts that reflected increased self-esteem. Note that a change such as Matthew experienced can help to transform the implicit self, but for more enduring change it was also necessary to address his painful past that brought about his feelings of inferiority and helplessness, along with the corresponding saggy posture.

Proximity

Infants and children need the proximity of a supportive other to meet their survival needs and protect them from danger. The psychobiological attachment system organizes proximity-seeking behaviors to secure the nearness of caregivers. This innate system of the child adjusts to the behavior of attachment figures and significant others in the child's community of belonging. If the attachment figure is unreliable or many significant others are inconsistently available, the proximity-seeking behaviors may become hyperactive. If the attachment figure is neglectful or unavailable, if there are no other people to reach out to, or if important people are punishing in the face of need or vulnerability, the proximity-seeking behaviors may become hypoactive.

A variety of factors in addition to attachment history contribute to personal proximity preferences: the situation, the specific individuals involved, and the nature of their relationship, gender, age, familiarity, content, and so on. Culture and privilege/oppression dynamics are also important factors in determining preferences in personal, social, and public norms of proximity-seeking action. Depending upon the factors above, too much or too little distance between interactants can be regarded as equally negative (Hall et al., 1995, p. 21). For example, it is acceptable for people considered to have more status to reach out and touch people thought to have less status, but not the other way around (Freeman et al., 1995). Caregivers may respond to the child's proximity needs by providing either too much or too little distance or vacillate between these extremes. These clients have particular difficulty navigating proximity and seem to not recognize a felt sense of the appropriate distance between themselves and others.

Therapists can help develop clients' awareness of somatic barometers that indicate appropriate proximity (cf. Ogden & Fisher, 2015) in different contexts. One female client, Jill, told me that close proximity made her feel safe and requested that I move my chair nearer to her. However, when I did so, Jill's muscles tightened, her breath became shallow, her body pulled back in her chair, and her eyes looked away. Jill and I agreed to contrast increased proximity with increased distance, and, to her surprise, she found that her body relaxed more when the distance was increased. Jill had initially thought that close proximity was preferable, but her implicit self told another story in its somatic narrative. Continuing the experiment, Jill eventually discovered a felt sense of "rightness" in her body in terms of the distance between us, which turned out to be about 8 to 10 feet apart. Jill described this felt sense as one of relaxation, with deeper breathing, easier eye contact, and an internal feeling of well-being.

Setting boundaries and seeking proximity go hand in hand. Negotiating physical distance and proximity in therapy teaches clients about their needs and preferences with others in support of their being able to form and maintain satisfying relationships. Clients who have experienced early relational trauma as well as those who are not traumatized struggle with being able to appropriately balance their needs for proximity and distance with the needs of others. Sensorimotor Psychotherapists frequently ask clients how close or far they prefer them to sit. Experiments (moving toward and away from the client, or moving an object such as a pillow closer and farther away) can be conducted to explore automatic responses to proximity, such as bracing, moving backward, holding the breath, or changes in orienting or attention. With clients for whom the above experiments are too provocative, introducing simple exercises such as rolling a therapy ball or gently tossing a pillow toward them while they use their arms to push the object away can strengthen the capacity to execute the protective action of pushing away that was usually not allowed in early relationships. If we do not have a felt sense of being able to push away, set boundaries, or protect ourselves, we usually do not feel safe to reach out to others. These two actions go hand in hand.

One cisgender female client from Brazil first stood immobile, allowing the pillow gently thrown by the therapist to hit her torso. Slowly, she practiced lifting her arms in a gesture of protection against the pillow hitting her body. Note that when protective actions incited the perpetrator to more violence in the past, as they did in her extremely abusive childhood, protective actions are abandoned; executing them in the safe context of therapy can be terrifying, and clients need encouragement and practice to execute these actions. As this client executed defensive actions, she gradually developed a somatic sense of empowerment, which helped her feel safer. This built the foundation upon which proximity-seeking could be introduced, such as making a beckoning gesture while the therapist slowly walked toward her, until she experienced a felt sense in her body that her therapist was close enough and should not come closer. Then she could tell the therapist to stop with her voice or by lifting her arms, palms open and extended outward in a stop gesture. It is important that the sense of suitable proximity is founded on the felt sense of preference, safety, or protection, in the body rather than on analysis or ideas.

Proximity in the therapy room—the degree of physical distance between therapist and client, whether they are sitting side by side, at an angle to, or directly across from one another, the amount of eye contact, and so forth—will need to be adjusted depending on the culture of the client. For instance, in the example of the Brazilian client above, after addressing her trauma history, therapist and client noticed that the personal space of the client was much closer than that of the therapist, a white U.S.-born woman, was accustomed to. Therapist and client used further exploration of space to help the client read cues of boundaries in others, starting with the therapist, to adjust her use of space when relating to others in the United States, and how that proxemics changed once she was back in Brazil.

SELF-STATES AND ENACTMENT

All animals adapt to their environments. Thus, actions will be revised or discontinued altogether when they consistently fail to provoke the hoped-for or needed response from others. Proximity-seeking actions will be truncated when others are not available or react to our reaching out in negative ways. If need is met with rejection or otherwise harsh treatment, we will defend against our own vulnerability and will stop seeking help or comfort when we feel needy. If we are discriminated against or bullied when we occupy too much physical space, we may learn to shrink our bodies, keeping them small. A sense of pride and self-esteem may be reflected by length in our spines and squared shoulders, but if we are shamed, discriminated against, or faced with oppressive circumstances, our shoulders may round and our spine may sag. Each of these movements and postures will reflect self-states that may be "inhospitable and even adversarial, sequestered from one another as islands of 'truth,' each functioning as an insulated version of reality that protectively defines what is 'me' at a given moment and forcing other self-states that are inharmonious with its truth to become 'not-me'" (Bromberg, 2010, p. 21). In any of these instances, exploring contrasting actions can bring forward a variety of self-states.

When Robert, the client described previously, explored reaching out, the self-state that had learned to inhibit that action became frightened and oppositional. Having made up its mind that others were never to be relied upon to respond to his needs, this part of him believed reaching out to be hopeless and even threatening. New actions, like new words, "are often initially perceived from an adversarial perspective by at least one part of the self, sometimes with grave misgivings, sometimes with outright antagonism, and sometimes even with rage" (Bromberg, 2006, p. 52). Keep in mind that these actions are not simply physical exercises: They are rich with strong emotions that were not regulated by the attachment figures or by other significant people, charged with social meaning and/or with trauma-related emotions of terror and rage that accompany instinctive defenses. Processing these actions and their effects can ultimately encourage self-states to get to know one another and increase the ease of transitions between states.

It warrants reiterating that the therapist's own nonverbal expressions and the self-states they represent have a strong impact on what takes place within the therapeutic relationship. Therapists tend to invite and interact with the parts of the client with which they are most comfortable, disconnecting from and ignoring the client's self-states that they would rather not address (Bromberg, 2006). Physical actions that are familiar, easy for the therapist to execute, and do not challenge or stimulate a therapist's not-me self-states are those that they are likely to explore with the client, ignoring or rejecting actions would make the therapist uncomfortable. If therapists are uneasy with reaching out to others for support, and/or uneasy when others reach out to them, they will be unlikely to explore this action with their clients. If a client attempts to do so, the therapist will probably be unable to demonstrate an emotionally and physically integrated reaching action, so the exploration will have little chance of producing the explicitly desired outcome. But this is not cause for undue concern for therapists who are interested in learning about their own participation in what takes place beyond the words. In fact, when therapist and client together successfully negotiate the tacit, implied effect of each party upon the other, which encompassess personal and sociocultural histories of both, the alchemy and healing potential of therapy can be actualized.

Therapy can be conceptualized as consisting of two mutually created, simultaneous journeys (cf. Ogden, 2014; Chapter 11, this volume). One journey is explicit and includes the interventions that the therapist is aware of, which are employed based on theory and experience. These inform clinical strategy and intervention by providing the conscious rationale for what takes place in the therapy hour. The second journey is implicit, consisting of the communication that takes place between the implicit selves of therapist and client, beneath the words in a nonverbal conversation. Although it may feel slightly familiar, the evasive and non-conscious implicit journey cannot be clearly identified or verbally described. This journey is traveled unawares by both therapist and client, and usually produces surprising consequences that neither anticipated. Because this venture is ambiguous, unclear, and often unsettling, the implicit selves of therapist and client, who may have opposing agendas, can collide in therapeutic enactments.

For one client, Ellen, a white cisgender unemployed female in her 50s, who was not able to complete her high school education, our implicit journey together became clear. Ellen had been forced to submit to extreme abuse during her childhood. A pattern of compliance continued into adulthood, long after that abuse was over. Ellen stated that she had great trouble feeling anger, and that when she did, she often turned it against herself through self-harm. As we explored her anger, Ellen discovered an impulse to push outward, along with the words, "Leave me alone." She immediately felt strong and powerful, and I felt relieved because the urge to self-harm seemed to be replaced by a fight defense of pushing. Ellen stated that she had not had much of a chance to practice any assertive action because doing so would have made the abuse at the hands of her caregivers much worse.

I suggested that we practice this action in therapy by standing up and giving her the opportunity to push away a pillow as I moved it toward her. Ellen agreed, but she seemed a little reluctant. I asked if it was okay with her to practice this movement, but I did not give the attention needed to the part of Ellen that (still) could not say no. She became compliant, and I, in my effort to do more, did not attend to her compliance. I realized (later) that my pushing her was a reflection of my own childhood with a demanding mother who conveyed that "more was better." But in session, I failed to notice that Ellen was approaching the limit of her window of tolerance (Siegel, 1999) and at risk of dissociating. Our two histories collided in an enactment that continued to intensify until finally we realized together that Ellen was complying and becoming dysregulated.

Another enactment occurred in Ellen's treatment when I used psychoeducation to explain bottom-up and top-down processes. Ellen seemed to understand my explanations and responded with a small smile, so I kept talking. After a few minutes, I noticed that Ellen subtly changed her posture, adopting a less aligned spine, and also requested more advice than normal regarding her current life. The interpersonal dynamics had shifted, and I redirected Ellen's attention to her slumped posture. Eventually she said the posture was connected to the words "I don't know enough; I am stupid." I realized that the part of me that wanted her to understand the concept of bottom-up and top-down collided with the part of Ellen that felt inferior because she had not been able to continue her education. Along with the part of me that was invested in her understanding my points, our differing social locations were significant as well. The fact that I was in a position of power as the therapist, had a doctoral degree, and was an author, all of which Ellen knew, contrasted with her own marginalized location in terms of education, employment, and economics, and may have contributed as well to her compliance.

The past is commonly reworked in a more powerful and substantial manner through processing an enactment than if the enactment had not occurred. The presence of both our pasts implicitly contributed to these two enactments. My part reflected my childhood attempts to please my mother by doing more and a need to be understood, and Ellen's part reflected her childhood pattern of submitting and complying to the wishes of others, as well as shame due to her marginalized locations, specifically her lack of education. Processing the enactment is possible when the therapist or the client (or both) " 'wakes up' and feels that something is going on here and now between them, rather than continuing to believe that the phenomenon is located solely in the client, who is 'doing the same thing again' " (Bromberg, 2006, p. 34). I woke up the first time as Ellen's arousal rose, her eyes widened fearfully, and she abruptly sat down after she pushed away the pillow. I realized that we had gone too far, and that interactive regulation was needed to bring her arousal back into a window of tolerance. At that moment, I was able to acknowledge the part of Ellen that was terrified and provide the reassurance that nothing bad was going to happen from executing that action. In the second enactment, I woke up again when she was agreeing to my explanations, but her spine slumped, which didn't match her words. This led to an exploration of the part of Ellen that felt inferior, grief about not being able to continue her education, and to a discussion about our differing locations. If Ellen had not experienced her hyperarousal and compliance, and I had not failed to notice her dysregulation or her acquiescence, the enactments and subsequent interactive repair could not have occurred. It is the repair and working through of those enacted experiences that often provide the most beneficial therapeutic impact.

Bromberg (2006) emphasized that the environment in which change can take place must be "safe but not too safe" for both therapist and client. If the emotional and physiological arousal consistently remains in the middle of the window of tolerance (e.g., at levels typical of low fear and anxiety states), clients' arousal will not arousal will not become dysregulated, and thus they will not have the chance to develop their regulatory capacity by returning arousal to the window. Distressing experiences must be stimulated for clients to learn to regulate and expand their windows. Therapists too are challenged by the residue of past histories they thought were already resolved, but that emerge in enactments and empathic failures within the relationship. Arousal of each party is at the regulatory boundary of their windows of tolerance (Schore, 2009). By working at the edges of the regulatory boundaries, the windows of both can be expanded.

It is the processing of each person's implicit self within the relationship that provides the raw material for new experiences, new actions, and new meanings for both parties. Ellen and I participated together in unfolding interactions within which we co-created a new experience and challenged early unsymbolized implicit relational knowing for both of us. Eventually, I woke up and recognized Ellen's self-states that I had heretofore ignored—the one that was terrified of making an assertive action and the one that was feeling ashamed of her lack of education—by directly acknowledging her fear and shame and reassuring her that this situation was different from her past in the first enactment, and exploring the part that felt inferior and discussing the impact of our differing locations in the second. These acts of recognition challenged both the part of Ellen that felt inferior and her relational knowing that her fear and shame would not be tended to and that she needed to comply with others' wishes rather than asserting herself. It also challenged my early relational knowing of never being "enough" and that I had to do more. Since the intimate relational processes of enactment emerge from what takes place in the moment between therapist and client, they cannot be foreseen. They are murky and confusing and, when they occur, require that the therapist is able to step into unknown territory, suspend interpretation, and uncover the meaning together with the client.

CONCLUSION

Visible and tangible nonverbal behaviors tell their own inimitable stories of past and current trauma, privileged and marginalized social locations, attachment disruptions, relational strife, resources, and sociocultural priming. They provide a continual source of implicit and explicit exploration in therapy. The therapist listens not only to the verbal narrative, but also to the somatic narrative for the purpose of making the unconscious conscious, as well as for "interacting at another level, an experience-near subjective level, one that implicitly processes moment to moment socio-emotional information at levels beneath awareness" (Schore, 2003, p. 52). Along with the therapist's implicit participation in the nonverbal conversation, explicit exploration of specific nonverbal behaviors provides an avenue to the client's unconscious and to the effects of privilege/oppression dynamics both in the client's history and within the therapeutic dyad. When we experiment with new actions to challenge outdated procedural learning, we challenge habitual implicit processing, including enactments, both explicitly through the use of words and also implicitly at a level at which words are not available and sometimes not needed for therapeutic change to occur. The intimacy and transformative power of this therapist-client journey can be heightened by thoughtful attention to what is being spoken beneath the words, by the story the body tells.

REFERENCES

Aposhyan, S. (1999). *Natural intelligence: Body-mind integration and human development.* Baltimore, MD: Williams and Wilkins.

Aposhyan, S. (2004). *Body-mind psychotherapy: Principles, techniques, and practical applications.* New York: Norton.

Aviezer, H., Hassin, R., Ryan, J., Grady, C., Susskind, J., Anderson, A., Moscovitch, M., & Bentin, S. (2008). Angry, disgusted or afraid? Studies on the malleability of emotion perception. *Psychological Science, 19,* 724–732.

Bainbridge-Cohen, B. (1993). *Sensing, feeling and action.* Northampton, MA: Contact.

Barrett, L. F., Adolphs, R., Marsella, S., Martinez, A. M., & Pollak, S. D. (2019). Emotional expressions reconsidered: Challenges to inferring emotion from human facial movements. *Psychological Science in the Public Interest, 20,* 1–68. doi:10.1177/1529100619832930

Beebe, B., & Lachmann, F. M. (1998). Co-constructing inner and relational processes: Self- and mutual regulation in infant research and adult treatment. *Psychoanalytic Psychology, 15*(4), 480–516. https://doi.org/10.1037/0736-9735.15.4.480

Bennett-Leighton, L. (2018). The trauma of oppression: A somatic perspective. In C. Caldwell and L. Bennett-Leighton. Oppression and the body: Roots, resistance and resolutions (pp. 17–30). Berkeley, CA: North Atlantic Books.

Bouisset, S. (1991). Relationship between postural support and intentional movement: Biomechanical approach. *Archives Internationales de Physiologie, de Biochimie et de Biophysique, 99,* A77–A92.

Burgoon, J. K., Guerrero, L., & Floyd, K. (2016). *Nonverbal communication.* New York: Routledge.

Brazelton, T. (1989). *The earliest relationship.* Reading, MA: Addison-Wesley.

Bromberg, P. M. (2006). *Awakening the dreamer: Clinical journeys.* Mahwah, NJ: Analytic Press.

Bromberg, P. M. (2010). Minding the dissociative gap. *Contemporary Psychoanalysis, 46*(1), 19–31.

Courtois, C. (1999). *Recollections of sexual abuse: Treatment principles and guidelines.* New York: Norton.

DeCasper, A. J., & Fifer, W. P. (1980). Of human bonding: Newborns prefer their mothers' voices. *Science, 208,* 1174–1176.

Desmond, J. (1997). Embodying difference: Issues in dance and cultural studies. In J. Desmond (Ed.), *Meaning in motion* (pp. 29–54). Durham, NC: Duke University Press.

DiCorcia, J. A., & Tronick, E. Z. (2011). Quotidian resilience: Exploring mechanisms that drive resilience from a perspective of everyday stress and coping. *Neuroscience and Biobehavioral Reviews, 35*(7), 1593–1602.

Dijkstra, K., Kaschak, M. P., & Zwann, R. A. (2006). Body posture facilitates retrieval of autobiographical memories. *Cognition, 102*(1), 139–149.

Dosamantes-Beaudry, I. (1999). Divergent cultural self construals: Implications for the practice of dance/movement therapy. *Arts in Psychotherapy, 24*(2), 129–135.

Dunham, Y., Baron, A. S., & Banaji, M. R. (2008). The development of implicit intergroup cognition. *Trends in Cognitive Sciences, 12,* 248–253. doi:10.1016/j.tics.208.04.006

Ekman, P. (1978). Facial signs: Facts, fantasies, and possibilities. In T. Sebeok (Ed.), *Sight, sound and sense* (pp. 124–156). Bloomington: Indiana University Press.

Ekman, P. (2004). *Emotions revealed: Recognizing faces and feelings to improve communication and emotional life.* New York: Henry Holt.

Fogel, A. (1993). *Developing through relationships: Origins of communication, self and culture.* Chicago: University of Chicago Press.

Frewen, P. A., Neufeld, R. W., Stevens, T. K., & Lanius, R. A. (2010). Social emotions and emotional valence during imagery in women with PTSD: Affective and neural correlates. *Psychological Trauma: Theory, Research, Practice, and Policy, 2*(2), 145–157.

Fuertes, J. N., Gottdiener, W. H., Martin, H., Gilbert, T. C., & Giles, H. (2012). A meta-analysis of the effects of speakers' accents on interpersonal evaluations. *European Journal of Social Psychology, 42*(1), 120–133. doi:10.1002/ejsp.862

Gallese, V., Fadiga, L., Fogassi, L., & Rizzolatti, G. (1996). Action recognition in the premotor cortex. *Brain, 119,* 593–609.

Grigsby, J., & Stevens, D. (2000). *Neurodynamics of personality.* New York: Guilford.

Hall, J., Harrigan, J., & Rosenthal, R. (1995). Nonverbal behavior in clinician-client interaction. *Applied and Preventive Psychology, 4,* 21–37.

Henley, N., and Freeman, J. (1995). The sexual politics of interpersonal behavior in women: A feminist perspective. London: Mayfield.

Janet, P. (1925). *Principles of psychotherapy.* London: George Allen and Unwin.

Kahalon, R., Shnabel, N., & Becker, J. C. (2018). "Don't bother your pretty little head": Appearance compliments lead to improved mood but impaired cognitive performance. *Psychology of Women Quarterly, 42*(2), 136–150. https://doi.org/10.1177/0361684318758596

Kurtz, R. (1990). *Body-centered psychotherapy: The Hakomi method: The integrated use of mindfulness, nonviolence, and the body.* Mendocino, CA: LifeRhythm.

Kurtz, R. (2010, January). Readings in the Hakomi method of mindfulness-based assisted self-study. Ron Kurtz Hakomi Educational Materials. http://hakomi.com/wp-content/uploads/2009/12/Readings-January-2010.pdf

Kurtz, R., & Prestera, H. (1976). *The body reveals: An illustrated guide to the psychology of the body.* New York: Holt, Rinehart and Winston.

Lapides, F. (2010, May). The implicit realm in couples therapy: Improving right hemisphere affect-regulating capabilities. *Clinical Social Work Journal.* https://link.springer.com/article/10.1007/s10615-010-0278-1

Lyons-Ruth, K. (1998). Implicit relational knowing: Its role in development and psychoanalytic treatment. *Infant Mental Health Journal, 19,* 282–289.

Lyons-Ruth, K., Bronfman, E., & Parsons, E. (1999). Atypical attachment in infancy and early childhood among children at developmental risk: IV. Maternal frightened, frightening, or atypical behaviour and disorganized infant attachment patterns. *Monographs of the Society for Research in Child Development, 64*(3), 67–96.

Mampe, B., Friederici, A. D., Christophe, A., & Wermke, K. (2009). Newborns' cry melody is shaped by their native language. *Current Biology, 19*(23), 1994–1997.

McGilchrist, I. (2009). *The master and his emissary: The divided brain and the making of the Western world.* New Haven: Yale University Press.

Moore, C. L., & Yamamoto, K. (2012). *Beyond words: Movement observation and analysis* (2nd ed.). New York: Routledge.

Nazzi, T., Bertoncini, J., & Mehler, J. (1998). Language discrimination by newborns: Toward an understanding of the role of rhythm. *Journal of Experimental Psychology: Human Perception and Performance, 24*(3), 756–766. https://doi.org/10.1037/0096-1523.24.3.756

Nespor, M. (2010). Prosody: An interview with Marina Nespor. *ReVEL, 8*(15). http://www.revel.inf.br/files/entrevistas/revel_15_interview_marina_nespor.pdf

Ogden, P. (2007, March). *Beyond words: A clinical map for using mindfulness of the body and the organization of experience in trauma treatment.* Paper presented at Mindfulness and Psychotherapy Conference, UCLA/Lifespan Learning Institute, Los Angeles.

Ogden, P. (2009). Emotion, mindfulness, and movement: Expanding the regulatory boundaries of the window of affect tolerance. In D. Fosha,

D. Siegel, & M. Solomon (Eds.), *The healing power of emotion: Affective neuroscience and clinical practice* (pp. 204–231). New York: Norton.

Ogden, P. (2011). Beyond words: A sensorimotor psychotherapy perspective on trauma treatment. In V. Caretti, G. Craparo, & A. Schimmenti (Eds.), *Psychological trauma: Theory, clinical and treatment.* Rome: Astrolabio.

Ogden, P. (2013a). "Oltre le parole: La psicoterapia sensomotoria nel trattamento del trauma." In V. Caretti, G. Craparo, & A. Schimmenti (Eds.), *Memorie traumatiche e mentalizzazione: Teoria, ricerca e clinica* (pp. 183–214). Rome: Astrolabio.

Ogden, P. (2013b). Technique and beyond: Therapeutic enactments, mindfulness, and the role of the body. In D. J. Siegel & M. Solomon (Eds.), *Healing moments in psychotherapy* (pp. 35–48). New York: Norton.

Ogden, P. (2014). Embedded relational mindfulness: A sensorimotor psychotherapy perspective on trauma treatment. In V. M. Follette, D. Rozelle, J. W. Hopper, D. L. Rome, & J. Briere (Eds.), *Contemplative methods in trauma treatment: Integrating mindfulness and other approaches* (pp. 227–242). New York: Guilford.

Ogden, P., & Fisher, J. (2015). *Sensorimotor psychotherapy: Interventions for trauma and attachment.* New York: Norton.

Ogden, P., Minton, K., & Pain, C. (2006). *Trauma and the body: A sensorimotor approach to psychotherapy.* New York: Norton.

Porges, S. W. (2005). The role of social engagement in attachment and bonding: A phylogenetic perspective. In C. Carter, L. Ahnert, K. Grossman, S. Hrdy, M. Lamb, S. W. Porges, & N. Sachser (Eds.), *From the 92nd Dahlem Workshop report: Attachment and bonding: A new synthesis* (pp. 33–55). Cambridge, MA: MIT Press.

Porges, S. W. (2011). *The polyvagal theory: Neurophysiological foundations of emotions, attachment, communication, and self-regulation.* New York: Norton.

Schachner, D., Shaver, P., & Mikulincer, M. (2005). Patterns of nonverbal behavior and sensitivity in the context of attachment relationships. *Journal of Nonverbal Behavior, 29*(3), 141–169.

Schnall, S., & Laird, J. D. (2003). Keep smiling: Enduring effects of facial expressions and postures on emotional experience and memory. *Cognition and Emotion, 17*(5), 787–797.

Schore, A. N. (1994). *Affect regulation and the origin of the self: The neurobiology of emotional development.* Hillsdale, NJ: Lawrence Erlbaum.

Schore, A. N. (2001). The effects of early relational trauma on right brain development, affect regulation, and infant mental health. *Infant Mental Health Journal, 22,* 7–66

Schore, A. N. (2003). *Affect regulation and the repair of the self.* New York: Norton.

Schore, A. N. (2009). Right-brain affect regulation: An essential mechanism of development, trauma, dissociation, and psychotherapy. In D. Fosha, D. Siegel, & M. Solomon (Eds.), *The healing power of emotion: Affective neuroscience, development & clinical practice* (pp. 112–144). New York: Norton.

Schore, A. N. (2010). The right brain implicit self: A central mechanism of the psychotherapy change process. In J. Petrucelli (Ed.), *Knowing, not-knowing, and sort-of-knowing: Psychoanalysis and the experience of uncertainty* (pp. 117–202). Washington, DC: American Psychological Association.

Schore, A. N. (2011). The right brain implicit self lies at the core of psychoanalysis. *Psychoanalytic Dialogues, 21,* 1–26.

Schore, A. N. (2012). *The science of the art of psychotherapy.* New York: Norton.

Schore, J. R., & Schore, A. N. (2007). Modern attachment theory: The central role of affect regulation in development and treatment. *Clinical Social Work Journal, 36*(1), 9–20.

Siegel, D. (1999). *The developing mind: Toward a neurobiology of interpersonal experience.* New York: Guilford.

Stepper, S., & Strack, F. (1993). Proprioceptive determinants of emotional and nonemotional feelings. *Journal of Personality and Social Psychology, 64*(2), 211–220.

Stern, D. (1985). *The interpersonal world of the infant: A view from psychoanalysis and developmental psychology.* New York: Basic Books.

Tronick, E. Z. (2007). *The neurobehavioral and social-emotional development of infants and children.* New York: Norton.

Tronick, E. Z. (2009). Multilevel meaning making and dyadic expansion of consciousness theory: The emotional and the polymorphic and polysemic flow of meaning. In D. Fosha, D. Siegel, & M. Solomon (Eds.), *The healing power of emotion: Affective neuroscience, development and clinical practice* (pp. 86–111). New York, NY: Norton.

Tronick, E., & Beeghly, M. (2011). Infants' meaning-making and the development of mental health problems. *The American psychologist, 66*(2), 107–119. https://doi.org/10.1037/a0021631

Tronick, E. Z., & Cohn, J. F. (1989). Infant-mother face-to-face interaction: Age and gender differences in coordination and the occurrence of miscoordination. *Child Development, 60,* 85–92.

Chapter 10

TECHNIQUE AND BEYOND: THERAPEUTIC ENACTMENTS*

*All journeys have secret destinations of
which the traveler is unaware.*

MARTIN BUBER

Full of possibility for great intimacy and personal growth as well as painful misunderstanding and empathic failure, human communication is multilayered. Most obvious and transparent is the explicit exchange of words, but the implicit conversation that goes on beneath the words is arguably more compelling. Unintended and spontaneous, this wordless tête-à-tête usually remains undetected by the conscious minds of both parties, but speaks clearly in the language of gesture, posture, prosody, facial expressions, eye gaze, and unconscious affect. This nonverbal call and response between implicit selves is the music for the dyadic dance between therapist and client.

A renewed interest in what is being articulated implicitly while something else is being verbalized is emerging in the field of psychotherapy—not only to bring awareness to the client's unconscious, but also to shed light on the role of implicit processing in

* I wish to thank Dr. Philip Bromberg for his contribution to this chapter.

clinical practice and how to restructure unconscious regulatory mechanisms through what takes place within the therapeutic dyad (Schore, 1994). This dance between therapist and client includes the therapist's unconscious interpretation and response of their own implicit self/selves to the communications of the client's implicit self/selves. Therapeutic action thus extends beyond understanding and interpreting clients and their behavior to participating in and negotiating with what is enacted beyond the words.

This chapter considers two simultaneous clinical journeys, each traveled to discover the implicit self: one is a conscious journey, the other is unconscious. The explicit, conscious journey pertains to what the therapist believes they are doing as a clinician, supported by theory and technique. Therapeutic methods, meant to be learned and then set aside, and not reflected upon explicitly in the therapy hour, guide interventions that emerge spontaneously within the dyad. With somewhat predictable outcomes, this journey can easily become conscious, and thus explained, rationalized, reflected upon, and even voluntarily changed midstream. For this journey, body-oriented mindfulness interventions from Sensorimotor Psychotherapy bring to light the implicit self of the client, and new physical actions that foster integration between explicit and implicit parts of the self can be discovered and executed.

On the explicit journey, the therapist's intention includes "to develop the skill of seeing [the] internal world, and then being able to shape it toward integrative functioning" (Siegel, 2010, p. 223). In contrast, the implicit journey explores what happens when the internal world cannot be seen or understood, but is enacted beneath the words, beyond technique. Elusive and unconscious, this journey may feel vaguely familiar to one or both parties, but leads relentlessly to outcomes that were not intended or predicted. Eluding explicit clarity, at least initially, this journey involves the body-to-body conversation between the implicit parts of client and therapist that takes place unawares. It is a messy journey that leads to collusions, collisions, and therapeutic enactments that, when negotiated, are central to therapeutic change.

The explicit and implicit material that emerges in the therapy hour is informed and sustained by contextual factors embedded in our sociocultural realities. We all carry with us current and cumulative historical identities of our groups of belonging, to paraphrase Anna Julia Cooper (1892, in Giddings, 1984/2008, p. 3) with regard to being Black: "when and where I enter, my entire race enters with me." Each individual brings to the therapy room their transgenerational inheritance and their own experiences of their gender, socioeconomic status, race, ethnicity, immigration status, sexual orientation, and every other marker of their identity. The implicit and explicit dialogues do not exist in isolation but are interconnected with the journeys of privilege and oppression that both therapist and clients have respectively traveled as individuals and historically situated human beings.

CORE CONCEPTS

The past is "remembered as a series of unconscious expectations" (Cortina & Liotti, 2007, p. 205). Because the memories, both personal and sociocultural, that shaped them are not always available for reflection and revision, these expectations are even more robust and influential. A child learns to predict which vocalizations, expressions, or actions will be welcomed or rejected, thus acquiring "implicit relational knowing"—"how to do things with others" (Lyons-Ruth, 1998, p. 282). This knowing is reflected in physical action sequences rife with intersecting personal, sociocultural, and contextual history and unconscious meaning. When certain actions are persistently ineffective in producing the desired outcome, they are abandoned or distorted. If no one is there to reach back, we may stop reaching out, literally and figuratively, or we may reach out hesitantly, with bent elbow, as if we do not expect our need to be met. If our attachment figures ridiculed us when we were vulnerable, we may stop seeking proximity altogether when we feel needy. If standing upright with our heads held high elicited abuse, ridicule, or bullying, we may develop a habit of slouching and lowering our gaze instead. Our bodies may shut down or become numb in the face of overwhelming adversity, such as historical trauma, poverty, ongoing oppression, or forced migration. If we experience discrimination and racism, our bodies may become habitually tense and ready to protect ourselves in anticipation of future assaults.

These physical habits profoundly affect our self-perception and identity, how we perceive and interact with the world, and how the world perceives and interacts with us. A slumped posture conveys implicit expectations to both self and other, possibly telling a story of diminished self-esteem and contributing to, if not inducing, feelings of shame, helplessness, and fear associated with the past (Ogden et al., 2006). However, it should be noted that these physical patterns may be adaptive in relation to sociocontextual factors such as privilege or, conversely, oppression, hence still eliciting best outcomes in certain social contexts or environments.

These nonverbal physical indicators are unconscious, unintended actions—"a piece of behavior or an element of style or anything that suggests . . . a connection to character, early memories, or particular [unconscious] emotions" (Kurtz, 2010, p. 110). They reflect and sustain the right-brain implicit self that "represents the biological substrate of the human unconscious mind and is intimately involved in the processing of bodily based affective information associated with various motivational states" (Schore, 2009, p. 114). Therapist and client can interrupt the automaticity of these indicators of the implicit self when they become mindful of them "not as disease or something to be rid of, but in an effort to help the patient become conscious of how experience is managed and how the capacity for experience can be expanded" (Kurtz, 1990, p. 111).

Mindfulness (cf. Chapter 4, this volume), as understood in

Western contexts, is "an active search process, a purposeful seeking in the field of awareness" (Siegel, 2010, p. 108). The general notion of mindful attention as being receptive to whatever elements emerge in the mind's eye gives way to mindful attention directed specifically toward nonverbal indicators of the implicit self. Instead of allowing clients' attention to drift randomly toward whatever emotions, memories, thoughts, or physical actions they might be drawn to, therapists actively use directed mindfulness to guide the clients' awareness toward particular indicators that provide a jumping-off point for conscious exploration of the implicit self they represent (Ogden, 2007, 2009). Mindfulness in therapy seeks to increase clients' integrative capacity by helping them get to know parts of themselves that were dissociated in order to support adaptation when the capacity or necessary social support to integrate traumatic experiences and memories was lacking (Van der Hart, 2012).

Mindfulness can also increase awareness of the sociocontextual factors that underpin our implicit selves and diverse identities. For example, when exploring gender with a female client, mindful awareness of the constriction in her body and slump of her shoulders led to the discovery that these patterns were partially associated with the lack of safety she felt around demanding, authoritative men. In another case, an undocumented client realized through mindfulness that the stress and heaviness in their shoulders were in part associated with the terror of being apprehended and possibly deported because of their immigration status.

Obviously, only those indicators that register consciously for therapist or client can be explored explicitly. But many, if not most, indicators are emitted, received, and interpreted unconsciously, shaping what happens within the relationship without conscious thought or intent. The unconscious collusions and collisions between therapist and client that often arise from this implicit dialogue can sabotage therapeutic gain, but also hold the potential for growth, when negotiated successfully in the course of therapy. Stark (2009) suggests that empathic failures

> are not just a story about the therapist and her lack of perfection, but also a story about the patient exerting pressure on the therapist to participate as the old bad object [and vice versa]. This mutual enactment can either result in retraumatization, if it's not properly processed at the intimate edge between patient and therapist, or it can lead to a better resolution and integration on a higher level.

ENACTMENTS AND PRIVILEGE/ OPPRESSION DYNAMICS

In the context of asymmetrical circuits of power and privilege/ oppression dynamics that include the intersectional identities and sociocultural histories of therapist and client, navigating therapeutic enactments requires the therapist to practice both discernment and rigorous honesty. Without these, from their positionality in the clinical encounter, therapists can easily bypass the operations of racism, sexism, homophobia, classism, xenophobia, transphobia, and similar dynamics of oppression that contribute to enactments.

Sociocultural context, privilege, and oppression affect us all and contribute to everything that occurs in the therapy room, including enactments. Though the impact is experienced very differently for those in dominant versus marginalized groups, none of us are immune to these dynamics. The experiences of oppression vary depending on many factors such as country of origin, region, or stage of life, to name a few. We all, psychotherapists included, must contend with the fact that we constantly participate in overt and covert ways in the dynamics of privilege and oppression. We take part in many ways—at times as a perpetrator, at times as a victim, at times as a rescuer, and at times as a bystander. As psychotherapists, we may perpetrate oppression by denying services to those that cannot afford our fee, may feel victimized when a client makes a derogatory remark about people with whom we share group membership, or participate as a bystander by providing services only to those that share social identities similar to ours. We also participate as bystanders when we do not explicitly acknowledge the contributions of structural and systemic forms of injustice and oppression to the client's psychological distress, thus aligning with a historical and highly individualized perspective of mental health.

In the following example, the therapist participates as a victim. A heterosexual client makes a derogatory comment to his gay, masculine-presenting therapist. The therapist feels hurt, spacey, and momentarily emotionally disengaged from the client and the session. Because the therapist had chosen not to disclose his sexual orientation to the client, he hesitates to address the impasse and his own reaction with the client at this time. The therapist freezes and experiences an emotional coldness, immobility in his body, and difficulty staying present in the session. The therapist and client have entered an enactment where the therapist feels victimized by the client's comment. The feelings and body sensations are familiar to him, having experienced them many times throughout his life when dating and in childhood, when he learned to be still and "lay low" as to "pass undetected."

The next example describes the therapist participating as a bystander. A white male therapist is meeting with a white female client. During a session that takes place early in treatment, the client casually makes a disparaging remark about her Jewish boss, whom the client feels is mistreating her. The client pauses and looks at the therapist as if wondering about the therapist's opinion in response to her comment. The therapist is startled and intuitively wants to address the comment therapeutically and within an anti-oppression framework. The therapist listens to the client with bewilderment at the implication of the statement and experiences in his body some activation in his chest and his legs. He struggles to remain present and engaged as his body tenses and there is a momentary pulling back of his upper body. He hesitates over whether to address the derogatory remarks and ultimately chooses not to, thinking that his silence will foster a greater therapeutic alliance. Internally he begins to rationalize the statement and tell himself that therapy is not the place to discuss such issues. The client leans forward, as she proceeds to generalize her disparaging opinions to all Jewish people while adding a minor disclaimer to her comments: "I'm not racist . . . but . . ." The therapist and client are now participating in an enactment in which the therapist has chosen to be a bystander to the client's anti-Semitism.

In the following example, the therapist acts as a perpetrator. A white male therapist working in a community-based agency is meeting with a Mexican American male adolescent client referred by his school. The young man appears withdrawn, disengaged, and uninterested in the therapy. He comes late to sessions and sits slumped in the chair. The therapist has attempted to engage him in treatment with very little success. As per agency protocol in working with minors, the therapist requests that the young man's primary caretaker come in for a collateral consultation. The client quickly states, "I don't want that," and appears uncomfortable and angry. His eyes momentarily avoid the therapist's gaze and his fists clench, while his feet move slightly in opposite directions. As the therapist attempts to explore with the client his uncertainty about having his caregiver come to session, he mistakenly interprets the young man's response as resistance. The therapist identifies in himself feelings of frustration and powerlessness. With every attempt to engage the client, the client appears more disengaged and shut down. As the therapy hour is about to end, the frustrated therapist announces that, per agency protocol, if the client's caregiver is unable to come to a session, his case will be closed. The teenager does not return for their follow-up appointment and fails to respond to outreach. In speaking to the school social worker about the client not showing up for their follow-up session, the therapist learns that the young man lives with his single mother and two younger siblings. His mother is an undocumented immigrant who does not speak English and works two low-wage jobs, one in the daytime and one a night shift, to make ends meet. In that moment the therapist understands that by indiscriminately enforcing the agency's policy without knowledge of the teenager's social context, he has acted as a perpetrator. Perhaps the teenager was protecting his mother from having to come to a session due to her limited availability or perhaps he was worried about her undocumented status.

Therapists are also at risk of taking on the role of rescuer, as illustrated in the following example. A documented immigrant female therapist is working with an undocumented female client who has suffered sexual harassment and rape by her male boss. The client was referred by her doctor for panic attacks, insomnia, and skin rashes associated with stress. The client expresses that it has taken her several months to come to therapy because of the fear and shame of disclosing what happened. The therapist feels outraged toward a boss who threatened to report the client's undocumented status if she did not respond to his sexual advances. The therapist informs the client that by collaborating with the police, she can get official papers to remain in the country. Even though this would be a good course of action to follow, the therapist's zealous approach to achieving justice does not consider the repercussions for the client, who has not disclosed the sexual abuse to her sister who works under the same boss. The therapist connects the client to services before it is clinically appropriate; the client does not follow up with the referrals. The therapist/client alliance is disrupted; the client becomes silent whenever action steps are mentioned, while the therapist feels resentful and martyred, falling into a rescuer enactment with the client.

It should be noted that these various kinds of enactments are inevitable. In all the examples above, the dynamics described reflect implicit self-states, or parts, of both therapist and client that reside in the unconscious recesses of the self, and that have different agendas. These "clashes of subjectivity" inevitably arise because the dissociated self-states of both therapist and client eventually find their voices which need to be heard, not silenced (Bromberg, 2006). The critical element is the relational negotiation of enactments once it is recognized that something is amiss. Thus, although attunement and safety are necessary to establish a context in which psychotherapy can begin, they are impossible to sustain, and are not the only agent of therapeutic change. Current approaches are making increasing use of the inevitable enactments during which the therapist and client find themselves feeling stuck, bored, annoyed, frustrated, or even hostile toward one another. As illustrated in the examples above, these relational clashes can be relevant to privilege/oppression dynamics, sociocultural contexts, and the intersecting social locations of both therapist and client. The following account of a therapy session delves into the murky waters of negotiating the inescapable enactment that percolates beneath the surface, while the explicit journey of working with nonverbal indicators simultaneously takes place.

CASE STUDY AND APPLICATION

Linda was a single, white, cisgender, heterosexual woman, from a middle-class background who was in her 40s when she sought consultation with me, a therapist who shared similar social locations with the client in terms of gender, race, economic status, and sexual orientation. She had attended a series of my seminars and asked to be a client for a videotaped consultation. With a string of difficult relationships behind her, Linda reported that intimacy and friendships had always been a painful struggle: "Social phobia used to be sort of my whole existence. I didn't 'do friends' for a long, long time; I didn't know how to. I couldn't get out there to places where I could even meet people." She attributed these difficulties to growing up as an isolated only daughter of an intrusive alcoholic mother and absent stepfather. She had been repeatedly admitted to psychiatric hospitals for major depression. Stating that she had learned early on to be totally numb, Linda considered herself an expert at disconnecting from her body. Her four years of psychoanalysis were life-changing in terms of her becoming more in touch with her cognitions and emotions, but her body had been completely left out of treatment and she wanted to learn to be more "embodied."

Linda recounted a childhood memory of pretending to be asleep while her mother entered her room at night looking for the alcohol she had hidden under her daughter's bed. As Linda spoke, her body tightened and jerked slightly, especially her arms and legs. I directed her mindful awareness toward her physical experience, asking her if she could describe what was occurring in her body as she talked about her mother's alcoholism. She reported that her shoulders and upper arms were tightening, and she felt that she could not move. Typically, as clients begin to talk about past trauma, the physical responses that were operative at the time of the original event emerge, and it was easy to imagine that Linda had frozen in her bed when her invasive mother had entered her room.

Linda's tense and immobile upper body seemed to relate to an instinctive freeze defense, elicited under threat in which the muscles become tight, the senses alert, and movement ceases. The immobilizing freeze defense comes into play when mobilizing defenses of cry-for-help, fight, and flight have been ineffective, and can become a default defense if repeatedly engaged. The tension seemed to implicitly predict that no one would respect her wishes and that any attempt she might make at action would not have a positive outcome. Her immobility was also possibly coupled with the restrictions imposed on her gender during Linda's upbringing in the 1950s, as white women in Western patriarchal societies were traditionally socialized to be more reserved and less assertive than men. Taking all these considerations implicitly into account, Linda's best choice (made automatically and unconsciously) was to become compliant, submissive, and immobile in the face of trauma or relational adversity. Since tension is a precursor to action, I reasoned that the tension in Linda's arms might be an indicator of assertive actions (such as reaching out or pushing away) that "wanted" to happen but were being held back because they had been ill-advised or unsuccessful in her childhood and through her socialization into womanhood. I hoped that as Linda became mindful of the tension, these impulses and the part they represented would rise to awareness as physical urges to move, ready to be further developed into full-blown physical actions that would mitigate her freezing response.

Hypothesizing to myself that if Linda could translate the language of her frozen body into words, movement would follow, I asked, "I wonder if the tension could talk instead of tighten, what would it be saying?" I encouraged Linda to sense her body and allow words to emerge spontaneously from the tension itself, rather than thinking about what it would say. Linda replied, "Go away. That is what came to mind. And I don't know if it's the feeling [pause] to make the feeling go away?" At this point she paused again and looked at me questioningly. In the moment, I was assuming that her reply pertained only to her past, and not to her experience with me. So I leaned forward slightly and finished her sentence for her: "Or your mother to go away." Linda nodded and said, "Yeah." However, her jaw tightened and thrust sideways, which I recognized later as an action that contradicted her words.

Therapists tend to invite and interact with the parts of the client that they are most comfortable with, and often fail to recognize parts that they would rather not deal with (Bromberg, 2006). I had not noticed Linda's jaw until I watched the video after the session, because I had not been receptive to the part of Linda that disagreed with my explicit perspective. Thus, I had been unable to acknowledge a part of her that I now believe wanted me to "go away" during the session, as she had wanted her mother to go away as a child. This part of Linda seemed to have perceived me as demanding something from her that she could not directly provide, which seemed to trigger a reenactment of her compliant part. As the session progressed, I came to recognize that the sideways thrust of Linda's jaw meant that she did not concur with my view, but could not say so—presumably because her explicit self was either unaware of, or unwilling to voice, her disagreement. Taking the risk to directly express her desire for distance in our relationship probably represented a threat to Linda's explicit sense of herself as well. Instead, this need was walled off into a dissociative part that emerged implicitly in the enactment, finding its voice in unconscious prosody, affect, and movement, such as the tension in her jaw.

This budding enactment, signaled by our body-to-body conversation of my leaning forward and her tightening her jaw, remained unconscious to us both, so we could not address it directly. I decided to continue to see if we could draw on the tension in her upper body to stimulate physical action. I wondered aloud if she could ask her body how the tension wanted to move: "Did it want to pull in, push out, or push away?" Providing a menu like this often catalyzes the protective physical impulses that were not implemented during the original event. As such an impulse emerges in the therapy hour, it can be further developed into an assertive defensive action that supports a sense of efficacy and empowerment that is absent in frozen immobility. Linda reported that she saw an image in her mind's eye of her hands lifting straight up off her lap. But she added that when she saw the image, the tension increased and she felt paralyzed, as if something were preventing the movement. The more I directed her to be mindful of the tension, the more the immobility and tension increased.

When a particular part of the client emerges, a corresponding part of the therapist comes forth, and vice versa. As Linda became more frozen, I became more persistent, trying harder to elicit movement and forgetting to ask her how various parts reacted to my interventions. She in turn became increasingly tight and immobile. We were caught in a cycle that we could not escape because neither of us could reflect on it, since we were not aware of it. Looking back, I believe the power and privilege of my positionality as the therapist leading the session intersected with Linda's acquiescence and her efforts to answer my unwanted questions. So I continued on the explicit journey of trying to stimulate movement by using my own body to demonstrate her visualized action of arms lifting upward, hoping to activate the mirror neurons in Linda's brain so that her frozen arms would perform in kind, mirroring my motions. Instead, Linda now reported that her arms from her elbows down to her wrists felt as if an outside force were holding them down, although of course she knew that was not true, and she had no explicit recollection of this ever occurring in her past.

I was rapidly losing my confidence that what I was doing had any therapeutic value, but I persevered. Eager to arouse a part of her that could resist being held down, I asked, "What happens if you stay with this feeling of being held down? What does your body want to do?" Linda said, "I'm sort of shaking . . . uh . . . and still feeling paralyzed . . . but I think that I'm sensing wanting to move—part of the shaking is sort of this attempt to get the hands off of me and . . . and literally not being able to move . . . and I'm sad." Linda then began to weep, partly in frustration, partly in sadness, it seemed. When her tears were spent, she said that she still felt frozen.

My lack of recognition of the part of Linda that had also been unacknowledged by her family—the part that needed distance and was upset and angry at the invasiveness of others—seemed to exacerbate Linda's compliance. I felt protective of what I perceived as a hurt, mistreated child part of her, and wanted her to feel empowered. Both of us unconsciously ignored her underlying anger, which was directed not only toward her mother but also toward my unintended intrusiveness. This collusion seemed to be an implicit agreement between us that perpetuated the avoidance of the not-me parts with which we were both uncomfortable. My not-me part was my implicit need for her to respond and feel better that led to my being intrusive; Linda's not me part was her unexpressed need for distance led to her feeling angry. In retrospect, I realized that my part of this collusion stemmed from my own early attachment with my somewhat withdrawn mother, with whom I achieved the contact I needed when I tenaciously tried to reach her and draw her out. However, as noted previously, the collusion could have also come from, or been coupled with, other factors stemming from my identity such as gender, phenotype, height, weight, or teacher role, to name a few, which protected certain parts from being revealed and recognized.

Linda's implicit sense of being invaded wreaked havoc with her nervous system, which vacillated from a state of sympathetic hyperarousal to parasympathetic hypoarousal. Eventually, she lost the integrity of her erect posture: Her spine slumped, and she shut down and became numb. Her implicit self seemed to forecast her relational future as grim (including her future with me); the possibility of taking action held no hope of positive outcome. Since the spine is the physical core of the body that serves as an axis around which the limbs and head can move, the possibility for movement diminished even more as Linda's spine sagged.

I felt desperate to find a way to alleviate not only her frozen body but also her emotional pain. Bromberg describes that this dilemma I experienced often leads to the intensification of the enactment: "Experiencing the pain and causing the pain begin to merge, and the [therapist's] escalating failure to do something about the patient's pain gradually leads him to become, in fact, the person that the patient already experiences him to be" (2006, p. 91). By now, Linda perceived me as invasive, and I became even more so: I leaned forward and asked her to notice what would happen to the freezing if she made eye contact with me, hoping against hope that our eye contact would provide the safety she needed to allow her arms to relax. She opened her eyes, which she had spontaneously closed at some unknown point, and blankly looked at me, reporting, "Nothing changes in the freezing." I asked, "What happens?" She replies, "I'm pretty numb. It's sort of . . . I can see you . . . uh . . . but it's not a sense of . . . uh . . . I don't have a sense of keeping you out but you're certainly not . . . I'm certainly not feeling connected either." Linda sighed deeply. In an attempt to encourage intersubjectivity and joining, I asked her if she could sense inside how she was not connecting with me. She sighed and mumbled, "Uh . . . uh . . . I'm . . . it's just that I'm sort of blank," and sighed again.

In addition to intersections of identity, enactments occur in the realms where interactive regulation has failed for both parties, where each craves what the other cannot provide, thus proving (again) that the need is invalid and will not be met. My leaning forward and suggesting to Linda that she make eye contact came in part from my own need for contact, which had its origins in my childhood when I yearned to reach my rather withdrawn and reserved mother. My desire that Linda have a meaningful experience with me and my eagerness to feel helpful to her were implicitly present in this session. Linda had grown up with an invasive mother who did not allow her daughter the freedom to set distance between them. I implicitly experienced Linda as not letting me in, whereas she implicitly experienced me as intrusive. Our primitive needs had gone unmet and, as Solomon states, "experiencing needs that are reminders of childhood can be shameful or humiliating" (1994, p. 248). Both of us implicitly felt the shame of having "illegitimate" needs that could not be met, reminiscent of what we had felt as children. Our two histories had collided in a hand-in-glove enactment. But none of this was reflectively available to either of us on an explicit level during the session itself. And since every intervention I tried only made things worse, I was rapidly losing confidence in my ability as a therapist. Bromberg describes the situation:

> Trapped in a shared dissociative cocoon, the [therapist] is now being forced, little by little, to relinquish his confidence that what he is doing as an analyst has validity. . . . The enactment will continue or escalate until the [therapist] runs out of ways to "understand" it and runs out of techniques to deal with it. (2006, p. 99)

As long as I continued to believe that Linda's persistent immobility pertained solely to her own history, the enactment continued to escalate. I was challenged to "wake up" (Bromberg, 2006) and realize that what was taking place in the therapy hour had to do with my own history as well as Linda's. For me, in the session, this realization did not occur explicitly, but implicitly, through a stroke of intuition. Instinctively, without reflection, I asked Linda to notice what happened if I closed my eyes. This intervention emerged spontaneously from what transpired experientially and implicitly from within the relational unconscious that Linda and I had created together. The idea of closing my eyes was not a premeditated or generic intervention. It came to me unbidden, arising from what transpired in the here and now between Linda and myself, the result of "direct knowing that seeps into conscious awareness without the conscious mediation of logic or rational process" (Boucouvalas, 1997, as cited in Schore, 2011, p. 13). As Schore states, "the therapist's moment-to-moment navigation through these heightened affective moments [occurs] not by left brain explicit secondary process cognition but right brain implicit primary process affectively driven clinical intuition" (2011, p. 1). When I closed my eyes, Linda immediately took a deep breath (which I could not see until I watched the video, since my eyes were shut), and she reported, "I'm much more relaxed in my arms—it took a few seconds, but now all that's frozen is my wrists and hands." This was the healing moment. The act of closing my eyes at last conveyed recognition of the part of Linda that needed distance.

I felt immense relief that finally her body had begun to unfreeze, and my own body began to relax as well. The part of me that had been trying so hard to elicit a response began to soften, thereby allowing a different experience and relationship to emerge. I slowly expanded on the experiment of creating distance by moving my chair away from her, both of us rejoicing in her unfreezing with each increase in the distance between us. Negotiating the enactment, as we did, is "all about developing the capacity of patient and [therapist] to move from experiencing the other as an object to control or be controlled by, to being able to play with each other" (Bromberg, 2011, p. 18). Once Linda and I ceased trying to control each other, we began to laugh and play together, in part from relief that finally there was movement, in part from each of our needs being implicitly validated (mine for connection, hers for distance and control in the relationship) and in part from the absurdity of the entire situation. Her shoulders, arms, and wrists relaxed with each progressive increase in the distance between us, but Linda's fingers remained tense. She laughingly exclaimed, "You'd probably have to be across the room for my fingers to unfreeze!" As I moved my chair further and further away from her, Linda's fingers too began to relax. She stated that the words that came to mind were that she had some control, which she had never had in her relationship with her mother.

Linda and I participated joyfully together in an unfolding interaction that was both playful and profound, within which we cocreated a new experience and challenged our early unsymbolized implicit relational knowing. My recognition of the part of Linda that needed distance, communicated through action as I closed my eyes and moved my chair away, challenged her relational knowing that others would be intrusive and that she had no control over this. As she became more interactive and even playful, my early relational knowledge that I must work hard to be empathic and draw the other person out for contact to occur was similarly challenged.

When the needs of the implicit self are recognized, actions that were previously perceived as futile or even dangerous spontaneously emerge. Linda began to engage actions she had long ago forsaken with more joyful laughter. Her posture became upright, and instead of tension and immobility, her previously frozen arms and hands began to dance in the air. Finally, when my chair was about 20 feet from hers, she giggled and asked me to open my eyes. As I did so, both her arms spread open with her palms upward in an expansive, welcoming gesture, a movement unfamiliar to her usually tightly closed body posture. With a chuckle and steady eye contact, Linda said, "Now you feel too far away, now that I'm unfrozen," and beckoned me closer with her arm and hand. These proximity-seeking actions, abandoned in her childhood because they did not bring about the desired outcome, surfaced spontaneously, infused with new hope for present-day satisfaction and enlivening a part of Linda that had long been kept at bay. We ended the session laughing quietly together and marveling at the simplicity of resolution and increased connection that closing my eyes and moving my chair away had created.

CONCLUSION

The real magic and healing power of clinical practice often come about from navigating the unformulated, unconscious impact of therapist and client upon one another, which includes the influence of past childhood histories and sociocultural context of both parties. If Linda had not experienced my attempted interventions as intrusive, interactive repair could not have occurred, and it was the repair and working through of the enacted experience that provided the most beneficial therapeutic impact. Although the ending of the session would probably be considered by many as its most therapeutic feature, the entire process—including the unavoidable messiness of the enactment—was therapeutic, because it encompassed a dissociated collision cocreated and worked through together, supporting the growth of the implicit selves of both of us.

It is essential to understand that enactments are not mistakes but rather mysterious, non-conscious strivings for a higher level of growth and organization, and their negotiations are a function of the developing and emerging relationship. The processing of each person's implicit self/selves within the relationship provides the raw material for new experiences, new actions, and new meanings for both parties. This intersubjective process of joining and cocreation cannot be defined, identified, or predicted ahead of time, because it occurs within the context of what transpires unexpectedly within the dyad, and thus requires a leap into the unknown not only for the client but for the therapist as well.

Mindfulness, language, and explicit exchange as well as the participation of the implicit selves of therapist and client are all indispensable elements in clinical practice. By bringing the felt experience into the therapy hour, attending to nonverbal indicators consciously on the explicit journey and unconsciously on the implicit one, negotiating the enactments and making new actions that challenge outdated relational knowing, the implicit self can be recognized, understood, and integrated.

REFERENCES

Aposhyan, S. (2004). *Bodymind psychotherapy: Principles, techniques, and practical applications*. New York, NY: Norton.

Boucouvalas, M. (1997). Intuition: The concept and the experience. In R. D. Floyd & P. S. Arvidson (Eds.), *Intuition: The inside story* (pp. 3–18). New York: Routledge.

Bromberg, P. M. (2006). *Awakening the dreamer: Clinical journeys*. Mahwah, NJ: Analytic Press.

Bromberg, P. M. (2011). *The shadow of the tsunami and the growth of the relational mind*. New York: Routledge.

Buber, M. (1955). *The legend of the Baal-Shem*. Princeton, NJ: Princeton University Press.

Cortina, M., & Liotti, G. (2007). New approaches to understanding unconscious processes: Implicit and explicit memory systems. *International Forum of Psychoanalysis, 16*, 204–212.

Giddings, P. (2008). *When and where I enter: The impact of black women on race and sex in America*. Harper-Collins e-Book. https://caringlabor.files .wordpress.com/2010/12/when-and-where-i-enter-_-the-impact-of-b -paula-giddings.pdf (Original work published 1984)

Kurtz, R. (1990). *Body-centered psychotherapy: The Hakomi method: The integrated use of mindfulness, nonviolence, and the body*. Mendocino, CA: LifeRhythm.

Kurtz, R. (2010, January). Readings in the Hakomi method of mindfulness-based assisted self-study. Ron Kurtz Hakomi Educational Materials. http://hakomi.com/wp-content/uploads/2009/12/Readings -January-2010.pdf.

Lyons-Ruth, K. (1998). Implicit relational knowing: Its role in development and psychoanalytic treatment. *Infant Mental Health Journal, 19*, 282–289.

Ogden, P. (2007, March). *Beyond words: A clinical map for using mindfulness of the body and the organization of experience in trauma treatment*. Paper presented at Mindfulness and Psychotherapy Conference at UCLA, UCLA/Lifespan Learning Institute, Los Angeles.

Ogden, P. (2009). Emotion, mindfulness, and movement: Expanding the regulatory boundaries of the window of tolerance. In D. Fosha, D. Siegel, & M. Solomon (Eds.), *The healing power of emotion: Affective neuroscience and clinical practice* (pp. 204–231). New York: Norton.

Ogden, P., Minton, K., & Pain, C. (2006). *Trauma and the body: A sensorimotor approach to psychotherapy*. New York: Norton.

Schore, A. N. (1994). *Affect regulation and the origin of the self: The neurobiology of emotional development.* Hillsdale, NJ: Lawrence Erlbaum.

Schore, A. N. (2009). Right-brain affect regulation: An essential mechanism of development, trauma, dissociation, and psychotherapy. In D. Fosha, D. J. Siegel, & M. Solomon (Eds.), *The healing power of emotion: Affective neuroscience, development and clinical practice* (pp. 112–144). New York: Norton.

Schore, A. N. (2011). The right brain implicit self lies at the core of psychoanalysis. *Psychoanalytic Dialogues, 21,* 1–26.

Siegel, D. J. (2010). *The mindful therapist: A clinician's guide to mindsight and neural integration.* New York: Norton.

Solomon, M. (1994). *Lean on me: The power of positive dependency in intimate relationships.* New York: Simon and Schuster.

Stark, M. (2009, March). *Optimal stress: Stronger at the broken places.* Paper presented at the 8th annual conference at UCLA, Los Angeles.

Todd, M. E. (1937/1959). *The thinking body.* New York, NY: Dance Horizons.

Van der Hart, O. (2012). The use of imagery in phase 1 treatment of clients with complex dissociative disorders. *European Journal of Psychotraumatology, 3,* 8458.

Chapter 11

MOVEMENT VOCABULARY, PLAY, AND CREATIVITY

Go and play. Run around. Build something. Break something.
Climb a tree. Get dirty. Get in some trouble. Have some fun.

G. BROM

To be creative is to experiment with new ideas, concepts, activities, and actions in ways that transcend rules and habitual modes of thinking, feeling, and moving. Existing norms must be inhibited in favor of taking the risks that will challenge learned ways of being. As Anna Freud said, "Creative minds have always been known to survive any kind of bad training." We must relinquish what we know as we go outside our comfort zone to teeter on the edge of our "windows of tolerance" (Siegel, 1999) where uncertainty reigns. However, human beings are clearly creatures of habit. The manner in which we think, feel, and act is based on early learning, in the context of our families and sociocultural groups, and established into routines over time. Habits, including those of movement, gesture, and posture, afford us a sense of security and safety in that they are adaptations to environmental conditions (familial and sociocultural), implicitly designed and proven to produce optimal outcomes. At the familial level, for example, if a child's attachment figures tout stoicism, the body and breath of the child may constrict in an effort to conceal vulnerable emotions, winning the acceptance of attachment figures. Similarly, if a child is a member of a marginalized group, such as a refugee in a country where people are prejudiced against refugees, physical patterns will be affected. The child may also conceal emotions and constrict their movements and breath in preparation for unsafe interactions with members of the dominant culture. Such habits, if unexamined, persist into the future and across contexts regardless of whether they are adaptive to current conditions or not, squelching our vitality and inhibiting novelty.

To be playful and creative is to challenge fixed, habitual responses so we can move, think, and feel in new, unfamiliar ways—to seek out and grapple with the risks that enliven us by their unpredictability and expand our windows of tolerance. This requires a spacious window to start with, and then meeting the challenges expands the window further. However, the width of each person's window changes according to context, the people they are with, and their relative sense of safety. A person's window of tolerance generally narrows in unsafe contexts and, in turn, their hypervigilance may increase with alertness to possible threat cues, which compromises the capacity for play and creativity. Those who belong to marginalized groups may be vigilant for signs of discrimination, prejudice, or incipient aggression and violence from members of the dominant culture, which also compromises the width of the window.

The borders of a window of tolerance lie at the edges of hyper- and hypoarousal. If our windows are wide enough, we can tolerate and be present with the uncertainty and novelty inherent in play and creative endeavors without our arousal reaching extremes of hyper- or hypoarousal. The width of each window is directly related to how much stimulation is required to elicit a threshold

The novelty of play and creativity challenges habitual responses, which can stimulate both arousal and emotions to the edges of the window of tolerance. By hanging out with the unpredictability of arousal at the edges, we challenge our comfort zone and expand our windows.

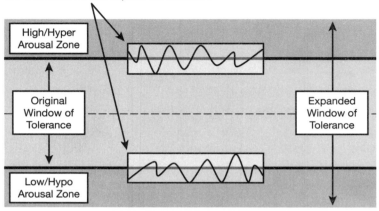

Figure 11.1: The Expanded Window of Tolerance   *Source: Ogden and Minton (2000); term coined by Daniel J. Siegel (1999)*

of response. If we have a generally wide window, meaning our threshold of response to stimulation is relatively high, we welcome and even relish the greater extremes of both high and low arousal even as the regulatory boundaries of the window are challenged. If our window is narrow, we have a lower threshold of response and are likely to experience arousal at the edges as unmanageable and dysregulating. Moreover, the width of our windows naturally fluctuates throughout the day and across contexts, but if we have a relatively spacious window, we can process complex and stimulating information more effectively. It is worth noting that the width of our windows of tolerance is inevitably dependent on historical, past, and present stressors and trauma experiences, including those current triggers related to our social identities and the dynamics of power and privilege.

If we had caregivers and communities to which we felt we

belonged who provided either comfort or stimulation as needed to prevent our arousal from remaining uncomfortably high or low for long periods of time, we are likely to have generally more spacious windows. Such caregivers and community not only help a child recover from negative states of distress, fatigue, and discomfort, but also actively engage in play, producing "an amplification, an intensification of positive emotion, a condition necessary for more complex self-organization" (Schore, 2003, p. 78). Through these salubrious early experiences with attachment figures and other persons of significance, we develop an internal confidence in our ability to regulate wide variances in arousal and respond flexibly to any number and kind of stimuli. This nourishes a safe base inside ourselves that can be relied upon throughout the life span as the ground from which we can effortlessly seek out the novelty that expands our windows even more. In the face of oppressive and hostile situations, this base provides a cushion we can rely on, which can potentially mitigate further stress and trauma.

In 1952, Roger Sperry stated, "The brain is an organ of and for movement. The brain is the organ that moves the muscles. It does many other things, but all of them are secondary to making our bodies move" (p. 298). In fact, only organisms that move from one location to another require a brain; and the brain depends on movement for its development (Ratey, 2002). The immediate action we make, whether reaching for a paintbrush or shaking our heads "no" at the thought of an art class, is determined by what we expect to happen in the very next instant or the future in general. Our brains continually compare the wealth of sensory stimulation from our immediate environment to memories of the past in order to make an action adaptive to present circumstance (Llinas, 2001). Movement habits reflect predictions about what is to come based on the repeated experiences of our past, the result of fitting sensory input into learned categories. Ratey (2002, p. 55) has pointed out that "we are constantly priming our perceptions, matching the

world to what we expect to sense and thus making it what we perceive it to be."

Movement patterns are also affected by our caregivers' history,
through transgenerational transmission of that history, epigenetics,
and because as children we imitate the movement of attachment
figures. When actions become routine, they are relegated to procedural learned behaviors, and we no longer use top-down cognitive processes to regulate them, leaving our minds free to learn and
tend to novel stimuli. Without the expectations that influence perceptual priming, each experience would be completely novel, and
although we might engage in unique and creative ways with the
world, we could become quickly overwhelmed by the vast amount
of new information. So procedural habits are necessary, but they can
constrain our movement vocabulary, which is analogous to verbal
vocabulary: If we know a variety of words and are capable of using
them effectively in different contexts, we have an extensive verbal
vocabulary. If we have a wide variety of different movements at our
disposal and can use them effectively to express ourselves in different contexts, we have an extensive movement vocabulary. Movement vocabulary is not linked to our physical ability or body ability,
but to the extent of physical expression, from micromovement to
macromovement, from the internal experience of a slight movement to those that are more visible externally.

When our movement vocabulary is truncated or limited, so are
impulses to play and inhabit our creativity. Our movement vocabulary can also be constrained when the context is not welcoming
or feels unsafe, as might be the case when a member of a marginalized group interacts with persons of the dominant culture. In
this instance, the movement vocabulary might be expressed differently by the two groups, since the movement for the marginalized
group may show more constriction when interacting, while dominant group members in general have greater permission to exhibit a
wider movement vocabulary, for instance, taking up more space or

touching more readily and frequently (Johnson, 2015; Johnson et al., 2018). An extensive movement vocabulary of flexible and variable physical actions, the capacity to intuitively know when to engage those movements, and the awareness to interrupt procedural habits when different actions could be more adaptive all support creativity. However, we must keep in mind that social and cultural priming strongly influence intuition, and may in fact be the basis for intuitive decision and movements (Wippich, 1994). Thus, priming may induce intuition that engenders a movement that may or may not be the most adaptive response in a particular context or to a particular stimulus. This chapter explores the interface between arousal tolerance, movement vocabulary, creativity, and play, and how to use movement to inspire the creative impulse that resides within us all.

THE ROLE OF MOVEMENT

Through movement, the fetus, infant, child, and adult continually learn about themselves, others, and the world in an ongoing interactive dance. Each interaction, each movement adjustment, communicates one's location in space, the nature of human relationships, and one's place in the world. Over time, we develop movement memory,

> achieved from a sophisticated feedback system that detects errors made as the movement is learned. The feedback system uses these errors as a basis from which to generate a new, more accurate [or adaptive] sequence of commands, eventually leading to a successful performance. We modify and learn through movement every second of our waking day whether we are active or inactive. (Ratey, 2002, p. 205)

Movement memory develops gradually and is obvious in such tasks as tying shoelaces or playing a musical instrument, but often not so clear in subtle physical accommodations to environmental, sociocultural, and interpersonal cues. For instance, if a child enthusiastically gesticulates and puffs up their chest while describing their latest fantasy but is met with the caregiver's admonishment to stop making things up, a disapproving facial expression, or a pulling back of the caregiver's body, the child's expanded chest may deflate, the movements become restricted, and the excitement may vanish from the child's voice and eyes. Likewise, a similar constriction can occur in a child of color who is subject to racial profiling or repeated microaggressions such as messages from from teachers, peers, or the media that the child's ideas are not worthy or welcomed. Any child who does not conform to the norm may become a target of microaggressions, microinvalidations, prejudice, or discrimination that are so impactful that movement habits are affected. Based on cultural prejudice, these attitudes are often communicated to the child nonverbally, such as by disapproving facial expressions or the pulling back of the other person's body. If such interactions are repeated over time, the child's body may become habitually constrained in dominant spaces, or possibly chronically constrained no matter the context. Mable Todd (1959) emphasized that function precedes structure: The same movement made repeatedly will ultimately mold the body. A constrained movement vocabulary does not fully support these qualities, thus imagination, playfulness, and spontaneity may be truncated, especially in particular contexts, for children who endure hurtful or demeaning experiences.

An embodied sense of self develops through the call and response of movement dialogue between the child and significant others, including attachment figures, peers, and sociocultural groups. "Good enough" attachment figures support the child's movement complexity so that "action sequences remain to some extent fluid and flexible throughout life; the nature of the consequences that are anticipated for a given action will change as the context of interaction changes and with development of the individual's powers"

(Bucci, 2011, p. 6). Thus, as our brains compare current information with past data, there is the possibility of an "upgrading" (Llinas, 2001, p. 38) of our movement, which expands our movement vocabulary further. However, schemas become more and more rigid in increasingly less functional environments, impeding new learning (Bucci, 2011) and constraining movement flexibility. Whether expansive or curtailed, the movement habits we form over time reflect and sustain implicit meanings and expectations, and thus can either encourage or inhibit creativity and play. The legacy of trauma, attachment failure, and sociocultural oppression, with their consequential neuropsychological deficits, impacts our bodies, can inhibit the development of our movement vocabulary, and restrict a fluid response to novelty.

Winnicott posited that psychotherapy clients could benefit from opportunities for "formless experience, and for creative impulses, motor and sensory, which are the stuff of playing" (1971, p. 64). It has been widely shown that movement can affect creativity. Lakoff and Johnson (1999) assert that concrete embodied experience is at the root of cognition, and that concepts are embodied in sensorimotor systems. For example, gestures can provide a direct representation of spatial relationships and have been shown both to boost the ability to solve spatial problems and to improve the ease and facility of verbal expression (Goldin-Meadow & Beilock, 2010). Even a repetitious movement like walking enhances creativity. Opezzo and Schwartz (2014) found that going for a walk, especially outdoors, increased creative thinking by over 50%, as measured by the ability to generate an analogy. They concluded, "Walking opens up the free flow of ideas, and it is a simple and robust solution to the goals of increasing creativity" (p. 1142). Cognitive scientists often correlate fluidity of thought with creativity and play (Hofstadter, 1995). Slepian and Ambady hypothesized that "fluid, creative thinking is grounded in fluid movement" (2012, p. 1). They explored the relationship between fluid movements of the arm (while the subject drew continuous, curved, and smooth patterns) and creative thought, finding that three areas were strengthened by fluid movement: creative generation, cognitive flexibility, and the ability to make remote connections. The authors noted, "Fluid movement enhanced creative but not analytic performance (only the former requires fluid thought)" (p. 4).

Similarly, a variety of cross-cultural and cross-species studies show that spontaneous, fluid movements are characteristic of play and signal other members of the social environment to play as well. These include a relaxed, open body posture and a tilting of the head, often accompanied by a whimsical expression on the face (Bekoff & Allen, 1998; Caldwell, 2003; Donaldson, 1993). The physical movements of play are more random, fluid, and nonstereotyped. They change quickly and are spontaneously expressed in children and animals in a variety of leaps, rolls, and rotational movements (Goodall, 1995). In contrast, movements characteristic of non-playful or overly serious interactions tend to be constrained, stereotyped, rigid, agitated, or nervous (Bekoff & Byers, 1998; Brown, 1995).

It follows that psychotherapy that directly works to expand movement awareness and vocabulary might enhance the capacity for play and creativity. As clients explore their movement vocabulary and practice movements that are unfamiliar, the new action becomes easier and more familiar, thus increasing the availability of a wider variety of actions. Clients increase their intuitive options in response to internal and environmental cues, although this choice is not cognitive; it arises from a felt sense in the body of expanded movement possibilities.

Bainbridge-Cohen's (1993) five fundamental movements—yield, push, reach, grasp, and pull—provide a useful map for exploring physical actions that may have been interrupted or curtailed by familial and sociocultural constraints. Expanding movement repertoire to include varieties of all five actions in turn can foster the capacity for creativity and play. Each action is described below and illustrated through case examples of clients who either overuse the action or have difficulty engaging it. How the therapist worked to help clients explore these movements is explained, with the understanding that reclaiming these actions and engaging them effectively and with ease, would increase creativity and play.

Yield

To yield means to let go, to release the body into contact with an object, the ground, or another person. We yield our weight to the force of gravity, letting go into the support of the ground; we yield to the care of another, or to the comfort of our beds as we fall asleep at night. When securely attached, infants experience a sense of safety in the arms of the caregiver, they are able to sink into the caregiver's body and receive support and care. The capacity to actively relax in contact rather than passively becoming immobile is the hallmark of yielding (Aposhyan, 1998). This relaxation is accompanied by a slight increase in muscular tone in the part of the body in contact with the person or object (Bainbridge-Cohen, 1993, para. 2). Yield is a restful, alert state that encompasses qualities of receptivity, trust, surrender, release, and the taking in of nourishment. Although Frank (2011) asserts that a releasing or letting-go action is a sixth fundamental movement, distinct from yielding, their qualities are equivalent; both letting go and release pertain to a relaxed, alert sense of surrender, of being rather than doing. Thus, releasing and letting go are considered to be subsumed into the movement of yielding (Aposhyan, 2004). The body is at peace, the muscles let go, the breathing is deep, perhaps with an extended exhale. The dorsal vagal system, a primitive branch of the parasympathetic nervous system that promotes rest and low or hypoarousal, is co-opted for quiet contact with the environment, with another, or with ourselves. When others induce or join us in these deeply pleasurable low-arousal states, our window of tolerance expands.

To be grounded—to make a physical connection with the force of gravity, so that the energy of the body is drawn downward—is to yield. Grounding is the concrete sensation of connecting to the earth, as our body responds to the pull of gravity by settling downward, much as the water in a pitcher sinks to the bottom, the lowest level. Yielding necessitates trust and relinquishing control; we yield not only to gravity, but to another's ministrations (as in relaxing into a hug or massage), to an internal impulse, such as to curl up, or to an external stimulation like enjoying the sound of beautiful music. In such a receptive state, the mind can wander and the imagination can flourish. We become open to receive new ideas, new ways of thinking, feeling, envisioning, and acting. Possibilities expand. The ah-hah moment often emerges from yield in which the mind drifts, the body relaxes, and both become deeply receptive to information that is unavailable in an active doing state. The ability to yield is thus an essential quality of certain elements of creativity.

Associated with letting go, releasing, and letting down, yielding requires an even, relaxed muscle tone, with a natural slight increase of tone at points of contact. However, if our muscles are lax and our bodies collapsed, yielding is compromised. Alternatively, if our muscles are tense and our bodies braced, yielding is also compromised. Some of us may fluctuate between these two conditions.

Lucy, a cisgender, African American woman, found it difficult to relax, especially at her job as a case manager at a nonprofit serving young adults in foster care. Lucy had hoped that the leadership of such an organization would be aware of organizational racism and the risks of meritocracy. However, it became evident that Lucy's colleagues of color were often passed over for promotions even when their job performance exceeded that of white case managers. In session, her body was stiff and her movements were constricted, telegraphing a nonverbal message of discomfort and stress. The tension throughout her body, and especially across her hunched shoulders, echoed her words that she could not let down her guard. She shared that she moved quickly from one task to the next, her best friend called her a workaholic, and her husband complained that she could not enjoy downtime. Lucy reported that as a child she was constantly worried about failing to meet her parents' dictum that as an African American child, she needed to "work twice as hard to get half as far." She had been full of silent anxiety and although she did perform well, her high-achieving family had sometimes pushed her ahead faster than her developmental skills warranted. Lucy's energy was mobilized up and out, rather than settled down into a restful and rejuvenating yield. This pattern was developed from learning that she must work harder than others and avoid making mistakes to excel in a white-dominated world. Her fear of disappointing her parents and not being successful were impediments to her creativity, spontaneity, and playfulness.

On the other hand, Jerry, a white, cisgender male, raised in an affluent family by a heterosexual couple, experienced a chronic shutdown or feigned death response, and he described himself as collapsed and "spaced out." Yielding is a form of inaction or immobilization without fear, but the feigned death response to trauma is immobilization with fear, when the dorsal vagal system is aroused to foster stillness in the hope of preventing demise (Porges, 2011). Jerry grew up in a verbally and occasionally physically abusive environment from which there was no escape, nor the possibility of fighting back, so the feign death or shut-down defense was the most viable. In addition, Jerry contended with high expectations that he perform well to make the family proud, as his father was a renowned surgeon. Jerry experienced chronic anxiety from being unemployed (i.e., laid off) and had a constant feeling of failing. Thus, several factors contributed to his collapsed posture: the feelings of failure, the shut-down response to abuse, and his emulating the carriage of his mother, who displayed a similar collapsed posture in response to the father's abuse. Jerry said he felt stuck, collapsed, and shut down when he tried to relax and became anxious when trying to fall asleep at night, which might be due to increased dorsal vagal tone, which can promote relaxation but is coupled with fear in the face of trauma. Instead of a true yield, Jerry experienced immobilization with fear, which induces flaccid muscles that accompany a feigned death response to threat, leaving him feeling collapsed, uncomfortably numb, and often unable to think clearly. Receptivity to novelty was lost, and the renewal that can come from a true yield was compromised.

Both Lucy and Jerry needed to learn the action of yielding. In therapy, Lucy explored "doing nothing" by allowing her body to rest into the sofa and taking slow breaths with a slightly longer exhale. Lucy first noticed impulses to move, uneasy emotions (nervousness, anxiety), and thoughts of, "You're lazy. You're wasting time." She and her therapist worked through the pressure she had felt from her parents that had been present "as far back as I can remember," which impeded her ability to yield. At the same time they acknowledged acknowledged her experience that she did need to work harder as an African American woman in a white-dominant society, as her parents had said. She placed her hands gently on her torso, using her own touch to soothe her anxiety and connect with the core of her body, sensing herself more deeply. Lucy felt compassion for the stress she had experienced that had continued until today. Gradually, Lucy began to feel and enjoy the sensations of her muscles relaxing and her breath deepening as her energy settled, releasing the weight of her body to the force of gravity, sensing the points of contact. Yielding provided her with more range of movement overall, instead of just upward and forward movements. In contrast, Jerry learned to sense the support of the chair under him, feeling how his thighs and buttocks met the surface of the chair. Tuning into the sensation of his body and the support of the chair helped Jerry find an active yield, and he spontaneously sat taller instead of slumping. This posture was very different from his usual collapsed body and shutdown state, which he had described as "letting go into nothingness," because he learned to let go, not collapse, into support. His ability to yield continued to develop as he worked with the pushing action.

Push

Yielding allows for the release of weight into a solid foundation of support beneath us, which provides stability and leverage to push against, and thus is the foundation for pushing actions. Pushing, to be fully effective, emerges from letting go of the yield, and requires a contraction of the body. Pushing is executed as the infant comes into contact with the environment and feels the sensation of the body against an external boundary. Pushing occurs in many ways. The fetus pushes with head and feet, lengthening the body, to be born, and later, the same pushing action enables an upright posture. Aligned posture requires a gentle push upward with the top of the head and downward into the pelvic floor in a seated position, or into the soles of the feet in a standing position. This upright posture supports the spine to do its job as the physical core of the body that provides support and stability to the entire physical structure and serves as an axis around which the limbs and head can move.

The first movements of an infant are initiated in the core of the body and radiate out to the periphery, then contract back inward to the core. These movements strengthen the core (Aposhyan, 2004; Bainbridge-Cohen, 1993), and later the vertical push when sitting and standing also develops the core. Kurtz and Prestera (1976, p. 33) note that the core of the body, the spine, has a psychological meaning as the "place inside" to which we may "go for sustenance." Frank explains that as we push, "the experience of weight condenses at the origin of the push, whether at head or tailbone, arms and hands, or legs and feet, as the act of pushing compresses tissues of the body" (2011, p. 26). Our physical sensation is intensified with a pushing action, which helps us experience the density of our bodies.

We push out in a variety of ways—with our arms, legs, spine, eyes, energy, and even breath. We push to create distance, separate, set a boundary, to protect and defend ourselves. The pushing action asserts our will and is often associated with the word "no," which facilitates not only protection but also differentiation, self-identity, and self-support. We learn who we are by saying no (pushing away) to some stimuli while being receptive (yielding) to others. From an individualistic development perspective (cf. Chapter 1, this volume), pushing is critical for differentiating from others and developing our self-identity as autonomous. From this viewpoint, the ability to push is seen as nourishing a locus of control inside ourselves, and a feeling of command over our participation with the environment, which is considered essential in playful interactions (Fisher et al., 1991; Levy, 1978). However, from a collectivist perspective, the focus is less on autonomy and more on connectedness, which can include self-awareness, sensitivity to others' needs, and ability to listen and work together for the good of all. Under this construct, what is important is not just the push, but the creative interplay between the person, the others, and the environment, shown as the capacity to push and let go alternatively in a dialogue.

Pushing is compromised by pushing either too much or too little, both of which limit the capacity to listen and respond creatively to both internal and environmental cues. If our spines remain chronically slumped (insufficient push from head to feet), the core may remain undeveloped, and the sense of one's boundaries and preferences indistinct. Without the foundation of an upright posture and the capacity to respond relationally and creatively to others and the environment through the yield-push dialogue, play and creativity are absent, or at least jeopardized. We may feel uncertain, inadequate, needy, or passive. Jerry's spine was perpetually slumped, turning his yield into a collapse, as previously described. He also had trouble saying no to any requests that came his way. In contrast, a military stance is an exaggerated push, inducing feelings of inflexibility, being on guard and ready to defend. This comes with a price if the stance is chronic. For marginalized people, being vigilant to the ever-present possibility of threat, especially in dominant spaces, can be a necessity. Being on guard, with concomitant tension and arousal, is likely a factor in studies showing that racism and oppression are linked to adverse mental and physical health outcomes (Williams et al., 2019). Sometimes, an overstated push without a chance to let down or yield, can diminish emotional intimacy in that it conveys a consistent message of "keep out" or "no."

Jonah, a South Asian cisgender male, often made the gesture of putting his hands up, palms out, in front of his body. This habitual gesture, along with a stiff, rigid posture, reflected a need to be in control and keep stimuli, including other people, at bay, habits that Jonah had developed during his demanding childhood. Jonah was the oldest of three children whose parents both worked long hours, thus making many caregiving and household tasks Jonah's responsibility. Both Jerry and Jonah needed to yield, then to develop a balanced, integrated push. As described above, Jerry first learned to yield by connecting with the support of the chair under him, and then sensing the support of the ground in a standing position. He learned to push off this base as he pressed into the ground with the soles of his feet, and he also pushed upward through the top of his head, which strengthened his core and aligned his posture. Maintaining an upright posture, he practiced a "no" gesture by pushing with his arms against a pillow held by his therapist, an action that was weak and ineffective from a collapsed posture but strong and clear from the upright posture gained by pressing downward and upward simultaneously. Jonah learned to yield by relaxing his tense body and releasing his weight into the ground so that he could rest or yield into the support beneath him. Again, from this yield action, he could develop a relaxed and flexible push through his spine. He practiced inhibiting his exaggerated and off-putting (to others) pushing motion in favor of letting go into a yield, and then executing the pushing motion while sensing support. This allowed the capacity to interact with the therapist and with others in a more resourced, connected, playful, and creative way.

Reach

Seeking proximity is the hallmark of attachment behavior. Bowlby (1982) observed that the attachment drive secures the nearness of attachment figures through approach behavior, such as reaching, which, along with grasping and pulling, is designed to bring one closer to another person. Whether or not a child reaches out is "based on that person's forecasts of how accessible and responsive his attachment figures are likely to be should he turn to them for support" (Bowlby, 1973, p. 203). Reaching is also connected to desire and satisfaction of needs; when the child feels safe to explore their environment, they can reach for what they need (food, water, connection, and so forth.). The norms of what can be reached for or not are defined by both family dynamics and the culture that the family is embedded in. Thus, reaching, like all of the five movements, is adapted and modified in accordance with the response of caregivers and other important people in a child's life, as well as sociocultural and community norms.

However, to reach has implications beyond seeking nearness to attachment figures. Aposhyan writes, "Reaching is the way we extend out into space, toward others, toward objects. It is our ability to go beyond ourselves. Psychologically, reaching manifests curiosity, longing, desire, compassion" (1998, p. 69). A reaching movement speaks to the desire to connect with another person or object in the environment. As we reach, we act on that desire, lengthening our limbs or spine to extend toward what we want. When a reach is supported by the previous action, a push, the reach can be full and grounded. The reach could be thought of as symbolically saying yes to a person or object, but even that yes can be only partially embodied if not supported by the push. Without the support of a push (evident in a lengthened spine), the reach may have an empty, needy, or demanding quality that is not grounded. As previously stated, the push helps us differentiate ourselves and determine what we want to say no to, without which we cannot fully say yes with a reach.

When an object or person is available for contact, literally within reach, then we can develop confidence in this action's efficacy. However, reaching, like all actions, is strongly influenced by culture and privilege/oppression dynamics. We can consider, for example, who is encouraged or even allowed to reach toward what they want in the larger sociocultural context, and who is not. If a person from a marginalized location reaches out for what they desire and want, their reach may be consistently unmet or penalized by society at large or individuals of the dominant culture. For example, if an African American reaches out to their banker to obtain a loan, their application may be met with unfounded rejection—studies show that African American loan applicants are denied more than twice as often as white applicants (Yale, 2018, para. 1). Reach can also be associated with a sense of power of ownership as well as feelings of entitlement, which can lead to reaching for what one wants without regard for others. For example, historically, men have been socialized to feel they are entitled to free access to women's bodies, which can cause them to ignore a woman's protest as they reach out for physical contact, and can contribute to sexualized violence. Such dynamics, and more, may come into play to impact the therapeutic relationship.

Depending on the previous two actions (yield and push) and the negative repercussions of past attempts to reach, we may be unable to reach out to others in a relaxed, tenacious, confident manner: with palms up, our arms fully extended in a way that conveys openness and assurance that our reaching will have a positive outcome. We may have a willingness to extend, but reach out with a stiff arm, palm down, braced shoulders, or a rigid spine, already expecting an undesirable result. Or we may show reluctance and reach out weakly, shoulders rounded, holding the elbow close to the waist rather than fully extending the arm. These styles of reaching inhibit creativity in different ways: One might symbolize a bracing against the unknown; the other might symbolize a "why bother" or giving-up attitude. We may withdraw from relationships and from the world, shun physical contact, and have a hard time extending ourselves. Without the confidence to reach into the unknown, and tolerance for the positive stress that accompanies uncertainty, our creativity and capacity to play can be hampered. Reaching, like all actions, is context dependent. As we mentioned above, belonging to a marginalized group can make the reach harder to embody in certain situations when the probability is high that reaching out for help or for connection may lead to disappointment, ridicule, or even violence. Reaching also may be perceived as a threat by people in the privileged culture, and thus the person may be punished for reaching, whereas in the context of family and close friends, reaching is received and can be easily embodied.

Mike, a 30-year-old white cisgender man, was a self-described loner. He suffered from chronic pain following injuries sustained from a car accident in adolescence that left him bedridden for several months and ended his dreams of becoming a basketball star. Mike said reaching out to others had never been a positive experience, especially after his accident. He struggled with depression and negative self-image following the collision, which led him to withdraw from others. In his current life, Mike was reluctant to initiate conversations, avoided eye contact, and often tightened his shoulders and leaned away from the other person when approached. Mike reported that he was averse to participating in playful or creative activities with others. He sought therapy at the request of his wife, who expressed a wish for more connection with him. When his therapist asked him to try reaching out, he found it unfamiliar and uncomfortable and did so awkwardly and stiffly, palm facing down. During his therapy Mike experimented with reaching out toward his therapist, with and without eye contact, noticing and processing his physical reactions, emotions, beliefs ("I am not normal"), and early memories of rejection. Through this often emotionally painful work, Mike's expectation of being rebuffed if he sought connection became less absolute, and after a time he could reach toward his therapist without ambivalence, which carried over to more contact with his wife.

On the other hand, Blanca (a Latina) and her partner, Jenn (white), came to therapy to improve their intimacy and communication. Blanca said she felt "crowded" because Jenn was "demanding and needy." When their therapist asked Jenn to reach out to Blanca, she leaned forward enthusiastically, with full extension of her arms and eager eye contact. She said she wanted to move closer to Blanca, who pulled back, which Jenn interpreted as rejection. As the therapist instructed Jenn to sit back in her chair and try reaching with a slightly bent elbow, Jenn said she didn't think Blanca would "be there" unless she really "engaged." In fact, the opposite was true; Blanca felt the impulse to reach back when Jenn's reach was less intense. Jenn reported that in childhood she needed to "create a fuss" in order to get her parents to pay attention to her, but she slowly learned that when she reached out in a more spacious and relaxed manner, Blanca was able to move toward her more fully instead of pulling away.

Grasp

Once a reach is executed, the obvious progression of that action is to grasp or hold on to the object of the reaching and, through the grasp, to discover the nature of the thing or person. Thus, grasping is reaching fulfilled, the natural outcome of reaching, and these two actions are complementary. Frank (2011, p. 29) clarifies: "Whereas reaching brings with it the risk of moving to the edge of and beyond one's kinesphere, grasping can reestablish balance by holding on to what is grasped." A child needing reassurance reaches for and holds on to the caregiver, who responds in kind, reaching back and grasping the child, who then regains a sense of security and equilibrium. Once the reached-for object is within grasp, holding on to it affords exploration with senses not only of

392 THE POCKET GUIDE TO SENSORIMOTOR PSYCHOTHERAPY IN CONTEXT

sight but also of touch, smell, and sometimes sound or taste. In a sense, to grasp is to hold on to the object of our desire and to gain understanding through discovery, as in the colloquialism "to have a solid grasp of something." To grasp something is to increase our understanding of it, to get to know its quality and significance through our senses. If the object is consistently out of reach—either physically or psychologically, as in too many restrictions levied by caregivers—confidence in this fulfillment and knowledge is truncated. A child also cannot reap the benefits of grasping if control is exerted such a way that the child in only allowed to explore what the caregiver chooses, rather than what the child chooses. Objects and opportunities can also be unobtainable because of cultural norms, racial biases, and oppressive systems that hold back groups of people in a variety of ways—financially, professionally, personally, and socially.

While reaching out can be a challenge for many clients, grasping and holding on can be equally challenging. Francine, a cisgender granddaughter of Holocaust survivors, did not want to hold on to anything. She had not sustained a relationship longer than a year, kept most of her friendships superficial, and was not attached to her possessions. When her best friend told her he felt "disposable," Francine sought help for her "commitment problem." In therapy, Francine chose a pillow to symbolically represent her friend. She placed the pillow in her lap, resting her hands on top of it, although her therapist had suggested that she try grasping it while imagining it as a symbol for her friend. Squirming as she struggled to grasp the pillow, Francine was clearly uncomfortable. She discovered she correlated holding on with being needy: "Better to let go than hold on" were her words. Francine had heard stories of loss during her entire childhood from stoic parents who had learned to survive, as had their parents, by keeping their grief and their needs at bay. Neediness was an unacceptable trait in Francine's family, which she associated with holding on, and which manifested in her inability to commit. Learning to hold on meant acknowledging that the person or object was important to her, facing her own need and the unresolved grief from the losses of historical and transgenerational trauma.

For Marshall, a white, cisgender gay man, reaching, grasping, and clinging were much more comfortable than pushing-away and letting-go/yielding actions. His boyfriend told him that he was too clingy and implied that this drove him away. As a child, Marshall had been teased by the older children, so much so that he did not want to leave his mother. He was afraid to go on playdates, a fear his parents brushed off, saying, "Don't be silly—you'll have fun." He remembered clinging to his mother and pleading with her not to make him go outside to play with the neighborhood children. In therapy, Marshall explored clinging (an easy, comfortable action for him) to a pillow. Slowly, he tried to release his grip, into an exploratory grasp instead of a desperate holding on, a simple action that he described as surprisingly scary. Grasping tightly gave him a sense of security, but grasping loosely thrust him back into implicit memories of his early years, just as holding on tightly did for Francine. Over several sessions, Marshall explored grasping tightly and loosely in slow motion, which brought the painful issues of his childhood that had led to clinging behavior to the surface so that they could be processed. Eventually loosening his tight grip into a more exploratory holding one became comfortable and even nourishing for him.

Pull

Pulling involves bringing an object or person closer to oneself, and/or bringing oneself closer to an object or person, and thus is also a proximity-seeking action. Pulling makes one thing or person move toward another person. Early actions of grasp and pull occur as the baby grasps the nipple with the mouth and pulls the milk by sucking, or as a tiny fist grasps the caregiver's little finger and pulls it to the mouth. We can pull with the mouth, eyes, or facial expression, as well as with the hands and arms. Pulling actions symbolize the satisfaction of getting what we want, of claiming it and owning it for ourselves. Pulling enables close proximity, which facilitates deeper exploration of the sensory elements of the object or person— smell, taste, and possibly sound. Thus, it expands knowledge of the object or person through the senses.

Margaret, a white cisgender client who had recently graduated from college, was worried about finding a good job. As she spoke about her desire, her therapist asked her to make motions of reaching out and then bringing her arms toward her torso as if drawing something that she wanted in toward her chest. Her therapist asked her to repeat that motion mindfully, exploring it for meaning and memories. Margaret found words that went along with this pulling movement: "taking in" and "claiming what I want." She talked of growing up "poor" and being raised by a single mother. Working minimum wage jobs meant that Margaret and her mom were always on the brink of not having enough to meet their basic needs. Margaret remembered feeling ashamed as a child because she wanted more than what her mom could provide for them. Her learned beliefs and shame in reaction to poverty conditioned her relationship with current opportunities, impairing her openness to take advantage of what was available. Practicing a pulling motion while imagining having the right to claim what she wanted challenged the belief that she didn't deserve wealth. Eventually, engaging this motion fully expanded her confidence in getting a job she wanted and enabled a more creative response to opportunities that came her way.

To pull something or someone toward us means to literally take what we believe to be our right. From this perspective, to pull has to do with positive entitlement. In pulling an object toward our person, we actualize the sense of having a right or claim to that which is pulled. It speaks to an inherent sense of deserving to have that object or person. In the negative sense, it can pertain to claiming something that is not our right to claim. Tanner, a white, upper-class, cisgender male, came to therapy because he felt great remorse after coming to the realization that having sex with his partner when she was intoxicated and unable to give consent constituted rape. His partner did not want to end the relationship but required couple therapy. As Tanner explored the pulling motion with a rope held by his partner, he pulled rather aggressively and said, "She is my girlfriend. I have a right to her." Tanner could not discriminate what was appropriate to pull toward himself or to feel satisfied (yield) from the pulling action. In therapy, Tanner revealed that men had dominated the women in his family; he had learned that women were there to serve him. To challenge this socialization, he and his partner tried a pulling motion with the rope, taking turns pulling the other closer, noticing and adjusting to the other person, and addressing their own reactions. Over time Tanner developed sensitivity to his partner, and could engage a graceful give-and-take, pull-and-yield motion that was mutually satisfying.

Alan, a young Asian American man, found it easy to reach and grasp a pillow that represented something he wanted, held by his therapist. But as his therapist encouraged him to pull the pillow toward him, he said, "Why? It will just get taken away." Alan had problems following through with his actions—he would begin going for what he wanted, such as learning to play the saxophone, but would soon abandon the activity. He grew up as an army brat, and his family had constantly changed locations. He had learned not to go after what he wanted since he would lose it anyway when they moved yet again. In addition, he acutely experienced a feeling of futility that opportunities were denied him that were available to his white counterparts, reporting being passed over for a job he wanted in favor of a white man who was less qualified. The simple act of reaching for, grasping, and then pulling a pillow toward himself brought up his grief for all he had lost, the hopelessness he experienced in a white-dominated society, and elucidated his strategy of not trying to claim anything as his own. Once he was able to process his grief and gain insight into his strategy, pulling in what he wanted became easier.

A pulling action should naturally lead to a yield as it is the completion of the action cycle of yield, push, reach, grasp, and pull. We spontaneously relax into the satisfaction of accomplishment and of receiving once we reach for, grasp, and pull to ourselves that which we want, whether it is a job, a person, or an object. However, when we are able to pull toward us what we want and perhaps achieve success after success in our lives, but are unable to experience the satisfaction of completion of that action, we cannot yield into and savor the satisfaction of our success.

CONCLUSION

It should be clear by now that these five basic movements spontaneously emerge in sequence (yield, push, reach, grasp, and pull) and each depends on the previous ones for its ultimate execution. The support afforded by yielding enables pushing; a full push is the foundation for reaching, and the natural outcome of reaching is grasping, which is organically followed by pulling whatever is grasped toward oneself. And, finally, pulling morphs into releasing the object that was pulled, in an action of yielding. All the actions we make can be conceptualized as intricate combinations of these five fundamental movements.

Our movement continually emerges in response to our ever-changing experience with others, the world, and ourselves, shifting moment to moment depending on whom we are with, our circumstances, internal state, predictions, and many other variables. Our actions, at their best, are economical and efficient, with effort appropriate to the task at hand. The movement itself proceeds efficiently beginning with its initiation, carried out through its execution, and ending with its completion, progressing easily into the next movement. Unnecessary muscular tension, flaccidity, or movements that contradict each other, like reaching out with the arms while pulling back with the upper body, are eliminated. When movement sequences are flexible and dynamic, we are better able to enthusiastically respond creatively to diverse and novel stimuli of varying intensity.

However, as illustrated, we develop habits of executing each of the five movements, as well as habits of moving through a combination or sequence of actions, that are useful for coping and filtering information but may limit our creativity and playfulness. As we have seen, these habits are also developed in response to contextual sociocultural circumstances and the interplay of the dynamics of power and privilege with oppression and marginalization. Thus, movement habits need to be explored, examined, and changed when they have become default behaviors over other actions that would be more adaptive and innovative in current contexts. A resilient movement vocabulary, with fluid access to the five fundamental movements and their combinations, enables us to welcome appropriate risks and respond to novelty in imaginative, life-enhancing ways. Our clients' response to novelty becomes ever more creative and playful when we can help them challenge their physical habits and develop expansive, innovative, flexible, and fluid movement vocabularies.

REFERENCES

Aposhyan, S. (1998). *Natural intelligence: Body-mind integration and human development*. Baltimore: Williams and Wilkins.

Aposhyan, S. (2004). *Body-mind psychotherapy: Principles, techniques, and practical applications*. New York: Norton.

Bainbridge-Cohen, B. (1993). *Sensing, feeling and action*. Northampton, MA: Contact Editions.

Bainbridge-Cohen, B. (n.d.). Yield versus collapse. Body-Mind Centering. https://www.bodymindcentering.com/yield-verse-collapse/

Bekoff, M., & Allen, C. (1998). Intentional communication and social play: How and why animals negotiate and agree to play. In M. Bekoff & J. Byers (Eds.), *Animal play: Evolutionary, comparative, and ecological perspectives* (pp. 97–114). New York: Cambridge University Press.

Bekoff, M., & Byers, J. (Eds.) (1998). *Animal play: Evolutionary, comparative, and ecological perspectives.* New York: Cambridge University Press.

Bowlby, J. (1973). *Attachment and loss: Vol. 2. Separation: Anxiety and anger.* New York: Basic Books.

Bowlby, J. (1982). *Attachment* (Vol. 1, 2nd ed.). New York: Basic Books.

Brown, S. (1995). Through the lens of play. *Revision, 17*(4), 4–14.

Bucci, W. (2011). The role of embodied communication in therapeutic change: A multiple code perspective. In W. Tschacher & C. Bergomi (Eds.), *The implications of embodiment: Cognition and communication* (pp. 209–228). Exeter, UK: Imprint Academic.

Caldwell, C. (2003). Adult group play therapy. In C. Schaefer (Ed.), *Play therapy with adults* (pp. 301–316). Hoboken, NJ: John Wiley & Sons.

Donaldson, F. (1993). *Playing by heart: The vision and practice of belonging.* Deerfield Beach, FL: Health Communications.

Fisher, A., Murray, E., & Bundy, A. (1991). *Sensory integration: Theory and practice.* Philadelphia: Davis.

Frank, R., & La Barre, F. (2011). The first year and the rest of your life: Movement, development, and psychotherapeutic change. New York: Routledge.

Goldin-Meadow, S., & Beilock, S. L. (2010). Action's influence on thought: The case of gesture. *Perspectives on Psychological Science, 5,* 664–674. doi:10.1177/1745691610388764

Goleman, D., P. Kaufman, & M. Ray. (1992). *The creative spirit.* New York: Penguin. Au: Not cited.

Goodall, J. (1995). Chimpanzees and others at play. *Revision, 17,* 14–20.

Hofstadter, D. R. (1995). *Fluid concepts and creative analogies: Computer models of the fundamental mechanisms of thought.* New York: Basic Books.

Johnson, R. (2015). Grasping and transforming the embodied experience of oppression. *International Body Psychotherapy Journal, 14*(1), 80–95.

Johnson, R., Leighton, L., & Caldwell, C. (2018). The embodied experience of microaggressions: Implications for clinical practice. *Journal of Multicultural Counseling and Development, 46*(3), 156–170.

Kurtz, R., & Prestera, H. (1976). *The body reveals: An illustrated guide to the psychology of the body.* New York: Holt, Rinehart and Winston.

Lakoff, G., & Johnson, N. (1999). *Philosophy in the flesh: The embodied mind and its challenge to western thought.* New York: Perseus.

Levy, J. (1978). *Play behavior.* New York: Wiley.

Llinas, R. (2001). *I of the vortex: From neurons to self.* Cambridge, MA: MIT Press.

Opezzo, M., & Schwartz, D. L. (2014). Give your ideas some legs: The positive effect of walking on creative thinking. *Journal of Experimental Psychology: Learning, Memory, and Cognition, 40*(4), 1142–1152.

Porges, S. W. (2011). *The polyvagal theory: Neurophysiological foundations of emotions, attachment, communication, and self-regulation.* New York: Norton.

Ratey, J. (2002). *A user's guide to the brain: Perception, attention, and the four theaters of the brain.* New York: Vintage.

Schore, A. (2003). *Affect dysregulation and disorders of the self.* New York: Norton.

Siegel, D. J. (1999). *The developing mind.* New York: Norton.

Slepian, M. L., & Ambady, N. (2012). Fluid movement and creativity. In *Journal of Experimental Psychology, 141*(4), 625–629. http://ambadylab.stanford.edu/pubs/Slepian-Ambady_Fluid-Movement-and-Creativity_%20in-press_JEPG.pdf

Sperry, R. W. (1952). Neurology and the mind-brain problem. *American Scientist, 40,* 291–312.

Williams, D. R., Lawrence, J. A., & Davis, B. A. (2019). Racism and health: Evidence and needed research. *Annual Review of Public Health, 40,* 105–125.

Winnicott, D. W. (1971). *Playing and reality.* London: Tavistock.

Wippich, W. (1994). Intuition in the context of implicit memory. *Psychological Research, 56,* 104–109. https://doi.org/10.1007/BF00419717

Yale, A. J. (2018, May 7). Black home buyers denied mortgages more than twice as often as whites, report finds. *Forbes.* https://www.forbes.com/sites/alyyale/2018/05/07/mortgage-loan-denials-more-common-with-minorities-new-report-shows/#3c8f3390509a

Chapter 12

A HEALING CONTEXT

Philosophical–Spiritual Principles of Sensorimotor Psychotherapy

> *The impulse to heal is real and powerful and lies within the*
> *client. Our job is to evoke that healing power, to meet its tests and*
> *needs and to support it in its expression and development. We are*
> *not the healers. We are the context in which healing is inspired.*
>
> RON KURTZ

The implicit context, or atmosphere, in which therapy takes place is the most essential and influential element of clinical practice. Every psychotherapist adheres to certain assumptions that define the quality of the therapeutic relationship, influence the maps and strategies used, and guide technique. These assumptions determine the overall relational climate in the therapy room. Whether learned explicitly or implicitly, foundational principles are established during formal training and by the characteristics of the specific methods used in practice, commonly accepted as the "best" or "right" way to engage with the client and to conduct therapy. They are, in turn, uniquely interpreted and embodied in different ways and to various degrees by practitioners. Underneath these learned concepts are the often unconscious beliefs and viewpoints of therapists themselves about the essence of the human condition, what circumstances facilitate change, the nature of interpersonal relationships, and the inspiration for healing. These perspectives constitute a paradigm unique to the individual therapist that exerts a powerful influence on clinical practice. Often unacknowledged and unconscious, myriad points of view—individual and collective, implicit and explicit, learned through education and personal experience—combine into a set of principles that determine the general climate in which therapy occurs, and are deeply felt and experienced by therapist and client alike.

Whatever the composition of a therapist's foundational principles, they provide a philosophical-spiritual ground for clinical practice. They shepherd the overall orientation of the therapist; thus the lenses or maps that inform therapeutic strategy as well as the specific time-limited interventions used in the clinical hour emerge from this orientation. By creating the overarching paradigm that shepherds the process of therapy, the foundational principles are the most critical and highly influential elements of any clinical practice, even more so when they remain unarticulated and unexamined.

The Sensorimotor Psychotherapist takes to heart a collection of six principles. Five are adapted from the work of Ron Kurtz (1990): organicity or inner wisdom, nonviolence, unity or interconnectedness, mind/body/spirit holism, and mindfulness. More recently, I expanded mindfulness to add "presence," on a continuum with mindfulness, and added a sixth principle, "relational alchemy." These principles are interrelated and overlapping: If you fully resonate with one principle, you are likely aligned with all of them. With roots in Buddhist, Taoist, and Indigenous traditions, these six principles are a credo of sorts, implicitly guiding therapeutic action and anchoring the emotional attitude and mind-set that underlie technique, not as a goal, a sequence of steps, or an end-point, and not through effort or conscious thought. Rather, they are emergent: The therapist's process of aligning with the principles inspires a particular state of consciousness that we trust will encourage the conditions in which growth is optimized, allowing clients to take their next step in their own evolution.

The foundational principles are age-old concepts that are interpreted and adapted to clinical work in explicit and implicit ways and operationalized in the process of therapy. The intention to embody these principles vitalizes a way of being in the world, with ourselves, and with each other that generates a context for healing and evolution. Thus, to align oneself with these foundations invites personal engagement. Therapists examine their affinity for each principle, curiously identify when they have transgressed the guidance of one of them, and muse on their ability to embody them in a process of self-awareness and growth.

These principles are the very heart, soul and spirit of Sensorimotor Psychotherapy. However, they do not remain static; they are emergent and aspirational in nature, held as ideals that we strive to embody, expressed differently in different contexts, relationships, and situations. As the nucleus of Sensorimotor Psychotherapy, our methodology, maps, and techniques emanate from this philosophical-spiritual base. The effectiveness and meaning of a Sensorimotor Psychotherapy session reflect first and foremost the therapist's affinity for and ability to practice within the guidance of the principles, and only second the mastery of theory and technique. This chapter describes each of the six principles, discusses their origins, and elucidates their influence on therapeutic action and technique in terms of how they are operationalized in the clinical hour.

ORGANICITY

> I can give you nothing that has not already its origins within yourself. I can throw open no picture gallery but your own. I can help make your own world visible—that is all.
>
> HERMAN HESSE

> During my life journey I've discovered an interesting thing; once you stop seeking outside you discover what already resides within.
>
> RASHEED OGUNLARU

Deep within, there is something profoundly known, not consciously, but subconsciously. A quiet truth, that is not a version of something, but an original knowing.

T. F. HODGE

Healing is not science, but the intuitive art of wooing nature.

W. H. AUDEN

"Organicity," a term drawn from the work of Gregory Bateson (1979), conveys that all living systems possess an inherent evolving intelligence that guides their own unique unfolding. Humans, as living systems, are self-organizing, complex, and nonlinear. To be self-organizing is to naturally and without conscious intention generate a kind of order as various parts of a system interact (Bateson, 1979). This process is not linear, does not progress predictably or evenly, and may appear to advance simultaneously in various directions. The complexity of living systems is described by Prigogine (1997) as nondeterministic, rendering the future unpredictable. At the same time, this complexity also embraces the intricate relationships that can catalyze patterns. As living systems, humans are responsive to their sociocultural environment, participating in an ongoing, natural interaction with the things and people surrounding them (Kurtz, 1990).

In my beginning years as a psychotherapist in the early 1970s, I learned from Ron Kurtz that it is not the therapist's job to find answers or solutions for clients' problems; people cannot be "fixed" or healed. Doctors can set a bone or remove a tumor, but living systems heal themselves. Under the best conditions, doctors provide the support that catalyzes healing from within, but they do not do the healing. Similarly, the therapist does not cure the client; rather, the healing power lies inside each person, who is endowed with their own unique, mysterious, and emergent growth path. This wisdom is enigmatic, continually unfolding, and the form it takes cannot be fully anticipated nor forecasted. We must draw forth the needed intelligence from clients, first by recognizing and trusting in its existence and second by co-creating with them the conditions in which it can emerge.

The principle of organicity conforms to the Chinese Taoist perspective of the ancient philosopher Lao Tzu, who is credited with saying, "At the center of your being you have the answer; you know who you are and you know what you want." According to Taoist teachings, one only needs to have faith in the wisdom that resides inside oneself, and facilitate the connections so that this wisdom, which already exists, is revealed. In Sensorimotor Psychotherapy, it is the therapist who shepherds this process so that the system— the client—changes spontaneously, without force, in the progressive direction of healing and wholeness.

Organicity acknowledges that every culture inherently contains its own unique wisdom, and that the wisdom of each individual is filtered through personal and collective experiences shaped by their culture. Cultural wisdom is extremely diverse, the result of experiencing different environments and interactions, socioeconomic conditions, privilege/oppression dynamics, the transgenerational transmission of trauma and resilience, and much more. Indigenous and Western cultural wisdom are different from each other, although there is no "one" intelligence for either group. Levac and colleagues (2018, p. 4) caution that "it is easy to fall into the traps of 'homogenizing' and 'othering' by approaching these vast ways of knowing [Indigenous and Western] in general terms." That said, there are differences between these two cultural orientations that powerfully impact personal and collective organicity. Generally speaking, the organicity experienced by Indigenous cultures is more relational and inclusive of past generations, both living and dead, than Western cultures. Indigenous knowledge emphasizes one's relationship with the Earth rather than viewing it as an object to explore or study, a more commonly held Western perspective (Smylie et al., 2014). The knowledge of many Indigenous cultures and people, across contexts, is more holistic, prioritizing relational, spiritual, and symbolic wisdom that carries across generations (Chilisa & Tsheko, 2014; Levac et al., 2018). Intelligence is considered to be a process, not an object or thing. A Western approach to intelligence is typically more fragmented, divided into separate disciplines, with an emphasis on logic and science and a rejection of metaphysical perspectives. Clearly, culture impacts our personal experience of organicity. The way in which we interact with the world and the world interacts with us, influenced by the generations before us, embraces the sociocultural values and socialization of our communities of belonging that implicitly guide us as to how to live, how to relate to others, what is possible for us, and so forth.

Organicity encompasses a non-pathologizing perspective. It challenges the medical viewpoint that is rooted in a disease model, which is focused on determining what is wrong and implementing procedures to fix the problem. The medical model attends to the parts rather than the whole, and to pathology and what is amiss. In contrast, the principle of organicity teaches that people make the best choices given the impact of their circumstances, social location, cultural conditioning (expansive and constraining), resources and information available to them. We do not see the client in terms of disease. Rather, we view clients and their presenting problems and symptoms with curiosity and compassion, understanding that each complaint, each symptom, and each problem holds within it a salubrious intent and purpose. We seek to discover the underlying adaptive function of the presenting issues, including behaviors and physical habits such as a slumped posture, as well as cognitive distortions and emotional biases.

The principle of organicity is aligned more with Indigenous perspectives that look to the natural environment and understand developmental processes as both nonlinear and emergent, linked to unknown, unseen, yet powerful intelligence that cannot necessarily be validated by the scientific method. Thus, importantly, as therapists, we cannot know what is best for our clients. As Kurtz (1990, p. 26) states, "When you embrace the organicity principle you look for and follow natural processes. You do not impose a structure or agenda on the process." We must find it in ourselves to rest in not knowing, to trust the client's unfolding process even when, and especially when, we do not understand it.

Symptoms that are usually perceived as liabilities are acknowledged as survival resources formed in attempts to regulate arousal and cope with adverse experiences, thus challenging the client's tendency to pathologize their difficulties and symptoms as shameful or as innate faults (Ogden & Fisher, 2015). Clients who come with complaints about relational issues learn to reframe them as survival resources, shaped at the intersection of one's unique developmental niche and privilege/oppression dynamics, rather than as personal deficits. Others who are dysregulated and contend with difficulties that often cause shame, such as self-harm, addictions, and so forth, can learn that these are survival resources—attempts to self-regulate and cope with their distress. For example, one young African American man was disturbed by his inability to stay calm in the face of watching reports of police violence on the media, and turned to alcohol to regulate. Through our work, he became aware of how these unsettling feelings lived in his body, and about how his earlier experiences, and those of his ancestors, propelled his dysregulation and anger. He learned that his "short fuse" had to do with a healthy protective part of himself that was both angry and grief-stricken at the injustice of racial profiling and racialized violence. He began to recognize these emotions in his body (tightness in his chest, pounding heart, clenched fists, etc.) and to channel them in more empowering ways by going for a run and putting pen to paper rather than by "exploding." By qualifying the behaviors clients are trying to change or the symptoms that destabilize them as survival resources used to cope, new options more easily open up for addressing them and finding other, more creative resources to fulfill their purpose.

A non-pathologizing perspective that trusts in a client's organicity is not meant to deny or minimize the severity of personal problems and struggles or potential risks presented by these difficulties that need attention. However, when they are understood as formed in reaction to specific circumstances and sociocultural influences with the intent to fulfill a particular function that at its core is health supporting, organicity will be revealed. We recognize that every culture has its own wisdom and that the organicity of each individual is filtered through experience and is thus shaped by social location and culture. For example, a Native American woman degraded herself for her "giving up" attitude surrounding the discrimination and oppression she and her people experience. However, this strategy can be adaptive in the context of systemic historical and current oppression when the forces of systemic oppression are perceived as too strong to fight against (Sue et al., 2019). She was able to reframe her passive attitude as adaptive and validate her capacity to take effective action in other arenas of her life. When strengths and competencies are acknowledged and embellished, difficult situations will be easier to face. Then resolving past suffering and dealing with ongoing stress and trauma will go more smoothly.

The therapist's task becomes one of being alert to the natural process of evolution, of helping clients turn inside deeply enough, in the context of an attuned therapeutic dyad, so that the right kind of information becomes available from within (Kurtz, 1990). The therapist resists being the "expert," giving advice, or controlling the session or the clients, but rather looks for their natural impulse to take the next step in their growth and guides them toward experiences that they are ready for. As this takes place, the system—the client, and often the therapist as well—changes spontaneously, without force, in a progressive direction of healing and wholeness.

To operationalize organicity in clinical practice, we recognize that all living systems follow their own path. When clients appear stuck, we assume the presence of a simultaneous impetus toward growth. We meet our clients where they are in their development, pacing to their needs, honoring their strengths, reframing their limiting beliefs and procedural patterns as salubrious adaptations and survival resources. We demonstrate faith that the client's spontaneous sensations, movements, images, emotions, thoughts, and impulses hold valuable information even when we do not understand them or the organicity that drives them (Ogden, 1986). Allowing time and space for the client to connect to their inner wisdom and refraining from giving advice are essential to operationalize organicity in clinical practice. It can be as simple as the therapist saying, "Where would you like to sit?" in response to the client asking, "Where should I sit?" at their first meeting. This implicitly communicates that the client knows what is right for them and simultaneously sets the stage for a particular kind of therapeutic relationship in which the client is encouraged to discover their own answers to their questions rather than seeking answers from the therapist.

We do not try to force clients into a direction they do not want to go or are not ready for, assume there is wisdom in resistance, and refrain from giving advice or solving problems. Even perceiving a client's symptom or issue as a problem instead of recognizing its adaptive purpose goes against organicity. Thus, we continuously help clients orient to their own locus of control within themselves, demonstrating a deep and radical respect for their freedom to be as they are and choose for themselves. The therapist learns what clients want to accomplish, validates the wisdom of their choices, and helps them turn inward to find the answers they are seeking, recognizing the value of whatever spontaneously emerges as grist for the therapeutic mill.

NONVIOLENCE

> *By having a reverence for life, we enter into a spiritual*
> *relation with the world. By practicing reverence*
> *for life we become good, deep, and alive.*
>
> ALBERT SCHWEITZER

> *Nonviolence is not a garment to be put on and off at will. Its seat*
> *is in the heart, and it must be an inseparable part of our being.*
>
> MAHATMA GANDHI

> *A liberation movement that is nonviolent sets the*
> *oppressor free as well as the oppressed.*
>
> BARBARA DEMING

> *Every relationship of domination, of exploitation, of oppression is*
> *by definition violent, whether or not the violence is expressed by*
> *drastic means. In such a relationship, dominator and dominated*
> *alike are reduced to things—the former dehumanized by an excess*
> *of power, the latter by a lack of it. And things cannot love.*
>
> PAULO FREIRE

> *Nonviolence is a powerful and just weapon, which*
> *cuts without wounding and ennobles the man*
> *who wields it. It is a sword that heals.*
>
> MARTIN LUTHER KING JR.

Nonviolence operationalizes organicity in clinical practice through the active creation of a relational and emotional context in which organicity can emerge. Recognizing the natural impulse of living systems for more complex levels of organization, nonviolence taps into the natural urge to evolve, grow, and heal. It is closely related to the Taoist concept of "Wu Wei," which literally translated means "non-doing." However, Wu Wei does not mean literally doing nothing; instead it speaks to following the way of nature—the organic flow or direction that is already taking place, which proves to be the most effective and effortless course of action. By creating the right conditions, living systems change by themselves; once the soil is prepared and sun and water are provided, the plant will grow on its own. Instead of doing more, doing less easily accomplishes more because the doer is simply supporting the unfolding process that is already in motion. Therefore, efforting and trying both become unnecessary and even counterproductive. Rather than manipulating or struggling to make something happen, nonviolence means we go with the grain, with what wants to happen, the incipient next step. There is no need to work against this natural inclination or to use force, which only creates resistance when applied to living systems (Kurtz, 1990).

The concept of nonviolence can be traced back almost 4,000 years to a significant ethical tenet of Jainism, Hinduism, and Buddhism called "ahimsa," which means "non-injury" in Sanskrit. Originating in the Vedic wisdom of India (Deshpande, 2019), ahimsa advocates respect for, and restraint from doing harm to, a living being. Ahimsa is interpreted in many different ways, but it is most commonly associated with nonviolence. Although both ahimsa and nonviolence are sometimes correlated with peace and non-action, these terms more precisely refer to the absence of violent methods, or to using the least harmful method, in any situation where action is called for, rejecting the use of force to effect change.

Perhaps the most visible face of ahimsa in history, Mahatma Gandhi opposed using force and instead used nonviolent resistance to end colonialism in India, inspiring similar crusades for freedom and human rights around the globe. Influenced by Gandhi, Albert Schweitzer coined the phrase "reverence for life" as an affirmation that expressed his conviction that all living beings should be respected. Schweitzer (1965, para. 4) wrote, "Ethics is nothing else than reverence for life. Reverence for life affords me my fundamental principle of morality, namely, that good consists in maintaining, assisting and enhancing life." In keeping with this way of thinking, nonviolence as applied to therapy "is born of an attitude of acceptance and an active attention to the way events naturally unfold" (Kurtz, 1990, p. 29).

Gleaned from these traditions to become relevant to psychotherapy practice, nonviolence is expressed in therapy through a deep respect for clients' experience. The ways in which experience is organized by habits of thought, emotion, posture, and movement are based on our experiential history, shaped into patterns over time, but they outgrow their utility when circumstances change. These once-adaptive behaviors and habits are not obstacles to growth, but can become default behaviors still in effect after the conditions that shaped them are over. Rather than trying to urge or coerce change or solve a problem, emphasis is placed on how clients organize their experience physically, emotionally and mentally, which is recognized as having meaning and purpose, and as holding the keys for their personal evolution. As Kurtz said, "Clients are experiences waiting to happen, not problems to be solved." Discovering the next step in the client's evolution—what already "wants" to happen—is a task of nonviolence. Therefore, the way clients organize experience, and thus everything that emerges spontaneously in the moment, are welcomed as interesting and valuable indicators of the natural experience waiting to happen that can be explored to advantage in the therapeutic journey.

The dynamics of violence in therapy can be nuanced, revealed in critical or judgmental attitudes toward the client, in subtle dismissal of their emotions, thoughts, desires, gestures, appearance, social locations such as sexual orientation, gender expression, ability, ethnicity, and so forth. Nonviolence requires the cultivation of a nonjudgmental attitude that accepts and welcomes all parts and responses of clients with compassion, especially those aspects clients themselves cannot accept. Rather than criticizing, judging, or pathologizing behavior, we are attentive to clients' emerging experience, and help them to also become curious about their internal landscape as it unfolds, to observe and learn about themselves more fully and compassionately in relationship with the therapist.

The therapist conveys appreciation for all aspects of the client for their original adaptive and empowering function. Even psychological defenses, which Kurtz (1990) refers to as attempts to manage painful experience, are validated for their purpose, such as for their regulating capacities. Kurtz points out that calling these behaviors "defenses" conjures up images of force, as if the client were trying to fight against themselves. These management behaviors are viewed as creative, if outdated, adaptations to life events, and thus the therapist does not seek to modify or change them. Instead, the client is helped to learn about how these behaviors are organized internally, through becoming aware of present-moment thoughts, emotions, images, posture and movements, tracking for what emerges naturally or is available to change. The attention to this unfolding experience leads to fresh, in-the-moment experiential knowledge, bringing forth new information that often inspires the so-called defenses to yield by themselves.

Nonviolence should not be interpreted as passivity, allowing anything to happen, or as neglecting to act when action is needed. The therapist can be both nonviolent and an active participant in the therapeutic process. It is the therapist's job to deliberately support the client in their evolution, to bring awareness to destructive tendencies and to interrupt them when necessary. For instance, there are times when direct action is called for to prevent harm to the client or to others. But nonviolence is more concerned with how the action is executed than with the action itself. If a client is homicidal, the therapist must act to protect both the target and the client, but the way in which the therapist acts is imbued with respect, compassion, and understanding for the person and all the factors that have led them to this point in their life. The attitude of nonviolence thus renders a harmful action itself as unacceptable, but affirms the person. Similarly, if clients are suicidal, protecting them may be paramount (while honoring situations that may indicate otherwise, for example in cases of terminal illness), yet the therapist's recognition of their extreme hurt and sorrow—bearing witness to their pain—reflects the principle of nonviolence. Simultaneously, the therapist and client work collaboratively toward understanding how the client is organizing experience and toward the possibility of a concomitant, perhaps deeper, life-affirming organicity that is also inclusive and accepting of the destructive impulse.

The client's organicity is discovered and revealed through a nonviolent approach that adheres to no preconceived definitive agenda. We realize that the therapist's own agenda, even one as indirect and seemingly innocuous as the desire to be helpful, can be subtly violent, exert pressure on the client, and complicate the unfolding of the client's organicity. As therapists, we relinquish ideas of how we think the therapy is supposed to look or proceed. Even a desire for change to take place "can interfere with nonviolence by creating a subtle pressure for something to happen" (Ogden 1986). Although we may have a treatment plan with general goals, we recognize that impromptu possibilities will emerge in the course of therapy that we could not have anticipated. We do not allow our plan to supersede opportunities that spontaneously come up in the moment. By letting go of agendas and of our desire that therapy proceed in a certain way, the door can remain open for the unexpected, and for organic unfolding.

Thus, we strive to become aware of and inhibit our hidden agendas and judgments. We recognize that lack of knowledge of culture and awareness of our own implicit bias can render aspects of clients' experience invisible to us and lead to unintended violence. The attitudes and prejudices we harbor toward others can be explicit and conscious, or implicit and unconscious. While we can challenge and inhibit our conscious biases, implicit bias, because it is outside our awareness, can insidiously wreak havoc on our intention to act nonviolently. Implicit bias often emerges in microaggressions, which verbally or behaviorally convey disrespect, hostility, or otherwise negative attitudes about race, sexual orientation, religion, and so forth (Sue, 2010). These indignities can be subtle, such as an expression of disgust when a client speaks of their sexual orientation, or a comment that reflects a stereotype, such as, "I didn't think Jewish people were good at sports" or "I'm surprised you don't like to dance, since you're African American." Microaggressions are more likely to occur when we are not aware of our bias and do not understand social locations, intersectionality, or privilege/oppression dynamics. When bias is unconscious, we do not recognize that unintentional microaggressions inflict harm, and thus also do not recognize the need to modify our behavior. If we want to work toward embodying the principle of nonviolence, it is our responsibility to engage in an ongoing process of self-examination to learn about the impact of privilege/oppression dynamics and uncover our own implicit bias with regard to differences between ourselves and our clients, including race, culture, gender, age, economics, and so forth, as well as the impact of intersectionality.

To act nonviolently requires great awareness from the therapist, both of their own bias and propensities, and of the here-and-now experience of the client. Noticing immediate signals of aversion or distress in the client, such as a fleeting facial expression or a slight pulling back of the body, combined with the therapist's self-awareness, provide the chance to recognize indicators of violence, and recover and repair. For example, eliciting more material than the client can integrate effectively (a subtle form of violence) can be remedied when the therapist tracks the signals, names what is noticed ("Seems like your breathing is becoming labored—maybe this is too much"). Through such awareness and adjustment, nonviolence is restored, and further supported as the therapist remains open to the spontaneous emergence of opportunities to follow the path of least resistance.

MIND-BODY-SPIRIT HOLISM

> *Being in touch with our bodies, or more accurately,*
> *being our bodies, is how we know what is true.*
>
> HARRIET GOLDHOR LERNER

> *The body is our general medium for having a world.*
>
> MAURICE MERLEAU-PONTY

> *the body is wiser than its inhabitants, the body*
> *is the soul, the body is god's messenger.*
>
> ERICA JONG

> *"The body is not a thing, it is a situation: it is our*
> *grasp on the world and our sketch of our project."*
>
> SIMONE DE BEAUVOIR

> *With neurology, if you go far enough with it, and*
> *you keep going, you end up getting weird. If you*
> *go a little further, you end up in the spirit.*
>
> OLIVER SACKS

The parts of any living system are intimately connected and continually interact with one another. Mind, body, and spirit are essential aspects of the human organism, and each can only be understood in relationship to the whole they constitute. All experience registers in the body, and mental/emotional and spiritual components are inherent in all significant bodily experience. The body houses the spirit in the broadest sense, and its habits of movement, posture, and expression reflect and sustain the habits of the mind in both thought and emotion. Our sense of ourselves, of ourselves in relationship with others, and of our place in the world emerges from these three ever-entwined elements that comprise the wholeness of who we are. Well-being arises from the health of each in communication with the others. A holistic approach to wellness considers the interrelationship between body, mind, and spirit in interaction with an environment that is constantly in flux.

Definitions and explanations of mind, body, and spirit vary enormously, and to delve into the vastness of these three dimensions is beyond the scope of this chapter. Keeping in mind that they can only be divided for conceptual purposes, working descriptions are briefly summarized as follows. Chopra (1989) wrote that our bodies are composed of energy and information that continually transforms. The mind, according to Siegel (2010), is an embodied relational process that regulates this flow of energy and information. It encompasses conscious and unconscious processes that combine thought, perception, emotion, imagination, memory, and so forth. The body as directly addressed in psychotherapy practice includes the autonomic nervous system, micromovements, and the more visible movement repertoire expressed in gestures, facial expressions, postures, and so forth. The spirit refers to the aspect of ourselves that is connected to something nonmaterial, larger than one's own existence, often associated with a sense of reverence, meaning, awe, and a greater encompassing purpose. For many, spirit includes an experience of or belief in the sacred. Although these dimensions carry their individual definitions, it bears repeating that they do not exist independently from one another and cannot be fathomed without considering their relationship to the whole.

For thousands of years, the unity of mind, body, and spirit has been reflected in the worldview and teachings of Indigenous people of various cultures, who have long understood that the health of each of these dimensions is mutually interdependent (Mark & Lyons, 2010). Gleaning wisdom from ancestral voices, animals, plants, and the land itself, drawing upon the spirit as a powerful healing force, and so much more, Indigenous people consider the communication between mind, body, and spirit as essential in wellness (McCabe, 2008). However, "proponents of Western science look at most indigenous knowledge as anecdotal at best and witchcraft at worst" (McCabe, 2008, p. 143). This rejection of holism can be traced back to the 1600s, when Descartes proposed that mind and body are distinct entities. Previously, even the Christian perspective had viewed humans as spiritual beings with a unified body and mind (Mehta, 2011). Their separation ushered in the beginning of modern science and its study of anatomy and physiology, doing away with the notion that disease was caused by nonphysical elements, such as personal or collective misconduct. But it closed the door to the unity of mind, body, and spirit in the Western world. Today, many Indigenous people have preserved their faith in holism, although the predominance of colonialism and Western science has "had the influence of sending traditional practices underground, and in some instances traditional healing practices were eliminated from the cultural vernacular altogether" (McCabe, 2008, p. 144). Conventional allopathic medicine still primarily focuses on treating parts of a person instead of considering the whole or taking into account the influence of the mind and spirit on the body. Although this is beginning to change, ailments of body, mind, and spirit are largely treated separately in the Western world.

Merleau-Ponty refutes the rejection of holism with his notion of the "lived-body," "that experience of our body which cannot be objectified" (in Gold, 1985, p. 664). The lived body holds an evolving wisdom that is already moving toward healing and health, and as therapists we intend to recognize and capitalize on this innate somatic intelligence. Our intention is recognized in Sensorimotor Psychotherapy's vision statement, "to harness the wisdom of the body to liberate human potential." This potential includes a sense of freedom and choice in body and mind, as well as the freedom and capacity to establish connection with that which is bigger than ourselves. As Gold (1985, pp. 664–665) states, "Human bodies...far from being Cartesian reductionist organ systems, can be better and more realistically envisaged as multiphasic, experiential beings of finite freedom.... [The body] is, most essentially, the centre of one's experiences, moods, expressions and thoughts: the very nexus of intentionality." Who we are, what we feel, and what we believe are intrinsically connected to our bodies.

Because the body is valued as the source of primary intelligence, intention, information, and change, it is an avenue to explore in therapy. It helps therapists and clients identify and address themes arising from spiritual, mental, and emotional realms. Sensorimotor Psychotherapy explores cues from the body that point to the strengths, spiritual connection, beliefs, emotions, and past hurts that show up in present-moment experience. Thus, the language of the body becomes a target of therapeutic action and a vehicle for understanding mental, emotional, and spiritual realms. The therapist seeks to experientially elucidate the intelligence of clients' sensations, postures, gestures, and movements with the intent to unveil an innate knowledge that goes beyond cognitive understanding.

The fact that the movement, posture, and physiology of the body adjust automatically, without conscious intent, to its environment to ensure survival and optimize resources is a potent indication of its intelligence. These adaptations result in patterns of tension, movement, gesture, posture, breath, rhythm, prosody, facial expression, sensation, physiological arousal, gait, and other action sequences. Developed in a sociocultural context, the effects of both negative and positive experiences, trauma and relational strife, spiritual communion and existential angst are held in bodily patterns. A crisis of spirit, for example—when people are "unable to find sources of meaning, hope, love, peace, comfort, strength, and connection in life or when conflict occurs between their beliefs and what is happening in their life" (Anandarajah & Hight, 2001, p. 84)—is reflected in the lived body through its posture, movement, expression, and physiology.

The story told by the body—the "somatic narrative" of gesture, posture, prosody, facial expressions, eye gaze, movement, and so forth—reflects both personal and sociocultural history. We keep in mind that culture has a powerful influence on one's perspective and experience of their own and others' bodies. Different cultures attribute more or different value to mind, body and spirit (e.g., logical thinking might be esteemed over emotions or vice versa; the body may be denounced or appreciated; spiritual life may be more or less emphasized and valued). The body from a Western perspective is usually perceived as lesser than the mind and its objectification is reflected in norms of physical attractiveness in terms of size, age, color, shape, and so forth (Hancock et al., 2000). These prejudices can lead those whose bodies do not conform to these standards to be viewed negatively, or to view their own bodies negatively. The determination of which bodies should be restrained or policed is also evidence of the norms of Western culture, particularly the perspective that diminishes Black and Brown bodies and elevates white bodies. Founded on inaccurate and harmful bias that bodies of color need to be controlled (Menakem, 2017) and white bodies need to be protected, this dangerous prejudice has contributed to and even sanctioned the incarceration and murder of Black and Brown people.

It is essential to address one's own bias toward the body so that we can challenge ourselves and not unwittingly enact our prejudice. Culture strongly influences the meaning we make from various movements and postures (Moore & Yamamoto, 2012). When movement patterns are familiar to us, we feel more security, but when they are not, we may sense discomfort or even threat. Burgoon, Guerrero, and Floyd (2010) point out that culture has a strong influence on duration of eye contact, proximity, and touch. These nonverbal patterns of communication, learned in one's particular sociocultural context, can reflect interpersonal dominance and subordination (Johnson, 2015). For example, dominance can be expressed by expansive movements and postures (Johnson, 2015) or by prolonged direct eye contact (Ellyson & Dovidio, 1985). Touch is used with more ease and frequency by those of privileged status, while those deemed to have lesser status learn to refrain from initiating touch in an asymmetrical relationship (Henley & Freeman, 1995). If we are unaware of the norms we have learned through our own sociocultural context, we are at risk of perpetuating privilege/oppression dynamics through our own movements and postures as well as through how we interpret and respond to the movements and postures of others. At the same time, we seek to respect that different individuals and groups have different relationships with and traditions concerning the body, and we seek to recognize and honor these differences in clinical practice.

When we grasp that our physical habits—the way we move, stand, sit, and so forth—are shaped by our personal and sociocultural histories, and these habits are also adjusted to our immediate internal state and external context, we understand that the body's wisdom is not static. It emerges from the constantly fluctuating interactions with others, the world, and our own internal experience. Our bodies shift from moment to moment depending on the state of our mind, emotions, spirit, who we are with, and so forth. Sometimes this shift is obvious and on a large scale, like a change in posture or gesture. Other times, this shift is subtle and almost negligible, but no less profound, like a micromovement or internal opening that may not be apparent to the observer.

The body is not only a resource for the client but a laboratory for self-awareness for therapists. When we are curious about the organization of our own bodies, we discover our physical habits, how they reflect the mind and spirit, and through this awareness we are more able to develop and model an expansive movement vocabulary. Implicitly, the therapist's own somatic resonance and awareness contribute to a safe, collaborative atmosphere in which to explore the body in interaction with the mind and spirit. We help clients to identify and understand their body as a powerful and honest avenue to self-knowledge, and to view its physical habits as intelligent adaptations. We support clients to expand their own movement vocabulary and, in doing so, to experience a corresponding expansion in mind and spirit, especially when physical patterns have become default behaviors over other actions that would be more integrative in current contexts. By developing a resilient, expansive, innovative, flexible, and fluid movement vocabulary, the overall vitality in all three dimensions of being also expands.

The intelligence of our bodies emerges out of our ever-changing experience with others, the world, and ourselves. To reveal the emergent wisdom of the body, mind, and spirit calls for a trust in the unknown and an orientation to process rather than outcome. With curiosity and willingness to explore the body, along with compassion and appreciation for ways the body adapted in the past, as well as awareness of sociocultural patterns of expression, we can better draw upon its wisdom. In Sensorimotor Psychotherapy, this means harnessing mindful awareness of the body and its relationship to emotion, cognition, and spirit, and discovering new movements and postures to support expansion in all three realms. The intelligence of the body, integrated with mind and spirit, is an emergent property, not a fixed one. Since the emergent knowledge of the body is always in transition, learning from the body is a continuous endeavor. The unity of body, mind, and spirit has different things to teach at different times as we go through various life processes, stages, and challenges. Over a lifetime, we can continue to tap the emergent intelligence of the body, allowing it to guide us beyond comfort and familiarity to reach for expansion in mind and spirit, and in all dimensions of our life.

UNITY

The fundamental delusion of humanity is to
suppose that I am here and you are out there.

YASUTANI ROSHI

Pull a thread here and you'll find it's
attached to the rest of the world.

NADEEM ASLAM

What if we all stopped fighting to belong
and realized that we already do?

VIRONIKA TUGALEVA

We are one, after all, you and I. Together we suffer,
together exist, and forever will recreate each other.

PIERRE TEILHARD DE CHARDIN

If you have come to help me you are wasting your time.
But if you recognize that your liberation and mine
are bound up together, we can walk together.

LILA WATSON

The unity principle underscores the fundamental interrelationship between all aspects of the universe: We exist in a constant state of being joined with all that is. Unity rejects the idea that we are separate and embraces interconnection and interdependence; it can be thought of as a beneficial force of nature that organizes disparate parts into wholes (Kurtz, 2004). Though individuals, we do not and cannot exist in isolation, but within a complex organic web of relationships. Each distinctive part of this web of self-organizing systems is generated in relationship to the whole and subsequently generates the whole. Without the activity of the whole, the parts would not exist, and vice versa. Thus, the universe is participatory: "All of us are embedded as co-creators, replacing the accepted universe 'out there,' which is separate from us" (Chopra & Kafatos, 2017). Each of us is an integral part of one unified, organic process that encompasses the whole of nature and the universe. Nothing exists outside of this complex web of relationships, and the individual cannot be separated from all that is. In the words of Thich Nhat Hanh (2001, p. 56), "'To be' is to inter-be. You cannot just be by yourself alone. You have to inter-be with every other thing."

Living systems carry within them an intelligence that cannot be explained by reductionist views that scale down complex dynamics to simple cause and effect. Advocates of reductionism propose that processes, even psychological processes, ought to be described according to science, such as through physiology and chemistry; in this view, a mental disturbance can be attributed to a chemical imbalance (McLeod, 2008). Dividing a living system into its parts, and then describing the whole in terms of the parts it contains, is the essence of reductionism, which unity contradicts. Unity acknowledges that a living system cannot be explained or understood in terms of its various parts.

The complexity of emergence in living systems is the process of something novel coming into being, which can be analyzed in retrospect, but cannot be fully predicted. Emergence occurs when a living system has attained a certain degree of complexity and then exhibits spontaneous intricate behaviors that arise from the interactions of its parts. Unanticipated behaviors or capacities are generated that the individual parts do not have on their own. Thus, emergent properties can come into being only when the parts interact with, and are reciprocally influenced by, all the other parts interacting within the larger whole. According to the principle of unity, living systems cannot be reduced to simple explanations, because multiple influences, known and unknown, seen and unseen, interact in initially mysterious ways that lead to unforeseen emergent properties.

What is brought into being cannot be reduced to or explained by the components.

Unity has roots in Indigenous, Taoist, and Buddhist teachings. The Buddhist concept of "dependent origination" teaches that everything exists because of everything else—nothing can be born, created, or survive on its own because all things are interdependent, and everything impinges upon all that is, and vice versa. A multitude of circumstances, elements, and interactions are needed for something to come into existence. As Thich Nhat Hahn (2001, p. 55) wrote, "you will see clearly that there is a cloud floating in this sheet of paper. Without a cloud, there will be no rain; without rain, the trees cannot grow; and without trees, we cannot make paper." Everything and everyone emerges and exists in parallel association with everything and everyone else; thus the sense of an isolated, independent self is an illusion.

Indigenous cultures also understand that each person is an integral part of all that is, summed up in the Native American expression "All My Relations," which means, "I cannot exist without you and you cannot exist without me. What I do affects you and others and what you do affects me. Everything we do has an effect on others and on our world" (Jansen, 2018, para. 4). Closely related is the South African concept of Ubuntu, which, loosely translated, means, "I am because we are," which recognizes that "we are all bound together in ways that are invisible to the eye; that there is a oneness to humanity" (Obama, 2013, para. 9). Transmitted through oral traditions for hundreds of years, Ubuntu is an ideology in which other people are seen as reflections of the self, thus recognizing that we are joined; our joys and our suffering are bound together. It "suggests to us that humanity is not embedded in my person solely as an individual; my humanity is co-substantively bestowed upon the other and me. Humanity is a quality we owe to each other. We create each other and need to sustain this otherness creation" (Eze, 2010, p. 191). With Ubuntu comes a sense of belonging to a larger whole; thus affirmation of other beings is naturally forthcoming. We rejoice in their joy and share in their pain and suffering, which is painful also to us (Tutu, 2000).

At the same time, the principle of unity recognizes individual and group differences. Kluckholn and Murray (1953) wrote that each person is, concurrently, like no other person, like some other people, and like all other people. Unity recognizes and celebrates differences within interconnectedness. Though nothing in nature is truly separate, to exist is also to have boundaries, whether we consider the membrane of a cell, the outer skin of an organism, or the borders of a nation. People also construct and maintain boundaries to be viable, healthy, and capable of experiencing fully the unity of which they are individual parts. The concept of unity acknowledges, respects, and values differences and boundaries. In unity, we become simultaneously aware of our differences and those of others, while also experiencing a sense of connectedness to others and to the universe.

Validation of both differences and interconnectedness is described by the term "unity in diversity," which can be traced to North American Indigenous people and Taoism (Lalonde, 1994). Unity becomes a felt reality when each person can safely and with acceptance participate in the whole, offering their unique talents and inspirations to contribute to local and global communities. This requires a felt sense of interconnection, a phenomenological recognition that injury inflicted upon one person or group of people harms everyone, and that joy experienced by one person adds to everyone's joy. But all too often the illusion of separation usurps an interconnected sensibility, bringing about boundless suffering and strife, seen in rampant exploitation, oppression, and violence. Manifestations of the denial of unity occur at every level of existence—in individual, collective, human, ecological, global, political, and sociocultural contexts. Racism, racialized trauma, war, sexism, and prejudice in all its forms reflect a painful and devastating inability to live the reality of our interconnectedness.

Unity itself becomes a lived reality when parts communicate; thus, although ever-present, it is recognized and experienced more fully through communication. A central goal of therapy is to facilitate communication interpersonally and intra-personally: communication between therapist and client and communication among parts, bringing special attention to those parts that are lost, hidden, or isolated. To operationalize unity collectively, bridges and affiliations need to be built that move beyond the interests of nationality, gender, race, ethnicity, and so forth, and effort needs to be made to discourage conceptualizations of the present-day dominant culture as better or universal (Lalonde, 1994). To actualize unity in diversity for all individuals and groups is described as "the highest possible attainment of a civilization, a testimony to the most noble possibilities of the human race. This attainment is made possible through passionate concern for choice, in an atmosphere of social trust" (Novak, 1983). Unity and freedom, therefore, are found within the choices we can make when we understand our undeniable interconnectedness within parts of ourselves and within the larger whole, and live from awareness of mutual interdependence, not by denying or trying to rise above it.

Thus, as therapists, we "work to get parts communicating, whether it's members of the family, the body and mind, or parts of the mind. It's an art, full of high skill, to coax these parts out of hiding, to help them speak openly and directly" (Kurtz, 1990, p. 32). Recognizing that all aspects are part of a larger whole, a central aim is to facilitate the communication between these parts—between each of us and within each of us. We help each person discover both how communication breaks down between internal parts and with external elements and how communication is supported and enhanced. When communication is restored between mind, body, and spirit, "me" and "not-me" self-states, emotion, thought, and body, implicit and explicit selves, and so forth, differences are resolved, integration is bolstered, one's connection to the greater whole is experienced more fully, and the energy used to maintain separation is freed for other endeavors.

Janet (1925) stated that therapists must encourage as much collaboration with the client as possible. To foster a felt sense of unity, collaborative communication between therapist and client is essential. In the therapy hour, a sense of co-creation or "being in it together" decreases separation, builds connection, and shifts responsibility for what occurs from the individual to the dyad. Unity is reflected in simple ways; for example, therapists use the collaborative language of "we" and "us" ("Maybe we could explore...") rather than "I" and "you." Instead of making therapeutic decisions on our own as therapists, we share our thinking and include our clients in the conceptualizing and decision-making process. We use psychoeducation to make sure we are on the same page with the client, check out our assumptions, honor our differences, and support the client's internal locus of control. We think out loud ("I wonder if....") as we appropriately convey our perceptions and intentions and we resonate with clients to share in their joy and pain.

We embody a sense of connectedness to others and the universe while also holding the simultaneous awareness of our separateness and our difference. We aim to be aware of and speak to our own biases and social locations, to be sensitive to those of our clients, and to bring these into the therapy hour as appropriate through honest communication. We remain receptive to all parts of ourselves and our clients in a stance of "radical openness," which entails an ongoing effort "to notice, question, and relinquish presumptions about oneself and the other" (Hart, 2017, para. 6).

In operationalizing unity, the therapist recognizes that everything that emerges in the therapy hour—thoughts, emotions, postures, movements, gestures, sensations, images, and so forth—are a part of the greater whole. They are "holons"—elements that "behave partly as wholes or wholly as parts, according to the way you look at them" (Koestler, 1967, p. 48). By understanding and experiencing each part, each element as a holon, as being a whole and a part at the same time, we recognize unity in everything that emerges in therapy. With this recognition comes a sense of choice and freedom. As Feldman (1999) states, "Understanding how things come together, how they interact, actually removes that sense of powerlessness or that sense of being a victim of life or helplessness" (para. 14). Through unity, we can act in accordance with the experience of our own and our client's relationship to all that is.

RELATIONAL ALCHEMY

An honorable human relationship is a process—delicate, violent, often terrifying to both persons involved. A process of refining the truths they tell one another. It is important to do this. It breaks down self-delusion and isolation and does justice to our own complexity. It is important to do this because we can count on so few people to go that hard way with us.

ADRIENNE RICH

She is a friend of mind. She gather me, man. The pieces I am, she gather them and give them back to me in all the right order. It's good, you know, when you got a woman who is a friend of your mind.

TONI MORRISON

The most empowering relationships are those in which each partner lifts the other to a higher possession of their own being.

PIERRE TEILHARD DE CHARDIN

My love has two lives, in order to love you: that's why I love you when I do not love you, and also why I love you when I do.

PABLO NERUDA

Relational alchemy, in alignment with the unity principle, appreciates that the distinctive and emergent qualities of each relationship spawn something greater than the individual components. The word "alchemy" describes an idiosyncratic process that brings about change by means that are not fully understood. Considered the forerunner of chemistry, alchemy was founded on the supposition that everything that exists is imbued with spirit and can be transformed. But when two or more substances are combined, the transformation that occurs is often unexpected. The same holds true for when humans interact. Relational alchemy describes the enigmatic transformation of two or more people that is inspired by their distinctive synchrony in the way in which they are connected. Because each person and each moment in time are unique, so is every human interaction. Thus, when people come together, novel and unexpected outcomes that cannot be understood by the rational mind are brought about.

Every human affiliation contains its own original and distinctive characteristics that bring forth content, communications, and outcomes that would not occur in any other interaction. Not only are human interactions impacted by each party's background, emotional valence, personality, perspectives, strengths, challenges, and so forth, but also by particular aspects of each person that are brought forward at discrete times, and in different relationship, generating an array of capacities, aha moments, struggles, and growth possibilities in every interaction. As living systems, relationships are self-organizing, self-directing, and self-correcting (Bateson, 1979)—thus constantly changing. Relational alchemy recognizes the mysterious forces that fuel these changes and transformations.

Human relationships are rife with opportunities for profound intimacy and expansion as well as for devastating miscommunications and ruptures, and everything in between. Relational alchemy encompasses the wonder of healing that occurs naturally, without effort, through the synergy of the dyadic dance of the therapeutic relationship. It also embraces the implicit, unformulated elements of both client and therapist that dovetail exquisitely to collide in therapeutic enactments that are incipient in any interaction but tend to blossom in long-term relationships. Powerful healing emerges from well-negotiated enactments, including collisions not only of family history but also of culture and social location. Each healing scenario—those that seem to happen magically on their own and those that are hard won through facing the challenges of enactments—holds awesome potential for transformation and liberation.

We humans have an essential and deep need for recognition, which Benjamin (1988, p. 12) defines as "that response from the other which makes meaningful the feelings, intentions, and actions of the self." Akin to what Schore (2009) calls the "interactive 'transfer of affect' between the right brains," and to what Stern (2004, p. 75) describes as when "two people see and feel roughly the same mental landscape for a moment at least," recognition is a mutual experience, a function of relational alchemy. Relational alchemy fuels both misrecognition and mutual recognition, which is as gratifying as misrecognition is painful (until it is relationally negotiated and transforms into recognition). Both can be profound change agents.

Therapy itself is "a nonlinear process [induced by relational alchemy] that endows both their relationship and their individual self-states with an ever-evolving experience of wholeness that is the primary source of healing and growth" (Bromberg, 2012). A shared moment of recognition is nourishing and growth enhancing to both therapist and client. Recognition is alchemical—a seemingly magical moment of expanding the capacity for self-other wholeness in which something spontaneous and novel is unexpectedly experienced: a "new reality is co-constructed and infused with an energy of its own" (Bromberg, 2006, p. 12). From these moments, new options are revealed, and new possibilities never before conceived spontaneously emerge.

Kurtz (2007) set the stage for acts of recognition in his initial orientation to a client: "My first impulse is to find something to love, something to be inspired by, something heroic, something recognizable as the gift and burden of the human condition, the pain and grace that's there to find in everyone you meet" (p. 13). Looking out for "something to love" instead of deficits or problems primes the pump for recognition of aspects of the client that need to be coaxed out of hiding and seen by another. Recognition can be thought of as occurring on a continuum from significant to profound. All along the spectrum are relational moments that are meaningful or significant. Such a moment might occur when a traumatized client tells their story of abuse for the first time to an attentive, attuned therapist, or when distorted limiting beliefs (e.g., "I am unworthy" or "No one will ever accept me"), learned in the context of early caregiving, are revised in an act of recognition that relationally challenges such beliefs so that the client experiences a felt sense of value and worth. Recognition can throw open the door to new possibilities, providing what is known as a corrective emotional experience that heals long-festering wounds. These moments are replete with "emotional attunement, mutual influence, affective mutuality, sharing states of mind," and an array of meanings may infuse them—validation, acknowledgment, affirmation, acceptance, understanding, appreciation, and so forth (Benjamin, 1988, pp. 15–16).

Approaching the extreme of the continuum, even more profound acts of recognition emerge as moments of heightened awareness in which both parties experience an expanded state of consciousness— a sense of spaciousness, beingness, love, reverence, gratitude, peace, or an encompassing sense of belonging (Ogden, 2007). Sometimes called "sacred moments" (Lomax & Pargament, 2011), these remarkable manifestations of relational alchemy may encompass, but are not confined to, a felt sense of spirit, holiness, blessedness, higher power, or divinity. Taylor (2013, p. 29) eloquently describes such a moment in her work with an African American adolescent in the juvenile carceral system:

> He often struggled to imagine his own future so I asked him to imagine what he thought I wished most for him. He inhaled deeply as his eyes rose slowly to the ceiling welling up with tears. He smiled and exhaled the word "freedom." All the air suddenly left the room. Something sacred and otherworldly had come to join us. Together we sat in silence.

"Freedom," particularly significant in an ancestral context of chattel slavery, was overflowing with layer upon layer of depth and meaning. Cultural history and spiritual practices, called "cultural kindling" (Cassaniti & Luhrmann, 2014), influence the meanings and connotations of such alchemical moments, and affect the nature of the unique relational alchemy in every therapist–client dyad. Cultural history and context may also prime physical experiences (such as trembling, spontaneous dancing, suspension of a sense of physical boundaries, tingling, or feelings of leaving the body), interpretation or meaning (such as liberation, safety, union), or the presence of other forces (God, spirit, ancestors, or totem animals) ascribed to a profound moment of recognition. For many clients and therapists, these experiences are "a source of meaning in life, feelings of connectedness with a larger community, and a sense of continuity bridging the past, present, and future" (Pargament et al., 2014).

These expansive experiences are life affirming, infusing clients and therapists alike with a sense of profundity that extends beyond mundane limitations. Pargament and Mahoney (2005) delineate four different categories of sacred moments. Transcendent experiences are extraordinary, rather than everyday, occurrences, such as the feeling of a greater presence. Boundlessness pertains to no longer being limited by temporal or dimensional boundaries, like the sense of time stopping or space expanding. The felt sense of an undeniable, ultimate truth refers to experiences like an unquestionable feeling of being blessed. A profound interconnectedness might be experienced in a rare depth of reciprocal understanding, attunement, and resonance between therapist and client. These various moments of heightened or sacred awareness may be accompanied by a sense of mystery, awe, humility, joy, serenity, being uplifted, peace, or other spiritual emotions (Pargament et al., 2014). However, as in the example described above, words and interpretation are often absent, for language itself is inadequate to describe these shared moments, and in fact can detract from their lived experience (Ogden, 1992/2007). Such numinous occasions are to be savored, not necessarily described.

The implicit elements or parts of both therapist and client that participate in relational alchemy exist in the depths of the unconscious, and may hold different versions of reality, beliefs, agendas, and predictions of relationships. In a reciprocal interchange between these unsymbolized elements of both participants, powerful therapeutic interchanges encompass both profound recognition and profound misrecognition. The same mysterious relational forces that lead to the recognition and sacred moments illustrated above also underpin the equally meaningful interpersonal conflicts and struggles that therapist and client come up against. As a function of relational alchemy, the implicit histories—recent, distant past, and intergenerational—of each person are reenacted through painful collusions, collisions, and enactments. These relational clashes reflect personal history, privilege/oppression dynamics, sociocultural contexts, and intersecting social locations, or all these factors combined. Mutually created, the enacted reliving of one person's relational experience calls forth a matching counterpoint in the other that reflects historical failures of relational transactions and resolutions for both. Because these historical events and their impact are not always available for contemplation and revision, and are thus enacted unawares, they have an even more potent and bewildering impact on the therapeutic relationship. These mutual enactments cause painful misrecognitions on both sides but also hold the possibility for extraordinary expansion when well negotiated (Bromberg, 2006; Ogden, 2013).

When a particular aspect of the client comes forward, a corresponding part of the therapist is drawn out to meet it, and vice versa, in an emergent process. There are infinite possibilities of enactment scenarios, all related to aspects of each person that are indirectly crying out to be heard and recognized. The alchemy that is forged as each part comes forward in interaction with its counterpart in the other usually leads relentlessly to aggravating degrees of misrecognition on both sides. If one person is needy, the other pulls away or resentfully takes care of them; when one is intrusive, the other withdraws or submits; if one is blaming, the other feels shame; if one becomes critical, the other feels inadequate or defensive, and so forth.

These relational systems also reflect the intersectional identities and sociocultural histories of therapist and client that exacerbate asymmetrical circuits of power and privilege/oppression dynamics. Oppressed and marginalized people—ethnic and racial minorities, migrants, refugees, Indigenous people, those with disabilities, the LGBTQ+ community, women and girls, the poor, and others who are persecuted by the privileged culture—suffer misrecognitions and nonrecognition in personal and sociocultural contexts that can have disastrous repercussions for generations to come. In an appalling and terrifying example, the abject lack of recognition of Black Americans as human beings with human rights during the time of chattel slavery in the United States is enacted today in incidents of police brutality and ongoing systemic oppression. The relational alchemy that brings people of different social locations together in the therapy room provides the opportunity to challenge deep-seated implicit and explicit sociocultural misrecognitions as client-therapist intersectional identities unconsciously come up against one another in a struggle experienced very differently by those of privileged locations and those of oppressed locations. These misrecognitions can manifest in ignoring difference ("We're all alike; we have the same opportunities"), emphasizing difference ("We will never really understand one another"), or misinterpreting difference ("Your anger stems from your interactions with your mother, not from systemic oppression"; "Your empathy is because you feel guilty because you are more affluent than I am"). As noted, each misrecognition brings about a corresponding reaction in the other, and vice versa. These nonconscious mutually created systems can escalate into full-blown enactments because the unresolved historical relational dynamics of one person fit together with the other's past in a way that exacerbates each one's current position. Because of this, a tremendous opportunity for healing of past and present is there for the taking if the enactment can be negotiated and implicit parts recognized.

Enactments are inevitable. Bromberg (2006) asserts, "...there is no way to avoid these clashes of subjectivity without stifling the emergence [in both therapist and client] of dissociated self-states that need to find a voice" (p. 24). If these voices are to be heard, relational safety will necessarily and inevitably be compromised or lost, at least temporarily. Large and small enactments lead to smoldering feelings of boredom, frustration, resentment, disappointment, or anger that can erupt into hostility and therapeutic impasses, even leading therapist or client, or both, to look for a way to exit the therapy. Enactments will percolate beneath the surface in misrecognitions, misattunements, and degrees of discomfort from slight to intense for both parties, communicated in body-to-body, emotional exchanges beneath the surface of consciousness while verbal content is addressed. The enactment will continue until one of the participants "wakes up" (Bromberg, 2006) to the fact that something is relationally not quite right. From there, an acknowledgment that the difficulty lies within the relationship, not solely in either person, can be nourished and the relational meaning coaxed forth from their reflective communications. If therapist and client persevere to search for mutually constructed meaning, the "failures in recognition can be addressed, acknowledged, and either repaired or mourned" (Benjamin, 2006, p. 120). The relational negotiation of an enactment, once it is realized that something is amiss, is the source of meaningful acts of recognition, and even of profound moments of transformation. Acknowledgment of a misrecognition and the hurt it inflicts, as well as active mutual mourning within the relationship, are both necessary before repair, but if done well, lead to something more than mere repair: a larger transformation that would not have been possible without the enactment. Although the unconscious collusions and collisions that emerge from the relational alchemy between the implicit patterns of therapist and client can defeat therapeutic progress, they can also lead to transformational acts of recognition when well negotiated. A well-negotiated enactment can legitimize each one's personhood, needs, and rights that have been invalidated in past relational and sociocultural contexts. Therefore, misrecognition and enactments are not errors but rather products of a deeper initiative within each person and within their relationship that seeks a higher level of communion and expansion.

In any relationship, the explicit verbal exchange pales in significance to the one that takes place implicitly, through prosody, body language, emotions, innuendo and so forth. Relational alchemy emerges from the interaction of implicit selves that hovers beneath the words, typically unrecognized and unarticulated by the conscious mind. This nonverbal communion is the elusive symphony of relational alchemy, enacted unawares through an implicit body-to-body emotional communication. Relational alchemy, the emergent and mysterious force that brings people together and guides their interactions, is the source of profound and unexpected sensations of being genuinely seen, whether emerging from spontaneous recognitions and sacred moments or from the hard struggles of negotiated enactments. Relational alchemy generates an intersubjective process of discovery—of knowing the other and being known by them—that occurs in a way that is neither predicted nor expected, and thus appeals to each person for the courage to step into unknown territory and trust what the journey will bring.

PRESENCE AND MINDFULNESS

*Maybe journey is not so much a journey ahead, or a
journey into space, but a journey into presence.*

NELLE MORTON

*...to be lost is to be fully present, and to be fully present
is to be capable of being in uncertainty and mystery.*

REBECCA SOLNIT

Beauty is the harvest of presence.

DAVID WHYTE

*The mind is a drama queen that gets too
embarrassed to continue acting up, after only a few
seconds of getting our undivided attention.*

MOKOKOMA MOKHONOANA

*Stop traveling to the past and future and come home to the
present moment. That is the only place you actually live.*

AKIROQ BROST

Although sometimes conflated, mindfulness and presence can be differentiated in terms of dual and nondual states of consciousness. For our purposes, in a simplistic distinction, mindfulness is conceptualized as a divided state and presence as a unified one. Mindfulness entails being aware of something in the here and now and thus encompasses both an observer who is aware and that which is observed. In contrast, presence is a participatory state of "being" rather than observing, of engagement with rather than awareness of an object or even noticing the engagement itself. As soon as we think about or observe our presence, our consciousness shifts to a dual state, and the full nondual consciousness of presence is compromised. The distinctive characteristic of presence is a wordless, unconsidered, direct sense of the present moment, whereas the hallmarks of mindfulness are noticing and accepting what is occurring in the present moment.

Presence is a felt sense of merging with each fleeting moment and participating completely. It has to do with "being" rather than "doing," and with being one with the doing. Presence exists only in the here and now rather than in the progression of linear time, as there is no time in the present moment. Thus, presence is not defined by the past nor impaired by expectations of the future. It is contrary to reacting through habit, or continuing to perceive things in familiar, comfortable ways. In a direct, unfettered experience of the here and now, we feel a sense of immediacy, as if we are residing inside the experience instead of being aware of it. We are immersed fully and completely with a sense of being "the very awareness, the very consciousness, that is present, that exists, in this very moment" (Almaas, 2008, p. 136). Describing presence as an "ability"'" diminishes its all-encompassing nature.

In its most desirable, unadulterated form, presence means we can circumvent the many permutations of mental constructs, conditioning, learned beliefs, and biases about ourselves, others, and the world that impinge on our expectations, predictions, and behaviors. Ideally, presence is a fresh and new experience in the here and now, independent of past conditioning and of future expectations, and thus open to and welcoming of novelty. Almaas and Johnson (2013, p. 39) describe it as "an actual sense of here-ness—beyond our emotions, beyond the mind, beyond our ideas. In presence, we can know ourselves in a way that is authentic, which means that we are knowing what is real in us." For thousands of years, various traditions have described compatible concepts: as "grace" or the "Holy Spirit" in Christianity; as "vital energy" or "chi" in Taoism; as "cessation" or the dissolution of boundaries between self and world in Buddhism; as wholeness or oneness in Hinduism; and as "opening the heart" in Islamic traditions such as Sufism (Senge et al., 2004).

In its essence, presence carries with it a sense of non-doing, as if we are one with what immediately surrounds us and with all that is. Senge and colleagues (2004, p. 14) describe it as generating a feeling of "letting come," receiving what is and engaging with a larger whole. Bortoft (quoted in Scharmer, 1999, p. 7) says it this way: "If the whole presences within its parts, then a part is a place for the presencing of the whole. ... a part is special and not accidental, since it must be such as to let the whole come into presence." We are able to sense the greater whole and experience our own unique place within that wholeness. This requires relinquishing control, habits, and preconceived ideas of things and letting go into a deep, attentive listening beneath what is on the surface, embracing a receptivity to the essence of things. When actions arise from this experiential and immediate sense of both the whole and the significance of each part within the whole, they can be made in service of whatever spontaneously comes forward in the moment in conjunction with how this fits into the greater picture.

When we are governed by habits formed from our history, or by "'machine age' concepts such as control, predictability, standardization, and faster is better" (Senge et al., 2004, p. 9), we will re-create the past in the present. Instead of being present, we "react" to the moment, which is "governed by 'downloading' habitual ways of thinking, of continuing to see the world within the familiar categories we're comfortable with" (Senge et al., 2004, p. 10). The brain's main function is often described as anticipation, enabling it to continually predict what will happen next so that we can make decisions and take appropriate action. Based on these forecasts, our unconscious decision-making process is an autopilot mechanism that is linked to our default mode network, by which we can make quick, timely decisions in predictable contexts in which we understand the rules of our environment (Vatenssever et al., 2017). The default mode network is related to making intuitive decisions, however intuition is often predicated on our past experience rather than the present moment, and thus our conditioning is a dominant influence.

When our minds wander, which they do about 50% of the time, our default mode network is active (Killingsworth & Gilbert, 2010), along with areas of the brain correlated with self-referential activity (Brewer et al., 2011). Half of our waking hours, we remove our awareness away from the present moment without knowing we are doing it. Even when we are engaged in pleasurable activities (except when making love), our minds will jump around (Killingsworth & Gilbert, 2010). While letting our minds wander may enhance creative problem solving and planning (Moondyham & Schooler, 2013), it can also lead to errors, poor decision-making, missing essential elements and so forth. As well, spending so much of our time on autopilot instead of being present seems to contribute to unhappiness, even when our minds gravitate toward thinking of positive things. Killingsworth and Gilbert (2010, p. 1) conclude that "a human mind is a wandering mind, and a wandering mind is an unhappy mind. The ability to think about what is not happening [in the moment] is a cognitive achievement that comes at an emotional cost."

Jha (2017, para. 20) asserts, "the opposite of a stressed and wandering mind is a mindful one." Concentration practices like mindfulness and music can help to train our minds to focus, and wander less, and thus can be a bridge from autopilot to presence. It should be acknowledged that to fit into a Western context, mindfulness practices have been altered from their original Buddhist meaning and intent. Through appropriation, Westerners, who have more resources, have adapted the symbols, practices, philosophy, spiritual intent, and so forth of primarily Buddhist mindfulness practices to suit Western purposes. In this way, mindfulness has become decontextualized from its initial cultural meaning and has lost much of its connection with its origin to benefit the group that has appropriated these practices (Kirmayer, 2015; Purser et al., 2016). When modifying mindfulness practices from Buddhism, it is honorable to reference their origin and to acknowledge that in appropriation, practices change their purpose. The Western adaptation of Buddhist mindfulness practices has turned away from the original intent of spiritual exploration and evolution, and from "the realisation of 'emptiness' and liberation from all attachments" (Anderson, 2015) and has redefined it as paying attention to the present moment with a nonjudgmental attitude of acceptance (Williams et al., 2007).

In this adaptation of mindfulness, we can begin to familiarize ourselves with our cognitive, emotional, and physical tendencies, and to learn how to let these go to return awareness to the present moment. But these endeavors still take place in dual awareness, as long as there is an observer and that which is observed, evident in most practices such as paying attention to the breath or sensation. However, over time, these efforts can act as an intermediary step that move us toward "being" and foster deepening our presence. Through mindfulness practices, we can become aware of ourselves, our thoughts, emotions, and body sensations, but in contrast, through presence we simply "be" ourselves, fully in the moment. Often in mindfulness exercises, practitioners experience a transition from observation to presence—to becoming one with the experience. But the moment they notice the oneness, they have reverted to dual consciousness, becoming the observer who notices experience.

Nevertheless, presence and mindfulness are not viewed as absolute separate states of consciousness. They can be conceptualized as occurring on a continuum with full presence or unified consciousness at one end, and mindful dual consciousness at the other. Our consciousness may lean more toward one end or the other moment by moment. On autopilot, our minds are wandering somewhere off the continuum, and mindfulness brings us back. But through practice, we learn that there is a choice in every moment to return to the here and now. We begin to identify thoughts, emotions, and body sensations as temporary and ever changing, rather than identifying with them (Ogden & Minton, 2000). Gradually we might naturally start to prefer a more prescient state over autopilot. If so, when we move away from being present, we will start to self-correct, returning to the state of mindfulness and developing a natural inclination to come back to the present moment more and more quickly when we wander, eventually to return to the unified consciousness of presence. With practice, presence becomes increasingly stabilized, "a state to which the system will, of itself, return after being perturbed away from it" (Naft, 2011, p. 172), which can mitigate the automaticity of the default mode network. For example, the default mode networks of experienced meditators are found to be consistent with less mind wandering, and to be more present in the moment as compared to non-meditators (Brewer et al., 2011).

However, presence cannot and should not be unchanging or consistent. For example, it is imperative that we therapists are aware of our own and our client's individual and transgenerational history in relation to social location, culture, and larger contextual events, and how privilege/oppression dynamics are played out in the therapy room. This requires us to be aware of our triggers and mindful of our internal reactions that interrupt presence, especially in working with clients who are "other"—of a different race, gender, socioeconomic status, sexual orientation, ethnicity, and so forth. Especially in the United States, but also throughout the world, to varying degrees we live in a culture where white supremacy and systemic oppression are the status quo, and conditioned bias toward difference is inescapable. Therefore, mindful awareness of the present-moment effect of this conditioning on our own internal patterns and processes is essential in order to dismantle implicit bias so that we do not unconsciously act on this conditioning, which would be inevitable without mindful attention. Additionally, when we are aware of differences and of the impact of privilege/oppression dynamics, we can address these issues directly with the client.

Thus, in clinical practice, therapists move back and forth along the continuum of mindfulness and presence. At times, we are more mindful of our own impulses, emotions, thoughts, and how our own history relates to that of the client, and at times we are more present. As we are aware of our effect on the client, we are also mindful of the effect the client has on us (Kurtz, 1990; Ogden, 1992/2007). However, if our attention is consistently divided (regularly too mindful and thus not present), we run the risk of hindering the dyadic dance of participation, synchronicity, and presence with our client. So primarily we lean toward the "presence" end of the continuum, in a deep resonance with the client, in an open state that is conducive to responsiveness and inspiration rather than analysis, interpretation, or logical thought. Through presence, the client senses we are with them, and we find ourselves acting without premeditation. Through mindfulness, we become aware of our own internal reactions that inform our embodiment of the foundational principles that guide therapeutic action.

PRINCIPLES DETERMINE TECHNIQUE

Nature does not hurry, yet everything is accomplished.

LAO TZU

You can't do what you want until you know what you're doing.

MOSHE FELDENKRAIS

Be brave. Be free from philosophies, prophets and holy
lies. Go deep into your feelings and explore the mystery
of your body, mind and soul. You will find the truth.

AMIT RAY

The most perfect technique is that which is not noticed at all.

PABLO CASALS

Therapy is complex. Determining clinical intervention with any given client at any given moment in time is not simple and rarely obvious. These principles offer the context from which to understand what treatment progress looks like for a client. Progress is less about pace and more about the emergent process; sometimes the change is slow and sometimes it happens quickly. In both cases, the principles help a therapist understand change and make it stick for clients because growth is a felt experience that emerges from their own awareness, in relationship to the therapist, within a context that is inherently health promoting. Without a strong intention to cultivate an atmosphere that is conducive to growth and evolution, and implement interventions in alignment with this atmosphere, true and lasting, self-generated healing within relationship does not occur. In Sensorimotor Psychotherapy, all technique is created from a firm grounding in the context generated by the study of, commitment to, and alignment with the principles.

In keeping with the concept of organicity—that living systems are intelligent, self-organizing, and self-correcting—the therapist helps clients learn about how they organize their experience in the present moment. Kurtz (1985, p. 7) states, "Perception is always an act of creation," constructed through habits that translate current events into experiential meaning, feeling, and action. "It is at the level of feeling and meaning [and bodily responses] that the conversion of events into experience becomes highly individual, creative, distinctly human, and sometimes unnecessarily painful and limiting" (Kurtz, 1985, p. 3). When the habits of conversion are discovered through mindfulness, therapists and clients together tap into the habitual meta-level of organization that underlies and shapes the quality of current experience. Although discussion can and does effect change through understanding and insight, it does not directly or explicitly target the habits that organize experience and ascribe significance to events, as mindfulness of these habits does. Focusing on how experience is constructed in the here and now represents a paradigm shift away from conversation and requires that talking about and focusing on content is suspended in favor of mindful awareness.

Mindfulness is gently (nonviolently) directed by the therapist in collaboration (unity, relational alchemy, presence) with the client toward the five building blocks of present experience—body sensation, movements, five-sense perception (e.g., internal images, smells, tastes, touch, and sounds), emotions, and thoughts (organicity, mind/body/spirit holism). These building blocks constantly fluctuate in response to internal and external stimuli in habitual patterns of organizing experience. Present-day reminders of the past can alter our internal experience in ways that abruptly bring our history into the experiential present, but generally we are not aware of the changes in the building blocks. If we do not notice these shifts, we are likely to respond as if the past were occurring in the present, which is usually at the root of why clients seek therapy. Discovering the internal habits of how events are converted into meaning begins with mindful awareness of one of the building blocks that is considered to be significant in the construction of experience. For example, instead of discussing the client's current conflict at work, the therapist directs attention to the tensing of the legs that occurs when the client talks about the work situation, and slowly, associations emerge: The client senses an impulse to run, sees in their mind's eye an image from childhood of being "bossed around" by their caregiver, hears the words, "I can't be myself," experiences feelings of anger, and so forth. These elements usually remain just under awareness, but they are indicative of powerful habits of thinking, feeling, and action, shaped by the past, that are imposed upon current events to convert them into meaning, albeit outdated.

Mindfulness as an intervention is passive, meaning that the intention is to notice internal experience rather than manipulate, change, interpret, or analyze it. The therapist and client suspend making meaning and forming conclusions in favor of simple observation, to stay with what at first may seem like unrelated bits of internal experience. Through mindfully sitting with these bits and noticing how experience unfolds by following the fluctuations in the building blocks, new elements that had not been noticed previously are discovered; new learning takes place, and unexpected meaning is revealed. In this way, within the context of the principles, the therapist helps the client turn inside deeply enough, toward important habits revealed in present-moment experience that convert events into meaning. Novel information becomes available from within. Because organicity is greater than what we can consciously know, "we trust that the [client] will take the new information and spontaneously incorporate it to the best advantage," (Ogden, 1986, p. 2), generating a natural internal reorganization.

Mindfulness adapted in Sensorimotor Psychotherapy is not a solo endeavor, but is embedded within the therapeutic dyad (Ogden, 2015). Instead of being taught as a meditation practice or solitary exercise, mindfulness entails therapist and client together becoming aware of the client's building blocks in the present moment. The therapist uses a specific set of skills or techniques to facilitate this, adapted from the work of Ron Kurtz (1990). Embodying the principles is the "being" part of the work, generating the skills that are the "doing" part—the specific, time-limited interventions that are used for a distinct purpose. These techniques can be observed by an outsider (except for tracking) and described.

The first skill—to track—is to be aware of the client's present-moment experience, reflected in the five building blocks as they fluctuate in response to certain stimuli—such as talking about a difficulty, remembering a trauma, sharing a recent incident of import, and so forth. Therapists do not "try" or struggle to notice anything specific, but through presence and the non-doing of nonviolence, maintain a receptive stance and find that certain elements jump out at them.

With the second skill—to make contact—the therapist then draws the client's attention to a building block considered (often implicitly) to be significant by naming it. For example, if the therapist notices that the client's shoulders tense as the topic of marriage is discussed, the therapist might say, "Seems like your shoulders are tightening as we talk about marriage." Therapeutic action does not emerge from efforting, analyzing or interpreting. Tracking and making contact reflect the principles in many ways: They emerge naturally from the absence of effort (nonviolence) and the synchronicity in the relationship (unity, relational alchemy, presence); the object of the contact statement is inherently acknowledged for its value (organicity), and as representing one aspect of mind/body/spirit holism. Tracking and making contact draw awareness to the client's present-moment experience, which initiates mindfulness. Additionally, qualifiers or adjunct clauses are used, such as "seems as if" or "looks like," to invite collaboration and modification by the client and ensure that therapist and client are in sync (unity, organicity, nonviolence).

When the client is interested in what has been named, the third skill—to frame—follows up on the contact statement by collaboratively defining the focus for exploration. The frame might be tension ("Let's stay with that tension in your shoulders"), thoughts ("How about we start with these thoughts you have about marriage?"), emotion ("Maybe we could explore this feeling of aversion to marriage"), and so forth. Note the collaborative, pensive tone and language of "we" (unity, relational alchemy, nonviolence, presence), the open-endedness of the frame inviting revision (organicity, unity, nonviolence), and the implicit acknowledgment that the frame will expand to include much more (mind/body/spirit holism).

If the client agrees to the frame, mindfulness questions are asked that directly focus attention on the target of the frame ("What do you notice as you stay with that tension?" "How is it pulling...in, up, back, or...?" "Are there any thoughts or feelings that go with the tension?"). To answer such questions, clients must become aware of present experience (mindfulness). The organization of experience is expanded as information related to the frame is gathered—the tension might hold fear, images of caregivers, sounds from the past, impulses such as to hide, thoughts and beliefs, and so forth. Mindfulness questions operationalize all the principles as a direct, collaborative, gentle, resonant inquiry into the organicity of each moment.

The fifth and final skill—to conduct experiments—guides mindful awareness to the internal fluctuations in response to a stimulus, and is prefaced by the phrase, "What happens when...?" Examples might be, "What happens when you exaggerate the tension?" "What happens when you see that image of your father yelling?" "What happens when you think about marriage?" "What happens when you sense this sadness?" The options are endless. Experiments are gentle investigations (nonviolence) into present experience (mindfulness) that elicit organicity, are adjusted as needed (unity, relational alchemy, presence), and are intended to reveal mind/body/spirit holism.

The application of these skills emerges organically as what action to take becomes apparent. The decision to intervene is not made rationally but from being receptive to what is revealed, until an action becomes obvious. In other words, action emerges from alignment with the principles, especially presence. The economist Brian Arthur (quoted in Senge et al., 2004, pp. 84–85) speaks of a "different way of knowing," claiming that,

In a sense, there's no decision-making....What to do just becomes obvious. You can't rush it. ... You need to "feel out" what to do. You hang back, you observe. ... You don't act out of deduction, you act out of an inner feel, making sense as you go. You're not even thinking. You're at one with the situation.

So it is with "deciding" what skills of embedded relational mindfulness to implement at any given moment. Therapeutic action takes place within a context created by the principles, without which it would be a rote exercise rather than a deep relational exploration into the client's internal landscape. Through this approach, the organization of experience is unveiled; new territory is discovered and mined for its intelligence and meaning. As this takes place, the system—the client, and often the therapist as well—changes spontaneously, without force, in a progressive direction of healing and wholeness.

CONCLUSION

We work in the dark—we do what we can—we give what we have. Our doubt is our passion and our passion is our task. The rest is the madness of art.

HENRY JAMES

The principles call for us to dwell in a place of uncertainty, of not knowing, to access a state of being that is open to the innovation of emergence. As Capra (2004, p. 41) writes, "Emergence results in the creation of novelty, and this novelty is often qualitatively different from the phenomenon out of which it emerged." We must relinquish the familiar so that we can experience something new. But this is not without risk. The quest to discover or, more precisely, to surrender to and receive, emergent wisdom and processes within ourselves, our relationships, and much more calls for the courage to step out of our comfort zones of what we think we know into unexplored, uncharted inner and outer domains without the security of being able to predict what might happen. Instead of seeking answers, we cultivate the ability to be with the questions, letting our minds and bodies become spacious and open to innovation, wonderment, and adventure. Instead of being task oriented, we are attuned to emergence, to what happens by itself. In relationship with others, stepping wholly and unabashedly into the fullness of the moment engenders what Tronick (2003, p. 476) calls a "dyadic state of consciousness [which] leads to feeling larger than oneself." If we can allow the principles to coax us into relinquishing the futile effort of trying to control a future that cannot be controlled, in our lives and with our clients, we might discover something infinitely more valuable than what we had expected or dreamed possible.

Every structure and every organism needs to exist within a context or foundation that will support its emergence and sustain its existence. This is true for physical structures, mental processes, people, relationships, life activities, spiritual pursuits, and everything else. In Sensorimotor Psychotherapy, this sustaining foundation is made up of the principles that provide guidance for how to "be" as a therapist. However, they not only guide us in clinical practice but also offer a kind of road map for thriving in relation to ourselves, to others, and in the world at large. As therapists, one of our tasks is to help clients bridge the gap between therapy and life so that the expansion and growth that blossom in the therapy room do not end there, but carry forward into full bloom in the real content and experience of daily life. The foundational principles provide the context and direction that allows this to happen for our clients, and for ourselves. They inspire an increasingly higher consciousness as we engage in the emergent process of aligning with their teachings. In their purest form, taken together, the principles are a map for love.

REFERENCES

Almaas, A. H. (2008). *The unfolding now: Realizing your true nature through the practice of presence.* Boston: Shambhala.

Almaas, A. H., & Johnson, K. (2013). *The power of divine Eros: The illuminating force of love in everyday life.* Boston: Shambhala.

Anandarajah, G., & Hight, E. (2001). Spirituality and medical practice: Using the HOPE questions as a practical tool for spiritual assessment. *American Family Physician, 63,* 81–89.

Anderson, L. (2015, June 5). Mindfulness has lost its Buddhist roots, and it may not be doing you good. *The Conversation.* https://theconversation.com/mindfulness-has-lost-its-buddhist-roots-and-it-may-not-be-doing-you-good-42526

Andrews-Hanna, J. R. (2012). The brain's default network and its adaptive role in internal mentation. *Neuroscientist, 18*(3), 251–270. https://doi.org/10.1177/1073858411403316

Bateson, G. (1979). *Mind and nature: A necessary unity.* New York: Bantam.

Benjamin, J. (1988). *The bonds of love: Psychoanalysis, feminism, and the problem of domination.* Toronto: Random House.

Benjamin, J. (2006). Two way streets: Recognition of difference and the intersubjective third. *Differences, 17*(1), 116–146. doi:10.1205/10407391

Brewer, J. A., Worbunsky, P. D., Gray, J. R., Tang, Y. Y., Weber, J., & Kober, H. (2011). Meditation experience is associated with differences in default mode network activity and connectivity. *Proceedings of the National Academy of Sciences, 108*(50), 20254–20259. doi:10.1073/pnas.1112029108

Bromberg, P. M. (2006). *Awakening the dreamer: Clinical journeys.* Mahwah, NJ: Analytic Press.

Bromberg, P. M. (2012). Credo. *Psychoanalytic Dialogues, 22*(3), 273–278.

Burgoon, J. K., Guerrero, L., & Floyd, K. (2010). *Nonverbal communication.* New York: Routledge. https://doi.org/10.4324/9781315663425

Capra, F. (2004). *The hidden connections: A science for sustainable living.* New York: Anchor.

Cassaniti, J., & Luhrmann, T. (2014). The cultural kindling of spiritual experiences. *Current Anthropology, 55,* S333–S343. doi:10.1086/677881

Chilisa, B., & Tsheko, G. N. (2014). Mixed methods in indigenous research: Building relationships for sustainable intervention outcomes. *Journal of Mixed Methods Research, 8*(3), 222–233.

Chopra, D. (1989). *Quantum healing: Exploring the frontiers of mind/body medicine.* New York: Bantam.

Chopra, D., & Kafatos, M. (2017). Why you and the universe are one. Chopra Foundation. https://www.choprafoundation.org/consciousness/why-you-and-the-universe-are-one/

Deshpande, R. (2019, November 8). What is ahimsa? *Yoga Journal.* https://www.yogajournal.com/lifestyle/what-is-ahimsa

Ellyson, S. L., & Dovidio, J. F. (1985). Power, dominance, and nonverbal behavior: Basic concepts and issues. In S. L. Ellyson & J. F. Dovidio (Eds.), *Power, dominance, and nonverbal behavior* (pp. 1–27). New York: Springer Verlag.

Emily. (2015, January 12). All my relations teachings. *Traditional Native Healing.* https://traditionalnativehealing.com/all-my-relations

Eze, M. (2010). *Intellectual history in contemporary South Africa.* New York: Macmillan.

Feldman, C. (1999, spring). Dependent origination. *Insight Journal,* 37–41. https://www.buddhistinquiry.org/article/dependent-origination/

Gold, J. (1985). Cartesian dualism and the current crisis in medicine—a plea for a philosophical approach: Discussion paper. *Journal of the Royal Society of Medicine, 78*(8), 663–666. https://doi.org/10.1177/014107688507800813

Hahn, T. N. (2001). *Essential writings.* Maryknoll, NY: Orbis.

Hahn, T. N. (2012). *Awakening of the heart: Essential Buddhist sutras and commentaries.* Berkeley, CA: Unified Buddhist Church.

Hancock, P., Hughes, B., Jagger, E., Paterson, K., Russell, R., Tulle-Winton, E., & Tyler, M. (2000). *The body, culture and society: An introduction.* Philadelphia: Open University Press.

Hart, A. (2017). From multicultural competence to radical openness: A psychoanalytic engagement of otherness. *American Psychoanalyst, 51*(1). https://apsa.org/apsaa-publications/vol51no1-TOC/html/vol51no1_09.xhtml

Henley, N., & Freeman, J. (1995). *The sexual politics of interpersonal behavior in women: A feminist perspective.* London: Mayfield.

Janet, P. (1925). *Principles of psychotherapy.* London: George Allen & Unwin.

Jansen, G. (2018). Living into all our relations. *Viewpoints, 22*(12). https://canadianmennonite.org/stories/living-all-our-relations

Jha, A. (2017, June 16). The science of taming the wandering mind in mindfulness: Healthy mind, healthy life. *Mindful.* https://www.mindful.org/taming-the-wandering-mind/

Johnson, R. (2015). Grasping and transforming the embodied experience of oppression. *International Body Psychotherapy Journal, 14*(1), 80–95.

Killingsworth, M. A., & Gilbert, D. G. (2010). A wandering mind is an unhappy mind. *Science, 330,* 923.

Kirmayer, L. J. (2015). Mindfulness in cultural context. *Transcultural Psychiatry, 52*(4), 447–469.

Kluckhohn, C., Murray, H. A., & Schneider, D. M. (Eds.). (1953). *Personality in nature, society, and culture* (2nd ed.). Knopf.

Koestler, A. (1967). *The ghost in the machine.* London: Hutchinson.

Kurtz, R. (1985). The organization of experience in Hakomi therapy. *Hakomi Forum,* no. 3, 3–9.

Kurtz, R. (1990). *Body-centered psychotherapy: The Hakomi method.* Mendocino, CA: LifeRhythm.

Kurtz, R. (2004). Principles and practices. Unpublished manuscript.

Kurtz, R. (2007). Readings on the Hakomi method of mindfulness-based assisted self-study. Unpublished manuscript.

Lalonde, R. (1904). Unity in diversity: Acceptance and integration in an age of intolerance and fragmentation. Bahai Library Online. https://bahai-library.com/lalonde_unity_diversity

Levac, L., Baikie, G., & Hanson, C. (2018). Learning across indigenous and western knowledge systems and intersectionality: Reconciling social science research approaches. University of Guelph. doi:10.13140/RG.2.2.19973.65763.

Lomax, J. W., & Pargament, K. I. (2011). Seeking "sacred moments" in psychology and in life. *Psyche and Geloof, 22*(2), 79–90.

Mark, G. T., & Lyons, A. C. (2010). Maori healers' views on wellbeing: The importance of mind, body, spirit, family and land. *Social Science and Medicine, 70,* 1756–1764.

McCabe, G. (2008). Mind, body, emotions and spirit: Reaching to the ancestors for healing. *Counseling Psychology Quarterly, 21*(2), 143–152.

McLeod, S. A. (2008). Reductionism and holism. *Simply Psychology.* https://www.simplypsychology.org/reductionism-holism.html

Mehta, N. (2011). Mind-body dualism: A critique from a health perspective. *Mens Sana Monographs, 9*(1), 202–209. https://doi.org/10.4103/0973-1229.77436

Menakem, R. (2017). *My grandmother's hands: Racialized trauma and the pathway to mending our hearts and bodies.* Las Vegas, NV: Central Recovery Press.Mooneyham, Benjamin & Schooler, Jonathan. (2013). The Costs and Benefits of Mind-Wandering: A Review. Canadian journal of experimental psychology = Revue canadienne de psychologie expérimentale. 67. 11-8. 10.1037/a0031569.

Moore, C. L., & Yamamoto, K. (2012). *Beyond words: Movement observation and analysis* (2nd ed.). New York: Routledge.

Naft, J. (2011). *The sacred art of soul making* (2nd ed.). Baltimore, MD: I.F. Publishing.

Novak, M. (1983). Epigraph. In C. L. Birch (Ed.), *Unity in diversity: An index to the publications of conservative and libertarian institutions* (p. 263). Metuchen, NJ: Scarecrow.

Obama, B. (2013, December 10). Remarks by President Obama at memorial service for former South African president Nelson Mandela. White House, Office of the Press Secretary. https://obamawhitehouse. archives.gov/the-press-office/2013/12/10/remarks-president-obama-memorial-service-former-south-african-president-

Ogden, P. (1986). *The principles and bodywork.* Boulder, Colorado [Unpublished manuscript].

Ogden, P., & Minton, K. (2000). Sensorimotor psychotherapy: One method for processing trauma. *Traumatology,* 6(3). www.fse.edu/-trauma/v6i3a3.html

Ogden, P. (2007). *Training for the treatment of trauma manual.* Boulder, CO: Sensorimotor Psychotherapy Institute. Unpublished manuscript.

Ogden, P. (2015). Embedded relational mindfulness: A sensorimotor psychotherapy perspective on the treatment of trauma. In V. Folette, J. Briere, D. Rozelle, J. Hopper, & D. Rome (Eds.), *Mindfulness-oriented interventions for trauma: Integrating contemplative practices* (pp. 227–239. New York: Guilford.

Ogden, P., & Fisher, J. (2015). *Sensorimotor psychotherapy: Interventions for trauma and attachment.* New York: Norton.

Ogden, P. (2013). Technique and beyond: Therapeutic enactments, mindfulness, and the role of the body. In D. J. Siegel & M. Solomon (Eds.), *Healing moments in Psychotherapy* (pp. 35–47). New York, NY: W. W. Norton & Company.

Ogden, P., Minton, K., & Pain, C. (2006). *Trauma and the body: A sensorimotor approach to psychotherapy.* New York: Norton.

Pargament, K., Lomax, J., Mcgee, J., & Fang, Q. (2014). Sacred moments in psychotherapy from the perspectives of mental health providers and patients. *Spirituality in Clinical Practice,* 1(4), 248–262.

Pargament, K. I., & Mahoney, A. (2005). Sacred matters: Sanctification as a vital topic for the psychology of religion. *International Journal for the Psychology of Religion,* 15(3), 179–198. https://doi.org/10.1207/s15327582ijpr1503_1

Prigogine, I. (1997). *The end of certainty: Time, chaos and the new laws of nature.* New York: Free Press.

Purser, R. E., Forbes, D., & Burke, A. (Eds.) (2016). *Handbook of mindfulness: Culture, context and social engagement.* New York: Springer.

Scharmer, C. O. (1999). Imagination becomes an organ of perception: Conversation with Henri Bortoft. McKinsey & Company and Society for Organizational Learning. https://www.presencing.org/assets/images/aboutus/theory-u/leadership-interview/doc_bortoft-1999.pdf

Schore, A. N. (2003). *Affect regulation and the repair of the self.* New York: Norton.

Schore, A. N. (2009). Right-brain affect regulation: An essential mechanism of development, trauma, dissociation, and psychotherapy. In D. Fosha, D. Siegal, & M. Solomon (Eds.), *The healing power of emotion: Perspectives from affective neuroscience and clinical practice.* New York, NY: W.W. Norton and Company. pp. 112–144.

Schweitzer, A. (1965, September 4). Schweitzer's struggle to find life's meaning: Doctor wrote of search. *Midland (Michigan) Daily News.* http://home.pcisys.net/~jnf/mdnstory.html

Senge, P., Scharmer, O., Jaworski, J., & Flowers, B. S. (2004). *Presence: Exploration of profound change in people, organizations, and society.* New York: Doubleday.

Siegel, D. J. (2010). *Mindsight: The new science of personal transformation.* New York: Random House.

Smylie, J., Olding, M., & Ziegler, C. (2014). Sharing what we know about living a good life: Indigenous approaches to knowledge translation. *Journal of Canadian Health Libraries Association, 35,* 16–21. doi:10.5596/c14-009

Stern, D. N. (2004). *The present moment in psychotherapy and everyday life.* New York: Norton.

Sue, D.W. (2010). *Microaggressions in everyday life: Race, gender, and sexual orientation.* Hoboken, NJ: Wiley.

Sue, D. W., Sue, D., Neville, H. A., & Smith, L. (2019). *Counselling the culturally diverse: Theory and practice.* New York: Wiley.

Taylor, S. (2013). Acts of remembering: Relationship in feminist therapy. *Women and Therapy, 36*(1–2), 23–34.

Tronick, E. Z. (2003). "Of course all relationships are unique": How co-creative processes generate unique mother-infant and patient-therapist relationships and change other relationships. *Psychoanalytic Inquiry, 23*(3), 473–491. https://doi.org/10.1080/07351692309349044

Tutu, D. (2000). *No future without forgiveness.* New York: Doubleday.

Vatanssever, D., Menon, D. K., & Stamatakis, E. A. (2017). Default mode contributions to automated information processing. *PNAS, 114*(48), 12821–12826. https://doi.org/10.1073/pnas.1710521114

Williams, M., Teasdale, J., Segal, Z., & Kabat-Zinn, J. (2007). *The mindful way through depression: Freeing yourself from chronic unhappiness.* New York: Guilford.

CREDITS

Chapter 1
SENSORIMOTOR PSYCHOTHERAPY IN CONTEXT: SOCIO-LOGICAL PERSPECTIVES © 2021 Pat Ogden, Sherri Taylor, Laia Jorba, Raymond Rodriguez, and Mary Choi

Chapter 2
THE IMPACT OF TRAUMA AND RELATIONAL STRESS ON PHYSIOLOGY, POSTURE, AND MOVEMENT

Reproduced from *Pat Ogden. The different impact of trauma and relational stress on physiology, posture, and movement: Implications for treatment. European Journal of Trauma & Dissociation 2020; 100172.* Copyright © 2021 Elsevier Masson SAS. All rights reserved."

Chapter 4
EMBEDDED RELATIONAL MINDFULNESS

From Ogden, P. (2014). Embedded relational mindfulness: A sensorimotor psychotherapy perspective on the treatment of trauma. In V. Folette, J Briere, D. Rozelle, J. Hopper, and D. Rome (Eds.), Mindfulness-oriented interventions for trauma: Integrating contemplative practices. (pp. 227–239). New York, NY: The Guilford Press.

Chapter 5
OPPRESSION, DEPRESSION, AND HYPOAROUSAL

From CLINICAL PEARLS OF WISDOM: 21 LEADING THERA-
PISTS OFFER THEIR KEY INSIGHTS edited by Michael Kerman.
Copyright © 2010 by Michael Kerman. Used by permission of W. W.
Norton & Company, Inc.

Chapter 6
A SENSORIMOTOR PSYCHOTHERAPY APPROACH TO
COMPLEX TRAUMA

This article was published in *Dissociative Disorders: An Expanding Window into the Psychobiology of the Mind,* Volume 29, Richard A. Chefetz, A
Sensorimotor approach to the treatment of trauma and dissociation,
pp. 263–279, Copyright © 2021 Elsevier.

Chapter 7
INTEGRATING BODY AND MIND

Adapted from Ogden, P & Fisher, J. (2014). Integrating body and mind:
Sensorimotor psychotherapy and treatment of dissociation, defense, and
dysregulation. In U. Lanius, S. Paulsen, & F. Corrigan (Eds.), Neurobiology and treatment of traumatic dissociation: Towards an Embodied Self
(pp. 399–422). New York, NY: Springer Publishing Company.

Chapter 8
THE ROLE OF THE BODY IN FORECASTING THE
FUTURE

Adapted from Ogden, P. (2015). 'I can see clearly now the rain has gone':
The role of the body in forecasting the future. In J. Pertrucelli (Ed.),

Body-states: Interpersonal and relational perspectives on the treatment of eating disorders. (pp. 92–103). New York, NY: Routledge.

Chapter 9
BENEATH THE WORDS: THE SOMATIC NARRATIVE

Adapted from Ogden, P (2011). Beyond Words: A Sensorimotor Psychotherapy Perspective on Trauma and Treatment. In in Caretti V., Craparo G., Schimmenti (eds.), Psychological Trauma. Theory, Clinical and Treatment. Rome: Astrolabio.

Chapter 10
TECHNIQUE AND BEYOND: THERAPEUTIC ENACTMENTS

Adapted from Ogden, P. (2013). Technique and beyond: Therapeutic enactments, mindfulness, and the role of the body. In D. J. Siegel & M. Solomon (Eds.), Healing moments in Psychotherapy (pp. 35–47). New York, NY: W. W. Norton & Company.

Chapter 11
MOVEMENT VOCABULARY, PLAY, AND CREATIVITY

Adapted from Ogden, P. (2017) Play, creativity and movement vocabulary. In T. Marks-Tarlow, M. Solomon & D. J. Siegel (Eds.). Play and creativity in psychotherapy (pp. 92–109). New York, NY: W. W. Norton & Company.

INDEX

Note: Italicized page locators refer to figures.

About the Author

Pat Ogden, Ph.D., (she/her), is a pioneer in somatic psychology, the creator of the Sensorimotor Psychotherapy method, and founder of the Sensorimotor Psychotherapy Institute (sensorimotor.org). Dr. Ogden is co-founder of the Hakomi Institute, past faculty of Naropa University, a clinician, consultant, international lecturer and groundbreaking author in somatic psychology. Her current interests include couple therapy, child and family therapy, social justice, diversity, inclusion, consciousness, and the philosophical/spiritual principles that underlie her work.

About the Author's Consultants

Mary Choi, (she/her), is a first generation Asian American, clinical social worker practicing in the Washington, D.C area. She incorporates psychodynamic, somatic, and spiritual approaches in her work with trauma, attachment, relationships, and culture. She has experience in a variety of community mental health based settings, and she facilitates workshops on race equity and social justice within her local community. Mary is an educator, consultant, and a faculty member at the Sensorimotor Psychotherapy Institute.

Raymond Rodriguez, LCSW-R, Rev., (he/him/his), is an Afro-Latino Clinical Social Worker, interfaith minister, and educator. He is the founder and clinical director of Aldea Counseling Services and has taught at the City University of New York, Columbia University, Smith College, and is a faculty member and consultant for the Sensorimotor Psychotherapy Institute. He lives in the Bronx with his partner and son.

Sherri Taylor, Psy.D., (she/they/femme), is a contemplative, scholar, consultant, and facilitator. She is core faculty in the Somatic Psychology department at California Institute for Integral Studies and also teaches in the Clinical Psychology doctoral program at The Wright Institute. She curates and hosts group trainings, playshops, and workshops for community and professional audiences in the areas of anti-racism, diversity and inclusion, the cultivation of joy and creativity, dream work, and spirituality.

Laia Jorba, Ph.D., (she/her/hers), is a Catalan teacher, counselor, and mentor, originally from Barcelona and currently residing in the U.S. She uses somatic and creative counseling approaches to explore trajectories of immigration and experiences of oppression and trauma on the body. She co-directs a community-based clinic, holds a private practice, and is a faculty member at the Sensorimotor Psychotherapy Institute. She has taught at different universities and lectures nationally and internationally.